Marketing for Sustainable Tourism

Tourism marketing has typically been seen as exploitative and fuelling hedonistic consumerism. Sustainability marketing can, however, use marketing skills and techniques to good purpose, by understanding market needs, designing more sustainable products and identifying more persuasive methods of communication to bring about behavioural change. This book summarises the latest research on the theories, methods and results of marketing that seeks to make tourist destinations better places to live, and better places to visit. It shares evidence on the motivations, mechanisms and barriers that businesses encounter, and on successes in changing consumer behaviour and pursuing sustainability goals. Particular attention is given to the methodologies of sustainable tourism marketing, to the subject's breadth and complexity, and to its many innovations. Further research is called for to fully understand what contextual aspects influence these pro-sustainability interventions to achieve which outcomes in other settings, in order to validate some of the exploratory studies discussed, and establish the feasibility of scaling up pilot studies for more general use.

This book was originally published as a special issue of the *Journal of Sustainable Tourism*.

Xavier Font is Professor of Sustainability Marketing at the University of Surrey, UK.

Scott McCabe is Professor of Marketing and Tourism at the University of Nottingham, UK.

Marketing for Sustainable Tourism

Edited by
Xavier Font and Scott McCabe

LONDON AND NEW YORK

First published 2018
by Routledge
2 Park Square, Milton Park, Abingdon, Oxon, OX14 4RN, UK

and by Routledge
711 Third Avenue, New York, NY 10017, USA

Routledge is an imprint of the Taylor & Francis Group, an informa business

Chapters 1-8 & 10-11 © 2018 Taylor & Francis
Chapter 9 © 2018 Xavier Font, Islam Elgammal and Ian Lamond. Originally published as Open Access.

British Library Cataloguing in Publication Data
A catalogue record for this book is available from the British Library

ISBN 13: 978-1-138-56031-4

Typeset in Myriad Pro
by RefineCatch Limited, Bungay, Suffolk

Publisher's Note
The publisher accepts responsibility for any inconsistencies that may have arisen during the conversion of this book from journal articles to book chapters, namely the possible inclusion of journal terminology.

Disclaimer
Every effort has been made to contact copyright holders for their permission to reprint material in this book. The publishers would be grateful to hear from any copyright holder who is not here acknowledged and will undertake to rectify any errors or omissions in future editions of this book.

Contents

CONTENTS

Citation Information

The chapters in this book were originally published in the *Journal of Sustainable Tourism*, volume 25, issue 7–9 (July–September 2017). When citing this material, please use the original page numbering for each article, as follows:

Chapter 7

The influence of trust perceptions on German tourists' intention to book a sustainable hotel: a new approach to analysing marketing information
Sindhuri Ponnapureddy, Julianna Priskin, Timo Ohnmacht, Friederike Vinzenz and Werner Wirth
Journal of Sustainable Tourism, volume 25, issue 7–9 (July–September 2017), pp. 970–988

Chapter 8

The role of travel agents' ethical concerns when brokering information in the marketing and sale of sustainable tourism
Alexa Mossaz and Alexandra Coghlan
Journal of Sustainable Tourism, volume 25, issue 7–9 (July–September 2017), pp. 989–1006

Chapter 9

Greenhushing: the deliberate under communicating of sustainability practices by tourism businesses
Xavier Font, Islam Elgammal and Ian Lamond
Journal of Sustainable Tourism, volume 25, issue 7–9 (July–September 2017), pp. 1007–1023

Chapter 10

Tourism, information technologies and sustainability: an exploratory review
Stefan Gössling
Journal of Sustainable Tourism, volume 25, issue 7–9 (July–September 2017), pp. 1024–1041

Chapter 11

An environmental social marketing intervention in cultural heritage tourism: a realist evaluation
Diana Gregory-Smith, Victoria K. Wells, Danae Manika and David J. McElroy
Journal of Sustainable Tourism, volume 25, issue 7–9 (July–September 2017), pp. 1042–1060

For any permission-related enquiries please visit:
http://www.tandfonline.com/page/help/permissions

Notes on Contributors

Nazila Babakhani is a PhD student at The University of Queensland, Australia. Her research interests are sustainable tourism and tourism marketing.

Susanne Becken is Director of the Griffith Institute for Tourism and Professor of Sustainable Tourism at Griffith University, Australia.

D. Scott Borden is Researcher and PhD student in the Department of Management at the University of Exeter, UK.

Alexandra Coghlan is Senior Lecturer in Tourism at Griffith University's Department of Tourism, Sport and Hotel Management, Australia.

Tim Coles is Professor of Management at the University of Exeter Business School where he is also the Director of Impact.

Ljubica Knezevic Cvelbar is Associate Professor of Tourism at the University of Ljubljana, Slovenia.

Sara Dolnicar is Research Professor of Tourism at The University of Queensland, Australia.

Islam Elgammal is Professor at Suez Canal University, Egypt.

Xavier Font is Professor of Sustainability Marketing at the University of Surrey, UK.

Stefan Gössling is Professor in the School of Business and Economics at Linnaeus University, Kalmar, Sweden.

Diana Gregory-Smith is Senior Lecturer in Marketing at the Birmingham Business School, University of Birmingham, UK.

Bettina Grün is Associate Professor of Applied Statistics at Johannes Kepler University Linz, Austria.

C. Michael Hall is Professor at the University of Canterbury, Christchurch, New Zealand; Visiting Professor at Linnaeus University, Sweden; Docent at the University of Oulu, Oulu, Finland; and Senior Research Fellow at the University of Johannesburg, South Africa.

Ian Lamond is Senior Lecturer at Leeds Beckett University, UK.

Danae Manika is Senior Lecturer in Marketing at the School of Business and Management, Queen Mary University of London, UK.

Scott McCabe is Professor of Marketing and Tourism at Nottingham University's Business School, UK.

David J. McElroy has a doctorate in Marine Ecology from the University of Sydney, Australia. He was Research and Evaluation Manager at Global Action Plan and is on the Board of Directors of the European Social Marketing Association.

Alexa Mossaz completed her PhD in the School of Environment at Griffith University, Australia.

Timo Ohnmacht is Lecturer at the Lucerne University of Applied Sciences, Switzerland.

Sindhuri Ponnapureddy is Research Associate and doctoral student at the Institute of Tourism at Lucerne University of Applied Sciences, Switzerland.

Julianna Priskin is Lecturer at the Lucerne University of Applied Sciences, Switzerland.

Brent W. Ritchie is Professor of Tourism at The University of Queensland, Australia.

Gareth Shaw is Professor of Retail and Tourism Management and Associate Dean of Research at the University of Exeter Business School, UK.

V. Dao Truong is Research Fellow in Tourism Research in Economic Environs & Society (TREES), North-West University, Potchefstroom Campus, South Africa.

Friederike Vinzenz is Researcher and doctoral student at the Institute of Mass Communication and Media Research at the University of Zurich, Switzerland.

Christopher Warren (MSc; PhD student) is the founder of Christopher Warren & Associates. He is a tourism practitioner, qualified trainer and assessor, and has contributed as a board member to community, local government, regional, state and national tourism bodies for over 14 years.

Victoria K. Wells is Professor of Marketing and Consumer Behaviour at the Management School, University of Sheffield, UK.

Werner Wirth is Professor of Empirical Research and Head of the Institute of Mass Communication and Media Research at the University of Zurich, Switzerland.

Sustainability and marketing in tourism: its contexts, paradoxes, approaches, challenges and potential

Xavier Font and Scott McCabe

ABSTRACT

Tourism marketing has typically been seen as exploitative and fuelling hedonistic consumerism. Sustainability marketing can, however, use marketing skills and techniques to good purpose, by understanding market needs, designing more sustainable products and identifying more persuasive methods of communication to bring behavioural change. This article summarises the latest research on the theories, methods and results of marketing that seeks to make tourist destinations better places to live in, and better places to visit. It explores sustainability marketing's two fundamental approaches, that of market development, using market segmentation, and that of sustainable product development. It introduces a Special Issue of the *Journal of Sustainable Tourism* on sustainable marketing, sharing evidence on the motivations, mechanisms and barriers that businesses encounter, and on successes in changing consumer behaviour and pursuing sustainability goals. Particular attention is given to the methodologies of sustainable tourism marketing, to the subject's breadth and complexity, and to its many innovations. Further research is called for to fully understand what contextual aspects influence these pro-sustainability interventions to achieve which outcomes in other settings, in order to validate some of the exploratory studies discussed, and establish the feasibility of scaling up pilot studies for more general use.

Introduction

There has never been a more opportune or important moment in which to address issues of marketing in sustainable tourism. At the time of writing, news agencies around the world reported that 2016 was officially the warmest year on record. A press release from the UK Met Office in conjunction with the University of East Anglia's Climate Research Unit stated that a particularly strong El Niño event was partly responsible; however, "...the main contributor to warming over the last 150 years is human influence on climate from increasing greenhouse gases in the atmosphere" (The Met Office, 2017). This coincided with the eve of Donald Trump's inauguration as the 45th President of the United States, who according to Ian Johnston writing in the UK newspaper, *The Independent*, has previously claimed "that climate change is a Chinese hoax, has appointed climate science deniers to key positions and spoken about withdrawing the US from the Paris Agreement on climate change" (Johnston, 2017). There is a sense that global politics and the world itself is at a precipitous moment in history, that decisions made in 2017 will significantly influence the direction of travel of businesses, consumer thinking and demand, and global governance for decades to come. The paradoxical nature of recent events, personified by the rise to power of more "sceptical" leaders, despite more powerful and concrete evidence on the damaging effects of human activity on the environment, point to an urgent need to evaluate practices, actions, theories and assumptions in every sphere of life. The role of tourism, both the industry and tourists as consumers, in shaping or responding to competing global forces is important for a number of reasons, including on the negative side, tourism's contribution to global carbon emissions, its impact on Indigenous and heritage cultures, its impacts on nature, "traditional" landscapes and townscapes and, on the positive side, its role in fostering peace, transferring wealth, creating jobs and developing stronger inter-cultural relations.

Yet, it may at first appear that the concepts of marketing and sustainability are antithetical, mutually incompatible (Jones, Clarke-Hill, Comfort, & Hillier, 2008; Smith, 1998). Marketing has been defined as the activity, set of institutions and processes for creating, communicating, delivering and exchanging offerings that have value for customers, clients, partners and society at large (American Marketing Association, 2013). This holistic definition suggests a benign view of marketing. Yet, it can be contrasted with an alternative, more maleficent perspective, which is critical of marketing's role in fanning the fires of consumer culture (see McDonagh & Prothero, 2014). Jones et al. (2008) point out that some commentators argue that marketing encourages unnecessary consumption, promoting a culture of materialism and a relentless search for unattainable lifestyles, to and by people who cannot afford them and for which ultimately their attainment would not make them happier. Furthermore, some areas of marketing activity, particularly advertising, have been criticised specifically for spurious claims in the promotion of sustainability, epitomised in the practice of "greenwashing"- misleading consumers about a company's environmental performance for business gains (Delmas & Cuerel Burbano, 2011; Laufer, 2003).

Tourism is most often conceived as a "want" rather than a "need", a luxury or a reward, as a non-essential, hedonic, aspirational consumption activity (reflected in advertising messages), such that tourism marketing is more readily associated with the more malign view of marketing practice. Indeed tourism is sometimes conceived as essentially pure marketing, as it is often based on packaging existing resources and assets of a destination, and subsequent promotion to new markets (McCabe, 2014). Additionally, the ubiquity of marketing in contemporary society, providing the wallpaper to social life, both online and off, plays into the notion that marketing is responsible for fuelling irresponsible levels and types of consumption. Yet, marketing is fundamental to tourism businesses and destinations. Thus, for example, effective marketing is largely responsible for the number, types and origins of tourists found in a destination, and for ensuring viable destinations which provide a valuable contribution to economic development and growth. Whilst the role of government and the industry in creating and shaping destinations is critical to the achievement of sustainability, marketing has an important function in determining how successfully destinations achieve their aims and objectives, in both the short and medium terms.

Sustainability on the other hand, whilst also, like marketing, plagued by varying interpretations and contrasting viewpoints, is generally associated with a more positive moral standing in academic discourse and social understanding. Sustainability provides a long-term view of the future, one that focuses attention on a set of ethical values and principles, which guides action in a responsible and harmonious way, incorporating the environment and societal consequences of actions, as well as economic goals. It is concerned with a balanced and holistic approach that recognises the role of all stakeholders and both present and future generations' entitlement to the use of resources. Sustainability has become an imperative: McDonagh and Prothero argue that; *"We have finally recognised that at our current levels of consumption the planet cannot sustain us or its carrying capacity for humanity ad infinitum"* (2014, p. 1186). It has become a "mega trend", spawning rafts of legislation from supranational and national governments, collective and individual actions by industries and individuals. McDonagh and Prothero cite GE, Marks and Spencer, Pepsico and others as spearheading sustainability initiatives in recent years. Additionally, they refer to the plethora of terms to describe consumer actions, such as; voluntary simplifiers, downshifters, ethical and sustainable consumers, to highlight the popularisation of responsible or alternative modes of consumption, or at the very least, an awakening of a critical consumer consciousness in global marketplaces.

Yet, the extent that true sustainable development is attainable is also questioned. Some argue the UN's Sustainable Development Goals (SDG) (http://www.un.org/sustainabledevelopment/sustainable-development-goals/), introduced in 2015 to replace the Millennium Development Goals, are too broad and diffuse. One example is the goal to reduce inequality within and among countries. This certainly appears to be unattainable in the light of recent statistics showing ever-increasing concentration of wealth among an ever-smaller number of global elites (Oxfam, 2017). Tourism also characterises these contrasts between ideals and realities. Some destinations are far from sustainable, based on short-term mass development models and with poor infrastructure to deal with environmental problems. Consumers may see sustainable alternatives as unappealing or too costly (involving sacrifices and inconvenience), or as "Catch 22" alternatives that could be encouraged even further by media reports of threatened ecosystems or species, to make perhaps damaging visits to destinations before they disappear forever (e.g. the Great Barrier Reef, or travel to the polar regions for polar bear viewing). And then there is the question of air travel and its contribution to carbon emissions.

Yet, tourism is both desired and required by developed and by many developing nations to enable development and to achieve sustainable economic growth. Tourism is often cited as a "green" industry, and rightly so in the context of extraction-based alternatives. It is these paradoxes and contrasts particularly that pose an important set of challenges and opportunities for debate on sustainability issues in tourism marketing. The idea that tourism marketing and sustainability can perhaps learn from each other may appear counter-intuitive. Marketing is generally associated with competitive business strategy, short-termism, and a profit imperative, promoting consumer choice in a way that advocates the benefits of self-gratification and instant satisfaction, which seems at odds with the ideals of sustainability. It is both despite and because of the inherent difficulties in reconciling sustainability issues with marketing theories, strategies and practices in a tourism context that more focused research is needed that seeks ways forward for theory development *and* practical solutions. This is the main purpose of this special issue. By focusing in on some of the most paradoxical and irascible issues, it may be possible to develop new ideas and propose research agendas to shape and direct future action. Whilst there is a rich seam of research and practice in the overall marketing literature on sustainable issues and responsible consumption (c.f. McDonagh & Prothero, 2014; Ulusoy, 2016; Wymer & Polonsky, 2015), this is less-well developed in tourism, but the wider literature attests to the potential role of marketing to understand and encourage consumer behaviour that is more sustainable, create and promote more sustainable tourism offerings, and ensure that tourism businesses operate in a more ethical way, congruent with the concerns of all stakeholders. We define sustainability marketing as the application of marketing functions, processes and techniques to a destination, resource or offering, which serves the needs of the visitor and stakeholder community today and ensures the opportunities of future visitors and stakeholders to meet their needs in the future. We follow the eighteenth-century cry (often attributed to radical church leaders in the UK from that period) "why should the devil have all the best tunes": we believe that sustainable tourism should and must be marketed if the concept is to make progress. Yet, before going on to explain how sustainability marketing can address issues and offer opportunities to deliver a more sustainable tourism, the context of marketing and sustainability is outlined.

Sustainability marketing in the tourism context

Although marketing has been criticised as fuelling irresponsible consumption, it is important to contextualise marketing as a function of corporate strategy and decision-making. There are two components to this, the extent that sustainability is commensurable with corporate strategy and the ability of marketing to influence corporate decisions. Some critical management scholars point out that

Corporate Social Responsibility (CSR) is poorly aligned to corporate capitalism. Prasad and Holzinger (2013) quote Milton Friedman's position on this: "[T]here is one and only one social responsibility of business—to use its resources to engage in activities designed to increase its profits so long as it stays within the rules of the game, which is to say, engages in open and free competition without deception or fraud" (Friedman, 1970, cited in Prasad & Holzinger, 2013, p. 1915). Prasad and Holzinger (2013) point out that CSR has become embedded within corporate culture and practice. Partly this is driven by legislation that has attempted to encourage firms to address social and environmental considerations alongside profit as part of the triple bottom line approach to firm strategy. In turn, this legislation has been a consequence of international treaties and laws on climate change, which has attempted to set limits on future carbon emissions. However, the critical management studies perspective argues that there is a fundamental tension at the heart of all CSR initiatives that are part of corporate marketing. That is the impossibility of caring for people who are at a great distance from the day to day activities of the firm. Globalisation has brought the distant into the everyday and yet it is perhaps beyond the capabilities of ordinary people to effect real changes for people who are far removed from them. Whilst we may argue that tourism brings these two sets of stakeholders together more readily than in other consumer contexts, the level of interaction and/or connections between them are inevitably limited and at the surface level. It is in this sense that sustainability marketing in a CSR context will undoubtedly fall open to accusations of greenwashing, however laudable the intentions (for more discussion on greenwashing, see Delmas & Cuerel Burbano, 2011, Smith & Font, 2014).

However, firms do not engage in CSR initiatives solely because they are legislated to do so. Much previous research has highlighted the market-based imperative for more sustainable corporate actions, including to meet increasing interest in, and levels of demand for, "green" products and services. On the one hand, there is a consumer push and on the other there is the influence of greater sustainability on firm performance (i.e. profits) or as a means through which they can satisfy some investors, or even justify their existence. Wymer and Polonsky (2015) summarise these competing dimensions underscoring the role of green marketing. They conclude that, whilst there is evidence to suggest that a greening of production can lead to cost-savings or to greater profit through adding value or increasing the competitiveness and attraction of the firm to the market, the profit motive is necessarily limited in scope. Similarly, whilst many firms understand and subscribe to the societal benefits of their actions, it would be contrary to good business sense to adopt a pure sustainable approach, which would impact negatively on profit, and so it is not a priority for firms. In terms of green consumerism, Wymer and Polonsky argue that despite much research on the potential of harnessing consumer's pro-environmental values and preferences, and the potential link to premium pricing, the actual uptake in the mass market has been limited. Greater sustainability would be achieved if consumers could be encouraged to adopt more responsible lifestyles and behaviours (Sheth, Sethia, & Srinivas, 2011). They argue that much more research is required to understand how to assist consumers in improving their decision-making, and how to increase the preference for green products in the mass market rather than in just the green consumer segment (2015, p. 255). While much is being learned about methods to nudge consumers to buy more sustainable tourism products (see, for example, Araña & León, 2016), the environmental psychology and behavioural economics literatures (e.g. Cialdini, 1993) have made little impact on the tourism literature (with the recent exception of Hall, 2014).

Two approaches can be broadly identified in sustainability marketing, the market development and product development approaches. Essentially, market development aims to increase sustainability-driven consumerism by selling products that are very sustainable to a small but growing market, and the efforts are primarily in finding ways to change the behaviour of the consumer so they purposefully purchase more sustainable products. In contrast, the product development approach aims to design and market products that are incrementally more sustainable to the entire market, as we explain below.

The market development approach

Much effort has gone into identifying market segments that have pro-sustainability values, beliefs and behavioural intentions, and finding persuasive methods to convince consumers in general to buy products identified as sustainable specifically because of such characteristics. Researchers are beginning to apply innovative psychological and sociological techniques to improve our understanding about the paradox between what consumer's state as their preferences, attitudes and intentions, and their actual behaviour as tourists, in order to identify market segments that are willing to purchase more sustainable products or behave in a more environmentally friendly way while on holiday, as shown by Babakhani, Ritchie and Dolnicar (2017) in this issue. A great deal of research has suggested that tourists value the environment, would like to act responsibly and favour greater sustainability (Miller, Rathouse, Scarles, Holmes, & Tribe, 2010). Some have suggested that tourists would even be willing to pay higher prices for more sustainable tourism experiences (Dolnicar, Crouch, & Long, 2008). Therefore, sustainable tourism segments could be targeted by tourism operators and destinations. In addition, if consumers are sympathetic to sustainable issues, this suggests that their behaviour could be steered towards more pro-environmental actions, or that the right types of marketing appeals (communications) could be effective in eliciting more sustainable consumption behaviour (Mair & Bergin-Seers, 2010). The mix and type of interventions or messages is important and can dramatically increase (or decrease) the effectiveness of pro-environmental appeals (Baca-Motes, Brown, Gneezy, Keenan, & Nelson, 2013).

Qualitative studies have attempted to understand the complex ethical and moral dilemmas facing those tourists who actively wish to act in a more responsible way. Recent studies have shown that responsibility in tourism is not something that has fixed meanings and definitions. Caruana, Glozer, Crane, and McCabe (2014) found that self-proclaimed responsible tourists thought that "responsibility" could be translated into many different dimensions, including "honest marketing" at one end of a spectrum and deeply immersive cultural and educational exchanges with locals people at the other. Not only does this show that there are varying levels of awareness about what concepts such as sustainability and responsibility mean to consumers, but it highlights the malleability of the ideas and ideals behind them, and demonstrates that consumers can adopt a range of styles and positions on different occasions and in different situations, highlighting the challenges of identifying specifically sustainable market segments. This makes the task of marketers and marketing more complex and calls for a better understanding of the varying "shades" of sustainability in the market.

A sustainability consumerism approach means that firms and social organisations will aim to meet the needs of consumers with relevant pro-environmental or responsible offers, often by highlighting their firm's sustainability based on certain criteria. This approach faces numerous challenges, such as raising awareness of consumers, often at a time when they are not predisposed to it, and convincing them that the alternative offered will fulfil their needs. It assumes that marketing and communication can make sustainability relevant to the decision-making and purchasing behaviour of the consumer. There is much evidence that shows this is weak in tourism, through evidence showing how ecolabels have not reached sufficient market impact (Chong & Verma, 2013) or because they have not been sufficiently market relevant (Rex & Baumann, 2007).

A further strand of related research and practice is that which attempts at influencing consumers to behave more sustainably. This special issue represents a coordinated effort to study the potential for behaviour change towards more sustainable tourism. Truong and Hall stand out for their previous contributions on this topic, and in their paper in this issue, they have studied 14 programmes that they consider to share some behavioural change strategies typical of social marketing. They found that despite the banner of social marketing, most programmes in practice are used to achieve business objectives (eight of the 14 seek to reduce water and energy consumption and improve waste management for example, which reduce operational costs for business), while those with clear altruistic benefits focus on a range of issues including preventing litter, preventing drug and substance abuse, reducing demand for rhino horn, and eating better and exercising more (Truong & Hall, 2017).

This special issue attempts to study in more detail the effectiveness of different social marketing interventions (Villarino & Font, 2015; Wehrli et al., 2014). We have learned so far that sustainability messages that appear overly moralising are off-putting to consumers. Messages based on fear, including campaigns highlighting potential consequences of climate change, have been shown to be less effective than other types of messages, since consumers cannot relate to those messages personally, and they find it difficult to envisage future scenarios. Despite the fact that companies know this, they lack the skills to write differently (Kreps & Monin, 2011). Emphasis needs to be on providing alternative desirable experiences that deflect consumers' attention from buying the most unsustainable products and actions by making them less attractive, particularly in situations where sustainability arguments are seen as a threat to one's freedom as consumer (Bögel, 2015; Font & Hindley, 2016; Petty & Cacioppo, 1986).

Some research has suggested that marketing messages should focus on empowering consumers' own capacities for change in order to be more effective (Van der Linden, 2014). Businesses and destinations are more likely to achieve behaviour change by using messages showing that they are on the same side as the consumer, by putting the emphasis on doing things together for an altruistic or collective benefit. This is because many direct sustainability messages which compel consumers to change their behaviour may backfire, since assertive messages are counterproductive when they are seen as an infringement of the consumer's freedom of choice (Dillard & Shen, 2005; Kronrod, Grinstein, & Wathieu, 2012), particularly when promoting sustainable behaviour (Meneses & Palacio, 2007). Examples of social marketing in tourism show how a range of positively and negatively framed messages, i.e. those highlighting benefits for the consumer and those asking the consumer to not do something bad (Truong & Hall, 2017), can be effective, despite the evidence that negatively framed messages turn off less environmentally conscious consumers (Huang, Cheng, Chuang, & Kuo, 2016). Studies in this issue provide specific examples of how to frame messages in a way to achieve better outcomes and choices, building on a nascent literature in tourism (Hardeman, Font, & Nawijn, 2017; Villarino & Font, 2015; Wehrli et al., 2014).

For example, Knežević Cvelbar, Grün, and Dolnicar (2017) provide a detailed account of different approaches reported in the literature to nudge consumers towards making more sustainable choices including educational approaches, or targeting segments more likely to behave sustainably either because of socio-demographic characteristics or internal factors. Borden, Coles, and Shaw (2017) found that social marketing initiatives requiring time and investment, or that were seen to potentially disrupt the customer experience, were not favoured by accommodation managers, while they generally found providing positive messages to be more acceptable, in three ways: by including some environmental explanation in the initial welcome introduction, by using feedback cards in the bedroom for customers to suggest further actions, and by using child focused messaging in the hope this also influences adults. We then delve deeper to study how interventions informed by specific theoretical constructs affect consumers. Babakhani et al. (2017)) demonstrate the importance of increasing attention and emotional arousal, together with broadening the range of benefits to include social norms, increase response to broader environmental concerns (Schultz, 2001); Mossaz and Coghlan (2017) show the potential of normalising the selection of sustainability suppliers, and focusing on the benefits of the consumer experience. Ponnapureddy, Priskin, Ohnmacht, Vinzenz, and Wirth (2017) find that general trust in others, specific trust in the hotel and the perceived usefulness of the hotel's brochure content are positively and significantly related to intentions to book a sustainable hotel. Babakhani et al. (2017)) found that textual messages fail to attract attention, whereas messages with images of people and the environment fared better.

While we have made much progress, the limitations of a market-led approach to sustainable tourism are numerous. The proportion of travellers that actually purchase sustainable tourism products remains rather limited (Karlsson & Dolnicar, 2016), and, considering the growth of the tourism industry, it is unlikely to be sufficient to have the transformative change that is needed to change the behaviours of tourism suppliers. Consumers that purchase more sustainable products often use this as an opportunity for moral licensing, that is, they will treat themselves to doing something unsustainable because they have "compensated" for it by doing something sustainable (Cascio & Plant, 2015; Hertwich, 2005). The two actions do not need to be equal in importance or impact, actually they will choose to act based on the "costs" - understood as time, money, convenience or comfort (Diekmann & Preisendörfer, 2003; Stern, 1992). Hence, businesses ought to communicate with customers using explicitly sustainable messages only for the most important actions that they want the customer to undertake, while for other actions, it may be advisable to avoid references to sustainability and frame all suggestions as part of a better holiday experience. Knowing that a product is sustainable is likely to actually increase consumption – for example using more water or energy in ecolodges, or consuming more food and drink with lower calories or alcohol content (Cascio & Plant, 2015; Hertwich, 2005), feeding their sense of sustainable hedonism (Malone, McCabe, & Smith, 2014) and causing a rebound effect. The lack of conclusive evidence confirming the existence of sustainable segments has meant that businesses have dismissed the need to change their products (Dolnicar et al., 2008). Sustainability marketing must offer more, if we are to even aspire to meet any of the Sustainable Development Goals.

The product development approach

The second strand of sustainability marketing, arguably less developed, considers how marketers have a responsibility to design products that are more sustainable, but that are sold to consumers based on other decision-making attributes. One example is the difference between selling travel by train instead of flying, based not on its smaller carbon footprint but on convenience. The purpose here is for businesses to take responsibility to normalise the consumption of products with more sustainable features, through a better understanding of market needs and the marketing skills required to survive in a market-based economy (Grant, 2007). This approach is driven by customer-relevant sustainable product design and places the responsibility for sustainable tourism marketing with the producer and not the market. Many consumers feel it is the responsibility of tour operators and destinations to become more active in ensuring sustainability. As such this approach focuses on finding methods to make sustainable products more appealing to the marketplace, or to introduce sustainability features to the products currently bought by the market, without negatively affecting demand. This requires a greater commitment from suppliers, as the business case cannot often be made internally on the basis of accessing new target markets, and instead the focus is on business resilience and reputational risk management.

This approach moves away from a segmentation approach, and focuses on establishing opportunities for *all* consumers to behave in a more sustainable way, irrespective of their attitudes. Mainstreaming sustainability is achieved by normalising the purchase of more sustainable products. The effort here is placed on product design and it differs from the sustainability consumerism, or market-led approach because it plays down sustainability benefits and emphasises personal benefits to the consumer instead. This approach has the advantage that the product can be continuously improved towards greater sustainability, without having to sacrifice commercialisation of the product until it meets certain standards, reducing fears of claims of greenwashing, and where effort is directed to continuously fine tune the sustainability features of the product in the background, ensuring that sales are maintained (Grant, 2007; Ottman, Stafford, & Hartman, 2006).

Two studies in this special issue help us make the case for a product design approach. Mossaz and Coghlan (2017) developed a framework to study how travel agents choose to speak about sustainability as part of their sales process, that looks at message framing, salience, cognitive effort, the role of affect, projection bias and false consensus. The nuanced account they provide gives a candid understanding of the importance of conservation to tourism professionals' social identity as professional safari travel agents, how selecting suppliers with conservation efforts has been normalised, and yet how these choices are not verbalised as part of the sales process for fear that they will jeopardise a focus on the hedonistic benefits of a unique experience, that just happens to be sustainable. This moral muteness and customer-centred experiential understanding (Kreps & Monin, 2011;

Malone et al., 2014) was elaborated in the study by Font, Elgammal and Lamond (2017) as green-hushing, that is, the deliberate underplaying of sustainability attributes in the marketing process, for fear that consumers will see the company as less competent or the product or service of lower quality. What they have in common is that they report on businesses that are not prepared to wait for the marketplace to demand sustainable products, and have found methods to take the initiative in supplying them as part of a better consumer experience (Font et al. 2017; Mossaz & Coghlan, 2017).

It is worth remembering that unsustainable behaviour is often a by-product of societal changes, and therefore the issues relating to sustainable outcomes need to be understood as part of product redesign. In this special issue, Gössling (2016) analyses the impact that internet-based platforms can have on sustainable tourism. He argues that information technology has further glamorised travel and has fuelled the desire for comparison of travel behaviours as well as being a mechanism for social connectedness, which feeds into identity and social status. This social trend, Gössling argues, feeds into a desire for conspicuous experience consumption, representative of a consumer culture that supports aspirational and acquisitive consumption. This consumer culture leads to increases in carbon footprint and wasteful behaviour in the quest for travel experiences that are readily acquired and showcased online through social media sites. Gössling also reflects on how information technology has brought about opportunities to serve ever more sophisticated segmented markets with diverse sustainable travel choices, yet with limited evidence on the impact these have on the global marketplace to date. Furthermore, digital technology has facilitated a sharing economy of travel, which is a mixed blessing for sustainability: it can increase the utilisation of resources, but also have unintended negative consequences. It is worth noting that sharing economy sites, such as Airbnb, Uber and BlaBlacar have grown faster than sites specifically promoting the sustainability options for travel. Information technology has led to increased market concentration and dominance, and the reputation of travel services is closely aligned with their online ratings and the temptation to over-state, or even fabricate, positive reputation. Technology platforms allow benchmarking that leads to competitive behaviours, which in turn has increased customer expectations on quality and service.

In a similar way, there is potential for different avenues to achieve more sustainable behaviour as a result of changing the way that products are designed and marketed, without presenting the products as sustainable per se. The emphasis here is an effort in making mainstream products slightly more sustainable. This is not marketing sustainable products, but marketing for sustainability benefits. The carbon footprint for travel to a destination is arguably the responsibility of the destination: it is their marketing efforts that will in part influence which markets visit the destination, and therefore the distances travelled, the mix of activities they will engage in, length of stay and so on. Therefore, a tourist destination can, for example, use their marketing efforts to reduce the carbon footprint of tourism, targeting markets for which there are direct flights rather than relying on hubs that increase the carbon footprint, or targeting segments that can access the destination through more environmentally friendly transport methods. This could be applicable to the private sector also, according to Knežević Cvelbar et al. (2017), who suggest that an understanding of the likely environmental footprint of different types of guests may become part of how hosts in networks such as Airbnb select guests, which would however constitute a further case of discrimination (Edelman & Luca, 2014), even if this is arguably for pro-environmental reasons. A tourist board would, therefore, have a new performance indicator for its marketing actions: carbon footprint of transport per visitor per night. Needless to say, we have not found any destination doing this, although Whittlesea and Owen (2012) produced and tested a bespoke tourism footprinting and scenario tool to make this possible for the UK's South West Tourism (a regional marketing agency).

Marketing can help us attract markets that have a more "normal" behaviour, that is, visitors that behave more like residents. Visitors that behave more like residents have a lower demonstration effect, reducing host–guest conflict, and also are more likely to spread their economic impact by buying more local products, and visiting a broader range of locations in the tourist destination rather than the key honeypots that suffer from overcrowding. One method that a tourist destination can use for this is to specifically target repeat visitors. Tourist boards might be reluctant to do this because part of their remit, and the justification for their existence, is through opening new markets, and also because repeat markets spend less per day. The statistics of tourist destinations on individual markets, however, tell us about expenditure, but not leakages and multiplier effects (and we all know that turnover is vanity whereas profit margins are sanity). A better understanding of how different markets spend and how such spending impacts on the destination may give us a different picture, and this could inform marketing efforts. A new performance indicator for tourist boards could well be the percentage of repeat visitors to the destination. While destinations may well have such data, the repeat market is not seen as a priority: it is often just taken for granted.

Tourist boards and businesses alike can also make tourism more sustainable by reducing geographical and seasonal pressures. Visitors often focus on very specific times and sites, which creates congestion, negative social and environmental impacts that are much higher than would be necessary if distributed more evenly. Congestion also means that the local economy cannot serve the needs of visitors efficiently, an opportunity cost, while the lack of visitors in low season is a second reason of sub-optimal performance. Destinations must change the way they promote themselves and stop relying on iconic attractions that are already saturated, and design packages so that iconic attractions can only be accessed as part of a longer stay. Explicit efforts at destination de-marketing will be more acceptable to consumers if they are found to fit well with the brand's environmental reputation (Armstrong Soule & Reich, 2015) and politically it is rather complex for destinations to do this, while private companies are unlikely to see a benefit in not showing the Eiffel tower in their marketing of Paris, for example, although they can suggest innovative ways of experiencing iconic sites that provide a better experience with a more acceptable impact.

Nudging consumers away from the most unsustainable choices may work better, and both Araña and León (2016) and Hall (2014) provide some promising examples such as the utilisation of attract and dispersal strategies, offering an increasing range of things to do, and marketing the personality of complimentary destinations that can serve different markets. The dispersion of tourism should also be diverting consumers away from peak demand periods in order to distribute demand to create a regular flow of visitors, which can be optimally accommodated. It is still surprising how many destinations seem to market their summer season in their brochures and websites, which is likely to be full anyway, and instead do not pay attention to their shoulder or low seasons. Ski resorts learned a long time ago to promote summer trekking, attractions as different as aquariums and museums are opening at night to provide more intimate experiences, and yet it seems odd that summer destinations have not always learned how to diversify their offer. The "Visit Amsterdam, See Holland" campaign to disperse tourism across the city and to neighbouring towns is a good example running since 2009 (Amsterdam Marketing, 2017), while numerous adventure tour operators are redesigning their tours for animal welfare reasons, and getting creative about providing activities that are both more humane and experiential (see, for example, G Adventures, 2017; TOFTigers, 2017).

Destination management organisations and distribution channels must introduce sustainability requirements in their supply chains, in order to make sustainability a de facto requirement to trade. In the same way that fair trade tea, coffee, cocoa, bananas and other commodities are becoming normalised, the tourism industry must use the lessons learned across other sectors to do the same. From humble beginnings (Schwartz, Tapper, & Font, 2008), companies as different as the largest leisure, travel and tourism company in the world, TUI, and the 1500 employee G Adventures are surveying their suppliers to identify and reward those that meet sustainability standards – both display their achievements in their brochures, but expect customers to buy their products for quality, not sustainability reasons. In mature destinations, with well-developed supply chains, sustainability certification must be the norm, not the exception. A destination cannot market their sustainability efforts with credibility when the majority of its product is not sustainable. Rather than expecting tourists to demand sustainable products, the public sector itself must acknowledge that they are often the largest buyer of catering, conference, event, hotel and transport services, and it is within their power to introduce sustainability criteria, that will then create a snowball effect. The city of Copenhagen is an example of good practice: over 70% of all its hotels are certified as sustainable, 18% of all food sold is certified as organic, and nearly 80% of all food purchased by the public sector as certified organic (VisitCopenhagen, 2017).

The cost of achieving a low carbon tourism sector by 2030 is estimated at US$11 per person per trip if costs are shared amongst international and domestic arrivals, or US$38 if only international arrivals pay (Scott, Gössling, Hall, and Peeters (2016). This relatively low cost of offsetting carbon emissions, together with the limited uptake of such programmes, begs the question of why the tourism industry relies on voluntary market mechanisms. Clearly raising awareness is likely to achieve some change, as well as showing the credibility of carbon offsetting, as found in tests conducted by Babakhani et al. (2017). But there is also an argument that such voluntary mechanisms are a way of avoiding regulation while also demonstrating the lack of appetite for further intervention by consumers. This is an example of the limits of product design mechanisms for sustainability marketing, in that issues without a clear win–win solution are unlikely to be addressed by businesses or destinations, and carbon suffers from not being a particularly attractive topic to sell to tourists, while absorbing the cost will only happen for the more committed businesses. The UK adventure tour operator Explore (www.explore.co.uk/about-us) is a good example of making a stand in this respect and including it in their price, hence reducing profit margins, because of their belief in taking responsibility.

These are just some further research avenues available to the tourism researcher that require a deeper understanding of the commercial realities of our industry, which in turn has potential to deliver scalable, impactful solutions.

Methods and impact in sustainability marketing

This special issue makes a contribution not only by identifying methods to make sustainable products more attractive and social marketing techniques more persuasive, but also by broadening the range of methods to study the effectiveness of such approaches (Doran & Larsen, 2014). Because of the evidence that environmental intentions are a poor predictor of behaviour (Juvan & Dolnicar, 2014), we must develop different methods to examine sustainability intentions (Dolnicar & Ring, 2014). Process evaluation helps understand what works for whom in what circumstances, rather than simply reporting on decontextualised outcomes. It is by looking into the "black box" of consumer behaviour that allows us to understand specific contextual factors that influence why certain mechanisms achieve desired outcomes in some cases but not in others. What the experimental and mixed methods approaches used in this special issue have in common is in their providing a greater depth of understanding, grounded in psychological theories that also have practical applications.

In this issue, Babakhani et al. (2017) develop communication methods that counteract previous limitations of engagement in carbon offsetting, writing messages to improve the effectiveness, transparency, choice and calculation of carbon offsetting. They test both the attention and activation of the respondents against these messages using psycho-physiological and attitudinal measures. Ponnapureddy et al. (2017) conduct a survey using the hypothetical scenario planning method to test purchase intentions, based on a fictitious 16-page online brochure. Borden et al. (2017) study how social marketing initiatives from small accommodation firms that encourage water efficient behaviour among guests impacts on the experience of those guests. This sequential mixed methods study has a minor qualitative element, studying the behaviours and attitudes of accommodation managers towards water saving initiatives, in order to complement a dominant quantitative part studying the response of guests towards such initiatives. Warren, Becken, & Coghlan (2017) conduct an action research experiment, developing a series of social marketing initiatives and testing their impact on consumer behaviour.

Most of these studies report a certain level of success in identifying methods to change consumer behaviour, and point towards theoretically valid constructs that may be operationalised in a broad range of contexts. Measuring the impact of social interventions is rare: Truong and Hall (2017) found that, besides the small operational savings, the majority of the campaigns studied did not seem to have a direct business benefit, such as increased purchases, other than vague reputational added value. Despite some rather vague claims about the effects of these programmes on positive behaviour change, actual evidence of effectiveness is rarely available. Truong and Hall (2017) found that results are not attributable, are vaguely generalised or simply not made available. It is also evident that studies tend to be highly context specific, and rarely consider the ways that contextual variables may have influenced results.

Borden et al. (2017) found some willingness to change behaviour in order to save water, but overall the results show that social marketing efforts (eight initiatives and five messages) would be more welcomed when they were supported by incentives and were found to not get in the way of positive guest experience. These incentives were, however, costly and therefore the least preferred initiatives by the accommodation owners. What is not clear at this point is the likely return on investment of different social marketing initiatives, which points the way to potential new lines for research. Warren et al. (2017) test a range of social marketing initiatives and are able to quantify the impact these have on resource consumption, while reporting limited negative impact on the guest experience. And yet despite reporting positive results, they also acknowledge that this type of intervention requires a level of dedication rarely seen in small accommodation owners, and that the positive response from consumers may be, in part, the result of the personal rapport developed between host and guest during the process.

Much further research is needed to provide realistic evaluations of the impact of campaigns on behaviour change, based on the bigger picture of how behaviour was formed or affected (Pawson & Tilley, 1997). Gregory-Smith, Wells, Manika, and McElroy (2017) establish that a thorough understanding of contextual factors can determine the ability of a social marketing project to achieve its outcomes (in this case, through internal communications via email, signage, toolkits, workshops, etc.) and how it can be used as an evaluative tool, and arguably also proactively as a diagnostic tool to reduce risks in project preparation. The study shows how outcomes are the result of multiple layers of decisions and how it is only by recognising the levels of complexity involved that we can fully appreciate the value of any intervention. Using data from interviews with the staff implementing the intervention as well as employees of the heritage tourism organisation involved, Gregory-Smith et al. (2017)) found that a number of contextual issues affected the ability of mechanisms to generate outcomes. For example, the lack of understanding of organisational culture in the implementation of pro-sustainability decisions meant that a blanket approach was taken; and the lack of pro-environmental infrastructure in the heritage properties did not allow certain objectives and initiatives to be translated into specific actions; agency issues of staff empowerment would prevent environmental awareness mechanisms from achieving their desired outcome, and so on.

Further research is needed to understand the conditions under which some of the studies included in this special issue achieved the outcomes reported. A pragmatic research approach should allow us to contextualise these social marketing initiatives, and help us assess their replicability and scalability.

Conclusions

Whilst this special issue represents merely the tip of the iceberg of the challenges facing tourism's sustainability and the role marketing can play in helping to achieve more sustainable outcomes, the articles brought together in this volume represent the cutting edge of research in this field. The research presented demonstrates the breadth of approaches that can be utilised to understand how consumers can be influenced to make more sustainable choices that do not compromise their main motivations, and also how we can mainstream sustainability into the wider tourism business through product design and more persuasive marketing messages. Globally, the industry is now at a pivotal point in its history. The research presented here shows that there are many innovative solutions to sustainability challenges and that there is a growing impetus for the development of more sustainable tourism products that can be marketed successfully. We hope that the range of issues covered, and the methods developed and applied will provide encouragement across the tourism marketing and sustainability fields to work more closely together in search of common goals for a prosperous, and environmentally responsible industry and marketplace, one that respects the needs of all stakeholders to achieve positive, successful and long-term outcomes, including tourists, residents, the tourism industry and related destination services. This special issue helps enable a platform for such greater cooperation and future research.

Some other wider ranging points need to be made. There is the problem of subject sub-division amongst researchers. An assessment of how best to market the concept of sustainable tourism to tourists, to the commercial world, and to those involved in the governance of tourism, requires many different subject specialists to work together. That is rare in the world of tourism academics. For example, this journal has encouraged papers and special issues on behavioural change. Its two most recent special issues on this subject (Volume 24, Issue 3, 2016 and Volume 21 (7) 2013) had very little discussion about the role of markets and marketing: papers concentrated on other questions, because those issues were promoted and populated by academics who had little experience in marketing. Given the commercial world's belief in marketing to secure tourist behaviour in their favour, that is surprising, but it is reality. This paucity of research into marketing may also reflect the failure of many sustainable tourism academics to work with the tourism industry (Lane, 2009). Higuchi and Yamanaka (2017), however, present a fascinating example of recent success in industry–academic cooperation. And there is a very important form of para-marketing in tourism – the role of travel writers and journalists, who have enormous but un-researched roles in influencing the image of sustainable tourism. McWha, Frost, and Laing (2017) have begun work on aspects of research into that area. Finally, there is a major implementation problem. How can the marketing specialists working in tourism promotion and marketing learn about the critical role of sustainable tourism in the future of the industry and the regions in which it works, and how can we, as researchers, disseminate our findings to them, and their clients?

Disclosure statement

No potential conflict of interest was reported by the authors.

References

American Marketing Association. (2013). Definition of marketing. Retrieved February 27, 2017, from https://www.ama.org/AboutAMA/Pages/Definition-of-Marketing.aspx
Amsterdam Marketing. (2017). Amsterdam metropolitan area visitors survey 2016. Retrieved February 25, 2017, from http://magazines.iamsterdam.com/boma-2016-english#!/amsterdam-bezoeken-holland-zien-copy-duplicate

Araña, J. E., & León, C. J. (2016). Are tourists animal spirits? Evidence from a field experiment exploring the use of non-market based interventions advocating sustainable tourism. *Journal of Sustainable Tourism, 24*(3), 430–445.

Armstrong Soule, C. A., & Reich, B. J. (2015). Less is more: Is a green demarketing strategy sustainable? *Journal of Marketing Management, 31*(13–14), 1403–1427.

Babakhani, N., Ritchie, B. W., & Dolnicar, S. (2017). Improving carbon offsetting appeals in online airplane ticket purchasing: Testing new messages, and using new test methods. *Journal of Sustainable Tourism,* 1–15. doi:10.1080/09669582.2016.1257013.

Baca-Motes, K., Brown, A., Gneezy, A., Keenan, E. A., & Nelson, L. D. (2013). Commitment and behavior change: Evidence from the field. *Journal of Consumer Research, 39*(5), 1070–1084.

Bögel, P. M. (2015). Processing of CSR communication: Insights from the ELM. *Corporate Communications: An International Journal, 20*(2), 128–143.

Borden, D.S., Coles, T., & Shaw, G. (2017). Social marketing, sustainable tourism and small/medium size tourism enterprises: Challenges and opportunities for changing guest behaviour. *Journal of Sustainable Tourism.* doi:10.1080/09669582.2016 1270952

Caruana, R., Glozer, S., Crane, A., & McCabe, S. (2014). Tourists' accounts of responsible tourism. *Annals of Tourism Research, 46*, 115–129.

Cascio, J., & Plant, E. A. (2015). Prospective moral licensing: Does anticipating doing good later allow you to be bad now? *Journal of Experimental Social Psychology, 56*, 110–116.

Cialdini, R. B. (1993). *Influence: The psychology of persuasion.* New York, NY: HarperCollins.

Chong, H., & Verma, R. (2013). *Hotel sustainability: Financial analysis shines a cautious green light.* Ithaca, NY: Cornell University. Retrieved February 27, 2017, from http://scholarship.sha.cornell.edu/cgi/viewcontent.cgi?article=1023&context=chrpubs

Delmas, M. A., & Cuerel Burbano, V. (2011). The drivers of greenwashing. *California Management Review, 54*(1), 64–87.

Diekmann, A., & Preisendörfer, P. (2003). Green and greenback the behavioral effects of environmental attitudes in low-cost and high-cost situations. *Rationality and Society, 15*(4), 441–472.

Dillard, J. P., & Shen, L. (2005). On the nature of reactance and its role in persuasive health communication. *Communication Monographs, 72*(2), 144–168.

Dolnicar, S., Crouch, G. I., & Long, P. (2008). Environment-friendly tourists: What do we really know about them? *Journal of Sustainable Tourism, 16*(2), 197–210.

Dolnicar, S., & Ring, A. (2014). Tourism marketing research: Past, present and future. *Annals of Tourism Research, 47*, 31–47.

Doran, R., & Larsen, S. (2014). Are we all environmental tourists now? The role of biases in social comparison across and within tourists, and their implications. *Journal of Sustainable Tourism, 22*(7), 1023–1036.

Edelman, B. G., & Luca, M. (2014). *Digital discrimination: The case of airbnb. com.* (Harvard Business School NOM Unit Working Paper (14–054)). Retrieved February 1, 2017, from http://www.hbs.edu/faculty/Publication%20Files/Airbnb_92dd6086-6e46-4eaf-9cea-60fe5ba3c596.pdf

Font, X., Elgammal, I., & Lamond, I. (2017). Greenhushing: The deliberate under communicating of sustainability practices by tourism businesses. *Journal of Sustainable Tourism.* doi:10.1080/09669582.2016.1158829

Font, X., & Hindley, A. (2016). Understanding tourists' reactance to the threat of a loss of freedom to travel due to climate change: A new alternative approach to encouraging nuanced behavioural change. *Journal of Sustainable Tourism, 25*(1), 26–42

G Adventures. (2017). G Adventures 50 in 5. Retrieved January 19, 2017, from https://www.gadventures.co.uk/twenty-five/50-in-5/.

Gössling, S. (2016). Tourism, information technologies and sustainability: An exploratory review. *Journal of Sustainable Tourism,* 1–18. doi:10.1080/09669582.2015.1122017.

Grant, J. (2007). *The green marketing manifesto.* Chichester: Wiley.

Gregory-Smith, D., Wells, V. K., Manika, D., & McElroy, D. J. (2017). A realist evaluation of an environmental social marketing intervention in cultural heritage tourism. *Journal of Sustainable Tourism.* doi:10.1080/09669582.2017.1288732

Hall, C. M. (2014). *Tourism and social marketing.* London: Routledge.

Hardeman, G., Font, X., & Nawijn, J. (2017). The power of persuasive communication to influence sustainable holiday choices: Appealing to self-benefits and norms. *Tourism Management, 59*, 484–493.

Hertwich, E. G. (2005). Consumption and the rebound effect: An industrial ecology perspective. *Journal of Industrial Ecology, 9*(1–2), 85–98.

Higuchi, Y., & Yamanaka, Y. (2017). Knowledge sharing between academic researchers and tourism practitioners: A Japanese study of the practical value of embeddedness, trust and co-creation. *Journal of Sustainable Tourism.* doi:10.1080/09669582.2017.1288733

Huang, M. C.-J., Cheng, Y.-H., Chuang, S.-C., & Kuo, K.-S. (2016). Framing makes tourists more environmentally conservative. *Annals of Tourism Research, 61*, 242–244.

Johnston, I. (2017). 2016 breaks record for hottest year ever. Retrieved January 19, 2017, from http://www.independent.co.uk/environment/dangerous-climate-change-time-running-out-2016-hottest-year-on-record-climatologist-gabi-hegerl-a7533211.html.

Jones, P., Clarke-Hill, C., Comfort, D., & Hillier, D. (2008). Marketing and sustainability. *Marketing Intelligence & Planning, 26* (2), 123–130.

Juvan, E., & Dolnicar, S. (2014). The attitude–behaviour gap in sustainable tourism. *Annals of Tourism Research, 48*, 76–95.

Karlsson, L., & Dolnicar, S. (2016). Does eco certification sell tourism services? Evidence from a quasi-experimental observation study in Iceland. *Journal of Sustainable Tourism, 24*(5), 694–714.

Knežević Cvelbar, L., Grün, B., & Dolnicar, S. (2017). Which hotel guest segments reuse towels? Selling sustainable tourism services through target marketing. *Journal of Sustainable Tourism*, 1–14. doi:10.1080/09669582.2016.1206553.

Kreps, T. A., & Monin, B. (2011). "Doing well by doing good"? Ambivalent moral framing in organizations. *Research in Organizational Behavior, 31*, 99–123.

Kronrod, A., Grinstein, A., & Wathieu, L. (2012). Go green! Should environmental messages be so assertive? *Journal of Marketing, 76*(1), 95–102.

Lane, B. (2009). Thirty years of sustainable tourism: Drivers, progress, problems and the future. In S. Gossling, C. M. Hall, & D. Weaver (Eds.), *Sustainable tourism futures: Perspectives on systems, restructuring, and innovations* (pp. 19–32). London: Routledge.

Laufer, W. S. (2003). Social accountability and corporate greenwashing. *Journal of Business Ethics, 43*(3), 253–261.

Mair, J., & Bergin-Seers, S. (2010). The effect of interventions on the environmental behaviour of Australian motel guests. *Tourism and Hospitality Research, 10*(4), 255–268.

Malone, S., McCabe, S., & Smith, A. P. (2014). The role of hedonism in ethical tourism. *Annals of Tourism Research, 44*, 241–254.

McCabe, S. (2014). Introduction. In McCabe, S. (Ed) *The Routledge handbook of tourism marketing* (pp 1–12). Oxon, UK: Routledge.

McDonagh, P., & Prothero, A. (2014). Sustainability marketing research: Past, present and future. *Journal of Marketing Management, 30*(11–12), 1186–1219.

McWha, M., Frost, W., & Laing, J. (2017). Sustainable travel writing? Exploring the ethical dilemmas of twenty-first-century travel writers. *Journal of Sustainable Tourism*, 1–17. doi:10.1080/09669582.2017.1281930

Meneses, G. D., & Palacio, A. B. (2007). The response to the commitment with block-leader recycling promotion technique: A longitudinal approach. *Journal of Nonprofit & Public Sector Marketing, 17*(1–2), 83–102.

Miller, G., Rathouse, K., Scarles, C., Holmes, K., & Tribe, J. (2010). Public understanding of sustainable tourism. *Annals of Tourism Research, 37*(3), 627–645.

Mossaz, A., & Coghlan, A. (2017). The role of travel agents' ethical concerns when brokering information in the marketing and sale of sustainable tourism. *Journal of Sustainable Tourism*, 1–18. doi:10.1080/09669582.2016.1198358.

Ottman, J. A., Stafford, E. R., & Hartman, C. L. (2006). Avoiding green marketing myopia: Ways to improve consumer appeal for environmentally preferable products. *Environment: Science and Policy for Sustainable Development, 48*(5), 22–36.

Oxfam. (2017). 62 people own same as half world. Retrieved January 19, 2017, from http://www.oxfam.org.uk/media-cen tre/press-releases/2016/01/62-people-own-same-as-half-world-says-oxfam-inequality-report-davos-world-economic-forum

Pawson, R., & Tilley, N. (1997). *Realistic evaluation*. London: SAGE.

Petty, R. E., & Cacioppo, J. T. (1986). *The elaboration likelihood model of persuasion*. New York, NY: Springer.

Ponnapureddy, S., Priskin, J., Ohnmacht, T., Vinzenz, F., & Wirth, W. (2017). The influence of trust perceptions on German tourists' intention to book a sustainable hotel: A new approach to analysing marketing information. *Journal of Sustainable Tourism*, 1–19. doi:10.1080/09669583.2016 1270952.

Prasad, A., & Holzinger, I. (2013). Seeing through smoke and mirrors: A critical analysis of marketing CSR. *Journal of Business Research, 66*(10), 1915–1921.

Rex, E., & Baumann, H. (2007). Beyond ecolabels: What green marketing can learn from conventional marketing. *Journal of Cleaner Production, 15*(6), 567–576.

Schultz, P. W. (2001). The structure of environmental concern: Concern for self, other people, and the biosphere. *Journal of Environmental Psychology, 21*(4), 327–339.

Schwartz, K., Tapper, R., & Font, X. (2008). A framework for sustainable supply chain management in tour operations. *Journal of Sustainable Tourism, 16*(3), 298–314.

Scott, D., Gössling, S., Hall, C. M., & Peeters, P. (2016). Can tourism be part of the decarbonized global economy? The costs and risks of alternate carbon reduction policy pathways. *Journal of Sustainable Tourism, 24*(1), 52–72.

Sheth, J. N., Sethia, N. K., & Srinivas, S. (2011). Mindful consumption: A customer-centric approach to sustainability. *Journal of the Academy of Marketing Science, 39*(1), 21–39.

Smith, T. M. (1998). *The myth of green marketing: Tending our goats at the edge of apocalypse*. Toronto: University of Toronto Press.

Smith, V., & Font, X. (2014). Volunteer tourism, greenwashing and understanding responsible marketing using market signalling theory. *Journal of Sustainable Tourism, 22*(6), 942–963.

Stern, P. C. (1992). What psychology knows about energy conservation. *American Psychologist, 47*(10), 1224–1232.

The Met Office. (2017). 2016: One of the two warmest years on record. Retrieved January 19, 2017, from http://www.metoffice.gov.uk/news/releases/2017/2016-record-breaking-year-for-global-temperature

TOFTigers. (2017). Travel operators for tigers. Retrieved January 19, 2017, from http://www.toftigers.org/

Truong, V. D., & Hall, C. M. (2017). Corporate social marketing in tourism: To sleep or not to sleep with the enemy? *Journal of Sustainable Tourism,* 1–19. doi:10.1080/09669582.2016.1201093.

Ulusoy, E. (2016). Experiential responsible consumption. *Journal of Business Research, 69*(1), 284–297.

Van der Linden, S. (2014). Towards a new model for communicating climate change. In S. Cohen, J. Higham, P. Peeters, & S. Gössling (Eds.), *Understanding and governing sustainable tourism mobility: Psychological and behavioural approaches* (pp. 243–275). London: Routledge.

Villarino, J., & Font, X. (2015). Sustainability marketing myopia: The lack of persuasiveness in sustainability communica-tion *Journal of Vacation Marketing, 21*(4), 326–335.

VisitCopenhagen. (2017). Sustainable Copenhagen. Retrieved January 19, 2017, from http://www.visitcopenhagen.com/copenhagen/sustainable-holidays/sustainable-copenhagen

Warren, C., Becken, S., & Coghlan, A. (2017). Using persuasive communication to co-create behavioural change–engaging with guests to save resources at tourist accommodation facilities. *Journal of Sustainable Tourism,* 1–20. doi:10.1080/09669582.2016.1247849.

Wehrli, R., Priskin, J., Demarmels, S., Schaffner, D., Schwarz, J., Truniger, F., & Stettler, J. (2014). How to communicate sus-tainable tourism products to customers: Results from a choice experiment. *Current Issues in Tourism.* doi:10.1080/13683500.2014.987732

Whittlesea, E. R., & Owen, A. (2012). Towards a low carbon future – the development and application of REAP Tourism, a destination footprint and scenario tool. *Journal of Sustainable Tourism, 20*(6), 845–865.

Wymer, W., & Polonsky, M. J. (2015). The limitations and potentialities of green marketing. *Journal of Nonprofit & Public Sector Marketing, 27*(3), 239–262.

Corporate social marketing in tourism: to sleep or not to sleep with the enemy?

V. Dao Truong and C. Michael Hall ⓘ

ABSTRACT

Social marketing is regarded as an effective consumer-oriented approach to promoting behavioural change and improved well-being for individuals, communities and society. However, its potential for tourism, especially sustainable tourism, remains under-researched. This article examines the utilisation of social marketing by tourism businesses. A search strategy identified 14 behavioural change programmes that involved tourism businesses. Half of these programmes label themselves social marketing; the others tend to be part of corporate social responsibility efforts, using a form of corporate social marketing (CSM). Most programmes seek to encourage pro-environmental behaviours in tourists, tourism businesses and other stakeholders including suppliers. Although tourism businesses can develop social marketing programmes alone, typically they collaborate with public and non-profit agencies as partners and sponsors. The strength of the tie between the promoted behaviour and the sale of a company's product varies considerably. It is suggested that social marketing can make significant contributions to environmentally sustainable tourism. However, this research also suggests that social marketing is not a substitute for, but rather an essential complement to, technological and regulatory approaches to climate change. Changing behaviour is a long process: without a long-term commitment from private sector companies, CSM programmes will fail to achieve behavioural change goals.

Introduction

Tourism's contribution to global environmental change is increasingly significant (Gössling & Peeters, 2015). This has been most clearly focused on climate change (Scott, Gössling, & Hall, in press), but also includes issues such as biodiversity loss, land-use change, water use and invasive species (Rutty, Gössling, Scott, & Hall, 2015; Scott, Gössling, & Hall, 2012). Given growth in tourist numbers, the potential detrimental impacts of tourism on the environment will only increase in the future if tourism follows a "business as usual" path (Scott, Gössling, & Hall, 2012, 2016; Scott, Gössling, Hall, & Peeters, 2016). The total annual number of tourist trips, both domestic and international, is estimated to likely exceed the world's population for the first time in 2017 (Hall, 2015). The annual number of international tourists is expected to reach 1.8 billion by 2030 (United Nations World Tourism Organisation [UNWTO], 2015). In the business-as-usual scenarios (i.e. with no changes to present policy) to 2050, the projected growth of tourism is likely to increase levels of energy consumption by 154%, greenhouse gas (GHG) emissions by 131%, water consumption by 152% and solid waste disposal by 251% (United Nations Environmental Programme [UNEP], 2015).

Industry advocates have primarily argued for technological and management solutions that focus on increased efficiency rather than any limits on tourism's growth to tackle resource use (Hall, 2009). However, while such measures may reduce, for example, emissions per passenger kilometre or guest night, the absolute amount of emissions continue to increase (Gössling, Scott, & Hall, 2013; Gössling & Peeters, 2015). The use of green labels and eco-labels that aim to encourage greater consideration of the environment in consumption practices also presents significant issues (Gössling & Buckley, 2016), often raising scepticism among consumers who may not think of holidays as an environmental harm (Villarino & Font, 2015). In the absence of legal mechanisms to reduce tourism's environmental effects, increased attention has turned towards mechanisms that encourage voluntary behavioural change by consumers (Cohen, Higham, Peeters, & Gössling, 2014), especially social marketing (Hall, 2013, 2014, 2016; Lane, 2009; Musgrave & Henderson 2015; Shaw, Barr, & Wooler, 2014; Truong, 2014; Truong & Hall, 2013, 2015a, 2015b; Truong, Dang, & Hall, 2016; Wearing & Schweinsberg, 2016), in the realisation that most environmental problems are caused by human behaviours and thus perhaps could be reversed by behavioural change (Gössling et al., 2012).

Social marketing utilises marketing techniques and methods to promote behavioural change in a target audience to engender public good (Kotler & Lee, 2008; Truong, 2014; Truong, Dang, Hall, & Dong, 2015). It generally falls within the purview of public agencies and non-profit organisations. The extent to which commercial entities can engage in social marketing, either alone or in partnership with non-profit organisations, to achieve social marketing objectives is strongly debated (Kotler, Hessekiel, & Lee, 2012), and is described by some scholars as a case of social marketing "sleep[ing] with the enemy" (Hoek & Jones, 2011, p. 39). Nevertheless, marketing and social marketing concepts have been further extended with the emergence of the corporate social marketing (CSM) concept, which is an activity that "uses business resources to develop and/or implement a behavior change campaign intended to improve public health, safety, the environment, or community well-being" (Kotler et al., 2012, p. 111), with such activities either being undertaken autonomously by a business or as a form of public—private partnership (PPP). Bloom, Hussein, and Szykman (1995) defined CSM as "an initiative in which marketing personnel who work for a corporation or one of its agents devote significant amounts of time and effort toward persuading people to engage in a socially beneficial behavior" (p. 10).

Although the context for promoting behavioural change in tourism appears favourable, with much emphasis on tourist market segments committed to environmental protection and tourism businesses supporting environmental initiatives (Peeters, Gössling, & Lane, 2009; Shang, Basil, & Wymer, 2010), in very few cases do tourism researchers demonstrate actual long-term behavioural change outcomes (Truong & Hall, 2015a). Despite strong advocacy for its adoption (Lane, 2009), tourism research into social marketing and associated behavioural interventions (i.e. "nudging" [Hall, 2013; Higham, Cohen, Cavaliere, Reis, & Finkler, 2016]) is limited in terms of published output and long-term tracking of interventions throughout the tourism system (Truong & Hall, 2013). Furthermore, even though there is substantial advocacy at a government, supranational and industry level for use of PPPs to achieve sustainable tourism goals, their capacity to achieve social marketing goals in tourism remains a significant research gap. For example, the UNWTO states:

> The Public-Private Partnership in the UN system and especially at UNWTO is critical to the Organization's efforts to address global challenges, related to sustainable tourism and development.

> An UN initiative, created in 2000 and called United Nations Global Compact engages with multinational companies and corporations to spot and evaluate the corporate social responsibility of their business activities, and

strives to advocate the inclusion, the monitoring and reporting of the UN sustainable development goals into their business operations. (United Nations World Tourism Organisation [UNWTO], 2016)

Although there is substantial research on PPPs in sustainable tourism with respect to governance (e.g. Lapeyre, 2011; Ruhanen, 2008; Spenceley, 2012; Zapata & Hall, 2012), and some aspects of destination marketing (Dinnie, 2011; Guzmán & Sierra, 2012), there is a paucity of studies specifically on tourism PPPs in relation to social marketing and behavioural change (Wearing & Schweinsberg, 2016). Such knowledge is important not only because of the extent to which it may underlie any behavioural intervention strategy in tourism settings but also because it may contribute to the evidence base of the potentially meaningful but neglected interrelationships between tourism and social marketing. Therefore, this study is a first step in seeking to understand CSM particularly within the context of PPP.

This article examines the adoption of social marketing by tourism businesses. First, it positions CSM within the social marketing field. Next, it reviews tourism research on social marketing. Then it describes the use of research methods and presents main research findings. Limitations to the present research are noted and opportunities for further studies suggested.

Social marketing, CSM, and PPPs

The concept of social marketing was introduced to refer to the application of marketing principles and methods to "the design, implementation, and control of programs calculated to influence the acceptability of social ideas" (Kotler & Zaltman, 1971, p. 5). Social marketing has received substantial attention from scholars in marketing and related disciplines and has been used to promote behavioural change in health, well-being and the environment (Hoek & Jones, 2011; Kotler et al., 2012; McKenzie-Mohr, Lee, Schultz, & Kotler, 2012; Truong, 2014; Truong & Hall, 2015b). Given that social marketing seeks to engender public good, it is generally undertaken by governmental and not-for-profit agencies, with the significance of PPPs being an ongoing theme (Truong et al., 2015). PPPs are "working arrangements based on a mutual commitment (over and above that implied in any contract) between a public sector organization with any other organization outside the public sector" (Bovaird, 2004, p. 200). This definition highlights the importance of the concept not just referring to cross-sectoral contractual engagement, i.e. via the contracting out of public services to the private sector, as is often mistakenly interpreted (Argento, Grossi, Tagesson, & Collin, 2009), but to the potential for synergies and mutuality in partnership relations, often through the creation of new hybrid structures and programmes. The nature of PPPs is illustrated in Figure 1. The PPP concept includes private–NGO partnerships as well as private business–public agency relationships (Mendel & Brudney, 2012). Given the range of mixed and hybrid models of service delivery, partnerships are also possible between all three sectors, as well as intra-sectoral partnerships, i.e. between different public authorities and agencies, sometimes in different jurisdictions (Bel, Brown, & Warner, 2014).

Although governmental agencies and non-governmental organisations (NGOs) possess valuable resources and expertise (e.g. communication and education networks, outreach capabilities), the sustainability of social marketing efforts often face long-term funding uncertainty (Lefebvre, 2012; Truong & Hall, 2013). Therefore, many of them are seeking to improve internal governance, broaden donor networks and/or increase income-generating activities, increasingly via partnerships with the private sector (Kotler et al., 2012; Lefebvre, 2012). Austerity measures and changes in philosophies of governance have also lead to greater use of private sector organisations for public service delivery, including tourism (Hall, 2014).

Although partly driven by a desire to deliver public services at a lower cost, and often criticised in terms of the loss of social service and public good functions, there remains an acknowledgement that in some cases public–private relationships can deliver public services appropriately (Bel et al., 2014; Bovaird, 2004). Such measures have also led to a significant blurring of the public–private

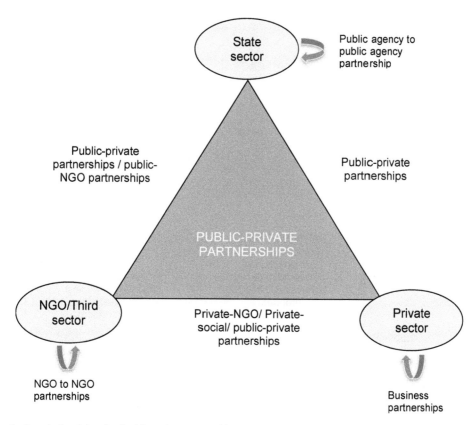

Figure 1 . Organisational domain of public–private partnerships.

dichotomy (Mendoza & Vernis, 2008), and changes in understanding of governance and state intervention (Hall, 2011, 2013).

Drawing on the extensive PPP literature, some of the different relationships between the public and private sectors in the delivery of social marketing programmes are identified in Figure 2 (Bel et al., 2014; Brinkerhoff, 2002; Brinkerhoff & Brinkerhoff, 2011; Hodge & Greve, 2009; Kivleniece & Quelin, 2012; Klijn, 2010). PPPs can be categorised with respect to organisational form and the mutual dependence that exists in the partnership relationship. Four main categories of partnership are identified from this perspective, with membership-based programmes and network partnerships arguably the most recognised in tourism (Hall, 2014).

At the same time as governments have sought to utilise businesses and NGOs to achieve social marketing objectives, many companies are increasingly supporting social causes while targeting their business goals (Andreasen & Drumwright, 2001; Kotler et al., 2012). Business support for social issues can move beyond philanthropic and volunteering initiatives to encompass mutually beneficial, long-term partnerships aimed at accomplishing strategic business and societal goals (Inoue & Kent, 2014; Kotler et al., 2012). However, private sector involvement in social marketing has been subject to much scrutiny and criticism. Numerous authors have argued that private sector companies do not fall within the domain of social marketing because for them profits are the most important outcome, not social change (Donovan, 2011; Fox & Kotler, 1980; Rangun & Karim, 1991). Hastings and Angus (2011) argue that the financial inputs of corporations into social marketing campaigns transform them into commercial marketing.

In contrast, Lefebvre (2012) contends that some social marketers may not be familiar with the ideas of markets even though social marketing draws upon principles and methods of commercial

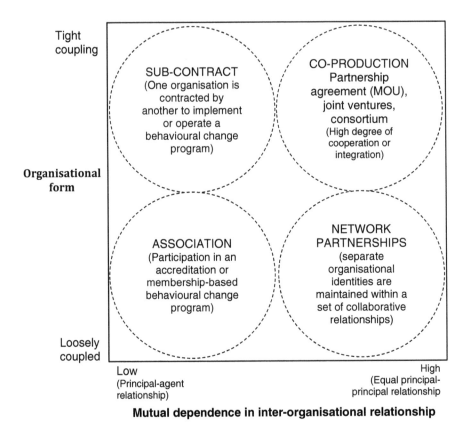

Figure 2. Frameworks for public—private partnerships in social marketing services.

marketing. A market is generally understood as any arrangement wherein some people sell products and services and others buy them. This includes the markets for behaviours and ideas where people consider various alternative behaviours, choices, models and experiences (Lefebvre, 2012, 2013; Rothschild, 2001). However, to operate effectively markets often need a range of other players to support the principal actors who are involved in the exchange process, including the private, non-profit and governmental sectors. Rothschild (2001) and Lefebvre (2012, 2013), therefore, argue that social marketing needs to move beyond a focus on non-profit and public entities to encompass all actors in the market system. Lee and Miller (2012) concur, arguing that lasting success in influencing behavioural change requires strategic, long-term partnerships between government agencies, NGOs and private companies.

The main goal of CSM initiatives is to promote behavioural change for the sake of improved health, safety, well-being or the environment (Kotler et al., 2012). The intended influence on behavioural change differentiates CSM from other corporate social initiatives such as cause promotion, philanthropy and volunteering whose main purpose is generally to raise funds, goodwill or awareness of the public or a consumer segment regarding a social issue and a brand, but not to change people's behaviours (Inoue & Kent, 2014; Kotler & Lee, 2005; Kotler et al., 2012; Table 1).

Given that it is focused on influencing behavioural change either directly by seeking to exchange one form of behaviour for another or indirectly by changing the market system within which exchange occurs (sometimes referred to as macro-marketing), CSM should create the most effective social benefits as compared to other corporate social initiatives (Kotler & Lee, 2005), although many CSM initiatives are included within corporate social responsibility (CSR) efforts, and may, therefore,

Table 1. Differences between CSM and other corporate social and environmental initiatives.

	Corporate cause promotions	Cause-related marketing	Corporate social marketing	Corporate philanthropy and sponsorship	Community Volunteering	Socially responsible business practices
Description	A corporation provides funds, in-kind contributions or other resources to increase awareness and concern about a cause or to support fundraising, participation, or volunteer recruitment for a cause.	A corporation commits to contributing or donating a percentage of revenues to a specific cause based on a product's sales over a specific period of time.	A corporation implements, sponsors, or participates in a behavioural change campaign using the tools and strategies of social marketing.	A corporation makes a direct contribution to a charity or cause, often in the form of cash, donation, or in-kind services. If explicitly undertaken with promotion of the corporation a major goal it is then sponsorship.	A corporation supports and encourages its employees and/or partners to volunteer their time and talents to support community issues and events.	A corporation adapts and conducts discretionary business practices and investments to support social causes aimed to improve community well-being and/or protect the environment.
Example	Established in 1987, the *Change for Good* programme, in which change is collected from passengers on board their flights, is one of UNICEF's best known and longest running partnerships As of August 2015 Aer Lingus, Alitalia, All Nippon Airways (ANA), American Airlines, Asiana Airlines, Cathay Pacific, Finnair, JAL and QANTAS are partners.	In early 2015, Hotel Metropole Hanoi donated 5% of proceeds from its "Gout de France" event to Operation Smile to support children suffering from facial deformities.	Hotels participated in Southwest Florida Water Management District's Water Conservation Hotel and Motel programme to encourage guests to reuse towels and linen.	Micato Safaris provided cash donations to develop educational services in the Mukuru slum in Nairobi, Kenya.	In 2009, Cathay Pacific Airways' staff arranged Christmas gifts and a party for poor children in Hong Kong. Volunteers also distributed recycled computers to 300 local poor students and trained them in basic computer skills.	Koto Vietnam, a social enterprise, provides training in tourism and hospitality skills to local poor children.

Sources: Authors and categories developed from Kotler and Lee (2005) and Kotler et al. (2012).

not be immediately recognised as CSM (Kotler et al., 2012). The next section reviews the tourism literature on social marketing.

The study of social marketing in tourism

Interest in the potential roles of social marketing in tourism can be traced back to the 1980s (Hall, 2014). However, it was only in the 2000s that social marketing became an explicit topic in tourism research (Bright, 2000). Social marketing has been examined with respect to its potential roles in influencing behavioural change in tourists (Dinan & Sargeant, 2000; Goldstein, Cialdini, & Griskevicius, 2008), tourism businesses (George & Frey, 2010), destination marketing organisations (Chhabra, Andereck, Yamanoi, & Plunkett, 2011), events (Musgrave & Henderson, 2015) and host communities (Truong & Hall, 2015b). Many of the studies are conceptual in nature and few demonstrate actual behavioural change that results due to social marketing interventions (Truong & Hall, 2015a).

Bright (2000) suggested that social marketing may have a role to play in the delivery of a range of recreation and leisure services by governmental agencies. Both Bright (2000) and Kaczynski (2008) also claimed that social marketing is congruent with the social welfare philosophy that drives the work of public recreation agencies, including tourism. In contrast, Dinan and Sargeant (2000) directly focused on the use of social marketing techniques by tourism organisations seeking sustainable tourist segments: those who are attracted primarily by natural beauty and historical values; and those who need to be encouraged to adopt a visitors' code of conduct. Peeters et al. (2009) also suggest the use of social marketing to influence tourists' behaviour in choosing destinations, travel modes and consumption patterns based on understanding their needs, wants and motivations.

One area of social marketing that has attracted considerable interest in tourism is that of demarketing (Hall, 2014; Orchiston & Higham, 2016). Demarketing is "that aspect of marketing that deals with discouraging customers in general or a certain class of customers in particular on either a temporary or permanent basis" (Kotler & Levy, 1971, p. 76). Beeton and Pinge (2003) suggested demarketing could be used to lead Australians away from gambling and towards spending money on domestic holidays. However, the strongest advocacy of demarketing in tourism is with respect to visitor management (Beeton & Benfield, 2002), an approach especially relevant for national parks and heritage sites (Armstrong & Kern, 2011; Benfield, 2001; McKercher, Weber, & du Cros, 2008; Wearing & Schweinsberg, 2016).

The potential contribution of social marketing to the development of environmentally-friendly behaviours is an increasingly significant topic (Barr, Gilg, & Shaw, 2011; Budeanu, 2007; Musgrave & Henderson, 2015). Several studies have discussed its application in event management (Kim, Borges, & Chon, 2006; Mair & Laing, 2013), while social marketing has also been investigated with respect to its potential in influencing behavioural change in tourism businesses. George and Frey (2010) examined the use of social marketing in encouraging tour business owners in Cape Town to adopt responsible tourism practices. Many hotels have adopted social marketing practices to encourage guests to reuse towels and linen, by the presence of a reuse request card, while also reducing operating costs and improving their image (Shang et al., 2010). Other hotels, notably those in the USA, use social marketing techniques to promote norms in order to engage guests in their environmental programmes, where descriptive norms that describe what other guests do (e.g. "the majority of guests reuse their towels") appear to be more effective than those that merely focus on ethically based environmental protection messages (Goldstein et al., 2008). Although, in contrast, Bohner and Schlüter (2014) found that in German hotels descriptive norms are not substantially more effective than standard norms with respect to impacts on guests who reuse towels and linen. Interestingly, the now well-recognised practice of many lodging businesses to encourage towel reuse may reflect the diffusion and adoption of social marketing practices by some operators without them necessarily being aware that they are engaged in social marketing.

Social marketing has also been examined in the context of gender issues in tourism advertising. Sirakaya and Sonmez (2000) and Chhabra and Johnston (2014) noted the potential implications of social marketing to encourage tourism marketing organisations to produce appropriately gendered tourism advertising. Chhabra et al. (2011) indicate that the adoption of social marketing to remove inappropriately gendered advertising images would have two main benefits: first, attracting women as a target segment; second, improving awareness of marketing ethics.

Based on a systematic search and analysis of tourism project documents, Truong and Hall (2013) found that a number of projects do not label themselves in social marketing terms although they adopt social marketing principles in their design and implementation. They suggest that social marketing may be a potential tool through which tourism can contribute to sustainable development and poverty alleviation. However, the Vietnamese projects examined by Truong and Hall (2013, 2015b) and Truong, Hall, and Garry (2014) were primarily carried out by non-profit organisations with little business involvement in PPP. The use of behavioural change campaigns by tourism businesses remains substantially unexamined and hence the undertaking of this study.

Research methods

There is no readily available international database of social marketing or CSM programmes. Therefore, in order to gain a sample of CSM programmes to examine this study utilises a virtual expert panel approach (Benjamin, 2006; Ryan, 2012) to "crowdsource" potential examples of CSM in tourism (see Lee & Miller, 2012, who also used this method in a social marketing context) along with further search of literature and online sources. The virtual expert panel approach engages a group of experts in a discussion about a topic of interest (Victoria State Department of Sustainability and Environment, 2005). It is "virtual" because it is conducted in virtual research settings such as social networking sites (e.g. Facebook) and online communities (e.g. listserv) (Ryan, 2012). In this study, this approach was combined with a content analysis of media detailing behavioural change programmes together with interviews where possible (Pettigrew & Roberts, 2011; Truong, 2014).

In order to identify CSM-related initiatives, an email was sent to Georgetown University's Social Marketing Listserv that currently has more than 2000 international members who are social marketing researchers and practitioners. The email asked for examples of behavioural change programmes anywhere in the world that were implemented, sponsored or participated in by tourism businesses. Those who were aware of a programme were sent another email that asked them to provide details about that programme. Online searches were then used to collect further information about the identified programmes, with implementing agencies being contacted directly when relevant information was not available online (see Truong & Hall, 2013, who adopted a similar approach with respect to development projects in Vietnam; Figure 3). In addition, to ensure that search results were as inclusive as possible websites of major tourism businesses and associations (e.g. Green Hotels Association, American Hotel and Lodging Association, Association of British Travel Agents) were examined, given that prior research suggested that a number of CSM initiatives were part of CSR efforts (Kotler et al., 2012). Attention was also given to tourism companies that had implemented behavioural change campaigns that had been reported in the academic literature (Goldstein et al., 2008; Shang et al., 2010). These searches were conducted entirely in English with potential programmes identified via a filter of key words. As of the end of August 2015, 32 behavioural change programmes were identified that involved tourism businesses.

The identified programmes were then examined against Andreasen's (2002) six social marketing benchmark criteria (Table 2) which have been widely used in the social marketing literature as a means of distinguishing social marketing programmes from other behavioural interventions such as education campaigns or social communications even when they are labelled as social marketing (e.g. Luca & Suggs, 2013; Truong & Hall, 2013). Meanwhile, others may not self-identify as social marketing even though they adopt social marketing principles and methods in their design and implementation (Andreasen, 2002; Truong & Hall, 2013). Of the identified programmes, 14 satisfied all six social marketing benchmark criteria.

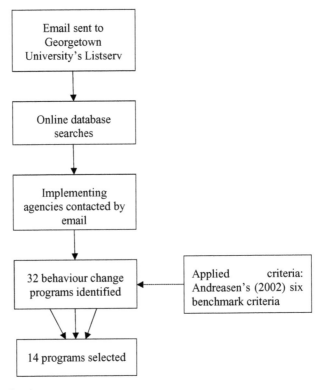

Figure 3. Search strategy flowchart.

Results

Of the 14 behavioural change programmes selected, 7 label themselves in social marketing terms. The other seven programmes are positioned more as part of broader company CSR efforts. Supplemental Table S1 (available in the online version of this paper, under the Supplemental Data tab on the paper's first page) provides programme details with respect to location, corporations' role, nature of partnership and organisational framework. In terms of location, five programmes are implemented

Table 2. Social marketing benchmark criteria.

Benchmarks	Description
1. Behaviour change goal	Programmes consider behavioural change as an objective and a primary outcome indicator.
2. Audience research and segmentation	Programmes are designed based on understanding of audience needs and wants. Formative research is conducted to achieve this target. Programme interventions are pre-tested. The audience are divided into homogenous segments.
3. Social marketing mix	Programmes use the set of four Ps in the traditional marketing mix (Product, Price, Place, Promotion). Programmes that only use the Promotion element are social advertising or communications. Other Ps may include People and Policy. These elements should be used flexibly.
4. Exchange	Something of value is offered to the audience to motivate behavioural change. It may be tangible (e.g. financial incentives) or intangible (e.g. emotional satisfaction).
5. Upstream targeting	Programmes seek to influence other people relating to the target audience (e.g. local authorities, professional organisations, policy-makers).
6. Competition	Competing behaviours are considered by programme interventions. They may be internal (e.g. the target audience's current behaviour) and/or external (e.g. weak policies). Strategies are used to eliminate or minimise these factors.

Sources: Authors and developed from Andreasen (2002) and Truong and Hall (2013).

in the USA, one in Fiji, one in Hong Kong and one in Vietnam. The remaining six programmes are transnational. A clear commonality among the identified programmes is that they predominantly involve large hotel groups and travel corporations.

Six programmes are organised by public agencies, where tourism businesses are partners (see Supplemental Table S1, available in the online version of this paper, under the Supplemental Data tab on the paper's first page). This form of involvement is popular among hotels that participate in social marketing programmes launched by public agencies to conserve water and energy through operational (high-efficiency facilities) and behavioural (guest-focused) mechanisms. Tourism businesses are involved in three programmes as sponsors (Don't Mess With Texas, Life Education Activity Programme [LEAP], and Fast Track Fiji). Significantly, they do not simply provide funding but are also engaged in programme activities. For example, the Dallas-based Southwest Airlines provides free tickets during Don't Mess With Texas' summer Road Tours, sponsors awards, and assists in communicating campaign messages to its customers (Kotler & Lee, 2005). The other five programmes were developed and implemented by tourism businesses (Inn Shape With Residence Inn, Environmentally Conscious Hospitality Operations, Planet 21, Sustainable Holidays Initiative, and Travellers Against Plastic), some in collaboration with public and non-profit agencies.

The nature of partnership (see Figure 1) varies across the identified programmes, where pair-of-sector relationships prevail. Partnerships between public (government) agencies and private sector companies tend to be the most popular (seven programmes), followed by business–business partnerships (three programmes), and an NGO–private partnership (one programme). Only three programmes involve partnerships between the public, private and NGO sectors (see Supplemental Table S2, available in the online version of this paper, under the Supplemental Data tab on the paper's first page). Networks and associations are the most widespread organisational framework for programmes (see Figure 2). Network partnerships occur where a large hotel group or travel company adopt social marketing practices within their network of managed and/or franchised companies often as a result of sponsorship relations. Associations exist where the programme is membership or accreditation based. For example, green labels are given to hotels participating in the Water-CHAMP^{SM} programme. Three programmes were co-produced and offer a high degree of integration between corporate goals and practice. The Sustainable Holidays Initiative had elements of both co-production and network partnerships. The subcontract category is found in the Chi campaign where Vietnam Airlines is contracted by TRAFFIC to communicate campaign messages to business passengers on board its flights (TRAFFIC, 2015). It is noted that these partnerships are identified at the time of writing and that they may change during programme implementation.

In terms of the type of behavioural change sought, 13 programmes sought to encourage pro-environmental behaviours with the target audience embracing tourists, tourism businesses' management and staff, and other stakeholders such as suppliers (See Supplemental Table S2, available in the online version of this paper, under the Supplemental Data tab on the paper's first page). Of these, eight programmes seek to reduce water and energy consumption and improve waste management, three involve litter prevention, one aims to prevent drug and substance abuse, and another focuses on reducing demand for rhino horn. The remaining programme encourages travellers to eat better and exercise more (Inn Shape With Residence Inn). All of the identified programmes undertake research to better understand their target audience and to inform programme interventions although the results of interventions are not always publically available or, where they are, they are often generalised to participants as a whole rather than individual firms or properties. This is significant, as programme participants do not want results to be publically used as a means of creating "league tables" or identifying "failure" (Anonymous, pers. comm., February 2016). Programmes also seek to identify barriers to the promoted behavioural change and adopt measures to eliminate or mitigate such barriers. A range of methods are employed, including literature reviews (e.g. Inn Shape With Residence Inn), focus group discussion (e.g. LEAP) and survey (e.g. Don't Mess With Texas), to gain insights into the target audience's knowledge, attitudes and behaviours. Site inspections and technical examinations are carried out particularly among hotel groups with the aim to identify potential areas where water and energy could be saved.

Different types of messages are used in the 14 programmes analysed. Positive messages that emphasise the potential benefits of the promoted behaviour are frequently used, such as "It's [bottling your own water] good for the earth", "Bottling your own water is good for your business" (Whole World Water), "Keep Texas beautiful" and "Keep America beautiful" (Don't Mess With Texas). By contrast, other programmes use negative messages to highlight the harmful impact of the undesirable behaviour. For example, the Fast Track Fiji campaign has displayed "Plastic kills" and "Do you like eating plastic?" messages on posters in an attempt to discourage its target audience from dumping plastic into the sea. Campaigns that promote towel and linen reuse in hotels have a common focus on providing specific guidelines to enable hotel guests to reduce water consumption. Such messages as "A towel hanging up means 'I will use again'" and "A towel on the floor means 'Please exchange'" are frequently found in these campaigns (the potential disadvantages of these messages are discussed later).

The strength of the tie between the behaviour sought and the purchase of a company's product varies considerably across the identified programmes. This tie is relatively strong in the case of the hotels that encourage extended-stay guests to reuse towels and linen, where hotels should have substantial water and energy savings. In contrast, the tie is rather weak in other cases. For example, American Southwest Airlines may not earn many direct benefits from its support for the Don't Mess With Texas campaign, although it may become perceived as a socially responsible and regionally committed firm over the long term given the length of association. Likewise, when Vietnam Airlines disseminates the Chi campaign's messages to its passengers and encourages them to stop consuming rhino horn, it does not link the behaviour sought with its product sales. This is despite possibilities of its corporate image being improved in some markets. This may also be as a result of the inter-organisational relationship being based on subcontracting with only a weak mutual commitment.

Influencing behavioural change requires something to be offered to the target audience ("exchange"). Since most of the identified programmes seek to promote environmentally-friendly behaviours, their benefits beyond the satisfaction in participating are generally not direct and cannot be realised in the short term. Many programme organisations, therefore, provide benefits that are more tangible in order to engage corporations or customers. For example, the WaterSaver Hotel and WaterCHAMP^{SM} programmes provide participating hotels with free materials such as linen/pillow cards and towel hangers and feature them in marketing and promotional activities. Reducing water and energy consumption should help hotels immediately save operating costs. However, a hotel guest may not get any direct personal benefits if he/she reuses towels and linen or stops littering. Therefore, a range of engagement and mobilisation activities are undertaken to encourage guests to adopt the proposed behaviours, including education (Fast Track Fiji) and awareness raising events and contests (Don't Mess With Texas, LEAP, WaterSense At Work). Prizes are often awarded to provide audiences a greater incentive to engage in the proposed behaviour. For example, some hotels offer a food and beverage voucher for each night that guests decline housekeeping service (Southwest Florida Water Management District, 2015).

The only programme that does not have a strong link between the sought-after behaviour and product sales but does encourage people to engage in behaviours that provide direct personal benefits is Marriott International's Inn Shape With Residence Inn. Partnered with the American Heart Association (AHA), this programme motivates extended-stay business travellers to adopt healthy eating habits and doing more exercise. Heart-healthy recipes are introduced and made available in guest rooms. In-room exercises were also developed with the professional assistance of the AHA (Bloom et al., 1995).

Outcomes of CSM programmes

Positive behavioural change outcomes have been reported by many of the identified programmes (see Supplemental Table S3, available in the online version of this paper, under the Supplemental

Data tab on the paper's first page), although as noted above, not all results are publically available. A number of different evaluation methods are employed. Surveys were used in two programmes to compare the attitudes and behaviours of the target audience before and after programme interventions (Don't Mess With Texas and LEAP). Surveys will also likely be conducted when the Chi campaign is completed, given that baseline surveys were carried out in 2011 and 2014 (N., TRAFFIC, pers. comm., August 2015; see also Table 4, online). Meanwhile, the participation and commitment of the target audience is used as an indication of achievement by the 'Travellers Against Plastic' program. By contrast, those programmes that involve hotel companies generally do not use surveys but instead undertake audits to measure actual levels of water and energy consumption before and after programme interventions. There appear two main reasons for this. First, these programmes combine technological and behavioural mechanisms. Second, although surveys are commonly used to assess the effectiveness of social marketing programmes, scepticism exists over the potential gap between what is reported by the target audience and what they actually do (Truong, 2014). Behavioural change outcomes are not (yet) available in two programmes (Inn Shape With Residence Inn and Fast Track Fiji).

Discussion

Social marketing is a potentially useful consumer-oriented approach to promoting behavioural change and improved well-being (Truong, 2014). Its potential for tourism remains under-researched, although motivating behavioural change is an issue that is now at the forefront of the sustainable tourism agenda (Cohen et al., 2014; Hall, 2014). As Lane (2009) stated seven years ago, "the whole area of Social Marketing, of how to promote behavioural change, seems to be a blank for sustainable tourism researchers" (p. 26). This argument is reflected by the review of literature presented in this paper, which indicates that in very few studies do tourism scholars provide details of the actual behavioural change outcomes that result due to social marketing interventions. That situation may also reflect Lane's (2009) contention, that sustainable tourism researchers rarely work closely with the tourism industry, and thus rarely get access to the industry's commercial information. Alternatively, it might reflect the lack of accurate record-keeping of relevant data over time by tourism businesses (Su et al., 2013).

This article examined a subset of social marketing by looking at CSM. Although tourism businesses can organise their own CSM programmes, collaboration with non-profit agencies appears common, a trend that reflects the broader social marketing field. One important aspect of the PPP nature of much CSM in tourism is that it appears to assist in greater transparency in reporting of the results of interventions with respect to actual change rather than just reporting on consumer awareness that a programme exists, something that has often been a criticism of public social marketing programmes (Hall, 2016). However, as noted substantial gaps remain in reporting. Although this may reflect the direct commercial imperatives of some partners another explanation relates more to how such results may be interpreted by consumers or others when taken out of the organisational context (Anonymous, pers. comm., February 2016).

Half of the identified programmes label themselves social marketing while the others tend to be regarded as part of CSR efforts even though they fulfil social marketing criteria. This research, therefore, supports previous studies (Truong & Hall, 2013) which indicate that the social marketing label is not necessarily effective in identifying CSM programmes in tourism settings, an issue that is significant for future research on social marketing in tourism. Andreasen's (2002) six social marketing benchmark criteria provide a useful framework for identifying and analysing social marketing interventions in tourism regardless of their label.

This research also suggests that CSM is often positioned by organisations as a special type of CSR programme or can be part of a larger social responsibility effort (Bloom et al., 1995; Kotler & Lee, 2005; Kotler et al., 2012). However, such a result is not completely surprising given that CSM is an extension of the application of commercial marketing management principles. Furthermore, to many stakeholders, including customers and staff, CSR is much more recognisable and understandable a concept than social marketing or CSM (Anonymous, pers. comm., February 2016). Given concerns from society and consumers over sustainability issues, as well as competition pressures, a greater number of tourism businesses may incorporate CSM as a component of their CSR strategies in addition to their traditional financial statement (Blose, Mack, & Pitts, 2015; Kim & Kim, 2014). As such, the distinction between CSM and CSR activities may become further blurred.

Kotler et al. (2012) suggest that businesses should promote a social behaviour that is compatible with their mission, products and brand, with the ideal scenario being that a strong tie exists between the promoted behaviour and increased sales of, or returns from, the company's product. This suggestion is confirmed by this study, since a number of hotels that encourage guests to reuse towels and linen have increased their total revenues as less water and energy is consumed while also mitigating emissions (see Supplemental Table S2 and S3, available in the online version of this paper, under the Supplemental Data tab on the paper's first page). At the same time, this can enhance corporate image resulting in improved recognition and intention to return and recommend by their customers. For example, Marriott International's customer surveys show 1.5 times the intention to return and 2 times the intention to recommend its hotels to others among those aware of its sustainability programme (Marriott International, 2014). Likewise, Lee, Hsu, Han, and Kim (2010) suggest that sustainability hotel branding helps enhance corporate image and increase guests' intention to visit and refer to others, as well as to pay premiums, while also serving as value and quality attributes. This study also suggests that the decision to support a behavioural change campaign may be driven by a desire to respond as a corporate citizen to an environmental or social issue. It may also be that companies seek to improve their image and/or customer relationships so as to increase sales over time (Kotler & Lee, 2005; Kotler et al., 2012). What is less clear, but which also may be significant in some circumstances, is the extent to which corporate participation is undertaken as a way of reducing the likelihood of regulatory intervention or taxation increases.

By implementing or supporting social marketing efforts, tourism businesses potentially enhance their employees' sense of belonging and feelings of making worthwhile contributions to achieving organisational objectives. Marriott International indicates that 9 out of 10 staff are proud of its environmental initiatives (See Supplemental Table S3, available in the online version of this paper, under the Supplemental Data tab on the paper's first page.). Bloom et al. (1995) suggest that when employees care about the social issue that is addressed by the company, they may feel better connected to the company, which may lead to higher productivity and lower turnover. In fact, these indirect benefits affect the company in the longer term than do direct benefits that are generated by strong product ties (Bloom et al., 1995).

Nevertheless, it is more challenging to engage the private sector when the tie between the proposed behavioural change and the sale of a company's product or promotion of brand is weak or non-existent. For instance, the Fast Track Fiji campaign is having difficulty engaging the participation of local tourism businesses in the prevention of plastic waste. While most local tourist boards have been "sitting on the fence", private hotels all want to be "on-board" but "putting their money where their mouth is, rarely happens" (A.M., Ocean Ambassadors, pers. comm., August 2015). This case suggests that private sector companies are concerned about the efficacy of social marketing programmes. This appears particularly the case when they do not (yet) recognise the benefits that the promoted behaviour change may bring about for their business. In other cases, it may also be equally difficult to involve the private sector even though the tie between the behaviour change sought and the sale of a company's product appears to be strong but the potential benefits seem limited. A good illustration of these is the WaterCHAMP^{SM} programme that has found it difficult to promote the involvement of small hotels. These hotels are concerned that water and energy savings are very limited while guests may be greatly inconvenience (See Supplemental Table S2, available in the online version of this paper, under the Supplemental Data tab on the paper's first page.). As such, it may be plausible to argue that private sector companies' involvement in and support for social marketing initiatives are not necessarily selfless but rather tend to be driven by the benefits that they may reap either directly or indirectly (Kotler & Lee, 2005; Kotler et al., 2012). The management and staff of Fast Track Fiji are, therefore, seeking to better involve the private sector, for example, through establishment of a more effective engagement model and support of local action groups.

In terms of outcome evaluation, some of the identified programmes draw upon the pre- and post-intervention model of effect, where surveys are often used. While it is recognised that surveys are a popular means through which social marketing outcomes are assessed (Lefebvre, 2013; Truong, 2014), they have also been subject to much criticism with respect to reliability. Indeed, Zaltman and Zaltman (2008) argue that when the audience group is asked to attach ratings of agreement to statements, the response reveals only thoughts about what the social marketer deem important but might not actually be the most relevant drivers of individual behaviour. Put another way, the audience are responding to ideas imposed on them, not generated by them. In addition, what is reported by the survey respondents may not be the same as what is actually done by them (Hall, 2014; Truong, 2014). This suggests that additional research methods should be employed to compliment survey results (i.e. data triangulation). It needs to be noted, however, that this methodological weakness is not limited to CSM initiatives in tourism but rather is common in the social marketing field as a whole (Truong, 2014). Therefore, further research in tourism settings and beyond is needed into how social marketing outcomes can be evaluated more rigorously.

Conclusion

This paper has examined tourism businesses' utilisation of social marketing to engender behavioural change. The identified programmes suggest that CSM can contribute meaningfully to the sustainable development of tourism. Even though efforts have been made to ensure that the search results are as comprehensive as possible, undoubtedly a greater number of CSM programmes have been undertaken in tourism settings. However, they are often not described in terms of social marketing and behaviour change, but are often treated more generically with respect to water or energy conservation, or waste reduction (Gössling, Hall, & Scott, 2015). Further research is thus needed to expand the findings of the present study by, for example, examining CSM initiatives that are reported in languages other than English (e.g. Su, Hall, & Ozanne, 2013). In addition, more long-term tracking of programmes is urgently required. The nature of PPPs may have important implications for the stability and lifespan of programmes. Co-produced programmes appear more stable than association-based inter-organisational relationships. Although the length of relationship for programmes, such as Don't Mess With Texas and LEAP, both linked to airlines, may appear to lie in other relationships and business factors, that needs to be explored further. Also of significance to the lifespan of CSM initiatives is their behavioural focus with some issues potentially being higher in public agendas and the issue–attention cycle than others. Indeed, a comment made in one interview was that "issues such as water and energy savings is of more concern to [the corporation] than it is to our customers. Most customers really don't care or they only do when there is something in the media" (Anonymous, pers. comm., February 2016). Moreover, although this research suggests that CSM can be an effective means of behavioural change, it is not a substitute for but rather an essential complement to technological and regulatory approaches to sustainable tourism, as well as downstream and upstream social marketing undertaken by governments and NGOs (Hall, 2016).

Changing behaviour is a long process and hence without a long-term commitment from private sector companies, it is likely that CSM programmes will fail to achieve desired behavioural change goals. In addition, as public agencies and private sector companies enter a long-term partnership, over time the former may become more dependent on the financial and/or technical assistance of the latter. A possible consequence is that corporate profitability could become the most important goal, rather than behaviour change. Where this happens CSM will likely be transformed into commercial marketing of corporate social and environmental initiatives (see Table 1), such as corporate cause promotion (Donovan, 2011; Hastings & Angus, 2011). A related issue is that social marketing programmes cannot just be copied with the expectancy of success even though there is a clear innovation—diffusion process involved with some programmes. Copying a hotel's messaging to its guests with respect to water and energy conservation, for example, does not make marketing sense as there is a need to understand customers and the messages that they relate to for that particular property and experience. The norms in one commercial setting, as well as the levels of exposure to messaging and the level of cynicism with respect to environmental practices and benefit, may be different to another. Such practices unfortunately may only increase consumer perceptions of "greenwash".

These issues highlight some of the very complex situations that surround the evolution of the social marketing field, including changes in governance and the respective roles of the public, private and third sectors in behaviour change. Such situations also create a substantial challenge for under-standing social marketing, the extent to which the private sector could, or should, be involved in social marketing initiatives, and the potential of social marketing for sustainable tourism. Although these issues are critical, this research is only a first step in their understanding and therefore offers significant potential avenues for future studies.

Disclosure statement

No potential conflict of interest was reported by the authors.

ORCID

C. Michael Hall ⓘD http://orcid.org/0000-0002-7734-4587

References

Accor. (2014). Sustainability report 2014. Retrieved 2 August 2015 from www.accorhotels-group.com

Andreasen, A.R. (2002). Marketing social marketing in the social change marketplace. *Journal of Public Policy & Marketing, 21*(1), 3—13.

Andreasen, A.R., & Drumwright, M. (2001). Alliances and ethics in social marketing. In A.R. Andreasen (Ed.), *Ethics in social marketing* (pp. 95—124). Washington, DC: Georgetown University Press.

Argento, D., Grossi, G., Tagesson, T., & Collin, S.O. (2009). The "externalisation" of local public service delivery: Experience in Italy and Sweden. *International Journal of Public Policy, 5*(1), 41—56.

Armstrong, E., & Kern, C. (2011). Demarketing manages visitor demand in the Blue Mountains National Park. *Journal of Ecotourism, 10*(1), 21—37.

Barr, S., Gilg, A., & Shaw, G. (2011). "Helping People Make Better Choices": Exploring the behaviour change agenda for environmental sustainability. *Applied Geography, 31*(2), 712—720.

Beeton, S., & Benfield, R. (2002). Demand control: The case for demarketing as a visitor and environmental management tool. *Journal of Sustainable Tourism, 10*(6), 497—513.

Beeton, S., & Pinge, I. (2003). Casting the holiday dice: Demarketing gambling to encourage local tourism. *Current Issues in Tourism, 6*(4), 309—322.

Bel, G., Brown, T., & Warner, M. (2014). Editorial overview: Symposium on mixed and hybrid models of public service delivery. *International Public Management Journal, 17*(3), 297—307.

Benfield, R.W. (2001). "Good things come to those who wait": Sustainable tourism and timed entry at Sissinghurst Castle Garden, Kent. *Tourism Geographies, 3*(2), 207−217.

Benjamin, C. (2006). Conducting technology commercialisation studies: A case study. *International Journal of Technology Transfer and Commercialisation, 5*(3), 237−250.

Bloom, P.N., Hussein, P.Y., & Szykman, L.R. (1995). Benefiting society and the bottom line: Businesses emerge from the shadows to promote social causes. *Marketing Management, 4*(3), 8−18.

Blose, J.E., Mack, R.W., & Pitts, R.E. (2015). The influence of message framing on hotel guests' linen-reuse intentions. *Cornell Hospitality Quarterly, 56*(2), 145−154.

Bohner, G., & Schlüter, L.E. (2014). A room with the viewpoint revisited: Descriptive norms and hotel guests' towel reuse behavior. *PLOS One, 9*(8), 1−7.

Bovaird, T. (2004). Public−private partnerships: From contested concepts to prevalent practice. *International Review of Administrative Sciences, 70*(2), 199−215.

Bright, A.D. (2000). The role of social marketing in leisure and recreation management. *Journal of Leisure Research, 32*(1), 12−17.

Brinkerhoff, D., & Brinkerhoff, J. (2011). Public−private partnerships: Perspectives on purposes, publicness, and good governance. *Public Administration and Development, 31*(1), 2−14.

Brinkerhoff, J. (2002). Government−nonprofit partnership: A defining framework. *Public Administration and Development, 22*(1), 19−30.

Budeanu, A. (2007). Sustainable tourist behaviour − a discussion of opportunities for change. *International Journal of Consumer Studies, 31*(5), 499−508.

Chhabra, D., Andereck, K., Yamanoi, K., & Plunkett, D. (2011). Gender equity and social marketing: An analysis of tourism advertisements. *Journal of Travel & Tourism Marketing, 28*(2), 111−128.

Chhabra, D., & Johnston, E. (2014). Dispelling gendered myths in tourism promotional materials: An upstream social marketing perspective. *Tourism Analysis, 19*(6), 775−780.

Cohen, S., Higham, J., Peeters, P., & Gössling, S. (Eds.). (2014). *Understanding and governing sustainable tourism mobility: Psychological and behavioural approaches.* Abingdon: Routledge.

Dinan, C., & Sargeant, A. (2000). Social marketing and sustainable tourism: Is there a match? *International Journal of Tourism Research, 2*(1), 2−14.

Dinnie, K. (2011). *City branding: Theory and cases.* London: Palgrave Macmillan.

Donovan, R. (2011). Social marketing's myth understandings. *Journal of Social Marketing, 1*(1), 8−16.

Environmental Protection Agency. (2015a). Putting WaterSense® to work: Olympic National Park Hotel reaches out and saves. Retrieved 30 July 2015 from www.epa.gov

Environmental Protection Agency. (2015b). Putting WaterSense® to work: Georgia Hotel saves $1 million annually by maximizing mechanical system. Retrieved 30 July 2015 from www.epa.gov

Environmental Protection Agency. (2015c). Putting WaterSense® to work: California Golf Resort hits hole in one with outdoor water efficiency efforts. Retrieved 30 July 2015 from www.epa.gov.

Environmental Protection Agency. (2015d). Putting WaterSense® to work: Hotel installs water-efficient sanitary fixtures. Retrieved 30 July 2015 from www.epa.gov

Environmental Protection Agency. (2015e). Putting WaterSense® to work: Laundry day means big savings for San Antonio, Texas, hotels. Retrieved 30 July 2015 from www.epa.gov

Environmental Protection Agency. (2015f). Putting WaterSense® to work: Texas hotel upgrades to four-star water efficiency. Retrieved 30 July 2015 from www.epa.gov

Fox, K., & Kotler, P. (1980). The marketing of social causes: The first ten years. *Journal of Marketing, 44*(4), 24−33.

George, R., & Frey, N. (2010). Creating change in responsible tourism management through social marketing. *South African Journal of Business Management, 41*(1), 11−23.

Goldstein, N.J., Cialdini, R.B., & Griskevicius, V. (2008). A room with a viewpoint: Using social norms to motivate environmental conservation in hotels. *Journal of Consumer Research, 35*(3), 472−482.

Gössling, S., & Buckley, R. (2016). Carbon labels in tourism: Persuasive communication? *Journal of Cleaner Production, 111*, 358−369.

Gössling, S., Hall, C.M., & Scott, D. (2015). *Tourism and water.* Bristol: Channel View.

Gössling, S., & Peeters, P. (2015). Assessing tourism's global environmental impact 1900−2050. *Journal of Sustainable Tourism, 23*(5), 639−659.

Gössling, S., Scott, D., & Hall, C.M. (2013). Challenges of tourism in a low-carbon economy. *WIRES Climate Change, 4*(6), 525−538.

Gössling, S., Scott, D., Hall, C.M., Ceron, J-P., & Dubois, G. (2012). Consumer behaviour and demand response of tourists to climate change. *Annals of Tourism Research, 39*(1), 36−58.

Guzmán, F., & Sierra, V. (2012). Public−private collaborations: Branded public services? *European Journal of Marketing, 46*(7/8), 994−1012.

Hall, C.M. (2009). Degrowing tourism: Décroissance, sustainable consumption and steady-state tourism. *Anatolia, 20*(1), 46−61.

Hall, C.M. (2011). A typology of governance and its implications for tourism policy analysis. *Journal of Sustainable Tourism, 19*(4−5), 437−457.

Hall, C.M. (2013). Framing behavioural approaches to understanding and governing sustainable tourism consumption: Beyond neoliberalism, "nudging" and "green growth"? *Journal of Sustainable Tourism, 21*(7), 1091−1109.

Hall, C.M. (2014). *Tourism and social marketing.* Abingdon: Routledge.

Hall, C.M. (2015). On the mobility of tourism mobilities. *Current Issues in Tourism, 18*(1), 7−10.

Hall, C.M. (2016). Intervening in academic interventions: Framing social marketing's potential for successful sustainable tourism behavioural change. *Journal of Sustainable Tourism, 24*(3), 350−375.

Hastings, G., & Angus, K. (2011). When is social marketing not social marketing? *Journal of Social Marketing, 1*(1), 45−53.

Higham, J., Cohen, S., Cavaliere, C., Reis, A., & Finkler, W. (2016). Climate change, tourist air travel and radical emissions reduction. *Journal of Cleaner Production, 111*, 336−347.

Hodge, G., & Greve, C. (2009). PPPs: The passage of time permits a sober reflection. *Economic Affairs, 29*(1), 33−39.

Hoek, J., & Jones, S. (2011). Regulation, public health and social marketing: A behavior change trinity. *Journal of Social Marketing, 1*(1), 32−44.

Inoue, Y., & Kent, A. (2014). A conceptual framework for understanding the effects of corporate social marketing on consumer behavior. *Journal of Business Ethics, 121*(4), 621−633.

Kaczynski, A. (2008). A more tenable marketing for leisure services and studies. *Leisure Sciences, 30*(3), 253−272.

Kim, H., Borges, M.C., & Chon, J. (2006). Impacts of environmental values on tourism motivation: The case of FICA, Brazil. *Tourism Management, 27*(5), 957−967.

Kim, S.-B., & Kim, D-Y. (2014). The effects of message framing and source credibility on green messages in hotels. *Cornell Hospitality Quarterly, 55*(1), 64−75.

Kivleniece, I., & Quelin, B. (2012). Creating and capturing value in public-private ties: A private actor's perspective. *Academy of Management Review, 37*(2), 272−299.

Klijn, E. (2010). Public private partnerships: Deciphering meaning, message and phenomenon. In G. Hodge, C. Greve, & A. Boardman (Eds.), *International handbook of public−private partnerships* (pp. 68−80). Cheltenham: Edgar Elgar.

Kotler, P., Hessekiel, D., & Lee, N. (2012). *Good works! Marketing and corporate initiatives that build a better world…and the bottom line.* Hoboken, NJ: Wiley.

Kotler, P., & Lee, N. (2005). *Corporate social responsibility: Doing the most good for your company and your cause.* Hoboken: Wiley.

Kotler, P., & Lee, N. (2008). *Social marketing: Influencing behaviors for good.* Thousand Oaks, CA: Sage.

Kotler, P., & Levy, S. J. (1971). Demarketing, yes, demarketing. *Harvard Business Review, 49*(6), 74−80.

Kotler, P., & Zaltman, G. (1971). Social marketing: An approach to planned social change. *Journal of Marketing, 35*(3), 3−12.

Lane, B. (2009). Thirty years of sustainable tourism: Drivers, progress, problems − and the future. In S. Gössling, C.M. Hall, & D.B. Weaver (Eds.), *Sustainable tourism futures: Perspectives on systems, restructuring and innovations* (pp. 19−32). London: Routledge.

Lapeyre, R. (2011). The Grootberg lodge partnership in Namibia: Towards poverty alleviation and empowerment for long-term sustainability? *Current Issues in Tourism, 14*(3), 221−234.

Lee, J.S., Hsu, L., Han, H., & Kim, Y. (2010). Understanding how consumers view green hotels: How a hotel's green image can influence behavioural intentions. *Journal of Sustainable Tourism, 18*(7), 901−914.

Lee, N., & Miller, M. (2012). Influencing positive financial behaviors: The social marketing solutions. *Journal of Social Marketing, 2*(1), 70−86.

Lefebvre, C. (2012). Transformative social marketing: Co-creating the social marketing discipline and brand. *Journal of Social Marketing, 2*(2), 118−129.

Lefebvre, C. (2013). *Social marketing and social change: Strategies and tools for improving health, well-being, and the environment.* San Francisco, CA: Jossey-Bass.

Life Education Activity Programme. (2014). 2013−2014 annual report. Retrieved 30 July 2015 from www.leap.org.hk

Luca, N., & Suggs, L. (2013). Theory and model use in social marketing health interventions. *Journal of Health Communication, 18*(1), 20−40.

Mair, J., & Laing, J. (2013). Encouraging pro-environmental behaviour: The role of sustainability-focused events. *Journal of Sustainable Tourism, 21*(8), 1113−1128.

Marriott International. (2014). 2014 sustainability report. Retrieved 30 July 2015 from www.marriott.com

McKenzie-Mohr, D., Lee, N., Schultz, W., & Kotler, P. (2012). *Social marketing to protect the environment: What works.* Thousand Oaks, CA: Sage.

McKercher, B., Weber, K., & du Cros, H. (2008). Rationalising inappropriate behaviour at contested sites. *Journal of Sustainable Tourism, 16*(4), 369−385.

Mendel, S., & Brudney, J. (2012). Putting the NP in PPP: The role of nonprofit organizations in public-private partnerships. *Public Performance & Management Review, 35*(4), 617−642.

Mendoza, X., & Vernis, A. (2008). The changing role of governments and the emergence of the relational state. *Corporate Governance, 8*(4), 389–396.

Musgrave, J., & Henderson, S. (2015). Changing audience behaviour: A pathway to sustainable event management. In C.M. Hall, S. Gössling, & D. Scott (Eds.), *The Routledge handbook of tourism and sustainability* (pp. 384–396). Abingdon: Routledge.

Ocean Ambassadors. (2015). *Plastic pollution – fast track Fiji*. Retrieved 4 August 2015 from www.oceanambassadors.org

Orchiston, C., & Higham, J. (2016). Knowledge management and tourism recovery (de) marketing: The Christchurch earthquakes 2010–2011. *Current Issues in Tourism, 19*(1), 64–84.

Peeters, P., Gössling, S., & Lane, B. (2009). Moving towards low-carbon tourism: New opportunities for destinations and tour operators. In S. Gössling, C.M. Hall, & D.B. Weaver (Eds.), *Sustainable tourism futures: Perspectives on systems, restructuring and innovations* (pp. 240–257). London: Routledge.

Pettigrew, S., & Roberts, M. (2011). Qualitative research methods in social marketing. In G. Hastings, K. Angus, & C. Bryant (Eds.), *The SAGE handbook of social marketing* (pp. 208–223). Thousand Oaks, CA: Sage.

Rangun, V., & Karim, S. (1991). *Teaching note: Focusing the concept of social marketing*. Cambridge, MA: Harvard Business School.

Rothschild, M. (2001). A few behavioral economics insights for social marketers. *Social Marketing Quarterly, 7*(3), 8–13.

Ruhanen, L. (2008). Progressing the sustainability debate: A knowledge management approach to sustainable tourism planning. *Current Issues in Tourism, 11*(5), 429–455.

Rutty, M., Gössling, S., Scott, D., & Hall, C.M. (2015). The global effects and impacts of tourism: An overview. In C.M. Hall, S. Gössling, & D. Scott (Eds.), *The Routledge handbook of tourism and sustainability* (pp. 36–63), Abingdon: Routledge.

Ryan, M. (2012). Federal ethics regulations governing Internet research. *Teaching Ethics, 12*(2), 127–136.

Scott, D., Gössling, S., & Hall, C.M. (2012). *Tourism and climate change*. Abingdon: Routledge.

Scott, D., Gössling, S., & Hall, C.M. (2016). A review of the IPCC Fifth Assessment and its implications for tourism sector climate resilience and decarbonization. *Journal of Sustainable Tourism, 24*(1), 8–30.

Scott, D., Gössling, S., Hall, C.M., & Peeters, P. (2016). Can tourism be part of the decarbonized global economy? The policy costs and risks of carbon reduction strategies. *Journal of Sustainable Tourism, 24*(1), 52–72.

Seattle Public Utilities. (2002). Hotel water conservation – a Seattle demonstration. Retrieved 30 July 2015 from www.seattle.gov

Shang, J., Basil, D., & Wymer, W. (2010). Using social marketing to enhance hotel reuse programs. *Journal of Business Research, 63*(2), 166–172.

Shaw, G., Barr, S., & Wooler, J. (2014). The application of social marketing to tourism. In S. McCabe (Ed.), *The Routledge handbook of tourism marketing* (pp. 54–65). Abington: Routledge.

Sirakaya, E., & Sonmez, S. (2000). Gender images in state tourism brochures: An overlooked area in socially responsible tourism marketing. *Journal of Travel Research, 38*(4), 353–362.

Southwest Florida Water Management District. (2015). *Water CHAMP water use survey results*. Brooksville, FL: Author.

Spenceley, A. (2012). *Responsible tourism: Critical issues for conservation and development*. London: Routledge.

Su, Y.-P., Hall, C.M., & Ozanne, L. (2013). Hospitality industry responses to climate change: A benchmark study of Taiwanese tourist hotels. *Asia Pacific Journal of Tourism Research, 18*(2), 92–107.

Texas Department of Transportation. (2010). *2009 litter attitudes and behaviors study*. Austin, TX: Author.

Texas Department of Transportation. (2014). *2013 litter attitudes and behaviors*. Austin, TX: Author.

TRAFFIC. (2015). *Chi campaign: Reducing demand for rhino horn in Vietnam (Year 1 report)*. Hanoi: TRAFFIC.

Travellers Against Plastic. (2015). Campaign overview. Retrieved 4 August 2015 from www.travellersagainstplastic.org

Truong, V.D. (2014). Social marketing: A systematic review of research 1998–2012. *Social Marketing Quarterly, 20*(1), 15–34.

Truong, V.D., Dang, V.H.N., Hall, C.M., & Dong, X.D. (2015). The internationalisation of social marketing research. *Journal of Social Marketing, 5*(4), 357–376.

Truong, V.D., & Hall, C.M. (2013). Social marketing and tourism: What is the evidence? *Social Marketing Quarterly, 19*(2), 110–135.

Truong, V.D., & Hall, C.M. (2015a). Promoting behaviour change for sustainable tourism: The potential role of social marketing. In C.M. Hall, S. Gössling, & D. Scott (Eds.), *The Routledge handbook of tourism and sustainability* (pp. 246–260). London: Routledge.

Truong, V.D., & Hall, C.M. (2015b). Exploring the poverty reduction potential of social marketing in tourism development. *Austrian Journal of South-East Asian Studies, 8*(2), 125–142.

Truong, V.D., Hall, C.M., & Garry, T. (2014). Tourism and poverty alleviation: Perceptions and experiences of poor people in Sapa, Vietnam. *Journal of Sustainable Tourism, 22*(7), 1071–1089.

Truong, V.D., Dang, V.H.N., & Hall, C.M. (2016). The marketplace management of illegal elixirs: Illicit consumption of rhino horn. *Consumption Markets & Culture, 19*(4), 353–369.

TUI Travel (2014). *Sustainable holidays report 2013*. Crawley: Author.

United Nations Environmental Programme. (2015). The 10YFP programme on sustainable tourism. Retrieved 15 July 2015 from www.unep.org/10yfp/tourism

United Nations World Tourism Organisation. (2015). UNWTO annual report 2014. Madrid: UNWTO.

United Nations World Tourism Organisation. (2016). Institutional relations and resource mobilization, public-private part-nerships. Retrieved 14 February 2016 from http://icr.unwto.org/content/public-private-partnerships

Victoria State Department of Sustainability and Environment. (2005). *Effective engagement: Building relationships with communities and other stakeholders*. Melbourne: Author.

Villarino, J., & Font, X. (2015). Sustainability marketing myopia: The lack of sustainability communication persuasiveness. *Journal of Vacation Marketing, 21*(4), 326–335.

Wearing, S.L., & Schweinsberg, S. (2016). *Marketing national parks for sustainable tourism*. Bristol: Channel View.

Whole World Water. (2015). Campaign overview. Retrieved 30 July 2015 from www.wholeworldwater.co

Zaltman, G., & Zaltman, L.H. (2008). *Marketing metaphoria: What deep metaphors reveal about the minds of consumers*. Boston, MA: Harvard Business Press.

Zapata, M.J., & Hall, C.M. (2012). Public–private collaboration in the tourism sector: Balancing legitimacy and effective-ness in local tourism partnerships. The Spanish case. *Journal of Policy Research in Tourism, Leisure and Events, 4*(1), 61–83.

Social marketing, sustainable tourism, and small/medium size tourism enterprises: challenges and opportunities for changing guest behaviour

D. Scott Borden, Tim Coles and Gareth Shaw

ABSTRACT

This paper investigates the impact on the guest experience of initiatives promoting water efficient behaviour in small/medium-sized enterprises (SMTEs) offering tourism accommodation. Interviews with 16 SMTE managers revealed businesses were unable to incorporate many initiatives previously examined in the literature, due to the small size of their businesses. In the interviews, however, they contributed three new ideas not previously examined in existing sustainable tourism dialogues. A subsequent questionnaire ($n = 408$) was administered to potential guests to better understand their water use behaviour, explore how initiatives might impact their accommodation experience, and to assess guest reactions to social marketing messages. Eight initiatives and five messages were tested. Cluster analysis revealed three distinct water user segments with one cluster showing the greatest promise for targeting to increase return on investment. Guests reported the highest positive impact on their experience from initiatives SMTEs stated were not operationally viable. This may indicate that larger firms have a competitive advantage over SMTEs if applying social marketing to change guest behaviour. However, the study found that two of the new initiatives, suggested by SMTE managers as more appropriate to their businesses, would be viable in engaging guests and at acceptably low costs.

Introduction

The tourism industry is a growing contributor to climate change and the degradation of resources (Scott, Peeters, & Gössling, 2010). One such vital resource is potable water where the industry has substantial impacts on fresh water systems (Gössling et al., 2012). Gössling, Hall, and Scott (2015) further acknowledge that the tourism industry generally increases per capita water consumption per individual; shifts water consumption between continents and regions; concentrates water use during certain times of the year; can cause injustices where visitors have greater access to, and use larger amounts of water than host peoples; and can negatively impact water quality through sewage discharge.

In the United Kingdom, where this research was conducted, practitioner led studies have predominantly focused on reducing home water use, finding "water usage is based on ingrained habits, beliefs that water is plentiful and a right, as well as a lack of conscious awareness and knowledge about the issue" (DEFRA, 2009, p. 10). Complementing DEFRA's research, five water user segments, also known as life-style groups, have been identified within the home by clustering similar water-related behaviours and attitudes (UKWIR, 2014). From "theory not practice" to "conscious consumers", each life-style segment is driven to use water in a particular manner and to embody certain barriers to change. Research into water behaviour in UK homes is aiding organizations advocating water efficiency to change home use behaviour (OFWAT, 2011) and a similar approach may aid the tourism sector.

Studies such as these have applied aspects of social marketing. Social marketing is "the adaptation and adoption of commercial marketing activities, institutions and processes as a means to induce behaviour change in a targeted audience on a temporary or permanent basis to achieve a social goal" (Dann, 2010, p. 151) and has been applied to a wide range of tourism issues (Hall, 2014). Their potential to contribute to sustainable tourism has been acknowledged, not least by encouraging pro-environmental behaviours among visitors (Dinan & Sargeant, 2000).

One area of growing interest is how social marketing may be applied within small- and medium-sized tourism enterprises (SMTEs). This paper investigates how initiatives encouraging water efficient behaviour among guests, developed through the process of social marketing with smaller firms, may impact the guest experience. Distinct challenges and opportunities are described and implications for both practitioners and researchers are discussed. To better understand the relationship between SMTEs and social marketing, a literature review is presented and results from two stages of empirical research are discussed. The first stage, interviews with managers of SMTEs, examined the willingness and ability of participating businesses to carry out initiatives within their accommodation. Managers were also asked to describe or create new initiatives not previously examined in the academic literature. In stage two, a questionnaire was administered to potential guests aiming to better understand their water use behaviour and how newly described initiatives may impact their experience.

Literature review

No consensus on the key points that define the social marketing process exists, as evidenced by variations within the literature (e.g. Corner & Randall, 2011; French, Blair-Stevens, McVey, & Merritt, 2010; Shaw, Barr, & Wooler, 2013; Truong & Hall, 2013). However, there are a number of commonly required stages highlighted in the literature: (1) define behavioural goal(s); (2) segment the audience; (3) use a marketing mix; (4) consider the importance of the exchange; and (5) incorporate balance between competing factors for behaviour.

Expanding on these points, when defining behavioural goals, it is important to target end point behaviours (McKenzie-Mohr, Lee, Shultz, & Kotler, 2012) as social marketing aims to promote measureable behavioural change and not just change in attitudes, awareness, or beliefs (Truong & Hall, 2013). Similarly, segmenting the audiences is a common marketing technique (Mazzocchi, 2008) used to understand unique desires and barriers expressed by groups of individuals and then developing tailored initiatives for those in each group (Shaw et al., 2013). While other research efforts have focused on expanding and redefining the marketing mix in the social marketing literature (Gordon, 2012), it is used during the process to define where, what and how to present initiatives to targeted segments (Andreasen, 2002). Next, tangible items (e.g. financial incentives, products) or intangibles (e.g. increased recognition within a peer group, regional pride) are exchanged for the desired change in behaviour based on the segments' unique motivations (French et al., 2010). All factors competing for a segments' responsiveness and willingness or ability to reach the defined behavioural goal(s) are considered and minimized (Shaw et al., 2013). Together these stages make up the foundation of the social marketing process which guided much of this current research and will be revisited in the discussion section of this paper.

This process, or parts of it, has previously been applied in research examining water consumptive behaviours within tourism accommodation. For example, towel and linen reuse programmes in tourism accommodation have been identified as a seminal example of applying social marketing efforts in tourism studies (McKenzie-Mohr et al., 2012). Work by O'Neill, Siegelbaum, and The RICE

Group (2002) represent the first research into this topic, concentrating on the Seattle hotel industry. Using two hotels as case studies, they identified a range of factors encouraging businesses to save water and implement towel reuse programmes. Similarly, Goldstein, Cialdini, and Griskevicius (2008) marked the first research into guest behaviour in this area, encouraging a plethora of similar work. Their research highlighted the ability to change guest behaviour through changing in-room messaging and found signage incorporating localized descriptive norms (i.e. "most guests in this hotel room participate in the programme") significantly increased participation in towel reuse schemes. This research was followed by Schultz, Khasian, and Zaleski (2008) whom replicated these studies adding a component of residents living in condominiums and found a combination of injunctive norms (what an individual feels they should do in a context) and descriptive norms (going along with everyone else) significantly increased participation. In addition, Mair and Bergin-Seers (2010) tested the need for informative texts to articulate the importance of reusing towels against providing incentives. They found participation rates significantly increased with the addition of information and not incentives.

Building in part on previous efforts, Shang, Basil, and Wymer (2010) applied a social marketing aspect to messaging, finding a statement of previously donating savings to a charity increased both participation and loyalty, while messages stating participation would provide savings for the business decreased participation and loyalty. They therefore recommended retrospective donations and use of personalized messages linked with the company logo to deter guest scepticism. In a slightly different approach, Blose, Mack, and Pitts (2015) tested the concept of loss aversion, (individuals are more likely to act to not lose something rather than gain the same amount) finding a significant increase in towel reuse scheme participation when loss aversion was added to messaging. These studies would be complimented by Reese, Loew, and Steffgen (2014) whom applied similar effort to hotels in Europe, finding altering messaging was also effective in changing guest behaviour in international destinations.

Other research in this area has focused on a variety of related topics. For example, Baca-Motes, Brown, Gneely, Kennan, and Nelson (2013) tested the impact on behaviour from guests making written, verbal, and/or public commitments to participate in reuse programmes. They found wearing a pin, as a form of public commitment, combined with a written commitment increased participation above participants making no commitment and those making only written commitments. More general findings and examples from practitioners are reported in Gössling et al. (2015), including the suggestion that seasonality is viewed as a potential variable to guest participation in saving water, as well as locality to certain activities (e.g. swimming pools and the ocean). Finally, in an effort to better understand messages currently being used by tourism accommodations to encourage guest participation in towel reuse schemes, Lee and Oh (2014) examined a diverse sample of messages from hotels and found a complexity of theory (such as those highlighted previously) already applied in practice.

This review has concentrated primarily on reuse schemes as this has been the primary focus in the literature to date. However, participation in these programmes is only one of many behaviours related to water consumption. Significantly, participation in reuse schemes and general water use behaviour (e.g. fitting low consumption showers and taps) have been found to be driven by different motivations and may therefore require varying interventions (Schultz et al., 2008). Furthermore, some research suggests changing water use behaviour may prove difficult as these behaviours are embedded in the social context of comfort, convenience and cleanliness (Shove, 2003) and guest behaviour in tourism accommodation is driven by hedonistic motivations (Miao & Wei, 2013). Therefore, clearly, a wider range of initiatives and a deeper understanding of the topic are needed to capture the complexities of water reduction within this context. This review has also highlighted some interconnected roles of both guests and managers in saving water, where initiatives (e.g. messages, commitments, incentives, etc.) encouraging guests to save water must first be adopted by and then effectively managed through businesses.

Since businesses are an integral part of this relationship, it is important to understand why they engage in such environmental initiatives. Here, we focus on SMTEs as they dominate the sector globally and their importance in generating (and reducing) environmental externalities from tourism has been widely acknowledged (Coles, Zschiegner & Dinan, 2014; Font, Garay, & Jones, 2016). The motivations for engaging in pro-environmental behaviour vary between firms, though much of the previous literature has stated larger firms engage in corporate social responsibility (CSR) to justify the business case (Font et al., 2016). However, smaller firms show both different motivations and barriers to engaging with CSR to those of larger firms (Morsing & Perrini, 2009). For example, Fassin, Rossem, and Buelens (2011) find decision-making in smaller firms is often not linked to profit and is instead an extension of the owner-manager's attitudes. Compared to larger firms, smaller firms may have the advantage of adopting or changing sustainable practices more quickly (Condon, 2004). However, their disadvantages have been described as possessing less capital, lacking information on market opportunities, having higher risk exposure, missing structured management systems, and not engaging in long term planning (Ateljevic & Doorne, 2000; Dewhurst & Thomas, 2003). Lack of information may also include exposure to academic and practitioner findings and recommendations, though Fassin et al. (2011) claim smaller firms commonly have a strong understanding of CSR issues without knowing specific theory.

More recently, Font et al. (2016) have expanded upon the current understanding of the motivations for SMTEs to engage in CSR, finding three distinct types of owners-managers based on their motivations to be sustainable. The first were competitiveness driven firms which reported the fewest efforts to be sustainable and were motivated by the business case. Next, firms driven by legitimization were motivated by social capital, a desire to please other stakeholders to gain value from their peers, and reported a variety of efforts. And finally, owner-managers driven by life-style and values reported the highest amount of CSR-related efforts.

Efforts to engage in CSR also include interacting with and encouraging guests to act responsibly. However, work by Coles, Warren, Borden, and Dinan (2017) describe a desire by SMTEs to avoid engaging in changing guest behaviour due to a fear of online negative comments. Font, Elgammal, and Lamond (2017) find similar patterns, reporting tourism accommodation in their study only communicated 30% of their efforts to their guests through their websites. They offer the term "greenhush" to describe this phenomenon where businesses communicate only the least contentious issues to display their efforts. These studies highlight the delicate balance businesses, including SMTEs, have with communicating their environmental efforts to guests. Further emphasising the importance of this issue, Coles et al. (2017) suggest avoiding promoting behaviour change with guests may actually increase unsustainable actions by indicating to customers that hedonistic behaviour is acceptable.

To better understand this delicate balance of engaging with guests, here, we investigated a wide range of behaviours and initiatives aiming to promote a diversity of water efficient actions (e.g. turning off taps, participating in schemes, taking shorter showers, etc.) with both managers and potential guests. The results are recommendations to practitioners and researchers on changing guest behaviour in SMTEs, informed through a multi-stakeholder approach, while attempting to minimize negative impacts on the guest experience.

Methods

Research was conducted through mixed methods as Molina-Azorín and Font (2016) identify that within sustainable tourism research, this approach may increase reliability in relation to social desirability bias, stakeholder comparisons, and transdisciplinarity. Social desirability bias refers to participants wishing to answer questions the "right" way. As such, two stages of data collection were conducted. In stage one, 16 semi-structured interviews with managers of SMTEs in South West England examined the nature and effectiveness of potential behaviour change initiatives within tourism accommodation. South West England was selected for this study as it is a primary UK holiday destination with a diversity of SMTEs business types (Coles et al., 2017). In stage two, a questionnaire was administered to potential guests examining general water behaviour and how initiatives, identified in stage one, might impact the guest experience.

Stage one: semi-structured interviews with SMTEs

Semi-structured phone interviews were conducted with 16 tourism accommodation managers to better understand how they may encourage guests to use water efficiently. Questions evolved through dialogue with participants, as is standard for semi-structured interviews (Barbour, 2013). General themes were established after review of findings from O'Neill et al. (2002) and four areas for discussion were used: water management within the accommodation; barriers to changing guest behaviour; feedback on initiatives previously investigated in the academic literature: and managers' ideas for initiatives to promote guest water efficient behaviour. Specifically, when discussing feedback on initiatives previously examined in the academic literature, managers were asked about the viability of implementing these efforts into their operations: donations to charity (Shang et al., 2010); money-off vouchers (Shang et al., 2010); water saving technologies (O'Neill et al., 2002); providing a personalized measurement of water use to each guest; and messaging (e.g. Goldstein et al., 2008; Schultz et al., 2008) using psychological theories (e.g. loss aversion, localized descriptive norms, and technical information on the subject).

Managers were selected by convenience from a list of customers from the area's water company (South West Water). This data-set was chosen because it represented all SMTEs receiving mains water in South West England. Figure 1 displays accommodation types represented by over 8500 South West Water customers. The data does not indicate size of the accommodation, however, Coles et al. (2017) observe that the South West of England is dominated by micro, small, and medium tourism accommodation businesses.

In an effort to collect a representative data-set, South West Water customer data were stratified by business size and type of accommodation. As defined by Storey (1994), micro-businesses have 0–9 full time equivalent (FTE) employees; small businesses, 10–49 FTE; and medium businesses, 50–100 employees. Businesses, where contact information was available, within each stratified grouping were emailed and interviews were held with the first respondents until saturation in findings was determined. The final sample size represented 16 managers: Hotels (3); B&Bs (3); self-catering (7), and tent/caravan (2). The sample was an effort to survey a group of businesses indicative of the diversity within the region, though due to convenience sampling, no claims are made that it is representative.

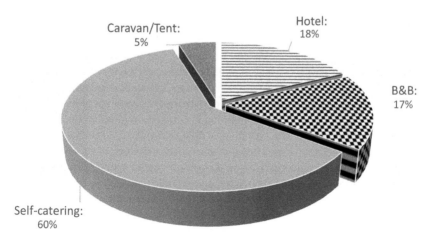

Figure 1. Type of accommodations recorded in South West Water customer database.
Source: Authors.

Table 1. Key information concerning participating accommodation managers in semi-structured interviews.

Business	Accommodation type	Accommodation size	GTBS level^	Star rating
T1	Tent/caravan	Micro	Gold	N/A
T2	Tent/caravan	Small	N/A	N/A
BB1	B&B	Micro	N/A	N/A
BB2	B&B	Micro	Gold	N/A
BB3	B&B	Micro	N/A	3
H1	Hotel	Small	N/A	3
H2	Hotel	Micro	Silver	N/A
H3	Hotel	Medium	N/A	3-4
SC1	Self-catering	Micro	N/A	N/A
SC2	Self-catering	Micro	Gold	5
SC3	Self-catering	Micro	N/A	4
SC4	Self-catering	Micro	Gold	5
SC5	Self-catering	Micro	Gold	5
SC6	Self-catering	Micro	N/A	N/A
SC7	Self-catering	Micro	N/A	N/A
SC8	Self-catering	Micro	N/A	4

^Green Tourism Business Scheme (GTBS) level indicates regional certification for environmental efforts.
Source: Authors.

A full list of interviews and key characteristics of each accommodation are presented in Table 1. Transcriptions were coded by theme and key words. Codes were allowed to be "in-vivo" (Barbour, 2007), enabling managers to define relationships with their own words. Labels representing each business have been used to preserve anonymity.

Stage two: guest questionnaire

Questionnaires were administered to individuals living in England and Wales concerning their water behaviours and the impact of potential initiatives on their experience when in tourism accommodation. Similar questionnaires have been used to better understand intentional water use behaviour in tourism accommodation previously by Shang et al. (2010) and Blose et al. (2015). Here, participants from England and Wales were combined as their water regulation is conducted by the same national organization: OFWAT, Scotland, Ireland, Northern Ireland, and all international destinations were excluded as they have different regulatory standards which may affect metering rates and behaviour. A market research company was hired to administer questionnaires as followed out in similar work by Dolnicar and Grün (2009) and Shang et al. (2010). Market research companies maintain internet panels representative of the UK's national census profile. Participants in these panels give their permission to be contacted for the purpose of research. Participants receive a small compensation based solely on the length of completed questionnaires. Within the panel, an on-line questionnaire was sent to randomly selected participants between the dates of 28 August and 30 August 2015. These dates were chosen to coincide with the end of a major holiday season in the United Kingdom, aiding participants in recalling more recent behaviour whilst in tourism accommodation.

To further aid in recalling past behaviour, potential participants were not able to complete the survey if they had not stayed in tourism accommodation in England or Wales in the past six months. For those participants able to complete the survey ($n = 408$), compulsory response questions collected information relating to: demographic and travel characteristics; the extent to which water consumptive services impacted their last booking decision (Cronbach's alpha 0.834); water behaviours in tourism accommodation (Cronbach's alpha 0.607); impact of initiatives aiming to reduce water use on their experience (Cronbach's alpha 0.816); the extent to which messages asking to help reduce water would encourage efficient behaviours (Cronbach's alpha 0.837); and the physical location where messages would most impact their behaviours (Cronbach's alpha 0.832). According to Drasgow (1984), a Cronbach's alpha score of 0.6 is sufficient for exploratory research and therefore all scales were considered valid.

The wording of water-related behaviours measured in this research was obtained from previous studies to allow for comparison (DEFRA, 2009; Miao & Wei, 2013; UKWIR, 2014). A small pilot survey ($n = 21$) was used to ensure wording clearly conveyed the researchers' intentions and some questions were later reverse coded to aid in interpreting results. SPSS version 22 was used to analysis the data. Analysis showed data were generally linear but non-parametric tests were determined to be most appropriate.

Segmenting the audience is an important step in social marketing campaigns where the aim is to better understand and then target specific groups most effectively (French et al., 2010). To accomplish segmentation, the statistical method of cluster analysis is routinely used. Cluster analysis applies numerous steps of combining observations and placing them together into "heterogeneous groups consisting of homogenous elements" (Franke, Reisinger, & Hoppe, 2009, p. 273).

Cluster analysis was performed to identify segments with homogenous water efficient behaviour within the tourism accommodation. In some previous efforts (e.g. DEFRA, 2009; Shaw et al., 2013; UKWIR, 2014), both attitudes and behaviours have been used for clustering. This method assumes there is a degree of translation from attitude to behaviour. To avoid this assumption, only behaviours were used to segment water users. To determine the number of behaviours to use during cluster analysis, recommendations from Dolnicar, Grün, Leisch, and Schmidt (2013) were used. Through a cluster analysis simulation study, Dolnicar et al. (2013) analysed data with known structure to determine appropriate sample size. Under all simulations, a ratio of 70:1, sample size to number of clustering variables, proved to be adequate for maintaining the known structure. To ensure best practice, this ratio was applied herein. With a sample size of 408, five behaviours within the tourism accommodation were used.

Prior to the final analysis, exploratory cluster analysis was conducted. During exploratory cluster analysis, Hair, Black, Babin, and Anderson (2010) recommend clustering variables with a range of methods and analysing results prior to determining the final protocol. Through this process, five behaviours were chosen based partly on their high variation between individuals, as recommended by Hair et al. (2010), and also through trial and error with the goal of discovering stable and valid clusters. The five behaviours meeting these criteria were: "I take efficient showers"; "I shower instead of bath specifically to save water"; "I take one or less showers/baths per day"; "If offered, I participate in towel reuse schemes"; and "I turn off the tap when brushing teeth". All behaviours were measured on the same five point Likert scale and the categorical data were standardized.

In the final analysis, a two-step procedure was applied where hierarchical cluster analysis determined the number of clusters and non-hierarchical cluster analysis (K-means) was used to place individuals within the determined number of clusters. This two-step procedure is recommended by Mazzocchi (2008) and Hair et al. (2010). During hierarchical clustering, Ward's method was used as it creates more similarly sized groups (Hair et al., 2010) and has been applied in similar types of research (e.g. Barr, Shaw, Coles, & Prillwitz, 2010; Coles et al., 2014). Squared Euclidean distance was applied as the measurement between observations as recommended for Ward's method by Hair et al. (2010). No single "stopping rule" has been found to best determine the number of clusters (Mazzocchi, 2008). Here, the dendrogram and percentage change in heterogeneity between clustering groups, using a calculated agglomeration coefficient, were used and a three or four cluster solution emerged as most valid. After exploring both outcomes, a three cluster solution was deemed most stable and valid. K-means cluster analysis was then run with a three cluster solution and was considered stable with only 3.6% of individuals changing cluster positions between the hierarchal and non-hierarchal test. Hair et al. (2010) classify cross tabulations of under 10% as very stable. All five behaviours used for clustering were significantly different between clusters.

Results and analysis

Stage one: semi-structured interviews with SMTEs

Sixteen managers participated in semi-structured interviews covering the topics of water management by the accommodation; barriers to changing guest behaviour; feedback on initiatives previously investigated in the academic literature: and their ideas for initiatives to promote guest water efficient behaviours. The sample contained both managers that actively managed their water and water use by their guests and those that did not, providing a diversity of feedback for this study. Perhaps surprisingly, responses were mostly consistent, transcending both type and size of tourism accommodation. Since type of accommodation varied greatly while size remained fixed to SMTEs in this study, this may further suggest SMTEs collectively have unique needs and contexts different to those of larger firms.

Barriers and drivers to changing guest behaviour

Managers were asked what barriers exist for implementing initiatives aiming to change guest behaviour. Overwhelmingly, guest satisfaction was most frequently identified with one managers stating: "If it was something that saved water but made the guest experience worse, frankly we wouldn't be doing it. When we focus on water we very much focus on how to help the environment without giving them a worse holiday (SC4)". In this context, the guest experience was principal.

Costs of implementing initiatives were the second most frequent response. This quote emphasis the general consensus of needing to preserve the guest experience and lower costs:

"You need something that makes their experience better, saves water and saves us money if you want it to be successful (SC2)". Other stated barriers of note were a belief that managers had already implemented all possible interventions; low levels of trust in suppliers and information from distributors; a desire to minimize messaging to not overwhelm guests; basic guest needs; and facility limitations.

This general consensus on barriers was in contrast to stated drivers. When asked about what would motivate managers to implement behaviour change initiatives they reported a variety of different answers. Some stated it was part of their personal values while others commented it made them feel a part of a group of concerned business owners. A smaller group identified the need to reduce costs.

Previously examined initiatives

All participants conceded they had no prior knowledge of previous academic findings on the topic of encouraging behaviour change among guests. However, they stated a high interest in the topic, such as in this quote from one participant: ".... I think it is something I should definitely see. I think there is a particular skill in putting that wording together and we would be very interested in seeing information on that (H3)".

Previous research, highlighted in the literature review of this paper, was reviewed with each manager. Managers were asked about the viability of each initiative at their establishment. Generally, managers showed lower interest in initiatives with higher financial cost and time investment. In particular, many managers stated donations to charity and voucher-off coupons would be too costly and implementing systems to account for guest participation were too complex for their small businesses. One manager stated, "no, personally I think that would take a lot of man-hours…" (BB3), while another remarked, "…but we just don't have the capital to make something like that work long term" (SC7). Providing personalized measurements was considered too invasive into the guest experience and technology able to measure water usage within each room was cited as a barrier. Costs and the potential to disrupt the guest experience were frequently cited as reasons for not using technological implementations such as waterless urinals in common areas and grey water recycling devices. While these barriers varied from technology to technology, this general theme emerged.

Managers showed the highest interest in providing messages promoting water efficiency as an initiative. One participant explained: "Yes, we would be very interested in seeing the messaging research and are currently doing only verbal requests. We have been thinking about messaging because our costs are high (BB1)". This was due to a general belief that messaging to guests as an initiative had a low cost and low impact on the guest experience as one managers stated: "They sound very subtle but effective. Doesn't sound intrusive at all but could have a big change (T2)".

However, when specific research on messaging was reviewed, managers were uneasy with the wording of previous efforts: "That sounds too boring, we need something more fun, they are on holiday after all (SC7)". They also cautioned about the tone, length, and amount of messaging: "We work really hard for them so they don't need to worry about it. We aren't expecting them to come on a week-long environmental lecture (SC2)". Instead they offered: "It is about focusing on the do's and not the don'ts. You have to engage with guests (SC1)". This feedback lead to a discussion concerning the ideas managers had for further engaging guests.

New contributions from SMTEs

Managers were asked to create or explain existing solutions to reduce water use in tourism accommodations that had not been previously researched. Since interviews were completed at different times, they were also presented with the previous ideas by managers in prior interviews and asked to comment on them. In this way, the later interviews were able to have a process of review, and in some cases recommended enhancements of their peer ideas. Perhaps not surprisingly, these newly explained ideas were generally endorsed by fellow managers. Whether this was due to a desire to conform and follow their peer group or because the ideas are more feasible for SMTEs is not resolved. However, several managers explained that these ideas seemed low impact on the guest experience, low investment and had potential to make large changes. Below are three of their ideas, representing their most collectively supported initiatives.

- Initial welcome introduction: while engaging guests on their initial walk through of the premises, staffs briefly (5–15 minutes) highlight environmental efforts in addition to the original pertinent information to show guests they are making an effort and hope guests follow suit. For example, while showing off the bathroom, the popularity of the towel reuse programme and the water saving shower heads would be emphasized.
- Feedback cards: cards located in guest rooms asking for additional ideas for saving water (and other environmental efforts) in the accommodation. This initiative would engage guests in the creation of solutions and may encourage them to use resources more efficiently if they are part of the "solution".
- Child-focused messaging: signs asking guests to use only the water they need directed towards children with the hope they will in turn influence their parents. This could also ensure the tone of the messages is more appropriate to the holiday experience.

Stage two: guest questionnaire

Cluster analysis was performed and three distinct clusters were identified through segmenting the data based on guests' water use behaviour. To summarize, the largest cluster, cluster 1 ($n = 165$), was generalized by a high effort to save water. Additionally, they scored highest for almost every intervention and message. Therefore, this cluster may represent the "most conscientious", needing little encouragement to save water. However, differences between cluster 2 and 3 presented the most fascinating data. The second largest cluster, cluster 2 ($n = 135$), represented individuals with the lowest overall effort and, specifically, the least effort to stop taps from running which is typically considered a habitual behaviour (DEFRA, 2009). Combined with placing the highest level of importance on all services, it may be expected that they were disinterested in saving water. However, they responded with a moderate level of positivity towards initiatives and messages. Therefore, they appeared unaware of their impacts but also receptive to engaging in behaviour change initiatives and were labelled, "overt users" due to the type of water use they displayed. This was in contrast to cluster 3 whom were labelled "disengaged" as they appeared least likely to engage in initiatives.

Table 2. Characteristics of the sample by cluster.

Characteristics	Most conscientious	Overt users	Disengaged
n	165	135	108
Gender			
Male	44.8%	45.9%	36.1%
Female	55.2%	54.1%	63.9%
Age[a]			
18–19	3%	3.7%	7.4%
20–24	8.5%	11.1%	12%
25–29	11.5%	28.1%	19.4%
30–34	15.2%	14.1%	18.5%
35–44	20%	17.8%	17.6%
45–59	21.2%	20%	16.7%
60–64	11.5%	2.2%	1.9%
65–74	7.9%	2.2%	5.6%
>74	1.2%	0.7%	0.9%
Average age[b]	42.3	36.18	36.5
Total household income[+]			
<£9999	7.3%	7.4%	8.3%
£10,000–£19,999	18.8%	18.5%	18.5%
£20,000–£29,999	14.5%	18.5%	16.7%
£30,000–£39,999	17.6%	20%	18.5%
£40,000–£49,999	14.5%	11.9%	13%
£50,000–£74,999	12.1%	11.1%	15.7%
£75,000–£100,000	3.6%	7.4%	0.9%
>£100,000	3%	2.2%	0.9%
Prefer not to say	8.5%	3%	7.4%
Average income[^]	£34,060	£36,315	£31,481
Highest educational qualification			
GCSE/NVQ	24.8%	25.2%	26.9%
A/AS level/GNVG	33.9%	25.2%	25%
Bachelor's degree	28.5%	30.4%	33.3%
Master's	9.1%	13.3%	13.9%
Doctorate	3.6%	5.9%	0.9%
Average number of individuals in household	2.81	3.06	2.94
Presence of children in household[a]	36%	53%	41%
Housing situation			
Home owned outright	24.2%	22.2%	25%
Home owned with mortgage or loan	36.4%	27.4%	31.5%
Shared ownership	1.8%	1.5%	0%
Let from council	12.7%	15.6%	11.1%
Let from private landlord or letting agency	18.8%	27.4%	22.2%
Other	6.1%	5.9%	10.2%
Water metrics			
With water meter in the home	52%	44%	54%
Differences in water company+	-	-	-
Occupation			
Higher managerial, administrative or professional	8.5%	9.6%	9.3%
Intermediate managerial, administrative or professional	20%	20.7%	17.6%
Supervisory or clerical and junior managerial, administrative or professional	30.9%	28.9%	29.6%
Skilled manual worker	10.9%	20%	12%
Semi and unskilled manual worker	4.2%	10.4%	10.2%
Casual or non-worker	25.5%	10.4%	21.3%

[a]Indicates a significant difference between clusters using a Kruskal–Wallis H test or Mann–Whitney U test ($p < 0.05$).
[b]Estimated using a life expectancy of 85.65 (UK Office for National Statistics, 2015).
[+]Excluded individuals that stated "do not know" or "prefer not to say" during Kruskal–Wallis H test.
[^]Estimated using an upper limit of £150,000.
Source: Authors.

Table 2 presents sample characteristics whilst Table 3 provides travel characteristics by cluster. Significant differences between clusters were observed between age; presence of children in the household; those visiting friends and relatives on their last overnight in tourism accommodation; the importance of all services (excluding en-suite bathrooms) on the booking process; and, overnight

Table 3. Travel characteristics by cluster.

Characteristics	Most conscientious	Overt users	Disengaged
Type of accommodation			
Hotel	48.5%	49.6%	53.7%
B&B	15.2%	20%	13.9%
Self-catering	13.3%	8.9%	13%
Campsite/caravan park	23%	21.5%	19.4%
Motivation for travel[b]			
To visit friends and relatives[a]	22.4%	39.3%	23.1%
Holiday	76.4%	67.4%	80.6%
Business or for work	4.8%	10.4%	6.5%
Mean score of services' importance on last booking*			
Swimming pool[a]	2.29	2.93	2.38
En-suite bathroom	3.89	4.01	3.74
Spa[a]	2.05	2.67	2.31
Separate shower and bath[a]	2.8	3.13	2.68
Fresh linen daily[a]	3.13	3.7	3.18
Fresh towel(s) daily[a]	3.29	3.81	3.33
Luxury shower[a]	2.74	3.21	2.74
Nights stayed in tourism accommodation per year for:			
Holiday-			
0–5	35.2%	38.5%	25.9%
5–10	25.5%	28.9%	29.6%
10–15	15.2%	18.5%	24.1%
15–20	9.7%	10.4%	15.7%
Over 20	14.5%	3.7%	4.6%
Average^	9.65	8.09	9.68
Business/work[a]			
0–5	90.9%	71.1%	81.5%
5–10	3.6%	20%	11.1%
10–15	3.6%	6.7%	4.6%
15–20	1.2%	0.7%	2.8%
Over 20	0.6%	1.5%	0.0%
Average^	3.35	4.57	3.94

[a]Indicates a significant difference between clusters using a Kruskal–Wallis H test or Mann–Whitney U test ($p < 0.05$).
[b]Question allowing multiple responses (e.g. tick all that apply).
*Items were measured on a scale from 1 (very unimportant) to 5 (very important).
^Calculated with an upper limit of 25 nights per year.
Source: Authors.

stays in tourism accommodation per year for business/work. Interestingly, the cluster "overt users" reported a greater desire for all seven services than the other clusters.

The most frequently reported behaviour was "I take one or less showers/baths per day", while the lowest reported was "I do not wait for the right temperature", meaning taps and showers are allowed to run until they were hot or cold. All behaviours measured in this study showed significant differences between clusters. Table 4 presents behavioural data for each cluster in descending order by most frequently reported.

The general profile demonstrates that the "most conscientious" cluster was the oldest group, with the least amount of households with children, visited friends and relatives least often during their last trip, placed the lowest importance on all seven services, and stay in tourism accommodation for business/work the least. This cluster also reported significantly higher effort to save water and greater effort for each of the eight behaviours.

The cluster, "overt users" was characterized as the youngest, with the most amount of households with children present, having the most respondents visiting friends and relatives, placing the highest importance of all seven services on their last booking, and staying in tourism accommodation for business/work most frequently. They also reported the lowest general effort to save water in tourism accommodation and the lowest scores for four of the five behaviours related to running taps.

The third cluster, "disengaged" was composed of individuals with a mean score between the others for age; households with children; respondents visiting friends and relatives; placing

Table 4. Mean scores of water efficiency behaviour at home and in tourism accommodation by cluster.

Item	$\bar{X}$	Most conscientious	Overt users	Disengaged
Overall effort to save water in tourism accommodation[φa]	3.06	3.56	2.64	2.81
Tourism accommodation behaviours[+]				
I take one or less showers/baths per day[Ra]	3.72	4.17	2.84	4.16
I turn off the tap when brushing teeth[Ra]	3.61	4.23	2.35	4.22
I take efficient showers[Ra]	3.51	4.07	2.73	3.64
If offered, I participate in towel reuse schemes[a]	3.47	3.96	3.16	3.12
I shower instead of bath to save water[a]	3.25	4.24	2.94	2.1
I control water when showering[a]	3.07	3.56	2.78	2.69
I prefer certified green businesses[a]	2.71	2.85	2.73	2.47
I do not wait for the right temperature[Ra]	2.51	2.65	2.27	2.63

[φ]Items measured on a scale from 0 (I make no effort to save) to 6 (I make every effort to save).
[a]Indicates a statistically significant difference between clusters using a Kruskal–Wallis H test ($p < 0.05$).
[R]Item has been reverse coded.
[+]Items measured on a scale from 1 (never) to 5 (always).
Source: Authors.

importance on services for their last booking; and, staying in tourism accommodation for business/ work. Additionally, they reported general effort to save water in tourism accommodation between that of the other clusters. However, they reported the least effort for behaviours not related to running taps (towel reuse; green-certified businesses; shower instead of bath). The only exception was the tap-related behaviour, "I control water when showering", where they reported the lowest effort.

Initiatives and messaging

Combining new ideas from SMTEs and previous ideas highlighted in this literature review, eight initiatives and five messages were presented to survey participants. Respondents indicated how each initiative would impact their experience. Impact on the guest experience was used here as it was the number one barrier to implementing initiatives stated by managers in stage one. These eight initiatives were designed to explore a diverse array of efforts (e.g. technologies, incentives, communication, and engagement).

Five messages were evaluated on how likely they would encourage individuals to use less water. An effort was made to include a diversity of messages found in the literature review of this study (e.g. drought, climate change, child-focused, standard message, use of psychological theory). A message of "Quack quack is duck for 'please save some water for me'" aimed to represent the SMTE recommendation to be "fun" while targeting children. Table 5 provides responses by cluster, ranked in descending order by overall sample mean. Significant differences for each initiative and message were observed between clusters. Participants were also asked where messages would be best located to encourage them to reduce water use. The bathroom was the number one reported location and significant differences between bathroom, website, verbally and "no message would be effective" between clusters were observed as seen in Table 6.

All clusters reported money-off vouchers and donations to charity would most positively impact their experience. For the "most conscientious", this was followed by highlighting efforts in the initial welcome and then feedback cards. However, the other clusters ranked feedback cards above highlighting efforts in the initial welcome. Mean scores for both of these manager lead initiatives were above the initiative "messages asking guests to help". This was surprising as managers expressed the highest interest in messaging and, as evidenced previously in this paper, a substantial amount of previous literature has focused on changing signage.

The "most conscientious" cluster reported that every initiative would more positively impact their experience than other clusters. They also stated every message would encourage them to save water to a greater extent than the other two clusters. Mean scores for "overt users" were between those of other clusters for every initiative except money-off vouchers which they ranked lowest. Following

Table 5. Mean scores of the impact on the guest experience from behaviour change initiatives and messaging.

Item	$\overline{X}$	Most conscientious	Overt users	Disengaged
Initiatives[*]				
A money-off voucher on concessions or your next stay if the towels or linens are not changed every day[a]	4.00	4.24	3.79	3.91
A donation to charity by the accommodation if the towels or linens are not changed every day[a]	3.57	3.78	3.46	3.40
A feedback card asking you for suggestions on how to improve the accommodation's environmental efforts[a]	3.45	3.65	3.41	3.20
Having the environmental efforts of the accommodation highlighted during your initial welcome introduction[a]	3.42	3.66	3.35	3.16
A messaging asking you to help use less water[a]	3.36	3.61	3.23	3.16
A light turning on in the shower when you have exceeded 5 minutes[a]	3.26	3.44	3.24	3.00
Personalized measurement of how much water you used during your stay made available for you to see[a]	3.18	3.41	3.16	2.84
Waterless urinals located in the facility[a]	2.76	2.81	2.99	2.40
Messages[^]				
Please promote our beautiful local environment by using less water[a]	3.62	3.84	3.47	3.45
Heating and transporting water consumes a large amount of electricity, increasing greenhouses gases. For example, according to the Environmental Agency, roughly 25% of electricity used in the home is for heating water. Please help us care for the environment by using only the water you need[a]	3.28	3.48	3.24	3.01
Amazingly, of the 22 water supply areas in England and Wales, the Environmental Agency classifies 12 as "seriously water stressed". This assessment is made by comparing current and forecast rainfall per person with current and forecast household demand per person. Please help us care for the environment by using only the water you need[a]	3.23	3.41	3.22	2.97
Other guests in this accommodation have expressed a desire for us to use less water, please aid us in this endeavour[a]	3.06	3.14	3.15	2.83
Quack quack is duck for "please save some water for me"[a]	2.93	2.98	3.08	2.67

[*]Items measured on a scale from 1 (very negatively) to 5 (very positively).
[a]Indicates a statistically significant difference between clusters using a Kruskal–Wallis H test ($p < 0.05$).
[^]Items measured on a scale from 1 (none) to 5 (very much).
Source: Authors.

that trend, for encouragement from messaging, the "overt users" cluster ranked between the other clusters for every message. Ranking lowest for all initiatives was the "disengaged" cluster (except money-off vouchers where they ranked in between other clusters). This cluster also contained the highest number of individuals stating no message would be effective in changing their behaviour.

All clusters agreed that the most general message starting with "Please promote…" would most encourage saving water. The child-focused message developed from manager feedback ("Quack quack…") received the lowest score. While it is important to note that all respondents to the survey were adults and the message was meant to target children, due to the low score, this initiative would not be recommended with the tourism accommodation.

Table 6. Reported location where messages would have a high impact on behaviour.

Location	Most conscientious	Overt users	Disengaged
Bathroom[a]	84%	68%	72%
Welcome packet	40%	44%	44%
Website[a]	28%	20%	16%
Verbally[a]	13%	24%	5%
Email	16%	14%	11%
Phone	6%	7%	1%
None, "no messages would be effective"[a]	4%	8%	9%

[a]Indicates a significant difference between clusters using a Kruskal–Wallace H test ($p < 0.05$).
Source: Authors.

Discussion

Due to the low sample size (16), geographical limitations and convenience sampling of SMTE managers in stage one, generalizing results for all SMTEs would be unwise. However, promisingly, results did support several findings from the literature. For example, managers reported the greatest barrier was potentially negatively affecting the guest experience (Coles et al., 2017), followed by costs. No consensus was found on motivations for such efforts which would support findings from Fassin et al. (2011) and Font et al. (2016) that SMTEs have a variety of drivers for engaging in CSR. Additionally, managers were concerned about the length and type of messaging with guests as reported by Font et al. (2017) and Coles et al. (2017).

While manager responses validated past literature, they also yielded two important new findings. First, participating managers reported many of the efforts previously explored in the literature to promote water efficiency behaviour were not viable within their current operations due to constraints related to their size. Importantly, donations to charity and money-off vouchers were deemed inappropriate to their operations due to financial constraints and a lack of technology and/or staffing to manage such complicated efforts. Instead, they offered three low resource intensive ideas not previously examined in the literature.

The subsequent guest questionnaires provided several novel findings as well. Most importantly, the majority of guests showed a willingness to exchange something for changing their water behaviour. Such an exchange should also consider competing factors for guests' behaviour (Shaw et al., 2013). Shove (2003) argues these competing factors are embedded in the needs and services of comfort, cleanliness and convenience. Here, these needs and services were identified by managers. Certainly no guest should be expected to refrain from showering or brushing their teeth and instead this research has focused on guests using only what they need. Since guests were willing to exchange for their change in behaviour, we therefore find the competing factors identified by Shove (2003) as helpful points in navigating this exchange and not necessarily impediments.

When viewed through the process of targeting audience segments, if resources are scarce, SMTEs focusing efforts on the "overt users" cluster to maximize return on investment. That is, this group showed the lowest effort on tap-related efforts (e.g. showering, sink use and inability to use dual flush toilets) which have been identified to be high water consumptive practices (South West Water, 2014; UKWIR, 2014). This group also showed a moderate level of positivity towards exchanging for a change in their behaviour. Additionally, targeting other clusters may provide lower returns as the "most contentious" is likely to follow any reasonable appeals while the "disengaged" are likely to ignore such requests all together. The "overt users" cluster, as others, reported the highest positive impact from money-off vouchers and donations to charity. However, if SMTEs are unable to offer incentives due to limitations explained earlier, feedback cards and then engaging this cluster in conversation, perhaps during the initial welcome introduction, would have the next most positive impact on their experience. Since they reported letting taps run, an emphasis during any conversations on the accommodation's efforts to reduce water waste from taps (e.g. implementing water efficient shower heads, low flow toilets, promptly fixing leaks, etc.) would be recommended.

These results may also have theoretical implications for how SMTEs apply social marketing. Importantly, guests reported the greatest positive impact on their experience from those initiatives requiring the highest financial and logistical investment (e.g. money-off vouchers and donations to charity). This supported previous findings by Miao and Wei (2013) that guest behaviour in tourism accommodation is driven by hedonic motivation, needing rewards to facilitate such an exchange. Some larger hotel firms (e.g. Starwood and ACCOR) have already begun implementing such programmes. Therefore, the financial constraints, lack of IT and staff to manage such programmes, as identified by SMTE managers in this study and the literature (Ateljevic & Doorne, 2000; Dewhurst & Thomas, 2003), could represent a difficult hurdle for them to contend with larger competitors in changing guest behaviour. This may indicate that in some instances, larger firms have a competitive advantage over SMTEs in applying social marketing to change guest behaviour. However, as displayed by the guest questionnaire, lower investment options, specifically feedback cards and the initial welcome introduction, may still be viable options.

Several limitations to the study need further discussion. First, in stage one, due to the convenience sampling method and request for interviews through email of SMTE managers, it is possible that participants were self-selecting. While results supported several findings in other recent research, this limitation is clearly acknowledged and future research on the topic could increase sample sizes and use randomized a-posteriori methods for segmenting their audience. As such, due to the limited geographical range and small sample size (16) of the current research, findings may not be applicable to all SMTEs. In stage two, the opportunity for an attitude-behaviour gap was possible. That is, claims that initiatives may positively impact the guest experience may not be true in practice. To minimize this concern, most behavioural questions were adopted from previous literature and each scale was subject to a Cronbach's alpha test for reliability. Additionally, a social desirability bias may have also existed. To minimize this bias, online questionnaires were conducted, as opposed to face to face questionnaires, as Kreuter, Presser, and Tourangeau (2008) find web-based surveying reduces this issue. Additionally, within the survey instrument, comment sections were provided for each question to allow participants to further express their answers. Finally, a pilot survey was conducted to check for understanding and clarity of the instrument. However, despite these efforts, these phenomena may have been present in this study, as is true of any research of this nature, and are acknowledged as limitations.

Conclusion

This paper investigated the impact on guest experience of initiatives designed to promote water efficient behaviour within SMTEs. Businesses stated they were unable or unwilling to incorporate many of the initiatives previously examined in the academic literature, in particular money-off vouchers and donations to charity, due to limitations related to their size. Instead they contributed three new ideas: feedback cards; highlighting their environmental efforts during the initial welcome introduction; and messaging focused on children.

To examine how these ideas may impact the guest experience, a subsequent online questionnaire was administered. While recent literature has suggested many SMTEs avoid engaging with their guests to change behaviour and communicate their efforts (Coles et al., 2017; Font et al., 2017), here most guests reported positively towards participating in initiatives. To further understand how to target guests, cluster analysis was used with three distinct segments of water users emerging: "most conscientious", "overt users", and "disengaged". Each cluster behaved significantly different with some more willing to engage in initiatives then others. The "overt users" cluster showed the greatest promise for targeting with the goal of increasing return on investment. This was due to their type of behaviour, allowing taps to run, and responsiveness to engage in an exchange.

Results also showed guests reported the highest positive impact on their experience from those initiatives SMTEs stated were not viable due to financial and logistical limitations. Specifically, money-off vouchers and donations to charity were reported to have the greatest positive impact. Some larger firms (e.g. Starwood and ACCOR) have already begun implementing such programmes. This may indicate, larger firms have a competitive advantage over SMTEs for applying social marketing to promote water efficiency. However, two initiatives deemed more appropriate by participating SMTEs (feedback cards and initial welcome introduction) represented more modestly acceptable opportunities for engaging the "overt users" at low cost to the business.

Findings also have implications for future research. Importantly, the "overt users" cluster reported the highest expectations for services on the tourism accommodation experience. Managers may therefore be advised to follow best practices supported by data driven research when engaging guests in initiatives to avoid scepticism as reported in Shang et al. (2010). However, SMTEs reported no previous exposure to findings from previous research efforts aiming to change guest behaviour. This was supported by observation from Coles et al. (2017) that many SMTEs avoid engaging guests. While Fassin et al. (2011) have identified that smaller firms may not need theory to have a strong grasp of CSR, it would appear there is a need here for more exposure to previous research findings for this particular aspect of CSR engaging guests in changing their behaviour. This may be due to the delicate balance of messaging to guests (Coles et al., 2017; Font et al., 2017). Therefore, clearly more impact driven research, studies developed with practitioners where findings are made readily available to those intended to use them, with SMTEs, is needed in this area if tourism systems are to become more sustainable.

While the findings offer strong conceptual and practical recommendations for the use of social marketing to change guest behaviour by SMTEs, discrepancies between reported behavioural scores and those actually occurring are always possible in any study of this nature. Moreover, whilst managers offered anecdotal evidence that, for example, highlighting environmental efforts during the initial welcome introduction changed guest behaviour, no data exists to evidence this claim. Therefore, while this study focused on how initiatives would impact the guest experience, identified as the greatest barrier to implementation by managers in stage one of this research, further research, preferably experimental in design to combat the attitude-behaviour gap, is recommended to determine impacts from these initiatives on changing behaviour.

Acknowledgments

The authors wish to thank the South West Water Company for their contributions.

Disclosure statement

No potential conflict of interest was reported by the authors.

References

Andreasen, A.R. (2002). The life trajectory of social marketing: Some implications. *Marketing Theory, 3*(3), 293–303.

Ateljevic, J., & Doorne, S. (2000). Staying within the fence: Lifestyle entrepreneurship in tourism. *Journal of Sustainable Tourism, 8*(5), 378–392.

Baca-Motes, K., Brown, A., Gneely, A., Kennan, E.A., & Nelson, L.D. (2013). Commitment and behaviour change: Evidence from the field. *Journal of Consumer Research, 39*, 1070–1084.

Barbour, R. (2007). *Doing focus groups*. London: Sage.

Barbour, R. (2013). *Introducing qualitative research: A students' guide*. London: Sage Publishing.

Barr, S., Shaw, G., Coles, T., & Prillwitz, J. (2010). "A holiday is a holiday": Practicing sustainability, home and away. *Journal of Transport Geography, 18*, 474–481.

Blose, J.E., Mack, R.W., & Pitts, R.E. (2015). The influence of message framing on hotel guests' linen-reuse intentions. *Cornell Hospitality Quarterly, 56*(2), 145–154.

Coles, T., Zschiegner, A.K., & Dinan, C. (2014). A cluster analysis of climate change mitigation behaviours among SMTEs. *Tourism Geographies, 16*(3), 382–399.

Coles, T., Warren, N., Borden, D.S., & Dinan, C. (2017). Business models among SMTEs: Identifying attitudes to environmental costs and their implications for sustainable tourism. *Journal of Sustainable Tourism*. doi: 10.1080/09669582.2016.1221414

Condon, L. (2004). Sustainability and small to medium sized enterprises – How to engage them. *Australian Journal of Environmental Education, 20*(1), 57–67.

Corner, A., & Randall, A. (2011). Selling climate change? The limitations of social marketing as a strategy for climate change public engagement. *Global Environmental Change, 21*, 1005–1014.

Dann, S. (2010). Redefining social marketing with contemporary commercial marketing definitions. *Journal of Business Research, 6*(2), 147–153.

Drasgow, F. (1984). Scrutinizing psychological tests: Measurement equivalence and equivalent relationships with external variables are the central issue. *Psychological Bulletin, 95*, 134–135.

DEFRA (2009). Public understanding of sustainable water use in the home. Retrieved from http://randd.defra.gov.uk/Default.aspx?Menu=Menu&Module=More&Location=None&ProjectID=16190&FromSearch=Y&Publisher=1&SearchText=ev0503&SortString=ProjectCode&SortOrder=Asc&Paging=10#Description

Dewhurst, H., & Thomas, R. (2003). Encouraging sustainable business practices in a non-regulatory environment: A case study of small tourism firms in a UK National Park. *Journal of Sustainable Tourism, 11*(4), 383–403.

Dinan, C., & Sargeant, A. (2000). Social marketing and sustainability: A planned approach to social change. *Progress in Tourism and Hospitality Research, 12*(3), 1–14.

Dolnicar, S., Grün, B., Leisch, F., & Schmidt, K. (2013). Required sample sizes for data-driven market segmentation analyses in tourism. *Journal of Travel Research, 53*(3), 296–306.

Dolnicar, S., & Grün, B. (2009). Environmentally friendly behaviour – Can heterogeneity among individuals and contexts/environments be harvested for improved sustainable management? *Environment and Behaviour, 41*(5), 693–714.

Fassin, Y., Van Rossem, A., & Buelens, M. (2011). Small-business owner-managers' perceptions of business ethics and CSR-related concepts. *Journal of Business Ethics, 98*, 425–453.

Font, X., Elgammal, I., & Lamond, I. (2017). Greenhushing: The deliberate under communicating of sustainability practices by tourism businesses. *Journal of Sustainable Tourism*. doi: 10.1080/09669582.2016.1158829

Font, X., Garay, L., & Jones, S. (2016). Sustainability motivations and practices in small tourism enterprises in European protected areas. *Journal of Cleaner Production, 137*, 1439–1448. doi:10.1016/j.jclepro.2014.01.071

Franke, N., Reisinger, H., & Hoppe, D. (2009). Remaining within-cluster heterogeneity: A metaanalysis of the 'dark side' of clustering methods. *Journal of Marketing Management, 25*(3–4), 273–293.

French, J., Blair-Stevens, C., McVey, D., & Merritt, R. (2010). *Social marketing and public health, theory and practice*. Oxford: Oxford University Press.

Goldstein, N.J., Cialdini, R.B., & Griskevicius, V. (2008). A room with a viewpoint: Using social norms to motivate environmental conservation in hotels. *Journal of Consumer Research, 35*(3), 472–482.

Gordon, R. (2012). Rethinking and re-tooling the social marketing mix. *Australasian Marketing Journal, 20*(2), 122–126.

Gössling, S., Peeters, P., Hall, M., Ceron, J.-P., Dubois, G., Lehman, L.V., & Scott, D. (2012). Tourism and water use: Supply, demand, and security. An international review. *Tourism Management, 33*(1), 1–15.

Gössling, S., Hall, C.M., & Scott, D. (2015). *Tourism and water*. Bristol: Channel View Publications.

Hair, J.F., Black, W.C., Babin, B.J., & Anderson, R.E. (2010). *Multivariate data analysis*. Upper Saddle River, NJ: Pearson Education.

Hall, M.C. (2014). *Tourism and social marketing*. London: Routledge.

Kreuter, F., Presser, S., & Tourangeau, R. (2008). Social desirability bias in CATI, IVR, and Web surveys the effects of mode and question sensitivity. *Public Opinion Quarterly, 72*(5), 847–865.

Lee, S., & Oh, H. (2014). Effective communication strategies for hotel guests' green behaviour. *Cornell Hospitality Quarterly, 55*(1), 52–63.

Mazzocchi, M. (2008). *Statistics for marketing and consumer research*. London: Sage.

Mair, J., & Bergin-Seers, S. (2010). The effect of interventions on the environmental behaviour of Australian motel guests. *Tourism and Hospitality Research, 10*(4), 255–268.

McKenzie-Mohr, D., Lee, N.R., Shultz, P.W., & Kotler, P. (2012). *Social marketing to protect the environment: What works*. London: Sage Publications.

Miao, L., & Wei, W. (2013). Consumers' pro-environmental behaviour and the underlying motivations: A comparison between household and hotel settings. *International Journal of Hospitality Management, 32*, 102–112.

Molina-Azorín, J.F., & Font, X. (2016). Mixed methods in sustainable tourism research: An analysis of prevalence, designs and application in JOST (2005–2014). *Journal of Sustainable Tourism, 24*(4), 549–573.

Morsing, M., & Perrini, F. (2009). CSR in SMEs: Do SMEs matter for the CSR agenda? *Business Ethics, 18*(1), 1–6.

OFWAT (2011). Push, pull, nudge: How can we help consumers save water, energy and money? Retrieved from www.ofwat.gov.uk

O'Neill & Siegelbaum and The RICE Group (2002). *Hotel water conservation: A Seattle demonstration*. Seattle, WA: Resources Conservation Section, Seattle Public Utilities. Retrieved from https://www.seattle.gov/util/cs/groups/public/@spu/@water/documents/webcontent/HOTELWATE_200407081359093.pdf

Reese, G., Loew, K., & Steffgen, G. (2014). Towel less: Social norms enhancing pro-environmental behaviour in hotels. *Journal of Social Psychology, 154*, 97–100.

Schultz, W.P., Khasian, A.M., & Zaleski, A.C. (2008). Using normative social influence to promote conservation among hotel guests. *Social Influence, 3*(1), 4–23.

Scott, D., Peeters, P., & Gössling, S. (2010). Can tourism deliver its "aspirational" greenhouse gas emission reduction targets? *Journal of Sustainable Tourism, 18*(3), 393–408.

Shang, J., Basil, D.Z., & Wymer, W. (2010). Using social marketing to enhance hotel reuse programs. *Journal of Business Research, 63*, 166–172.

Shaw, G., Barr, S., & Wooler, J. (2013). The application of social marketing to tourism. In S. McCabe (Ed.), *The Routledge handbook of tourism marketing* (pp. 54–64). London: Taylor and Francis Ltd.

Shove, E. (2003). Users, technology and expectations of comfort, cleanliness and convenience. *Innovation, 16*(2), 193–206.

South West Water (2014).: Draft water resources management plan, 2015–2040. Retrieved from https://www.southwestwater.co.uk/media/pdf/4/7/South_West_Water_Draft_Water_Resources_Management_Plan_March_2013.pdf

Storey, D.J. (1994). *Understanding the small business sector*. London: Thomson Learning.

Truong, D.V., & Hall, M.C. (2013). Social marketing and tourism: What is the evidence? *Social Marketing Quarterly, 19*(2), 110–135.

UK Office for National Statistics (2015). Retrieved from http://www.ons.gov.uk/ons/rel/lifetables/national-life-tables/2010–2012/sty-facts-about-le.html

UKWIR (UK Water Industry Research) (2014). *Understanding customer behaviour for water demand forecasting* (Report Ref. No. 14/WR/01/14). London: UK Water Industry Research Limited.

Which hotel guest segments reuse towels? Selling sustainable tourism services through target marketing

Ljubica Knezevic Cvelbar, Bettina Grün and Sara Dolnicar

ABSTRACT

This paper reviews and evaluates the wide range of supply and demand side measures employed and tested to reduce the environmental impacts of tourist accommodation. It focuses on the importance of understanding market segments and their pro-environmental behaviour by exploring the personal and travel characteristics significantly associated with pro-environment beneficial change, empirically investigating hotel guest characteristics associated with higher towel reuse. Towel use per day, per room, is modelled according to the number of adults in the room, the number of children, and the type and origins of guests. Observed actual towel use by 204 travel parties spending 480 nights in a four-star hotel in Slovenia reveals key personal and travel characteristics of hotel guests which are predictive of towel reuse: their country of origin, booking methods used, being a business traveller and not being a family. Results point to a-priori market segments which could be given booking preference in periods of high demand to reduce hotel environmental footprints. Results also point to promising leverage points for interventions designed to modify the behaviour of hotel guests on site. The approach and methodology used could be applied to marketing pro-environmental concepts more widely across other sustainable initiatives.

Introduction

Accommodation providers can reduce the burden of their operations on the environment in several ways. They can take supply-sided measures, such as equipping the hotel building with features that minimize the use of resources (Butler, 2008). Examples include the activation of electricity only when the room key card is inserted, the installation of feedback monitors displaying, in real-time, water and electricity consumption, the installation of water-efficient taps and showerheads, and the use of energy efficient lamps and appliances. Such technical equipment can be installed at the time of con-structing the hotel or be retrofitted, but it typically comes at an additional cost (Kirk, 1995). Many small and medium accommodation businesses choose not to install or retrofit such equipment (Beccali, La Gennusa, Coco, & Rizzo, 2009).

A second supply-side approach involves working with employees. Prior work in this area indicates that the pro-environmental behaviour of employees can be stimulated by corporate commitment to environmental protection codified in environmental policies or certifications (Andersson, Shivarajan, & Blau, 2005; Bohdanowicz, Zientara & Novotna, 2011; Tudor, Barr, & Gilg, 2008) and by company leaders' displaying pro-environmental behaviour (Cordano & Frieze, 2000; Robertson & Barling, 2013).

Factors intrinsic to the employee, such as their pro-environmental attitudes, norms, awareness, and beliefs, also contribute to explaining their behaviour (Ramus, 2002; Scherbaum, Popovich, & Finlinson, 2008; Tudor et al., 2008).

Arguably, the most effective supply-side approach is to change the default position. Changing the default has been shown to be successful in changing behaviours with environmental consequences (Pichert & Katsikopoulos, 2008). In the context of hotel towel use, however, it is not easy to implement in luxury hotels where guests have expectations of minimum standards of service provision.

Accommodation providers can also take demand-side measures, such as trying to convince tourists upon arrival to behave in an environmentally friendly manner. This approach assumes that educational measures can be set in place, and that they are effective (Ballantyne, Packer, & Falk, 2011; Lee & Moscardo, 2005; Luck, 2003; Powell & Ham, 2008). However, many studies show that the positive effects of educational measures on tourists' environmentally sustainable behaviour were conducted with samples of people who already had a high predisposition towards such behaviours. Evidence from other fields of research shows that increased knowledge and awareness will not necessarily lead to pro-environmental behaviour (Kollmuss & Agyeman, 2002). Recent findings indicate that even people who are actively engaged in environmental action at home do not behave particularly in an environmentally friendly way when on vacation (Juvan & Dolnicar, 2014). These findings combined cast doubt on the effectiveness of the educational approach for changing tourist behaviour.

Another possible demand-side approach involves proactively targeting tourists who are less likely to display environmentally harmful behaviour. Such a targeted approach has been proposed in the past (see Dolnicar, 2006). Several studies have attempted to profile segments of the market that would be suitable for such a targeted approach, by using socio-demographic characteristics such as age, gender, social and marital status, and income (see Diamantopoulos, Schlegelmilch, Sinkovics, & Bohlen, 2003); or internal factors such as motivations, pro-environmental knowledge, awareness, values, attitudes, emotions, locus of control, responsibilities, and priorities (see Kollmuss & Agyeman, 2002). The conclusion from a review of this body of work is that several environmentally friendly consumer segments with certain personal characteristics do exist. However, rarely has actual behaviour been used as a dependent variable. Most studies used stated behavioural intentions as the variable of interest. Intentions, however, are not good predictors of behaviour, especially behaviour that is subject to societal expectations or social norms. A recent study by Karlsson and Dolnicar (2016a), for example, demonstrates that most tourists who claim to consider the environment when making tourism-related decisions actually fail to do so when their behaviour is observed. Simultaneously, Karlsson and Dolnicar's study points to the existence of a small group of tourists – just over 10% – who indeed do consider the environment, even in the highly hedonistic context of vacation behaviour. Identifying such a segment specifically in the hotel context and proving that certain personal characteristics of segment members are linked to desired behaviours would open the door to a range of marketing approaches to reducing the environmental damage. In addition, hotels may benefit from a reduction in operational costs due to lower consumption of expensive resources such as water and electricity. Note, however, that such a targeting approach is likely to only be adopted by hotels in peak periods where demand is higher than the number of rooms available. In other contexts, such as accommodation offered on peer-to-peer accommodation networks (such as Airbnb), on the other hand, such a targeting approach could be immediately adopted. The reason is that, in peer-to-peer networks, rejecting booking requests is very common (Karlsson, Kemperman & Dolnicar, in press). Informing peer-to-peer network hosts of segmentation criteria that identify guests who will reuse towels and, therefore, have a lower environmental footprint and create lower operational costs, can immediately translate into changes in how hosts select their guests. In the longer term, as these criteria become known in the peer-to-peer network it is likely that guests will adopt less resource intensive behaviour in order to increase their booking chances. This is already clearly visible with guests now frequently offering a self-reference about their guest behaviour (Karlsson et al., in press). Currently such guest references are limited to issues of cleanliness, but there is no reason why this could not extend to behaviour with environmental consequences.

This study aims to identify personal and travel characteristics which are significantly associated with hotel towel reuse. Knowledge of these characteristics is a necessary condition to be able to implement any target segmentation action in view of reducing the environmental footprint of guests, at least with respect to resources used in relation to towel exchange. Such knowledge also represents the starting point for the identification of segments of guests which currently have very low levels of towel reuse and therefore represent primary target segments for behavioural interventions.

The study contributes to knowledge in sustainable tourism because it is the first investigation to prove, using behavioural measures, that hotel guests differ systematically in hotel towel use.

Literature review

Most studies of pro-environmental behaviour which measure actual behaviour conclude that pro-environmental consumers are more likely to have better general environmental knowledge and information (Arbuthnot, 1977; Vining & Ebreo, 1990; Winett, Leckliter, Chinn, Stahl, & Love, 1985), are more involved in environmental groups (Arbuthnot, 1977), have more past experience with pro-environmental behaviour (Macey & Brown, 1983), are more liberal (Arbuthnot, 1977; Webster, 1975; Weigel, 1977), and are more concerned about the future (Arbuthnot, 1977). They are also more likely to have higher social status and income (Arbuthnot, 1977; Gatersleben, Steg, & Vlek, 2002; Webster, 1975; Weigel, 1977), be female (Webster, 1975), have larger households (Gatersleben, et al., 2002), and be better educated (Weigel, 1977).

Most of these studies were undertaken in the home environment. Since the 1990s, the focus shifted toward using the theory of planned behaviour as the basis for the study of human behaviour (Ajzen, 1985, 1991). This theory postulates that behaviour can be predicted by behavioural intentions which, in turn, are determined by attitudes, social norms, and perceived behavioural control. This theory has been empirically shown to hold across a range of human behaviours; for example, intention to quit smoking (Norman, Conner, & Bell, 1999), condom use (Sutton, McVey, & Glanz, 1999), and exercising (Courneya, 1995). Combined with the increased ease of accessing survey data, the theory of planned behaviour may have led to the neglect of the study of actual behaviour, because behavioural intention was assumed to be a valid proxy for actual behaviour. Another prominent theory used to explain pro-social behaviour is norm activation theory (Schwartz, 1977). This theory explains pro-environmental behaviour based on four situation activators: awareness of need, situational responsibility, efficacy and ability and two personality activators: awareness of consequences and denial of responsibility. The norm activation process is based on self-expectations or personal norms expressed as moral obligation towards the environment. Personal norms have a central position in norm activation theory and function as mediator of situational and personality activators influence on behaviour (Harland, Staats, & Wilke, 2007). This theory has been tested in the context of a wide range of human pro-social behaviours including: energy conservation (Black, Stern, & Elworth, 1985), willingness to pay for environmental protection (Guagnano, Dietz, & Stern, 1994), shopping (Thøgersen, 1999), and choosing green accommodation (Han, 2015).

In terms of tourism-related research, only few studies have investigated actual behaviour, supporting the conclusion by Dolnicar and Ring (2014) that "Studies that measure real behavior are notably absent" (p. 43). Exceptions are the studies by Baca-Motes, Brown, Gneezy, Keenan, and Nelson (2013), Goldstein, Cialdini, and Griskevicius (2008), and Mair and Bergin-Seers (2010), which all used observed hotel towel use as the dependent variable and demonstrate that well-designed behavioural interventions can lead to a reduction of towel use. Baca-Motes et al. (2013) successfully used cognitive dissonance and social-identity theory to trigger hotel towel reuse; while Goldstein et al. (2008) show that descriptive and social norms are successful pro-environmental interventions in the hotel context. Meanwhile, Mair and Bergin-Seers (2010) found that persuasive communication encourages hotel guests to reuse the towels. In all these studies, hotel guest were seen as one homogeneous group. The possible existence of market segments among hotel guests which may differ in their pro-environmental behaviour or which may show different reactivity to the interventions set in those experiments was not investigated.

Other studies in tourism aiming to shed light on the reasons for environmentally friendly behaviour used self-reported past behaviour or behavioural intentions of tourists as their key variable of interest. Examples include profiling tourists who stayed at eco-certified accommodation (Dalton, Lockington, & Baldock, 2008; Fairweather, Maslin, & Simmons, 2005; Firth & Hing, 1999; Han & Kim, 2010; Jin-Soo, Hsu, Han, & Kim, 2010; Weaver & Lawton, 2002), visited eco-labelled attractions (Higham, Carr, & Gael, 2001; Karlsson & Dolnicar, 2016a; McKenna, Williams, & Cooper, 2011), participated in eco-friendly tours (Bergin-Seers & Mair, 2009; Dolnicar, 2010; Edwards & Griffin, 2013; Tierney, Hunt, & Latkova, 2011; Wearing, Cynn, Ponting, & McDonald, 2002), or chose sustainable modes of transport (Böhler, Grischkat, Haustein, & Hunecke, 2006; Dickinson, Robbins, & Lumsdon, 2010; Hergesell & Dickinger, 2013; Prillwitz & Barr, 2011). Those studies contribute critically to the understanding of tourists' pro-environmental behaviour, yet they are of limited use for developing marketing action to increase the environmentally friendly behaviour of the general tourist population because they were conducted with tourists predisposed to pro-environmental behaviours.

Another stream of research focuses on relating tourists' environmental awareness to pro-environmental behaviour, finding that the level of environmental awareness (Lee & Moscardo, 2005), the level of environmental knowledge and education (Powell & Ham, 2008; Luck, 2003), and tourist engagement in environmental learning outcomes (Ballantyne et al., 2011) impact on tourists' environmental behavioural intentions in protected areas.

Market segmentation has also been shown to have potential for triggering pro-environmental behaviour in tourism. Existing studies used either cognitive or social demographic characteristics to explain the pro-environmental behavioural intentions of tourists. For instance, Dolnicar and Leisch (2008) used reported past environmentally friendly holiday behaviour as a dependent variable, and found that the moral obligation to behave in an environmentally friendly way and pro-environmental attitudes are positively associated with membership in an environmentally friendly tourist segment. Fairweather et al. (2005) show that tourists who are concerned about the environment are more likely to choose eco-friendly tourism operators. Mair and Bergin-Seers (2010), Carrus, Bonaiuto, and Bonnes (2005), and Stanford (2014) found that eco-centric attitudes are a good predictor of pro-environmental behavioural intentions.

A range of findings have been reported with respect to the association of socio-demographics with higher levels of pro-environmental behavioural intentions. Overall, the past literature points to a few personal characteristics that may be useful in the search for a distinct segment of hotel guests who behave in a more environmentally friendly way: being older, female, and local (Carrus et al., 2005; Dolnicar & Leisch, 2008; Galley & Clifton, 2004), being highly aware of environmental issues (Lee & Moscardo, 2005), having pro-environmental attitudes (Dolnicar & Leisch, 2008; Carrus et al., 2005; Mair, 2011), being concerned about the environment (Fairweather et al., 2005), and feeling morally obliged to behave in a pro-environmental manner (Dolnicar & Leisch, 2008). These prior findings, combined with the availability of information about guests at the fieldwork location, drive the selection of predictor variables in this study.

Methodology

An empirical study using actual tourist behaviour with direct negative environmental consequences (specifically, towel use) was conducted in the four-star rated Bohinj Park Eco Hotel located in Bohinj (Slovenia). It should be noted that towel use is not the most environmentally harmful behaviour of tourists. There is general consensus that transportation is the largest contributor of greenhouse emissions, estimated to account for between 47% and 93% of tourism-generated carbon emissions (Dwyer, Forsyth, Spurr, & Hoque, 2010; Gössling & Schumacher, 2010; Gössling et al., 2005; Hoque et al., 2010; Kelly & Williams, 2007). There is no doubt, therefore, that changing people's travel patterns related to holidays would serve as the most efficient leverage point to reduce environmental impacts, as suggested by Dolnicar, Laesser, and Matus (2010). The problem with such an approach, however, is that it represents a major modification of people's holiday travel plans. Given recent studies that show that people's inclination to make major sacrifices to their holidays for the purpose of protecting the environment is low – even among people who volunteer for environmental organizations at home (Juvan & Dolnicar, 2014) – we may assume that attempts at changing people's travel modes and routes are unlikely to be successful. Aiming at behaviours that involve a lower level of sacrifice on the part of the tourist, such as towel reuse, represents an alternative. While each reused towel has a small impact, measures that could reduce towel use in the accommodation sector more broadly could have – in aggregate – a substantial global impact. Thus, this study focuses on towel reuse. Towel reuse can also act as a proxy for investigating many other small environmentally friendly activities.

The hotel in which the empirical study was conducted is located close to the Bohinj Lake in Slovenia. Slovenia is a relatively small country, with two million inhabitants, located in central-eastern Europe. Until 1990, part of former Yugoslavia, it underwent a successful transition from a social to a market economy and society, joining the European Union in 2004 and the European Monetary Union in 2007. Tourism is a major service export for Slovenia, contributing 40% of all service exports (Bank of Slovenia, 2015). Tourism also contributes 12% of GDP and 13% of total employment (Statistical Office of Republic of Slovenia, 2015).

Slovenia is one of the greenest countries in the world: 70% of Slovenian territory is covered by forest. Nature-based tourism is important for Slovenia, as is health and wellness-based tourism. City tourism is strong in Slovenia's capital Ljubljana (the Green Capital of Europe in 2016, and recipient of the World Travel and Tourism Council Best Destination award in 2015) as well as in its second largest city Maribor (European Capital of Culture in 2014). Seaside tourism is concentrated in two destinations along the Adriatic coast: Portorož and Piran. Statistics point to Slovenians being among the more environmentally friendly inhabitants in Europe: the Slovenian hospitality sector produces less food waste than any other European country (BIO Intelligence Services, 2010) and around 90% of Slovenians recycle their waste, placing them in the group of the most active recyclers in Europe (European Commission, 2014). Slovenians respect nature and spend on average more time visiting natural landscapes than the average European (Institute for Sustainable Development, 2015). Bohinj is located at the border of Triglav National Park in the Slovenian Alps. In 2015, it recorded 80,000 international tourism overnight stays (Statistical Office of Republic of Slovenia, 2015), primarily from Austria, Croatia, Germany, Serbia, and Russia.

Bohinj Park Eco Hotel was designed and built in 2009 with a vision of minimizing the environmental impacts of tourism – focusing on minimal use of water and electricity. It received several local environmental and innovation awards and the international Green Globe certificate in 2010. Bohinj Park Eco Hotel has 96 rooms and hosted 10,461 tourists in 2015.

Bohinj Park Eco Hotel represents a conservative location to conduct experiments in environmental sustainability. The bias that could be expected as a consequence of the hotel and location choice is that of overall higher levels of environmentally friendly behaviour by guests. There is no reason, however, to assume that interpersonal differences – which are the key focus of attention in this study – would be biased. It should be noted, however, that when we asked hotel staff to estimate the extent to which people self-select Bohinj Eco Park Hotel because of its environmental credentials, they all agreed that none of their guests did. This hotel is one of only two hotels in the Bohinj region, and its distinct features are that it is modern and offers a wide range of entertainment facilities which the other hotel does not offer, such as a bowling alley, a small movie theatre and an extensive water park. When asked how environmentally friendly the guests were, the chief of the cleaning department indicated that the amount of empty or half-empty plastic bottles left behind in the rooms to her is evidence of the low level of environmentally friendly behaviour in their guests.

The empirical study was conducted between 20 December 2014 and 11 March 2015. For this study, 26 hotel rooms were selected which were representative of the hotel room offerings, meaning that all types of rooms were represented in proportion to the frequency of their occurrence in the hotel. During the study period, 204 travel parties stayed in those rooms for a total of 480 nights. The experiment involved no interventions to trigger tourist behaviour. Rather, tourists' natural, uninfluenced behaviour was investigated.

The key variable of interest in this study was the number of towels used per room per night. This dependent variable was deliberately chosen to be behavioural in nature, because it is well understood that respondents do not always provide accurate responses to surveys (Dolnicar, 2013). Rather, a wide range of response sets can distort survey findings. Response sets are "test-taking habits which affect questionnaire responses" (Cronbach, 1950, p. 3). One such response set is known to occur when survey respondents are asked about topics on which society as a whole holds specific views. The bias resulting in such instances is referred to as social desirability bias. Social desirability refers to "Consensus judgments as to what behaviour, feelings, and attitudes win social approval" (Fordyce, 1956, p. 171). Social desirability bias, therefore, is the "systematic error in self-report measures resulting from the desire of respondents to avoid embarrassment and project a favorable image to others" (Fisher, 1993, p. 303). It has been repeatedly acknowledged that sustainable tourism is an area likely to be affected by social desirability bias (see Bergin-Seers & Mair, 2009; McKercher & Prideaux, 2011; Miller, 2003). Socially desirable responding in the context of self-report measures attempting to capture tourists' pro-environmental behaviours leads to over-reporting of such behaviours. Therefore, if a survey measure served as the dependent variable in this study, hotel guests would be likely to over-report towel reuse because of social desirability bias. In addition to generally leading to overestimating towel reuse of hotel guests, this social desirability bias might not affect all respondents in the same way. Certain tourists may have a higher tendency to engage in socially desirable responding than others, thus leading to differences between respondents in reported towel reuse that might not be present in their actual behaviour. Such a bias is particularly problematic if the aim is to detect market segments characterized by environmentally friendly behaviour. To avoid validity problems due to potential survey biases, the actual number of towels used per night in each of the hotel rooms was used as dependent variable. This measure was obtained with the assistance of hotel cleaning staff, who counted and recorded the number of towels used.

Towel use data were then matched with characteristics of the guests occupying the room. These personal characteristics and travel party characteristics served as independent variables. Note that this information was too basic to allow the identification of individual hotel guests. The following pieces of information were used: the number of adults staying in a room, the number of children staying in a room, and the type of hotel guest (individual tourist, guest who booked through a travel agency, guest benefiting from a reduced corporate rate), check-in and check-out date, and the country of origin of the registered hotel guest, coded as either being domestic (Slovenian) or not.

Ethical clearance for this study was obtained from the University of Queensland Human Ethics Committee (approval number 2014001411). Data were analysed by determining basic descriptive statistics and by using a Poisson regression model for the number of towels per room and night as the dependent variable (a generalized linear model with Poisson-distributed dependent variable and log-link). The following variables were used as co-variates in the regression: number of adults in the room, number of children in the room, type of guest, and whether or not the guest registered for the room was Slovenian.

Guests generally stayed in the hotel for more than one day. This led to the following two model specifications: (1) a variable indicating if the number of towels used were replaced on their last day of stay was included as a co-variate with main effect, but also with interaction effects because guests could only opt to not have their towels changed if they continued staying; and (2) a random effect for travel parties was included to account for the repeated measurements of guests staying in the same room for several nights, leading to a generalized linear mixed model being fitted. The model is fitted based on maximum likelihood estimation with the R (R Core Team, 2016) package lme4 (Bates, Maechler, Bolker, & Walker, 2015). Standard errors for the regression coefficients were obtained using the observed Fisher information matrix and asymptotic z-tests were used to determine p-values for the regression coefficients.

After analysis of the quantitative data, results were presented to seven hotel staff, including all reception staff and the head of the cleaning department. They were asked to provide observations and possible explanations for these findings.

Results

Table 1 provides descriptive information about the data: 43.6% of the travel parties included in the study were individual travellers, 20.1% booked their hotel through a travel agency; 36.6% came on a corporate rate. The average length of stay was 2.36 nights. Just over one-third were travelling alone, nearly two-thirds shared the room with a second adult, and in 14.7% of cases three adults shared a room. Nearly three-quarters of travel parties were travelling without children. Just under one-fifth of the travel parties (18.2%) included one or more children. Approximately half of the travel parties were Slovenian; half were not. On average, 3.74 towels were used per room per night, calculated at over 466 nights being available with 14 observations (3%) being missing; that is, not correctly entered by cleaning staff. Please note that this count includes all towels: bath towels, hand towels and face towels.

Details of the model results are provided in Table 2. The first six variables (last day of stay, number of adults, number of children, guests who booked through a travel agent, guests who were given a corporate rate, and whether the guest was Slovenian or not) represent main effects; all others are interaction effects of those same variables with this night being the last of their stay. The p-values in

Table 1. Data characteristics.

	N	%
Type of guests: individual	89	43.6
Type of guests: agency	41	20.1
Type of guests: corporate contracts	74	36.6
Number of adults: 1	74	36.3
Number of adults: 2	127	62.3
Number of adults: 3	3	14.7
Number of children: 0	150	73.5
Number of children: 1	37	18.1
Number of children: 2	17	0.1
Slovenian guest	99	48.5
International guest	105	51.5
	Mean	SD
Length of stay	2.36	1.67
Number of towels used	3.74	3.49

Table 2. Regression results of the fixed effects.

Dependent variable: number of towels used per tourist per night	Coefficient	Standard error	p-Value
Last day of the stay	0.823	0.293	0.004**
Number of adults	0.234	0.131	0.075 #
Number of children	0.271	0.079	< 0.001***
Type of guests: agency	−0.939	0.195	< 0.001***
Type of guests: corporate contracts	−0.319	0.159	0.045*
Slovenian	−0.254	0.118	0.032*
Last day: number of adults	0.204	0.134	0.128
Last day: number of kids	−0.127	0.080	0.114
Last day: type of guests agency	0.765	0.200	< 0.001***
Last day: type of guests corporate contracts	0.073	0.164	0.656
Last day: Slovenian	0.099	0.121	0.411
Constant	0.256	0.287	0.371
Number of observations	466		

***Significant at 0.001%; **significant at 0.01; *significant at 0.05; # significant at 0.1.

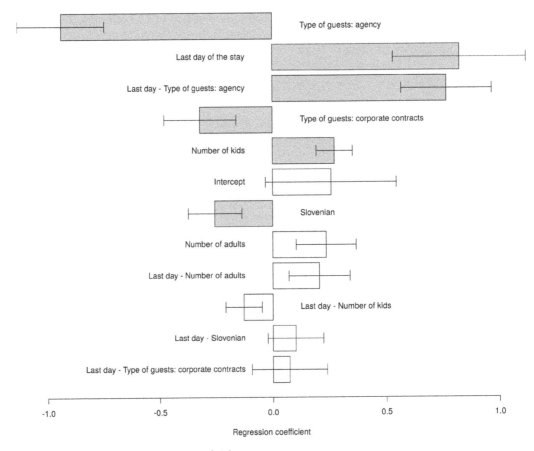

Figure 1. Impact on hotel towel use per room and night.

the third column indicate which of those variables are significantly associated with hotel towel use. As can be seen, five main effects and one interaction effect emerge as having a significant impact on the number of towels used per room per night.

The main effects include the number of children (with more children, not surprisingly, increasing the number of towels used), the type of guests (with individual tourists which are included in the constant using the highest number of towels), and whether it was the last day of the stay.

Figure 1 depicts the regression coefficients (bars) as well as the standard errors (lines). Independent variables are ordered by the size of the association from high to low. Significant associations are indicated by grey bars. What becomes very clear when inspecting Figure 1 is that being Slovenian is significantly associated with lower levels of towel use, but that being Slovenian is not the personal characteristic that has the strongest association with towel use. The number of children affects towel use to a higher degree, as does the booking mode of either booking directly, via a travel agent or using a corporate rate. This is interesting, because it points to a wider range of personal and travel characteristics which can be used by hotels if they wish to target a segment of guests with a smaller environmental footprint.

Hotel staff said that they felt that Slovenians may have been better at reusing towels because it is easier for them to talk to reception staff because there is no language barrier. Reception staff are happy to explain to them what the purpose and the benefits of hotel towel reuse are. Hotel staff also noted that business travellers were always the best in terms of towel reuse because – as opposed to families – they come in clean, spend all day in seminars and do not do any sports, thus they have very little need for more than one or two towels. Families, on the other hand, the staff observed, often arrive at the hotel after a long trip, needing a shower or a bath immediately upon arrival. Families also engage in more activities that, in turn, lead to additional showers and baths. Also, families spend much more of their time in the hotel room than business travellers and even couples travelling alone.

Conclusions, practical implications, limitations, and future work

Environmentally sustainable tourism is a key aspiration of tourism organizations, governments, and the tourism industry. However, this aspiration is difficult to implement in practice. Financial and practical constraints, as well as the inherently hedonic nature of tourism, represent key barriers.

This study investigates whether or not significant associations can be identified between hotel guests' personal characteristics and one specific behaviour with environmental consequences: hotel towel reuse. Key results from our study are that: (1) tourists differ systematically in their towel reuse; and (2) tourists – in our study – had a smaller environmental footprint in terms of towel use if they were domestic tourists, had booked their stay through a travel agent or their company, and had no children.

The fact that several personal characteristics emerge as being associated with environmentally friendly behaviour by hotel guests opens the door for a range of marketing approaches aimed at reducing the environmental impact of hotel visits, including targeting segments of the tourist market known to behave – intrinsically – in a more environmentally friendly way. In the traditional accommodation sector, such targeting approaches are likely to be useful primarily in times when supply is higher than demand (peak tourist seasons) because, ultimately, commercial accommodation providers must aim at high occupancy to maximize profit. This is not, however the case in peer-to-peer accommodation networks where accommodation providers state a wide range of reasons, many of which are not monetary, for making space available to tourists (Karlsson & Dolnicar, 2016b). The demand for peer-to-peer accommodation has skyrocketed in the last decade. The leading provider, Airbnb, did not exist a decade ago and now caters to 17 million tourists (Airbnb, 2015) and is worth twice as much as Expedia and more than Marriott Hotels (Carson, 2015). As such, managing environmental sustainability issues in accommodation provided through peer-to-peer networks is critical already now, but is likely to become even more critical in future.

Another approach to using marketing for the purpose of increasing the environmental sustainability of hotel operations is to develop targeted communication messages to attempt to change behaviour at the hotel among those segments inherently tempted not to behave in an environmentally friendly manner. Such communications could include awareness-raising for the behaviours that can easily be modified without sacrifice of holiday enjoyment, and awareness-raising of global resource shortages.

An example of such communication messages having been used successfully in the past to influence guest behaviour in hotels was provided in a study by Kallbekken and Sælen (2013) who achieved a 21% reduction in plate waste in 52 Finnish hotel restaurants by placing a sign on the tables saying: "Welcome back! Again! And again! Visit our buffet many times. That's better than taking a lot once". Other examples of the usefulness of communication messages in the context of increasing the environmental sustainability of tourism have been provided in the context of travel to national parks (Kim, Airey, & Szivas 2011; Stanford, 2014), reuse of towels in hotels (Mair & Bergin-Seers, 2010), and destinations (Araña, León, Moreno-Gil, & Zubiaurre, 2013). All these studies, however, treated all guests as one homogeneous group. Findings from this study would suggest communication messages be targeted at those market segments among hotel guests which are currently displaying the lowest base level of towel reuse.

Another possibility is to develop interventions, rather than communication messages, to achieve behavioural change. Such interventions could be targeted at children, for example, and could involve small rewards to acknowledge desirable behaviour. This study identifies which hotel guests would be the best targets for such communication messages or interventions given their low base level of towel reuse.

This study is limited in several ways. It investigates only one single dependent variable: the number of towels used. It would be of great interest to investigate the same research question using a wider range of dependent variables. A second limitation is that the study was conducted in one hotel and in one location only. Optimally, the study would have been conducted in many hotels, at many different locations, and in many countries in order to ensure more generalizable results. Furthermore, because all measures used in this study were objective and not based on self-reporting in surveys, it was not possible to test the effect of other personal characteristics mentioned in prior literature, such as motivation, pro-environmental knowledge, awareness, values, attitudes, emotion, locus of control, responsibilities, and priorities (Kollmuss & Agyeman, 2002). This could also be investigated in an extended replication study. Note, however, that all those characteristics are much more difficult to translate into immediate target marketing actions because it is not as easy to identify tourist motivations or their locus of control as it is to identify whether they are domestic travellers, how they book, and if they travel with children.

Additionally, and critically to guiding future research: this study can draw firm conclusions about systematic associations between guest characteristics and towel reuse, but it cannot prove the drivers behind it. For example, it can be hypothesized that Slovenian guests reuse their towels more because European statistics show that Slovenians are among the most active in terms of other pro-environmental behaviours, such as recycling (European Commission, 2014), but it cannot be proven that the fact that Slovenian people generally behave more environmentally friendly is the reason for their higher level of towel reuse in hotels. To be able to draw conclusions of this nature would require extensive analytic qualitative research (Rossiter, 2010) followed by experimental studies in which the hypothesized cause would be varied by the researchers. Propositions that lend themselves to such an investigation in relation to differences observed with respect to country of origin include that hotel guests behave in a more environmentally friendly way if they are staying in their own country because is it the environment of their country that is affected by their behaviour; that hotel guests behave in a more environmentally friendly way if they have previously experienced shortages of basic resources, such as water or electricity; that hotel guests behave in a more environmentally friendly way if they are repeat visitors because they feel a higher level of responsibility and attachment. In terms of the finding that people on corporate rates (business travellers) reuse their towels more, a possible explanation that could be tested in future work is that hotel guests behave in a more environmentally friendly way when they are on a business trip because a business trip is not a "timeout from life" where special behavioural rules apply, as is the case in the holiday context. In terms of children, a proposition that could be tested is that families with children behave in a less environmentally friendly way because they are overwhelmed by the situation and are thus unable to consider the environment in their decisions.

Future research should also undertake experimental intervention studies to test the effectiveness of alternative marketing approaches to reducing the environmental footprint of hotel guests, similar to that by Kallbekken and Sælen (2013) in the context of plate waste. Examples of such interventions could include offering a small reward for opting out of the entire room clean, introducing incentives for children for towel reuse which converts environmentally sustainable behaviour into a game for them, raising awareness for resource shortages on the planet among hotel guests who have no prior experience with such shortages themselves, and so on. Any measure that successfully alters tourist behaviour to be more environmentally friendly, rolled out on a large scale, has the potential to materially influence the environmental sustainability of the tourism industry for the better.

Finally, the approach, methodology and findings of this paper could have considerable transference value for the study of marketing for more sustainable forms of tourism generally, and of a range of pro-environment initiatives in the accommodation sector and elsewhere. The paper contributes to the growing literature on behavioural change.

Acknowledgments

The authors are grateful to the Australian Research Council (ARC) for supporting this research through salary funding under the Discover Scheme project DP110101347 and The University of Queensland for support under the Vice-

Chancellor's Research Focused Fellowship and Jim Whyte for enabling the collaboration under the Jim Whyte Fellowship. The authors thank Nazila Babakhani and Homa Hajibaba for feedback on previous versions of this manuscript. Most of all, the authors thank Anze Cokl, the General Manager of Bohinj Park Eco Hotel, for his active involvement in the implementation of this project. Finally, we thank Emil Juvan for pointing us to some interesting work in the area of food waste reduction.

Disclosure statement

No potential conflict of interest was reported by the authors.

Funding

The authors are grateful to the Australian Research Council (ARC) for supporting this research through salary funding under the Discover Scheme project [DP110101347] and The University of Queensland for support under the Vice-Chancellor's Research Focused Fellowship Programme.

References

Airbnb. (2015). Retrieved from http://blog.airbnb.com/wp-content/uploads/2015/09/Airbnb-Summer-Travel-Report-1.pdf

Ajzen, I. (1985). From intentions to actions: A theory of planned behavior. In J. Kuhl & J. Beckmann (Eds.), *Action control: From cognition to behavior* (pp. 11–39). Berlin, New York: Springer-Verlag.

Ajzen, I. (1991). The theory of planned behavior. *Organizational Behavior and Human Decision Processes, 50*(2), 179–211.

Andersson, L., Shivarajan, S., & Blau, G. (2005). Enacting ecological sustainability in the MNC: A test of an adapted value-belief-norm framework. *Journal of Business Ethics, 59*(3), 295–305.

Arbuthnot, J. (1977). The roles of attitudinal and personality variables in the prediction of environmental behaviour and knowledge. *Environmental Behaviour, 9*(2), 217–232.

Araña, J.E., León, C.J., Moreno-Gil, S., & Zubiaurre, A.R. (2013). A comparison of tourists' valuation of climate change policy using different pricing frames. *Journal of Travel Research, 52*(1), 82–92.

Baca-Motes, K., Brown, A., Gneezy, A., Keenan, E.A., & Nelson, L.D. (2013). Commitment and behavior change: Evidence from the field. *Journal of Consumer Research, 39*(5), 1070–1084.

Ballantyne, R., Packer, J., & Falk, J. (2011). Visitors' learning for environmental sustainability: Testing short-and long-term impacts of wildlife tourism experiences using structural equation modelling. *Tourism Management, 32*(6), 1243–1252.

Bank of Slovenia. (2015). *Annual Report*. Retrieved from https://www.bsi.si/iskalniki/letna_porocila_en.asp?MapaId=711

Bates, D., Maechler, M., Bolker, B., & Walker, S. (2015). Fitting linear mixed-effects models using lme4. *Journal of Statistical Software, 67*(1), 1–48.

Beccali, M., La Gennusa, M., Coco, L.L., & Rizzo, G. (2009). An empirical approach for ranking environmental and energy saving measures in the hotel sector. *Renewable Energy, 34*(1), 82–90.

Bergin-Seers, S., & Mair, J. (2009). Emerging green tourists in Australia: Their behaviours and attitudes. *Tourism and Hospitality Research, 9*(2), 109–119.

BIO Intelligence Services (2010). Preparatory study on food waste across EU 27. Retrieved from http://ec.europa.eu/environment/eussd/pdf/bio_foodwaste_report.pdf

Black, J.S., Stern, P.C., & Elworth, J.T. (1985). Personal and contextual influences on houshould energy adaptations. *Journal of Applied Psychology, 70*(1), 3–21.

Bohdanowicz, P., Zientara, P., & Novotna, E. (2011). International hotel chains and environmental protection: Analysis of Hilton's *we care!* programme (Europe, 2006–2008). *Journal of Sustainable Tourism, 19*(7), 797–816.

Böhler, S., Grischkat, S., Haustein, S., & Hunecke, M. (2006). Encouraging environmentally sustainable holiday travel. *Transportation Research Part A, 40*(8), 652−670.

Butler, L. (2008). The compelling "hard case" for "green" hotel development. *Cornell Hospitality Quarterly, 49*(3), 234−244.

Carrus G., Bonaiuto, M., & Bonnes, M. (2005). Environmental concern, regional identity and support for protected areas in Italy. *Environment and Behaviour, 37*(2), 237−257.

Carson, B. (2015). Retrieved from http://www.businessinsider.com/airbnb-15-billion-round-values-the-company-at-255-billion-2015-6?IR=T

Courneya, K.S. (1995). Understanding readiness for regular physical activity in older individuals: An application of the theory of planned behavior. *Health Psychology, 14*(1), 80−87.

Cordano, M., & Frieze, I.H. (2000). Pollution reduction preferences of US environmental managers: Applying Ajzen's theory of planned behavior. *Academy of Management Journal, 43*(4), 627−641.

Cronbach, L.J. (1950). Further evidence on response sets and test design. *Educational and Psychological Measurement, 10,* 3−31.

Dalton, G.J., Lockington, D., & Baldock, T.E. (2008). A survey of tourists' attitudes to renewable energy supply in Australian hotel accommodation. *Renewable Energy, 33*(10), 2174−2185.

Diamantopoulos, A., Schlegelmilch, B.B., Sinkovics, R.R., & Bohlen, G.M. (2003). Can socio-demographics still play a role in profiling green consumers? A review of the evidence and an empirical investigation. *Journal of Business Research, 56* (6), 465−480.

Dickinson, J.E., Robbins, D., & Lumsdon, L. (2010). Holiday travel discourses and climate change. *Journal of Transport Geography, 18*(3), 482−489.

Dolnicar, S., Laesser, C., & Matus, K. (2010). Short haul city travel is truly environmentally sustainable. *Tourism Management, 31,* 505−512.

Dolnicar, S., & Ring, A. (2014). Tourism marketing research − Past, present and future. *Annals of Tourism Research, 47,* 31−47.

Dolnicar, S. (2006). Nature-conserving tourists: The need for a broader perspective. *Anatolia, 17*(2), 235−256.

Dolnicar, S. (2013). Asking good survey questions. *Journal of Travel Research, 52*(5), 551−574.

Dolnicar, S. (2010). Identifying tourists with smaller environmental footprints. *Journal of Sustainable Tourism, 18*(6), 717−734.

Dolnicar, S., & Leisch, F. (2008). Selective marketing for environmentally sustainable tourism. *Tourism Management, 29*(4), 672−680.

Dwyer, L., Forsyth, P., Spurr, R., & Hoque, S. (2010). Estimating the carbon footprint of Australian tourism. *Journal of Sustainable Tourism, 18*(3), 355−376.

Edwards, D., & Griffin, T. (2013). Understanding tourists' spatial behaviour: GPS tracking as an aid to sustainable destination management. *Journal of Sustainable Tourism, 21*(4), 580−595.

European Commission (2014). Attitudes of European citizens towards the environment. Retrieved from http://ec.europa.eu/public_opinion/archives/ebs/ebs_416_en.pdf

Fairweather, J.R., Maslin, C., & Simmons, D. (2005). Environmental values and response to ecolabels among international visitors to New Zealand, *Journal of Sustainable Tourism, 13*(1), 82−98.

Firth, T., & Hing, N. (1999). Backpacker hostels and their guests: Attitudes and behaviours relating to sustainable tourism. *Tourism Management, 20*(2), 251−254.

Fisher, R.J. (1993). Social desirability bias and the validity of indirect questioning. *Journal of consumer research, 20*(2), 303−315.

Fordyce, W.E. (1956). Social desirability in the MMPI. *Journal of Consulting Psychology, 20*(3), 171−175.

Galley, G., & Clifton, J. (2004). The motivational and demographic characteristics of research ecotourists: Operation Wallacea volunteers in Southeast Sulawesi, Indonesia. *Journal of Ecotourism, 3*(1), 69−82.

Gatersleben, B., Steg, L., & Vlek, C. (2002). Measurement and determinants of environmentally significant consumer behavior. *Environment and Behavior, 34*(3), 335−362.

Gössling, S., & Schumacher, K.P. (2010). Implementing carbon neutral destination policies: Issues from the Seychelles. *Journal of Sustainable Tourism, 18*(3), 377−391.

Gössling, S., Peeters, P., Ceron, J., Dubois, G., Patterson, T., & Richardson, R. (2005). The eco-efficiency of tourism. *Ecological Economics, 54*(4), 417−434.

Goldstein, N.J., Cialdini, R.B., & Griskevicius, V. (2008). A room with a viewpoint: Using social norms to motivate environmental conservation in hotels. *Journal of Consumer Research, 35*(3), 472−482.

Guagnano, G.A., Dietz, T., & Stern, P.C. (1994). Willingness to pay for public goods: A test of the contribution model. *Psychological Science, 5*(6), 411−415.

Han, H., & Kim, Y. (2010). An investigation of green hotel customers' decision formation: Developing an extended model of the theory of planned behaviour. *International Journal of Hospitality Management, 29*(4), 659−668.

Han, H. (2015). Travelers' pro-environmental behavior in a green lodging context: Converging value-belief-norm theory and the theory of planned behavior. *Tourism Management, 47,* 164−177.

Harland, P., Staats, H., & Wilke, H.A. (2007). Situational and personality factors as direct or personal norm mediated predictors of pro-environmental behavior: Questions derived from norm-activation theory. *Basic and Applied Social Psychology, 29*(4), 323–334.

Hergesell, A., & Dickinger, A. (2013). Environmentally friendly holiday transport mode choices among students: The role of price, time and convenience. *Journal of Sustainable Tourism, 21*(4), 596–613.

Higham, J., Carr, C., & Gael, S. (2001). *Ecotourism in New Zealand: Profiling visitors to New Zealand ecotourism operations.* Department of Tourism Research Paper No. 10. Dunedin: University of Otago.

Hoque, S., Forsyth, P., Dwyer, L., Spurr, R., Ho, T.V., & Pambudi, D. (2010). *The carbon footprint of Queensland tourism.* Gold Coast: CRC For Sustainable Tourism.

Jin-Soo, L., Hsu, L.T., Han, H., & Kim, Y. (2010). Understanding how consumers view green hotels: How a hotel's green image can influence behavioural intentions. *Journal of Sustainable Tourism, 18*(7), 901–914.

Institute for Sustainable Development (2015). Slovenians' attitudes towards environment. Retrieved from http://www.itr.si/publikacije

Juvan, E., & Dolnicar, S. (2014). The attitude-behaviour gap in sustainable tourism. *Annals of Tourism Research, 48*, 76–95.

Kallbekken, S., & Sælen, H. (2013). 'Nudging' hotel guests to reduce food waste as a win–win environmental measure. *Economics Letters, 119*(3), 325–327.

Karlsson, L., & Dolnicar, S. (2016a). Does eco certification sell tourism services? Evidence from a quasi-experimental observation study in Iceland. *Journal of Sustainable Tourism, 24*(5), 694–714.

Karlsson, L., & Dolnicar, S. (2016b). Someone's been sleeping in my bed (refereed research note). *Annals of Tourism Research, 58*, 159–162.

Karlsson, L., Kemperman, A., & Dolnicar, S. (in press). May I sleep in your bed? Getting permission to buy.

Kelly, J., & Williams, P. (2007). Modelling tourism destination energy consumption and greenhouse gas emissions: Whistler, British Columbia. *Journal of Sustainable Tourism, 71*(1), 67–90.

Kim, A.K., Airey, D., & Szivas, E. (2011). The multiple assessment of interpretation effectiveness: Promoting visitors' environmental attitudes and behavior. *Journal of Travel Research, 50*, 321–334.

Kirk, D. (1995). Environmental management in hotels. *International Journal of Contemporary Hospitality Management, 7*(6), 3–8.

Kollmuss, A., & Agyeman, J. (2002). Mind the gap: Why do people act environmentally and what are the barriers to pro-environmental behavior? *Environmental Education Research, 8*(3), 239–260.

Lee, W.H., & Moscardo, G. (2005). Understanding the impact of ecotourism resort experiences on tourists' environmental attitudes and behavioural intentions. *Journal of Sustainable Tourism, 13*(6), 546–565.

Lück, M. (2003). Education on marine mammal tours as agent for conservation—but do tourists want to be educated? *Ocean & Coastal Management, 46*(9), 943–956.

Macey, S.M., & Brown, M.A. (1983). The role of past experience in repetitive household behavior. *Environment and Behavior, 15*(2), 123–141.

Mair, J. (2011). Exploring air travellers' voluntary carbon-offsetting behaviour. *Journal of Sustainable Tourism, 19*(2), 215–230.

Mair, J., & Bergin-Seers, S. (2010). The effect of interventions on the environmental behaviour of Australian motel guests. *Tourism and Hospitality Research, 10*(4), 255–268.

McKenna, J., Williams, A.T., & Cooper, J.A.G. (2011). Blue flag or red herring: Do beach awards encourage the public to visit beaches? *Tourism Management, 32*(3), 576–588.

McKercher, B., & Prideaux, B. (2011). Are tourism impacts low on personal environmental agendas? *Journal of Sustainable Tourism, 19*(3), 325–345.

Miller, G.A. (2003). Consumerism in sustainable tourism: A survey of UK consumers. *Journal of Sustainable Tourism, 11*(1), 17–39.

Norman, P., Conner, M., & Bell, R. (1999). The theory of planned behavior and smoking cessation. *Health Psychology, 18*(1), 89–94.

Pichert, D., & Katsikopoulos, K.V. (2008). Green defaults: Information presentation and pro-environmental behaviour. *Journal of Environmental Psychology, 28*(1), 63–73.

Powell, R.B., & Ham, S.H. (2008). Can ecotourism interpretation really lead to pro-conservation knowledge, attitudes and behaviour? Evidence from the Galapagos Islands. *Journal of Sustainable Tourism, 16*(4), 467–489.

Prillwitz, J., & Barr, S. (2011). Moving towards sustainability? Mobility styles, attitudes and individual travel behaviour. *Journal of Transport Geography, 19*(6), 1590–1600.

Ramus, C.A. (2002). Encouraging innovative environmental actions: What companies and managers must do. *Journal of World Business, 37*(2), 151–164.

R Core Team (2016). A language and environment for statistical computing. Vienna: R Foundation for Statistical Computing. Retrieved from https://www.R-project.org/

Robertson, J.L., & Barling, J. (2013). Greening organizations through leaders' influence on employees' pro-environmental behaviors. *Journal of Organizational Behavior, 34*(2), 176–194.

Rossiter, J.R. (2010). *Measurement for the social sciences: The C-OAR-SE method and why it must replace psychometrics*. New York: Springer Science & Business Media.

Scherbaum, C.A., Popovich, P.M., & Finlinson, S. (2008). Exploring individual—level factors related to employee energy conservation behaviors at work. *Journal of Applied Social Psychology, 38*(3), 818—835.

Schwartz, S.H. (1977). Normative influences on altruism. *Advances in Experimental Social Psychology, 10*, 221—279.

Stanford, D.J. (2014). Reducing visitor car use in a protected area: A market segmentation approach to achieving behaviour change. *Journal of Sustainable Tourism, 22*(4), 666—683.

Statistical Office of Republic of Slovenia (2015). *Annual Report*. Retrieved from http://www.stat.si/statweb

Sutton, S., McVey, D., & Glanz, A. (1999). A comparative test of the theory of reasoned action and the theory of planned behavior in the prediction of condom use intentions in a national sample of English young people. *Health Psychology, 18*(1), 72—81.

Tierney, P., Hunt, M., & Latkova, P. (2011). Do travelers support green practices and sustainable development. *Journal of Tourism Insights, 2*(2), 1—16.

Thøgersen, J. (1999). Spillover processes in the development of a sustainable consumption pattern. *Journal of Economic Psychology, 20*(1), 53—81.

Tudor, T.L., Barr, S.W., & Gilg, A.W. (2008). A novel conceptual framework for examining environmental behavior in large organizations a case study of the Cornwall National Health Service (NHS) in the United Kingdom. *Environment and Behavior, 40*(3), 426—450.

Vining, J., & Ebreo, A. (1990). What makes a recycler? A comparison of recyclers and non-recyclers. *Environmental Behaviour, 22*(1), 55—73.

Wearing, S., Cynn, S., Ponting, J., & McDonald, M. (2002). Converting environmental concern into ecotourism purchases: A qualitative evaluation of international backpackers in Australia. *Journal of Ecotourism, 1*(2/3), 133—148.

Weaver, D.B., & Lawton, L.J. (2002). Overnight ecotourist market segmentation in the Gold Coast hinterland of Australia. *Journal of Travel Research, 40*(3), 270—280.

Webster, F.E. Jr., (1975). Determining the characteristics of the socially conscious consumer. *Journal of Consumer Research, 2*(3), 188—196.

Weigel, R.H. (1977). Ideological and demographic correlates of proecology behavior. *Journal of Social Psychology, 103*(1), 39—47.

Winett, R.A., Leckliter, J.N., Chinn, D.E., Stahl, B., & Love, S.Q. (1985). Effects of television modelling on residential energy conservation. *Journal of Applied Behaviour Analysis, 18*, 33—44.

Using persuasive communication to co-create behavioural change – engaging with guests to save resources at tourist accommodation facilities

C. Warren, S. Becken and A. Coghlan

ABSTRACT

Unsustainable consumption of energy and water by tourist accommodation will escalate if incremental global tourism growth and business-as-usual approaches continue. Guests use more than half of the energy and water at accommodation facilities and so have a partnership role to play in saving resources. Our study is the first to measure the impact of persuasive communication on guests' resource consumption behaviour (energy and water use) and stay satisfaction. It used an innovative intervention based on interpersonal communication, sequential influence and eco-feedback. Guests' ($n = 759$) consumption of electricity, gas and water was monitored at four fully self-contained cottages using smart meters, over a period of 304 days. An ethnographic study, action research and departure survey examined if pro-environmental persuasion could encourage guests to save resources, how guests responded to the intervention and measured whether pro-environmental persuasion affected guest satisfaction. Results show that guests who received the intervention used significantly fewer resources, 80% claimed they tried to save and their overall satisfaction was not negatively affected, while reasons to save/not save were complex. A resource-saving persuasion model is proposed for further research, practitioners are recommended to install pro-environmental infrastructure, train staff to engage customers, and identify responsible channels for fiscal savings.

Introduction

Sustainability in tourism is becoming more mainstream, but an understanding of how businesses can engage guests to be active partners in reducing resource consumption remains elusive. Tourism is resource-intensive (Gössling et al., 2012), and without intervention, resource consumption may double by 2050 (Gössling & Peeters, 2015). While technology-based efforts to improve efficiency have shown potential for savings (Warren & Becken, in press), in isolation, these efforts are insufficient to make meaningful reductions (Melissen, Koens, Brikman, & Smit, 2016). As approximately half of direct resource consumption is related to guest rooms (City of Melbourne, 2007), involving guests in resource efficiency and conservation programs is critical (Hawkings & Vorster, 2014).

Previous research on guest engagement is limited, owing to hosts' discomfort with raising environmental concerns with their customers (Villarino & Font, 2015). Green hotels commonly do not ask guests to conserve resources, perhaps thus contributing to "myopic" sustainable marketing communication (Belz & Peattie, 2009, p. 153). Therefore, new guest engagement approaches that do not compromise the host's reputation need to be explored. Tourism operators need to move beyond one-way communication and develop a dynamic multidimensional process that co-creates experiences in service relationships (Brodie, Hollebeek, Juric, & Ilic, 2011). Thus, the focus is on influencing guest behaviour through interactive persuasion rather than standard pro-environmental messages. Guests may not be able to reduce consumption on their own because they lack specific knowledge of their environmental impacts (Juvan & Dolnicar, 2014; Warren, 2012), and monitoring their consumption is not sufficient to achieve reductions (Melissen et al., 2016). To be successful in conserving resources, guests require specific information, skills and opportunities (Lee & Moscardo, 2005). Earlier research has shown that the majority of guests are willing to receive such support (Warren & Coghlan, 2016).

An engagement approach using multiple steps can become a shared responsibility between hosts and guests (Warren, Gripper, & Claringbould, 2012). Engagement requires stepping beyond sharing green values to jumping forward into a reciprocal arrangement where the accommodation provider can apply "house rules" (Tucker, 2003) and persuasively communicate pro-environment information to help guests apply skills that deliver improved sustainability outcomes. This paper's original contribution reports on the first guest engagement study to measure response to persuasive techniques to save energy and water. The persuasive effort involves the innovative integration of interpersonal communication, and sequential influence including daily eco-feedback, which as a whole facilitates a co-created experience.

Literature review

Resource use in tourist accommodation

The literature on environmental management in tourist accommodation is considerable. Key studies have focused on the implementation of environmental management systems (Chan, 2009), audits and benchmarking (Becken, 2013), technological solutions (Mak, Chan, Li, Lui, & Wong, 2013), corporate and personal values (El Dief & Font, 2012), and economic outcomes resulting from environmental initiatives (Stipanuk, 2001). A few studies mention guest involvement in water and energy saving through the use of key tags (Nikolaou, Vitouladitis, & Tsagarakis, 2012), towel/linen reuse (Nicholls & Kang, 2012), offset opportunities (Levy & Park, 2011), sensor explanation cards (Baloglu & Jones, 2015), and environmental information or charging guests separately for energy (Leslie, 2007). However, in-depth studies of active guest engagement are lacking, despite recognition that effective environmental strategies involve all stakeholders, including guests, working with the hotel's efforts (Hays & Ozretić-Došen, 2014).

One key barrier to involving guests in reducing consumption relates to accommodation providers' scepticism that guests are interested in participating in programs, especially in luxury hotels (Jarvis & Ortega, 2010; Leslie, 2001; Vernon, Essex, Pinder, & Curry, 2003). Instead, providers focus on soft pro-environmental infrastructure which results in small savings without affecting guest satisfaction, such as in-room sensors and energy-efficient TVs (Susskind, 2014). The overall environmental benefits remain low. A more progressive strategy would be to encourage an awareness of consumption patterns through a process similar to mindfulness (Coles, Zschiegner, & Dinan, 2014; Garay & Font, 2013). Mindfulness refers to being in the present, using self-regulation and control to monitor one's thoughts and behaviours (Bishop et al., 2004; Langer & Moldoveanu, 2000), and has been linked to lower materialism (Brown & Kasser, 2005) and reduced ecological impact (Rosenberg, 2004). Barber and Deale (2014) suggested that mindful guests would like eco-feedback that puts them in control of consumption, while Cvelbar, Grün, and Dolnicar (2016) recommend targeting different messages at distinct guest groups, notions explored in more detail in this study.

To date, only seven studies have specifically focused on measuring guests' resource saving – specifically, in relation to towel reuse (Warren & Becken, in press). One of these is a large study ($N =$

2416) that involved interpersonal communication and commitment (Baca-Motes, Brown, Gneezy, Keenan, & Nelson, 2013). At check-in, guests who supported the hotel's environmental ethos (by ticking "YES" on a card) were given a Friends of the Earth pin to wear. Findings showed that these guests were more likely to keep their towel for reuse (80% for a general environmental commitment and 63% for a specific towel-reuse commitment) than those who had not committed (53%). The study successfully demonstrated that commitment-gaining and reciprocation can increase pro-environmental behaviour on a single service aspect. Nevertheless, to save energy and water across a multitude of amenities where resource usage levels are unfamiliar to guests requires an innovative step-jump in hospitality engagement.

Persuasive communication

Persuasive communication, which includes verbal, non-verbal and imagery components (Gass & Seiter, 2014; O'Keefe, 2016; Perloff, 2010), is more sophisticated than the asynchronous (one-way) approach of advertising. It involves "a symbolic process in which communicators try to convince other people to change their attitudes or behaviours regarding an issue through the transmission of a message in an atmosphere of free choice" (Perloff, 2010, p. 12). Persuasion can influence an individual's mental state through steps that seek to change attitudes, which may lead to a change in behaviour (O'Keefe, 2016). Persuasion differs from compliance gaining in that the latter is focused on changing behaviour without necessarily changing attitudes (Gass & Seiter, 2014).

Persuasive communication involves multiple contacts in a dialogue (Perloff, 2010), where perceived trustworthiness and credibility of the communicator can affect the success of influence or compliance techniques (McCroskey & Teven, 1999). As mood and age differences may also influence persuasion because of value differences or topic relevance, successful communicators modify their approach to match the audience (Curtin, 2010; O'Keefe, 2016). A defining factor is the persuasiveness of the communication context. Social situations include subtle cues found in face-to-face meetings (Gass & Seiter, 2014), and they may also be sensitive to direct and indirect messages, depending on culture (Wiseman et al., 1995).

Politeness theory (Brown & Levinson, 1987; Kitamura, 2000) provides a framework to further develop interpersonal communication tactics. Individuals seek to maintain two kinds of face: positive to gain respect and negative when feeling constrained by others. Understanding the politeness threshold for both the communicator and persuadee is essential to encouraging behaviour change. Individuals are less likely to comply with requests if their face is threatened (Gass & Seiter, 2014). Face-threatening acts can occur when a communicator does not care about the persuadee's feelings (Kitamura, 2000).

In situations where we cannot say exactly what we wish, we apply language techniques to convey a message without threatening (Holtgrave, 2008). Techniques include the friendly approach of positive politeness (indicating similarities or expressing appreciation) and a formal approach of negative politeness (by using advice or respecting another's right not to be imposed upon) (Brown & Levinson, 1987; Kitamura, 2000). Politeness tactics could therefore be incorporated into pro-environmental behaviour change strategies at tourist accommodations.

Reciprocation through persuasive social exchange

Like politeness, social exchange offers a powerful persuasive communication situation (Perloff, 2010), which can encourage reciprocation where individuals feel obliged to repay favours, gifts or helpfulness. Exchange relies on the potency of exchangeable items that individuals might possess and the value of these items for others (Callaghan & Shaw, 2002). Social structures enable individuals to employ persuasion as either reciprocal or negotiated exchanges (Cook & Rice, 2006). Reciprocation is "one of the most potent weapons of influence" (Cialdini, 2009, p. 19), as the process of reciprocation generates emotions (Cook & Rice, 2006) that can then contribute to sustained reciprocation. Feelings of trust can evolve as the exchange continues, increasing the positive affect between the actors and perpetuating the persuasive communication relationship. In the context of behaviour change, reciprocation is an important consequence of social exchange.

Earlier research has identified the importance of negotiated exchange within a hospitality context as a method of control (Lynch, Molz, McIntosh, Lugosi, & Lashley, 2011), for example, in the context of house rules of a smaller accommodation (Tucker, 2003). The question then arises as to whether reciprocal exchange could be a persuasive method for encouraging guests to save resources. Dolnicar and Grün (2008) concluded the best way to encourage visitors to take pro-environmental action was for hosts to ask them to behave as "guests", implying the accepted social protocol of following rules in unfamiliar places. The host–guest relationship offers an "intense social exchange" that could be a focus for tackling sustainability in tourism (Selwyn, 2000, p. 80). The negotiated host–guest exchange may, therefore, be the first step in what could be a positively reinforcing communication beyond passively opting into corporate social responsibility programmes (Levy & Park, 2011).

The medium: interpersonal persuasion

The social exchange framework entails a dynamic communication process that enables communicators to tailor their message to the receiver (Perloff, 2010). To be effective, the persuadee must perceive communicators as credible, conveying both expertise and trustworthiness (O'Keefe, 2016). A proposed third dimension of credibility is goodwill, where communicators convey understanding, empathy and responsiveness (McCroskey & Teven, 1999). Credibility is relevant in the context of hospitality, and is established from expertise of the host with regard to sustainable practices at his/her property (Nikolich & Sparks, 1995) and trust developed with the guest (Wang, Law, Hung, & Guillet, 2014). Hospitality employees who demonstrate expertise and have a relaxed tone improve customers' reciprocity (Kang & Hyun, 2012).

The message approach: sequential influence techniques

*Sequential influence technique*s involve multiple steps that can improve overall persuasiveness (Perloff, 2010). One such technique is *pre-giving* – providing a gift followed by requesting compliance (Gass & Seiter, 2014). The pre-giving approach encourages the persuadee to comply with the communicator's request by stimulating positive emotions like gratitude for the favour or a desire to reciprocate and repay the communicator (Burger, Sanchez, Imberi, & Grande, 2009). In the accommodation context, an established practice is for hosts to use initial guest contact to convey rules within exchange (McIntosh, Lynch, & Sweeney, 2010; Tucker, 2003). Such exchange could apply sequential influence techniques to encourage reciprocal pro-environmental behaviour. These techniques could be enhanced by applying social contact influences that "break the ice" and stimulate commitment (Guéguen et al., 2013; Joule, Bernard, & Halimi-Falkowicz, 2008), for example, through light physical touch (e.g. shaking hands) (Hornik, 1992) or smiling (Vrugt & Vet, 2009). Preparatory methods, like signing an agreement or being advised that the receiver is free to comply with a communicator's request, have been shown to increase commitment (Baca-Motes et al., 2013; Joule et al., 2008).

The message: technical information

To further increase message persuasiveness, the communicator can identify consequences of action, make recommendations and then state a conclusion. In other words, the message needs to be specific as to why the persuadee should take the desired action. Proposing a consequence resulting from an advocated action that is valued by the persuadee is more persuasive than consequences that are not valued (O'Keefe, 2016).

Currently our understanding of how to communicate sustainability to guests is limited. Most tourism businesses have conveyed facts about their sustainability practices rather than presenting customer-centred experiences (Villarino & Font, 2015). Graphs and technical content in sustainable tourism messages were found to be less appealing than emotional imagery and text (Wehrli et al., 2014), and while social influence may be important, it can be less effective if it raises feelings of guilt (Coulter & Pinto, 1995). The challenge is to frame a host's (technical) resource message in a way that is valued by guests.

Currently, guests have no way of learning their resource consumption level in a hotel room. Juvan and Dolnicar (2014) recommended that guests be given metered eco-feedback on their electricity use (as implemented in some accommodation sites, personal communication with manager of Eco-lodge, Chile, 15 June 2015). As how tourists respond to such eco-feedback has not been studied, research is needed to examine whether eco-feedback would result in normalising conservation behaviours (Noel, Schultz, Cialdini, Goldstein, & Griskevicius, 2008) without compromising satisfaction. To contribute to closing this gap, our study aims to measure the impact of persuasive communication on guests' pro-environmental behaviour and their stay satisfaction. We address three research questions:

(1) Can pro-environmental persuasive communication reduce guest resource use?
(2) How do guests respond to sequential influence techniques encouraging them to save resources?
(3) Does pro-environmental persuasive communication (negatively) affect guest satisfaction?

These questions contribute to the understanding of how to improve the sustainability of tourism, and specifically, hospitality, by inviting guests to be active participants in reducing resource consumption through an interpersonal persuasion process that breaks through societal barriers (Melissen et al., 2016).

Methodology

Overview of research design and study site

This section provides a brief summary of the quasi-experimental action-research design (Figure 1). Action research is well suited to problem solving and field-based research, and is emergent and responsive, relying on a reflective process to facilitate an adaptive research design (Zuber-Skerritt, 2012). Through reflection, the participants, and in particular the researcher, can engage in learning, critical analysis and practical improvements of the intervention to achieve the desired outcome. A mixed methods approach involved collecting guest profile data, monitoring electricity, gas and water consumption at each cottage, and using sequential influence techniques as an intervention. Observations, ethnographic methods and a departure survey completed the experiment.

The research had three distinct phases using two types of intervention (Table 1). A baseline of guests' profile and their resource use was maintained throughout. Phase 1 compared Intervention 1 with Control 1 (8 May–15 October 2015). Phase 2 compared the Intervention 1 with Control 2, using an ethnographic study and departure survey (16 October–29 December 2015). Phase 3 compared Intervention 2 with Control 3 and continued with the ethnographic study and departure survey (30 December–7 March 2016). Each of these elements is explained in the subsequent sections.

The site was Crystal Creek Meadows in Kangaroo Valley, New South Wales, Australia. The property has four 4.5-star-rated cottages that provide comprehensive self-catering facilities. Of critical importance to the validity of this research is that while the business holds sustainable tourism certifications, it is not marketed as an eco-resort. Potential customers are attracted by the rural setting, interior comforts, children's activities and day spa services. The hosts live on the property, but the accommodation reception is a separate building away from the main dwelling, and cottages are spread across the 16-acre site to maximise privacy. Guests can choose their level of interaction with the hosts after check-in.

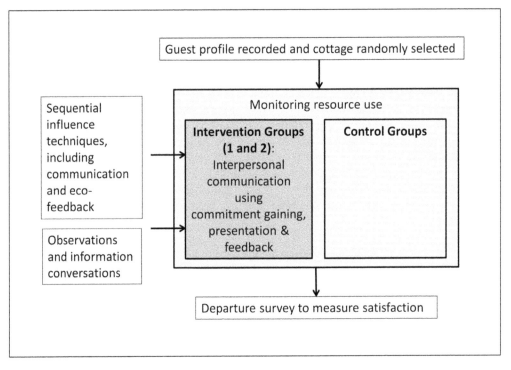

Figure 1. Overview of research design.

Table 1. Research timeline and phases.

Method	Description	Phase 1: Benefit-led					Phase2: Benefit-led with observations			Phase 3: Recommendation-led		
		May 2015	June	July	Aug	Sept	Oct	Nov	Dec	Jan	Feb	Mar 2016
Guest profile	Party size, tariff type, origin											
Monitoring	Cottages' electricity, gas, water use monitored by minute											
Control groups	No persuasive sustainability request											
Intervention groups	Commitment gaining, presentation, daily eco-feedback, occasional assistance											
Ethno-graphic study	Informal conversations, observations field notes, reflective notes											
Departure survey	Self-completion satisfaction survey after checkout											

Shading indicates methods applied to each stage. Change in shading tone indicates different intervention approaches and shows. Phase 1 did not have the ethnographic study or departure survey.

Data collection

Data on guest profiles, resource use, response to the interventions and satisfaction with the accommodation experience were collected across the three different phases.

Guest profiles and resource consumption data

After guests' reservation details were recorded, parties were randomly selected to participate in the intervention or to function as a control. This selection was important to randomise the potential impact of cottage type on resource use patterns. All cottages were monitored using smart meter technology. A total of 302 bookings stayed between 8 May 2015 and 7 March 2016, representing a total of 759 guests (644 adults, 117 children) with an average stay length of 2.3 nights.

Intervention

Two types of intervention were used. Intervention 1 was tested in Phases 1 and 2 ($N = 91$ vs. $N = 139$ bookings in the control group). Intervention 2 was examined in Phase 3 ($N = 28$ in the intervention vs. 44 in the control group). No differences were found between Intervention Groups 1 and 2 and the control groups, in terms of demographic and travel-related variables, providing evidence that the random assignment was effective. The interventions consisted of sequential influence techniques (summarised in the Supplemental Material Table S1, available in the online version of this paper) delivered by the host through (1) verbal commitment-gaining tactics at check-in, (2) presentation in the cottage, (3) encouragement of free-will commitment by asking guests to sign a pledge, and (4) printed daily eco-feedback with personalised messages delivered to the cottage at 07:30 each day.

Two presentation approaches were tested: in Intervention 1, the host focused on the guest's self-benefits by highlighting positive features of the cottage, whilst in Intervention 2, the host directly recommended that guests use the cottages' pro-environmental infrastructure and provided instructions on how to minimise resource consumption.

Ethnographic data/guest response

The ethnographic study (Phases 2 and 3, October–March) involved recording each guest interaction in detailed field notes (200–450 words covering commitment gaining, response to eco-feedback and informal conversations when offering assistance). Interventions 1 and 2 produced 55 guest-party bookings (93% of the total). Source materials were both verbal (speech acts, utterances, overlaps, incompletions in speech and changes in party speaking) and non-verbal communications (silence, gaze) (Krippendorff, 2013) and expressions of positive or negative face as well as examples of positive and negative politeness (Brown & Levinson, 1987). Time spent with guests was 5–20 minutes for commitment gaining/presentation. Additional time was spent with guests on demand (e.g. helping them set their fire). Daily observations were made when the first author delivered eco-feedback sheets and, through 41 analytical memos (110–480 words each), was able to compare all guest parties staying on the property along a timeframe that allowed comparisons across similar weather conditions.

Departure data/guest satisfaction with the accommodation experience

At check-out, guests were asked to complete a survey (one per booking), with 86% completed (Phases 2 and 3, October–March). Afterwards, in informal conversations, guests added to the ethnographic data. A limitation was that not all guests wished to converse at this time, as the rest of their party were often set to leave.

Analysis

Baseline analysis

Booking details were entered into the statistical software package SPSS 23. Resource use was measured in one-minute pulses, recorded for each guest party booking and verified by manual meter reading. Total consumption rates for each guest stay were measured from 15:00 (check-in time) on their day of arrival to 11:00 (check out time) on their day of departure. To normalise resource use data, the total amounts were then divided by the number of hours for each booking. Cleaning of data resulted in the removal of one outlier from the intervention group who used a very small amount of gas or water during their one-night stay. Data on use of water, gas and electricity were not normally distributed, and a non-parametric test (Mann–Whitney test, Field, 2013) was used to test differences amongst groups.

Ethnographic analysis

As part of the action research approach, the host was both actor (implementing the interventions) and researcher, observing guests at the time of the persuasive communication arguments, observing them during their stay and reflecting on persuasion theory, politeness theory and the concept of hospitality whilst on site. The ethnographic method is well suited to theory development, where theoretical constructs can be compared in the field to develop a deep understanding of the application of the relevant theory in practice (Snow, Morrill, & Andersen, 2003). The researcher noted how his tone, the guests' emotional state upon arrival and their negative face affected message delivery. As this research evolved, the content of the persuasive communication intervention was adapted from guest self-benefits (Intervention 1) to recommending use of pro-environmental infrastructure (Intervention 2). This "enhanced persuasion" was considered important, as the ongoing analysis of guest resource use indicated a ceiling on guests' savings during the first intervention.

Coding of field notes and analytical memos occurred in two ways (Saldana, 2013).The first cycle involved initial coding using NVivo to segment and breakdown the data and compare Interventions 1 and 2, followed by a reinterpretation of conversations and behaviour (Krippendorff, 2013). The second cycle of coding involved focused, axial and finally theoretical coding to find the central theme.

Departure survey analysis

Departing guests were asked to self-assess whether they actively tried to reduce their electricity, gas, water or firewood use. Interventions 1 and 2 participants were further asked whether the daily eco-feedback information added to or detracted from the experience of their stay. In addition, a pre-existing satisfaction scale was used to measure the cognitive, affective and conative aspects of satisfaction (Robinot & Giannelloni, 2010).

Guests were asked (1) "In general, how satisfied are you with the services supplied by the accommodation?" (2) "If a member of my family or a friend was looking for accommodation, I would readily recommend this accommodation?" and (3) "If you had the chance to come back, would you do so?" All three questions used a five-point Likert scale. An overall satisfaction index was created that ranged from 3 (very best) to 15 (very worst) and was then collapsed into three categories (highly satisfied, satisfied, less satisfied) to provide greater sample sizes.

Three further questions specifically assessed guests' perceptions of property attributes, again using a five-point Likert scale: (1) "How well do you think staff understood your specific needs?" (2) "Comparing (property name) with other self-contained accommodation you have stayed at, would you say the quality of services and facilities were (higher/lower)?" and (3) "Considering your overall experience at (property) how would you rate its value for money?" A service attribute index was created using the metric (3 to 15) described above. Again, to overcome issues associated with small sample sizes, respondents were collapsed into three groups. Chi-square tests assessed differences amongst groups.

Table 2. Results of the Mann–Whitney test, comparing resource use across groups.

Resource variable	Significance	Test statistic U	Effect size
Intervention 1			
Electricity per hour	<0.001	8318	0.267
Gas per hour	=0.049	7297	0.123
Water per hour	=0.091	7159	0.111
Intervention 2			
Electricity per hour	<0.001	1910	0.414
Gas per hour	=0.021	1805	0.271
Water per hour	=0.006	1846	0.326

Results

Reducing guest resource use through persuasive communication

Analysis of the resources consumption figures from control groups and the intervention groups shows that pro-environmental persuasive communication can be successful. For the benefit-led Intervention 1 (i.e. Phases 1 and 2), electricity use (median = 207 kWh per hour) was significantly lower than for the control group (median = 255 kWh per hour) (Table 2). The effect size indicates that 26.7% of difference in electricity use between these groups was due to Intervention 1. The differences for gas (Intervention 1 median = 0.016 cubic metre per hour vs. 0.018 cubic metre per hour for the control group) and water use (Intervention 1 median = 14.4 litres per hour vs. 15.1 litres per hour for the control group) were less pronounced. Accordingly, the effect sizes for gas and water were smaller, and for water consumption, the difference between the groups was significant at only the 10% level.

The test results comparing resource use of the recommendation-led Intervention 2 group with the control group during Phase 3 show more pronounced differences. The median electricity use of Intervention 2 guests was 175 kWh per hour versus 251 kWh for the control group. The median gas usage was 0.008 cubic metres per hour versus 0.013 cubic metres for the control group, and the difference in water use was 9.3 litres per hour versus 14.0 litres per hour for the control group. The largest effect was on electricity use per hour, with about 41.4% of difference in consumption being explained by Intervention 2.

The departure survey asked whether guest parties had actively tried to reduce electricity, gas and water use. A Chi-square test (χ^2 [1, 120] = 6.652, $p = 0.036$) shows that guests in Interventions 1 and 2 were considerably more likely to try to reduce their resource use (80% responded affirmatively) than those in the control group (58.5%).

Guest responses to sequential influential techniques

During the course of the intervention, none of the guests rejected the presentation, and none asked for the eco-feedback sheets to be stopped. Two guest parties did not sign the pledge, whilst in some instances, all members of guest party chose to sign.

Using the ethnographic data, the researchers coded and analysed guest responses to the sequential communication, and seven categories emerged. Six of these categories contribute to two key dimensions of resource-saving persuasion: guests' response to interpersonal pro-environmental communications and determinants of their own saving behaviour (Figure 2). The six categories are explained below. The seventh category related to the context.

Interpersonal pro-environmental communications

Commitment gaining. Three factors were important: flexibility, politeness and credibility. Guests arrived in different emotional states, requiring the host to be flexible when applying commitment-gaining tactics – using personalised approaches during ice-breaking and tailoring the pre-giving message to guests' personal needs. Guest states included being happy, friendly, relaxed, business-like, distant, shy, quiet, tired, unwell and adversely affected by the weather, suggesting that a standardised script would not be sufficient in engaging guests. From the outset, guests demonstrated flexibility and an openness to accept the host. All guests in the Intervention 1 group agreed to be part of the experiment. With Intervention 2, the host first asked "Have you ever stayed in an eco-friendly cottage before?" Four guest parties (Guest 39, 94, 123, 142) said yes, one said "must have" (Guest 36), and the remainder had not stayed in eco-accommodation. All agreed to take the tour of the cottage's resource-saving infrastructure and listen to the host's recommendations on its use. Meanwhile, the ethnographic data collected during check-in and cottage presentation revealed a wide range of non-verbal guest communication, which was interpreted using politeness theory. Guests applied formal negative face the majority of the time during the presentation, and friendly positive face for those already in a happy holiday mood.

The findings confirm that hosts must apply both negative and positive politeness tactics to improve persuasiveness. In the following negative politeness, for example, the host apologised and used common ground with tourists from the UK to improve persuasion.

Field Note for Guest 129: While they read the pledge certificate with Negative Face I said "Sorry you might think this is like selling double glazing." "No there should be more places like this."

Politeness tactics built naturally from the first encounter, where flexibility was applied. In addition, establishing the communicator's credibility, and their business credibility, were important. The host's flexible and polite approach through the early sequences helped build credibility and trustworthiness ("You seem the sort of person one can trust", Guest 28 said and signed).

Field Note for Guest 70: During the cottage tour X asked me to confirm his friend's advice that it was more efficient to have the ceiling fan on all day as it would use less power than to start/stop. (This demonstrated consumer confusion about ways to achieve energy efficiency and made me aware that this guest saw me as a credible host. I corrected his confusion and advised that to save energy fans should only be on when a room is occupied, when the occupant needs a cooling breeze and when required in tandem with an a/c to circulate cooler air.)

However, one guest (Guest 62) asked why the lounge light was on when they arrived, whilst another pointed out that a battery was missing from the gas stove's lighter, requiring matches and leading to environmental waste (Guest 39). They saw these errors as contradicting the presentation, indicating the importance of attention to details to maintain credibility.

Presentation. Components and delivery style of the presentation (Intervention 1 and Intervention 2) affected results. The benefit-led approach, Intervention 1, was well received by guests happy to see the indulgences (e.g. local produce, handmade chocolates and king-size bed) and many accepted the host's presentation (including technical graphs) as part of their holiday experience. Some sat down to listen, occasionally inviting the host to sit with them. Comparing Intervention 1 with 2, the host found that highlighting benefits restricted later communication to provide precise advice to guests to save resources, because the politeness threshold had been set at a lower level of eco-friendly resource consumption.

Field Note for Guest 18 (Intervention 1): X said they hoped "we can still have baths" [she had organised the trip and so may have been worried about how the pitch was coming across to her friends]. I said that of course they could still have baths [to suggest moderation would have been crossing a threshold] but it was about "not wasting." X says "yes I know you are" [she was gauging the situation].

Memo 6/1: The fact that I am making a stronger pitch at the beginning makes me feel I can be more instructional in the eco-feedback sheets, because the first encounter was a recommendation rather than a hospitality one where the customer comes first.

The more technical approach with Intervention 2 permitted the host to keep a negative face at key points during the presentation. This approach was felt to emphasise sincerity and normalise the message as guests expressed a wide range of emotional utterances, which – if the host joined in too far – derailed the conservation. Examples of emotions conveyed by guests indicated they were competitive, fun-loving, humorous, supporting, accepting, assessing, unsure, guilty, and fearful.

Eco-feedback. The host was able to personalise advice, which proved helpful for guests to learn and apply practices, making the eco-feedback a critical turning point in the persuasion sequence for the majority (see Table S1 available in Supplemental Material in the online version of this paper). Some guests were disappointed with their performance and keen to improve, while a small minority appeared to find the advice patronising. These findings highlight the challenge of balancing tone and content. Guest party 142, who displayed strong green values, rejected feedback, as it appeared to make them feel guilty across other lifestyle choices they made.

> **Field Note for Guest 55:** X commented on my pitch saying they were surprised upon arrival, but they found the eco-feedback good "especially this morning" when they were under target. He also mentioned they talked about the impacts of preparing their own dinner in the cottage.

> **Manageress' eco-feedback from departing Guest 130:** The guests said they loved getting reports every day to see how they were doing.

> **Field Note for Guest 60:** X said he found the figures comparing other guests' consumption "like big brother" and did a little grimace.

Saving behaviour

Personal circumstances. Three factors of personal circumstances influenced savings behaviour: needs, values and practicalities. Needs were non-negotiable, as for a number of guests, the ability to save was affected by physiological and safety concerns. Some who claimed to hold environmental values were constrained by their physical need to keep cool or other physical constraints. For others, security fears made them uncomfortable leaving windows open at night with only closed fly screens (Guest 84), with Guest 139 admitting to locking windows in the city and using air-conditioning at night as a consequence. Despite these constraints, several of these guests tried to reduce consumption after listening to the host's advice and achieved savings below targets (Guest 139) or generously donated to the charity box (Guest 22).

Guests' values were a key driving force that affected persuasion outcomes, and the host was able to work flexibly with guests' values to increase persuasion. Those introduced to sustainability at work or those with environmental concerns were open-minded to the intervention, just as those who saw how practicing new behaviours could be applied at home. Most guests examined the technical graphs carefully and with interest. While a few guests readily participated in the intervention, the process of reducing resource use for groups of adults often brought out "team captains" who encouraged others to modify their behaviour.

> **Field Note:** "Well I won't do very well" said the horse-riding sister. The other two sisters rallied and said "what do you do with your horse manure?" "We pass it on for potting mix." "Well then" they said.

Despite persuasion and infrastructure, guests face practicalities preventing them from saving resources. These include their travel party and the degree they can influence reciprocation, their desire to cook in rather than eat out, and their habits in terms of recharging electronic equipment. Such contexts appeared to pertain particularly to young families and guests from collectivist societies. Observations showed that guests' knowledge of infrastructure affected capacity to save, for example, not being aware that ceiling fans can be used in winter or not being able to use the wood fire. Likewise, some guests applied traditional practicalities to save.

Field Notes for Guests 34 and 24: "This will be interesting for this one [looking at X] as she leaves all the lights on" says Guest 34 who smiles and cups his wife's face in his hands.

did try (to save) with water but were less conscious with electricity, we used the bath but all used the same water. (Guest 24)

Persuasion can only be effective within the realm of what is practically feasible for guest parties, as many internal factors also make demands on the guest party's ability to save resources and keep harmony.

Applying "house rules." Overall, guests followed the house rules, even if they did not always agree: "well it's your business" (Guest 7). Many guests were prepared to reciprocate without challenging. In many cases, they felt the experience matched their own values ("We have to save our planet" [Guest 94]), felt obliged to comply with the host's requests, or chose to ignore them:

Field Note for Guest 60: X said they did not save and behaved as usual because it was their holiday.

Adoption, learning and contentment. Observation showed guests followed advice from the eco-feedback sheets. The most obvious adaption was the use of natural ventilation by the intervention groups. Guests from the control group had not received the presentation and were unaware of the techniques and skills, resulting in higher energy use. Several guests responded competitively.

Field Note for Guest 139: Despite their need for air conditioning at night and security fears, I saw their windows open early in the morning (they had been open all night to benefit from lower temperatures). They made an effort to change practices.

Some guests received more than four daily eco-feedback sheets during their longer stay (in a few cases during heatwaves). During this period, the host found guests content and consistently maintaining their resource saving.

Manageress' eco-feedback: Guests 136 told Z that they "found the reports 'interesting'. We were delighted that we 'smashed the record'", but they also felt concerned for others who would have to try and beat their figures.

Some departing guests showed positive emotions that may have helped sustain their reciprocation. While this may have also been positive politeness, they directly expressed interest, joy, pride, amusement and inspiration when talking about the experiment. Only a few instances occurred reflecting guilt or open dislike for the intervention. For example, Guest 36 noted "a tendency to over regimentation" in the departure survey.

Field Notes for Guest 125: "Strongly Disagreed" ticked for feedback information on departure survey; "Because I am aware of such issues and don't need to be reminded on holiday." Yet during the cottage presentation they were very supportive of the programme's principles, however, their eco-feedback showed them their consumption was above target.

Positive guest responses also helped sustain the host's performance throughout the action research study. Just as guests enjoyed recognition that they were consuming resources carefully, so the host felt happy or disappointed with guests' responses and performance. Many guests appeared to change their mental approach towards saving resources, arriving with holiday expectations that did not include intentions of saving, and leaving with an attitude of contentment at having made the effort. As this was by far the majority, the host felt a genuine sense of appreciation from guests.

In addition to the six categories that underpin the two key dimensions, context was found to be critically important. Thus, knowledge of infrastructure and weather are included as additional factors that contribute to sustainable outcomes.

Infrastructure and weather. Guests' responses to infrastructure indicated many actions were standard, common sense (sink vs. dishwasher) or nostalgic (gas kettle). Other items were greeted with good humour (bathroom clock facing the shower) or seen as innovative (toilet with integrated cistern), and in some cases people wanted to take photographs and expressed an intension to buy. The existence of infrastructure added to the host's credibility.

Extreme weather occurrences (e.g. heat waves), unexpected weather (e.g. cold nights) or weather not prepared for (e.g. rainy days) strongly influenced consumption. On occasion, guests resorted to using energy-intensive infrastructure instead of self-adapting. Feedback and advice were helpful in moderating guest consumption, but only as far as practicalities (and politeness) permit.

Field Note for Guest 88: As I was leaving the cottage X asked for my advice "how would you warm up this cottage?" (outside temperature 21C) I was surprised and said "you could put on more clothes (he was wearing a T shirt and shorts) or put the fire on." They appeared to be afraid to light the wood fire, fearing consequences for their 16-month-old son; 20 minutes later I delivered wood to find X wearing his jumper.

Guest satisfaction

Two indices were used in the departure survey: a satisfaction index and a service attribute index. Satisfaction was generally high for all groups (Table 3). The Intervention 2 group, who received a more technical form of communication, was slightly less satisfied than the two other groups, but the differences were not statistically significant (χ^2 [1, $N = 121$ valid cases] = 7.076, $p = 0.132$). Similarly, no statistically significant differences occurred between the three groups for the service attribute index (χ^2 [1, $N = 120$ valid cases] = 3.550, $p = 0.470$). The results therefore show that the interventions did not compromise guest satisfaction.

Guests who felt they reduced their resource use were no less satisfied than those who did not try (χ^2 [2, 118] = 15.102, $p = 0.128$). Interestingly, when it comes to satisfaction with service attributes, guests who tried to conserve resources appeared to value their stay more than those who did not reduce resource use ((χ^2 [2, 117] = 22.756, $p = 0.030$).

To further explore whether actual resource savings affected satisfaction, the quantitative monitoring data were compared with satisfaction levels. No significant differences were found between the satisfaction index or service attribute index scores and resource use (Kruskal–Wallis test for nonparametric data). So, while the median consumption level differed between the sample groups (Mann–Whitney: electricity $p = 0.000$, gas $p = 0.12$, water $p = .006$), their satisfaction rating was not dependent on the amount of resources used.

Finally, the intervention sample was asked whether the daily information sheet with personalised eco-feedback affected their experience. Guests responded that the sheet "strongly added" (24.5%), "tended to add" (49.1%) or was "neutral" (26.4%) to their experience. To overcome small sample size, this variable was collapsed into two responses, namely "added to experience" and "did not add to experience." Guests who believed the sheet added to their experience were also significantly more likely to say they saved resources ((χ^2 [2, 52] = 17.728, $p = 0.000$)), and they scored higher on the service attribute index (χ^2 [2, 53] = 6879, $p = 0.032$). They had a similar satisfaction index rating (χ^2 [2,

Table 3. Guest satisfaction by group.

	Intervention 1 Oct–Dec	Intervention 2 Jan–Mar	Control Oct–Feb
Satisfaction index			
Highly satisfied	60.0%	60.0%	80.3%
Satisfied	23.3%	16.0%	9.1%
Less satisfied	16.7%	24.0%	10.6%
Attribute satisfaction			
Highly satisfied	34.5%	29.2%	40.3%
Satisfied	34.5%	41.7%	43.3%
Less satisfied	31.0%	29.2%	16.4%
Sample size	$N = 30$	$N = 25$	$N = 66$

53] $= 3.585$, $p = 0.167$). Guests may consider eco-friendly features to be secondary factors and they may not have an overall impact on satisfaction (Robinot & Giannelloni, 2010).

Guests who felt the experience was positive wanted to share their experiences with others at departure (after the survey was completed) and might hold conversations, occasionally up to 45 minutes (Guest 86). Overall, none of the guests said the host's presentation was inappropriate.

Discussion

This study investigated how guests can become active partners in driving sustainability in tourism by focusing on whether pro-environmental persuasive communication could lead to resource conservation. It also sought to understand how guests respond to sequential influence that encourages them to save resources and whether saving affects their stay satisfaction. The findings indicate that emphasising the benefits to guests of saving (Intervention 1) and teaching guests how to utilise the available infrastructure to save (Intervention 2) resulted in use of significantly less electricity, gas and water than by the control groups. Overall, guests accepted the sequential influence techniques and satisfaction was not compromised.

Of particular note was the importance of social exchange and reciprocation (a "potent weapon", Cialdini, 2009, p. 19), as pre-giving and detailed explanation led guests to reciprocate the accommodation's efforts. In this study, customers accepted house rules (Tucker, 2003) and behaved as guests within the host's domain (Dolnicar & Grün, 2008). Despite negotiated exchange norms (Cook & Rice, 2006), the host was not challenged by any guest. Host credibility appeared to be established through expertise and trust (e.g. through the eco-feedback). A balance had to be found between establishing expertise through technical information and maintaining guests' interest. The majority of guests were prepared to study the graph and learn about infrastructure, and were impressed or surprised by the scope of technical eco-feedback. The provision of this technical information fostered reciprocation, as Intervention 2 guests saved most.

Understanding the politeness threshold (Brown & Levinson, 1987; Gass & Seiter, 2014) of guest and host appears essential in responding flexibly to the idiosyncratic nature of guests on arrival. An important finding for hospitality providers is that a negative face does not mean a negative view, but that a guest is concentrating on the message. Consequently, applying positive and negative politeness tactics enables the host to protect the guest and the host from losing face (Holtgrave, 2008). Using negative face can build integrity into the host's technical knowledge and encourages guests to focus their attention. Negative politeness helps the host be direct and to be seen as taking seriously any guest concerns, as he/she explains consequences of inaction and recommends a better approach.

Unpacking the process of persuasive communication and identifying thresholds leads to a better understanding of the two-way, interpersonal process of persuasive communication resulting from "spiralling engagement" through multiple and sequential steps of communication. This process and the ensuing model are detailed next.

Spiralling engagement

An important feature of this study was to test a process for engaging guests in resource reduction, using a sequential approach that could be replicated by tourism practitioners. Figure 2 illustrates how more sustainable outcomes can be achieved through a host–guest partnership. The first step is to build empathy by gaining commitment, followed by presenting a pro-environmental infrastructure and savings programme to encourage reciprocation and providing eco-feedback, and finally appreciating guest efforts.

Combined, these steps follow sequentially as communication spirals through the guests' stay using multiple personalised persuasive messages that contribute to a transition in interpersonal contact. The word "multiple" is essential and could help sustainable hospitality communication transition

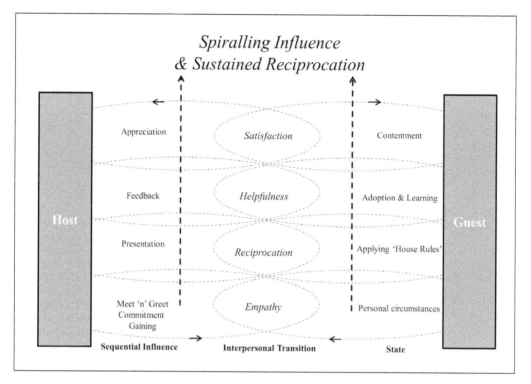

Figure 2. Model of spiralling pro-environmental sequential influence.

from its myopic focus (Belz & Peattie, 2009; Villarino & Font, 2015) to co-created experiences. The dynamic quality of spiralling communication permits guests to evolve as collaborative partners as they gain new knowledge (Juvan & Dolnicar, 2014; Warren, 2012).

The spiralling relationship can mediate the impact of eco-feedback. While the majority of guests in the study who received eco-feedback felt it added to their experience, 25% did not. Nevertheless, overall guests' satisfaction levels were similar between groups, suggesting that while eco-feedback was not welcome by some, overall sequential influence techniques were acceptable, as demonstrated by a similar high rating of staff's understanding of guests' specific needs. To be replicable in other accommodations, guest relations staff would need to be formally trained to deliver persuasion successfully, with infrastructure in place for guests to use.

Some guests demonstrated mindfulness by focusing their attention on consumption and controlling their practices. However, motivations were complex (e.g. environmental concerns, competitiveness, complying with social norms), as were their reasons for not being able to save, indicating the need for more research on constraints to guests' engagement. The focus of this study was on the interaction between host and guests, but further study should examine the application of character strengths and mindful consumption.

There appeared to be no link between how much guests consumed and their stay satisfaction. This study also showed that consumption is highly contextual. Both intervention and control groups were subject to factors such as outside temperature, water temperature in the property's water storage tank, or daylight savings. Future research might explore in greater detail how these factors moderate resource consumption and satisfaction. Importantly, for this study and its focus on guest engagement, the flexibility of the intervention and messages allowed the host to take advantage of these contextual variables and incorporate them into his persuasive communication.

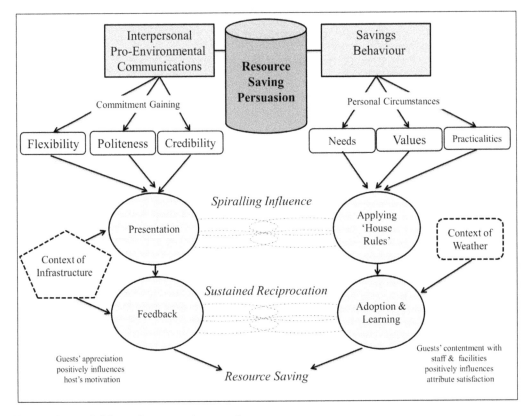

Figure 3. An extended theory of resource-saving persuasion.

A model of resource-saving persuasion

This study contributes to sustainable tourist accommodation development by proposing a conceptual model as a basis for future research to test and progress our understanding of reducing guest resource use (Figure 3). *Resource-saving persuasion* stimulates sustained guest efforts to conserve resources. Through a combination of *interpersonal pro-environmental communication* and *saving behaviour*, guests are influenced to conserve by reducing consumption. Interpersonal pro-environmental communication applies commitment-gaining steps that require hosts to employ a high degree of flexibility to their persuasive communication and judge suitable positive and negative politeness tactics to respect different guest groups' needs. The host must also be conversant with the pro-environmental infrastructure and the fiscal use of resource savings. Presentation and eco-feedback strongly link to the site's infrastructure and are conveyed as helpful tips multiple times during guests' stay.

Guests' saving behaviours are mediated by the personal circumstances of their needs, values and practicalities. To help adjust their message, practitioners could identify guests' specific needs and practicalities at the time of booking and find opportunities for guests to share their values during their stay. Provided the host has demonstrated empathy by being flexible and polite, and is seen as credible, guests can be persuaded to apply house rules. Sustained reciprocation depends on the quality of the eco-feedback and the advice to use pro-environmental infrastructure, especially in extreme weather conditions.

Comprehensive infrastructure and helpful advice can increase guests' appreciation and efforts to save, which also sustains the host's motivation. Positive feedback reinforces good performance. The model developed here could be applied by accommodation providers with suitable pro-environmental infrastructure. However, to accommodate face-saving acts, providers may need to train their staff to use a flexible format rather than a standardised speech.

The proposed model requires further testing at other accommodation types and in other environments. However, this study does represent consumption by different guest types during four seasons, thus providing a robust starting point for further study.

Conclusion

This study is the first to measure guest resource-saving behaviour as a response to sequential influence techniques and the effect of resource-saving persuasion on guest satisfaction at tourist accommodation. Findings show that guests who received this innovative intervention used significantly less resources. Guests who received specific saving recommendations conserved the most.

Using commitment-gaining steps, a presentation, eco-feedback and advice, the host requested that guests save resources. Guests reciprocated and 80% claimed to try to save resources. Understanding both guests' and host's face-saving threshold was found to be an important politeness aspect for delivering the communication and maintaining guest satisfaction. Eco-feedback is essential to motivate guests, but it must be part of a holistic multiple communications. Reasons to save/ not save were remarkably complex.

A preliminary model of resource-saving persuasion is proposed for further research. Tourism professionals should ensure they have adequate pro-environmental infrastructure for guests to use as alternatives to high resource-using systems. Also required is comprehensive staff training that facilitates multiple guest contact. Furthermore, local destination beneficiaries could be identified for the fiscal results of resource saving. Such an approach could "unblock" (Melissen et al., 2016) the societal tangle that restricts sustainable tourism accommodation and normalise partnership between hosts and guests.

Disclosure statement

No potential conflict of interest was reported by the authors.

References

Baca-Motes, K., Brown, A., Gneezy, A., Keenan, E., & Nelson, L. (2013). Commitment and behavior change: Evidence from the field. *Journal of Consumer Research, 39*(5), 1070–1084.

Baloglu, S. & Jones, T. (2015). Energy efficiency initiatives at upscale and luxury US lodging properties: Utilization, awareness, and concerns. *Cornell Hospitality Quarterly, 56*(3), 237–247.

Barber, N. & Deale, C. (2014). Tapping mindfulness to shape hotel guests' sustainable behavior. *Cornell Hospitality Quarterly, 55*(1), 100–114.

Becken, S. (2013). Operators' perceptions of energy use and actual saving opportunities for tourism accommodation. *Asia Pacific Journal of Tourism Research, 18*(1–2), 72–91.

Belz, F., & Peattie, K. (2009). *Sustainability marketing. A global perspective*. Chichester: John Wiley & Sons.

Bishop, S., Lau, M., Shapiro, S., Carlson, L., Anderson, N., Carmody, J., … Devins, G. (2004). Mindfulness: A proposed operational definition. *Clinical Psychology: Science and Practice, 11*(3), 230–241.

Brodie, R., Hollebeek, L., Juric, B., & Ilic, A. (2011). Customer engagement: Conceptual domain, fundamental propositions, and implications for research. *Journal of Service Research, 14*(3), 252–271.

Brown, K., & Kasser, T. (2005). Are psychological and ecological well-being compatible? The roles of values, mindfulness, and lifestyle. *Social Indicators Research, 74*, 349–368.

Brown, P., & Levinson, S. (1987). *Politeness. Some universals in language usage* (Studies in Interactional Sociolinguistics, Vol. 19). Cambridge: Cambridge University Press.

Burger, J., Sanchez, J., Imberi, J., & Grande, L. (2009). The norm of reciprocity as an internalized social norm: Returning favors even when no one finds out. *Social Influence, 4*(1), 11–17.

Callaghan, M., & Shaw, R. (2002). A theoretical application of exchange theory to online purchase decisions. In *Proceedings of the Australian and New Zealand Marketing Academy conference 2002* (pp. 3241–3249). Melbourne: ANZMAC.

Chan, W. (2009). Environmental measures for hotels' environmental management systems ISO 14001. *International Journal of Contemporary Hospitality Management, 21*(5), 542–560.

Cialdini, R. (2009). *Influence. Science and practice* (Vol. 5). Boston, MA: Pearson.

City of Melbourne (2007). *Energy wise hotels toolkit*. Melbourne: City of Melbourne.

Coles, T., Zschiegner, A., & Dinan, C. (2014). A cluster analysis of climate change mitigation behaviours among SMTEs. *Tourism Geographies, 16*(3), 382–399.

Cook, K., & Rice, E. (2006). Social exchange theory. In J. Delamater (Ed.), *Handbook of social psychology* (pp. 53–76). New York, NY: Springer.

Coulter, R., & Pinto, M. (1995). Guilt appeals in advertising. What are their effects? *Journal of Applied Psychology, 80*(6), 697–705.

Curtin, S. (2010). Managing the wildlife tourism experience: The importance of tour leaders. *International Journal of Tourism Research, 12*, 219–236.

Cvelbar, L., Grün, B., & Dolnicar, S. (2016). Which hotel guest segments reuse towels? Selling sustainable tourism services through target marketing. *Journal of Sustainable Tourism*. doi:10.1080/09669582.2016.1206553

Dolnicar, S., & Grün, B. (2008). Challenging 'factor-cluster segmentation'. *Journal of Travel Research, 47*(1), 63–71.

El Dief, M., & Font, X. (2012). Determinants of environmental management in the Red Sea hotels: Personal and organizational values and contextual variables. *Journal of Hospitality & Tourism Research, 36*(1), 115–137.

Field, A. (2013). *Discovering statistics using IBM SPSS statistics* (Vol. 4). London: Sage.

Garay, L., & Font, X. (2013). Corporate social responsibility in tourism small medium enterprises evidence from Europe and Latin America. *Tourism Management Perspectives, 7*, 38–46.

Gass, R., & Seiter, S. (2014). *Persuasion. Social influence and compliance gaining* (Vol. 5). Abingdon: Routledge.

Gössling, S., & Peeters, P. (2015). Assessing tourism's global environmental impact 1900–2050. *Journal of Sustainable Tourism, 23*(5), 639–659.

Gössling, S., Peeters, P., Hall, M., Ceron, J., Dubois, G., Lehmann, L., … Scott, D. (2012). Tourism and water use: Supply, demand, and security. An international review. *Tourism Management, 33*, 1–15.

Guéguen, N., Joule, R., Halimi-Falkowicz, S., Pascual, A., Fischer-Lokou, J., & Dufourcq-Brana, M. (2013). I'm free but I'll comply with your request: Generalization and multidimensional effects of the "evoking freedom" technique. *Journal of Applied Social Psychology, 43*, 116–137.

Hawkins, R., & Vorster, S. (2014). Green accommodation. In T. Delacy, M. Jiang, G. Lipman, & S. Vorster (Eds.), *Green growth and travelism* (pp. 59–82). London: Routledge.

Hays, D., & Ozretić-Došen, □. (2014). Greening hotels – building green values into hotel services. *Tourism & Hospitality Management, 20*(1), 85–102.

Holtgrave, T. (2008). *Language as social action: Social psychology and language use*. London: Lawrence Erlbaum Associates.

Hornik, J. (1992). Tactile stimulation and consumer response. *Journal of Consumer Research, 19*(3), 449–458.

Jarvis, N., & Ortega, P. (2010). The impact of climate change on small hotels in Granada, Spain. *Tourism and Hospitality Planning & Development, 7*(3), 283–299.

Joule, R., Bernard, F., & Halimi-Falkowicz, S. (2008). Promoting ecocitizenship: In favour of binding communications. *International Scientific Journal for Alternative Energy and Ecology, 6*(62), 214–218.

Juvan, E., & Dolnicar, S. (2014). Can tourists easily choose a low carbon footprint vacation? *Journal of Sustainable Tourism, 22*(2), 175–194.

Kang, J., & Hyun, S. (2012). Effective communication styles for the customer-oriented service employee: Inducing dedicational behaviors in luxury restaurant patrons. *International Journal of Hospitality Management, 31,* 772–785.

Kitamura, N. (2000). *Adapting brown and levinson's 'Politeness' theory to the analysis of casual conversation.* Paper presented at the ALS2k, the 2000 conference of the Australian Linguistic Society, Melbourne.

Krippendorff, K. (2013). *Content analysis. An introduction to its methodology* (Vol. 3). Thousand Oaks, CA: Sage.

Langer, E., & Moldoveanu, M. (2000). The construct of mindfulness. *Journal of Social Issues, 56*(1), 1–9.

Lee, W.H., & Moscardo, G. (2005). Understanding the impact of ecotourism resort experiences on tourists' environmental attitudes and behaviour intentions. *Journal of Sustainable Tourism, 13*(6), 546–565.

Leslie, D. (2001). Serviced accommodation environmental performance and benchmarks. *Journal of Quality Assurance in Hospitality & Tourism, 2*(2–3), 127–147.

Leslie, D. (2007). The missing component in the greening of tourism: The environmental performance of the self-catering accommodation. *International Journal of Hospitality Management, 26*(2), 310–322.

Levy, S., & Park, S. (2011). Analysis of CSR activities in the lodging industry. *Journal of Hospitality and Tourism Management, 18*(1), 147–154.

Lynch, P., Molz, J., McIntosh, A., Lugosi, P., & Lashley, C. (2011). Theorizing hospitality. *Hospitality & Society, 1*(1), 3–24. doi:10.1386/hosp.1.1.3_2

Mak, B., Chan, W., Li, D., Lui, L., & Wong, K. (2013). Power consumption modelling and energy saving practices of hotel chillers. *International Journal of Hospitality Management, 33,* 1–5.

McCroskey, J., & Teven, J. (1999). Goodwill: A re-examination of the construct and its measurement. *Communication Monographs, 66*(1), 90–103.

McIntosh, A., Lynch, P. & Sweeney, M. (2010). "My Home Is My Castel": Defiance of the commercial homestay host in tourism. *Journal of Travel Research, 50*(5), 509–519.

Melissen, F., Koens, K., Brikman, M., & Smit, B. (2016). Sustainable development in the accommodation sector: A social dilemma perspective. *Tourism Management Perspectives, 20,* 141–150.

Nicholls, S., & Kang, S. (2012). Green initiatives in the lodging sector: Are properties putting their principles into practice? *International Journal of Hospitality Management, 31,* 609–611.

Nikolaou, I., Vitouladities, H., & Tsagarakis, K. (2012). The willingness of hoteliers to adopt proactive management practices to face energy issues. *Renewable and Sustainable Energy Reviews, 16,* 2988–2993.

Nikolich, M., & Sparks, B. (1995). The hospitality service encounter: The role of communications. *Journal of Hospitality & Tourism Research, 19*(2), 43–56.

Noel, J., Schultz, W., Cialdini, R., Goldstein, N., & Griskevicius, V. (2008). Normative social influence is under-detected. *Personality and Social Psychology Bulletin, 34*(7), 913–923.

O'Keefe, D. (2016). *Persuasion theory and research* (Vol. 3). Thousand Oaks, CA: Sage.

Perloff, R. (2010). *The dynamics of persuasion* (Vol. 4). New York, NY: Routledge.

Robinot, E., & Giannelloni, J. (2010). Do hotels' "green" attributes contribute to customer satisfaction? *Journal of Services Marketing, 24*(2), 157–169.

Rosenberg, E. (2004). Mindfulness and consumerism. In T. Kasser & A.D. Kanner (Eds.), *Psychology and consumer culture: The struggle for a good life in a materialistic world* (pp. 107–125). Washington, DC: American Psychological Association.

Saldana, J. (2013). *The coding manual for qualitative researchers* (Vol. 2). London: Sage.

Selwyn, T. (2000). An anthropology of hospitality. In C. Lashley & A. Morrison (Eds.), *In search of hospitality: Theoretical perspectives and debates* (pp. 18–37). Oxford: Butterworth-Heinemann.

Snow, D., Morrill, C., & Anderson, L. (2003). Elaborating analytic ethnography: Linking fieldwork and theory. *Ethnography, 4*(2), 181.

Stipanuk, D. (2001). Energy management in 2001 and beyond. *Cornell Hotel and Restaurant Administration Quarterly, 42*(3), 57–90.

Susskind, A. (2014). Guest' reactions to in-room sustainability initiatives: An experimental look at product performance and guest satisfaction. *Cornell Hospitality Quarterly, 55*(3), 228–238.

Tucker, H. (2003). The host–guest relationship and its implications in rural tourism. In D. Hall, L. Roberts, & M. Mitchell (Eds.), *New directions in rural tourism* (pp. 80–89). Aldershot: Ashgate.

Vernon, J., Essex, S., Pinder, D., & Curry, K. (2003). The 'Greening' of tourism micro-businesses: Outcomes of focus groups investigations in South East Cornwall. *Business Strategy and the Environment, 12,* 49–69.

Villarino, J., & Font, X. (2015). Sustainability marketing myopia. The lack of sustainability communication persuasiveness. *Journal of Vacation Marketing, 21*(4), 326–335.

Vrugt, A., & Vet, C. (2009). Effects of a smile on mood and helping behavior. *Social Behavior and Personality, 37*(9), 1251–1258.

Wang, L., Law, R., Hung, K., & Guillet, B. (2014). Consumer trust in tourism and hospitality: A review of the literature. *Journal of Hospitality and Tourism Management, 21,* 1–9.

Warren, C. (2012). Positive connectedness: Encouraging pro-environmental behaviour change in responsible accommodation. *Progress in Responsible Tourism, 1*(2), 40–68.

Warren, C., & Becken, S. (in press). Saving energy and water in tourist accommodation: A goal-oriented systematic literature review (1987–2015). *International Journal of Tourism Research.*

Warren, C., & Coghlan, A. (2016). Using character-based activities to design pro-environmental behaviours into the tourist experience. *Anatolia*, 1–13. doi:10.1080/13032917.2016.1217893

Warren, C., Gripper, J., & Claringbould, L. (2012). World Responsible Tourism Day case study: Encouraging environmental awareness in children through ecotourism interpretation. *Progress in Responsible Tourism*, 2(2), 111–127.

Wehrli, R., Priskin, J., Demarmels, S., Schaffner, D., Schwarz, J., Truniger, F., & Stettler, J. (2014). How to communicate sustainable tourism products to customers: Results from a choice experiment. *Current Issues in Tourism*, 1–20. dx.doi.org/10.1080/13683500.2014.987732

Wiseman, R., Sanders, J., Congalton, K., Gass, R., Sueda, K., & Ruiqing, D. (1995). A cross-cultural analysis of compliance gaining: China, Japan, and the United States. *Intercultural Communication Studies, 5*(1), 1–17.

Zuber-Skerritt, O. (Ed.). (2012). *Action research for sustainable development in a turbulent world*. Bingley: Emerald Group.

Improving carbon offsetting appeals in online airplane ticket purchasing: testing new messages, and using new test methods

Nazila Babakhani, Brent W. Ritchie and Sara Dolnicar

ABSTRACT

Voluntary carbon offsetting by air passengers could help counteract environmental damage caused by air travel. But adoption rates among air travellers are low. This study (1) develops new communication messages which counteract barriers to carbon offsetting identified in prior studies, and (2) tests their effectiveness using psychophysiological and attitudinal measures, a technique new to sustainable tourism research methodologies. Results point to low levels of traveller awareness of carbon offsetting schemes, the primary need for any message to attract the air passengers' attention, the superiority of pictorial and short textual information as well as the identification of particularly effective content. The study makes three key contributions: (1) it highlights the critical importance of awareness raising as a precursor of behavioural change, (2) it offers tangible recommendations for improving carbon offsetting messages, and (3) it demonstrates the usefulness of psychophysiological measures for pre-testing alternative social marketing messages aimed at increasing environmentally sustainable tourist behaviour across a range of applications. Findings of considerable practical importance include refinements of current messages to increase both attention levels and emotional arousal, and the positive impact of promoting additional social co-benefits alongside environmental benefits. Future valuable research themes using psychophysiological and attitudinal measures are suggested.

Introduction

As air travel grows, so does its contribution to carbon emissions and global climate change. Recent modelling by Gössling and Peeters (2015) estimates that tourism CO_2 emissions will increase by 169% between 2010 and 2050. Although they acknowledge the contribution of the transport sector to the consumption of food, water and land resources, transport is associated mainly with energy consumption, passenger travel and CO_2 emissions. Travel accounts for 75% of all energy demand from tourism. Air travel's share of tourism emissions is expected to increase from 40% in 2005 to 52% in 2035 (UNWTO/UNEP/WMO, 2008) because both domestic and international travel are expected to grow significantly under business as usual forecasts (BITRE, 2009; Macintosh & Wallace, 2009; UNWTO/UNEP/WMO, 2008). Such growth poses potential risks to the environment through the production of carbon emissions directly from air travel. As Gössling, Haglund, Kallgren, Revahl, and Hultman (2009) argue, there are few human activities that produce as much CO_2 emissions as aviation travel in such a short period of time.

One strategy to address aviation-related carbon emissions are voluntary carbon offset schemes, which are argued to be an effective complement to mandatory regulation (Blasch & Farsi, 2014). Carbon offsetting schemes are popular with airlines because they raise awareness among air travellers of aviation's environmental impacts and allows passengers to directly contribute voluntary payments to environmental projects (Burns & Cowlishaw, 2014). In the aviation context, voluntary carbon offsetting allows passengers to offset the CO_2 emissions created by their flight by making a voluntary monetary contribution, calculated using fuel consumption and load factors. A passenger's share of the carbon emissions can be converted into a monetary value by dividing the flight emissions value by the number of passengers on a flight sector (Qantas, 2015). The emissions value includes the flight as well as ground activities. In some cases, air passengers can also use earned member mileage points to offset CO_2 emissions (Chen, 2013). The airline transfers the money earned from the sale of voluntary carbon offsets to an organisation that invests in projects to avoid, reduce or absorb CO_2 emissions through renewable energy, energy efficiency and forest restoration projects. Many carbon offset projects are accredited by independent third-party verifiers ensuring their compliance with strict regulations surrounding the reduction of greenhouse gas emissions (Qantas, 2015). The offset contribution varies based on load factors and other conditions. An average offset of a trip from Sydney to Brisbane in Australia costs approximately $1 per person. An average offset from London to Singapore costs approximately $10 per person.

Participation levels in carbon offset programmes are low. Only between 10% (Commonwealth of Australia, 2009; Qantas, 2011) and 16% (Mair, 2011) of Australians have purchased carbon offsets in the past. Internationally, purchase rates of between 2% and 3% have been reported (Choi, Ritchie, & Fielding, 2016; McLennan, Becken, Battye, & So, 2014). Although voluntary carbon offsets grew 14% since 2013, voluntary carbon markets transacted US$395 million in 2014, comprising only 1% of total global emissions (Peters-Stanley & Gonzalez, 2015). These low figures suggest that there is considerable scope to increase voluntary carbon offsetting amongst consumers.

Barriers to low adoption of voluntary carbon offsetting fall into two main categories: the lack of knowledge and awareness of such schemes (Chang, Shon, & Lin, 2010; Gössling et al., 2009; McKercher, Prideaux, Cheung, & Law, 2010) and the public perception that offsetting schemes are not credible, or transparent, but are confusing (Broderick, 2008; Gössling et al., 2007; Polonsky, Grau, & Garma, 2010).

Designing and communicating appealing carbon offsets to overcome these barriers could substantially increase uptake among air passengers. The present study takes a first step in this direction. Specifically:

(1) a number of alternative messages are developed aimed at overcoming the key barriers identified in prior research; and
(2) psychophysiological methods are used to test the effectiveness of these messages using attention and activation as dependent variables. Psychophysiological measures are employed because they reflect mental and affective processes in consumers and they cannot be manipulated by study participants, thus offering complementary insight to traditional attitudinal measures (See the Methodology section for further details of psychophysiological methods).

The results of this study contribute to knowledge about how people can be motivated to engage in voluntary behaviour which benefits society rather than the person who displays the behaviour. Key insights gained from this study are of immediate practical value as they point to clear recommendations on how new messages could be designed to increase voluntary carbon offsetting. In addition, this study illustrates the usefulness of psychophysiological measures in the context of testing messages aiming at changing human behaviour which has environmental consequences.

Finally, it should be noted that carbon offsetting is only one of many possible behaviours that air travellers and tourists can take to counteract the environmental cost of their travels. It was chosen for this study because (1) it is one of the few behaviours which, once promising communication messages have been identified, can be tested using actual behaviour rather than stated behavioural intentions or self-reported behaviour, both of which are known to be biased in contexts where society has certain expectations about people's behaviour; (2) it represents a behaviour that implies very low cost on the side of the traveller (a few dollars) and as such does not represent a major sacrifice (as opposed to, for example, not flying and taking a vacation closer to home); (3) millions of people book airline tickets online. Even the smallest of increases in the uptake of carbon offsetting would have a massive positive impact.

Literature review

Because carbon offsetting schemes are relatively new, they suffer from a lack of consumer knowledge and awareness. Furthermore, a number of barriers exist in relation to offset programmes themselves which affect intentions and actual adoption behaviour. Offset suppliers have tried to address some of these barriers in recent years, but such changes have not been effectively communicated to consumers.

Awareness and attitudes

Lu and Zhang (2012) conclude from their study that 65% of air travellers had no knowledge of carbon offset programmes and only approximately 6% were aware of such programmes. Gössling et al. (2009) find that – although 71% of respondents were worried about climate change and 82% believed air travel contributes to climate change – only 2% paid for voluntary offsets. In this study, 76% of respondents were unaware of carbon offsetting and only 5% knew that carbon offsets are offered by airlines. Fewer than 50% of respondents in Hooper, Daley, Preston, and Thomas' (2008) study were aware that they could offset carbon emissions from their flights. Attitudes toward aviation carbon offsetting were positive once the purpose and nature of offsetting was described (Choi et al., 2016; Gössling et al., 2009). Explaining voluntary carbon offsets to increase knowledge increases the desire and intentions to pay for aviation offsets (Gössling et al., 2009; Hooper et al., 2008; Kim, Yun, Lee, & Ko, 2016; Lu & Zhang, 2012), suggesting improvements in communication are a prerequisite for new green programmes such as carbon offsetting (Kim et al., 2016).

Drivers of carbon offsetting can also be related to individual beliefs including moral responsibility to address climate change, concerns about the environment and future generation, and worries related to environmental disasters (Brouwer, Brander, & Van Beukering, 2008). Some consumers feel, for example, that carbon offsetting is the right thing to do; a cheap and easy way to contribute to the environment (Mair, 2011). Others see it as a convenient excuse to maintain their present consumption patterns (Higham, Reis, & Cohen, 2015; Kollmuss & Bowell, 2007).

Barriers

Carbon offsets have drawn widespread criticism (Gillenwater, Broekhoff, Teexler, Hyman, & Fowler, 2007) for their lack of credibility and verification standards (Broderick, 2008). As Scott, Gössling, Hall, and Peeters (2016) note, carbon offsets must preclude leakage, where a project reducing emissions in one location simply increases emissions elsewhere, and must be permanent, independently verified and registered, to avoid double counting. The quality of carbon offset projects can lead to a low level of consumer credibility and transparency (Broderick, 2008), and may be perceived as not contributing to emission reduction (Haya, 2007). Only 5% of respondents in Lu and Zhang's (2012) study believed carbon offsets were effective. Similarly, Choi et al. (2016) find that perceived effectiveness significantly influences attitudes and subjective norms toward aviation carbon offsetting, which in turn influence adoption intentions.

A lack of transparency and standardisation in the offset market undermines consumer trust (Hooper et al., 2008). This is partly due to the existence of a large number of programmes and limited information on their effectiveness and compliance with national or international standards (Peters-Stanley & Gonzalez, 2015).

Consumer willingness to purchase and attitudes towards carbon offsetting are more positive when an environmental label is provided rather than calculating the fee composition via a carbon calculator (Liu, Chen, & He, 2015). Carbon calculation can look simple but is complex and ambiguous, thus confusing consumers and acting as a barrier to adoption (Gössling et al., 2007) rather than helping to improve price justification and increasing trust and credibility of the programme (Liu et al., 2015). Hooper et al. (2008) recommend that offset providers should communicate the purpose of carbon offsetting, provide information on the effectiveness of offset projects and clearly explain ways of calculating emissions to consumers.

Another way to motivate customers to purchase voluntary carbon offset is to develop and communicate programmes which meet customer preferences for specific segments of airline passengers, or allow consumers to choose which project is funded by their contributions. Heterogeneity in consumer offset preferences has been largely ignored to date (Blasch & Farsi, 2014). Evidence provided by Choi and Ritchie (2014) points to the importance of programme choice; respondents in their study expressed a higher willingness to pay if a range of different projects were available. Specifically, willingness to pay was higher for renewable energy projects, not for forest management projects. Yet, projects to avoid deforestation were most frequently used by offset providers in 2014 (Peters-Stanley & Gonzalez, 2015). Blasch and Farsi (2014) find that both forestry and renewable energy projects were preferred but in developing countries and offered by non-profit providers. They suggest that the context of carbon offsetting should, therefore, be considered in future research. Choi and Ritchie (2014) identify consumer preference for projects that provide carbon credits which are legally binding. This option is available in some countries, such as Japan but not in others, such as Australia (Nakamura & Kato, 2013), increasing confusion around carbon offset programmes and their effectiveness at a global level.

Co-benefits beyond offsetting carbon emissions, such as biodiversity protection, technology/market development and poverty reduction have also been identified (MacKerron, Egerton, Gaskell, Parpia, & Mourato, 2009) and can therefore attract consumer attention (Liu et al., 2015). In MacKerron et al.'s (2009) study, offset programmes with biodiversity co-benefits were more highly valued by consumers, whilst technology development was least valued. The study also concluded that emphasising co-benefits of offsetting could increase consumer willingness to pay, while willingness to pay can also be higher for certified programmes – but only after consumers were made aware of certification schemes (MacKerron et al., 2009). This suggests that understanding and matching offers with preferences is vital. Emphasising legal aspects and certification of carbon offsetting can reduce concerns outlined previously by enhancing trustworthiness and credibility of carbon offset programmes.

In summary, barriers may exist which are associated with (1) general awareness and attitudes toward the environment and carbon offsetting, and (2) programme-related barriers associated with the perceived effectiveness and transparency of specific offset programmes, including carbon offset programme types, confusing carbon calculators (Juvan & Dolnicar, 2014) and lack of choice over programmes. These barriers can influence the adoption of voluntary schemes negatively impacting upon their growth.

Communication messages are the primary avenue used to overcome barriers to desirable behaviour. The effectiveness of communication messages for changing human behaviour has been demonstrated empirically in a number of studies in marketing and social marketing. The social behaviours which were successfully influenced include physical exercise (Jones, Sinclair, & Courneya, 2003), not smoking (Hammond, Reid, Driezen, & Boudreau, 2012), the use of sunscreen (Detweiler, Bedell, Salovey, Pronin, & Rothman, 1999), weight loss (Kreuter, Bull, Clark, & Oswald, 1999) and helping behaviours such as donor card-signing (Skumanich & Kintsfather, 1996). Studies indicate that the framing and content of messages (images and text) can affect attention and emotions in target groups, and can also influence attitudes and behaviour. For instance, messages that are framed positively rather than negatively can be more effective (Jones et al., 2003). Messages that highlight gains rather than potential losses in undertaking the target behaviour have also been shown to be more effective at changing attitudes and behaviour (Detweiler et al., 1999). Similarly, studies have shown that message elements that have testimonials or narratives rather than statistical evidence may change attitudes and behaviour as they help people process information required for decision-making (Detweiler et al., 1999). However, in some cases, it is difficult to provide suitable narratives or testimonials as the time required for people to process information may be short or there is limited space to include a testimonial. Examples include cigarette packaging where space is limited and purchasing carbon offsets during online booking when time is limited. In these cases, the use of short text and images featuring real people has been found to be more effective in promoting behaviour change (Hammond et al., 2012).

Methodology

Psychophysiology is "the scientific study of social, psychological, and behavioural phenomena as related to and revealed through physiological principles and events in functional organisms" (Cacioppo, Tassinary, & Berntson, 2007, p. 4). Psychophysiological measures are physiological in nature and used to index psychological phenomena. These measures include one or more of the following: electroencephalogram (EEG, measure of brain wave activity), electromyogram (EMG, measure of muscle activity), measure of eye movement, electrodermal activity (EDA, changes in the electrical activity at the skin surface), heart responses, blood volume, blood pressure, respiration rate, skin temperature, and many other measures (Andreassi, 2007). These measures have been applied in many disciplines including marketing (Stewart & Furse, 1982), but are yet to be tested in sustainable tourism research.

Psychophysiological measures (1) are close to mental and affective processes associated with consumer inquiry, (2) avoid concealment of true consumer reaction because they measure automatic processes without any manipulation; and (3) monitor the thoughts and feelings in real time when one is unaware, which cannot be retrieved, or which would become changed in subsequent verbal elicitation (Bagozzi, 1991). Therefore, using psychophysiological measures can provide novel insights for consumer research including measuring consumer reactions to marketing stimuli.

Design

A within-subject design was conducted in a psychophysiological laboratory to assess alternative communication approaches. Twenty respondents – research students at the authors' university – participated in the study. This sample size is typical of eye tracking and skin conductance studies because collecting data from each study participant is extremely labour-intensive. The fact that participants were students is not expected to limit the generalisability of findings because there is no reason to assume the existence of a substantial difference in the effect of these particular messages on attention and activation across population groups. Screening questions were used (1) to ensure that participants had booked a flight online in the last 12 months and (2) to prevent including participants who engineered their responses to qualify for the study.

Five alternative messages were tested to measure attention, activation and attitude change as a consequence of exposure to the messages. They were designed on the basis of insights from prior work as well as a previous failed study by the authors where only textual messages were used. This failed study led to the insight that – in the first instance – the message had to attract attention. The textual messages consistently failed in this respect. Drawing on these insights and the social marketing literature outlined earlier, we designed messages that showed potential gains and positive benefits of carbon offsetting. A combination of images of people and the environment was used, along with short and long text-based messages. One message represents the current message airline passengers see when they book a flight online with Qantas, the Australian national carrier. The other four messages each target one of the key barriers to voluntary carbon offsetting as identified in prior work. The exact messages are provided in the Supplemental Data section of the online version of this paper. Each respondent was exposed to each message and messages were rotated among participants to avoid order effects. The analysis compares study participants' assessments and reactions to different messages.

Specifically, an "effectiveness" message was presented in a (3 × 4) matrix design, where four columns represented successful projects which have been implemented with funding raised through voluntary carbon offsets. The first row comprised pictures of each project, the second row contained short textual information explaining outcomes of each project, and the third row provided detailed descriptions of each project. The "transparency" message presented other projects where percentage of passengers' contribution on each project was determined. Similarly, the "choice" message included four other projects, with related pictures (first row) and names (second row), and descriptions of each project (third row). Within these messages, participants could choose the project they wanted to spend their money on. Finally, a "calculation" message verbally explained how the price of carbon offsetting is calculated.

Implementation

Participants entering the laboratory were given participant information and asked to sign a consent form if they were willing to participate in the study. Then, they were placed in front of a computer screen and first shown a few questions, including questions about their understanding of carbon offsetting, their belief about effectiveness and transparency of carbon offset programmes, and their assessment of the percentage of Australians they believe hold certain beliefs about carbon offsetting; this process revealed their assessment of Australians. This projective technique was used deliberately to avoid socially desirable responding (Crowne & Marlowe, 1960).

After those questions were answered, two Ag–AgCl electrodes pre-gelled with isotonic gel were attached on the distal phalanges of the index and middle fingers of the participants' non-dominant hand. EL507 disposable electrodes (Biopac Systems, Inc.) and GEL101 (Biopac Systems Inc.) were used.

After attaching the electrodes, participants performed a cycle of hyperventilation to check the autonomic nervous system reactivity. Subsequently, their eye movements were calibrated by asking participants to follow a calibration point on the eye tracker screen, where the distance between participants and eye tracker was around 60 cm. The task started after a resting period of one minute.

Visual attention captured by observing eye movements is related to different types of consumer behaviours. Visual attention is a significant predictor of choice (Lohse, 1997; Pieters & Warlop, 1999). For example, Russo and Leclerc (1994) use eye fixations to investigate the choice processes for non-durable products. In a lab simulation of supermarket shelves, Russo and Leclerc observe the complete scanpaths of eye movement across alternative products. Three distinct stages occur in the choice process: orientation (which involves gaining an overview of the product), evaluation (the longest stage which involves direct comparison between alternatives), and verification (which involves detailed examination of the already chosen brand). Looking at an item for longer is associated with a higher likelihood of choice (Krajbich, Armel, & Rangel, 2010). In a binary choice task between familiar options, individuals are more likely to choose the snack food option that they looked at more (Krajbich et al., 2010). Visual attention can also provide insight to many other cognitive tasks including information processing (Rayner, 1998), visual search (Janiszewski, 1998), and problem solving (Just & Carpenter, 1976).

Activation also plays an important role in explaining consumer behaviour (Kroeber-Riel, 1979; Groeppel-Klein, 2005). Investigating the impact of activation on consumers' overall processing of information, Kroeber-Riel (1979) finds in experimental studies that stronger activation is associated with a higher level of cognitive performance. Specifically, activation promotes pick-up of information and leads to higher recall. Activation is also an important construct for the explanation of buying behaviour at the point of sale (Groeppel-Klein, 2005). Buyers and non-buyers differ significantly in terms of activation, and different activation patterns are associated with different decision-making patterns.

The study participant was then shown the following instruction: *Qantas would like to see more of their passengers purchase carbon offsets for the flights they book. Passengers purchase the carbon offsets during the online booking process. You will now see five different ways the online invitation to purchase carbon offsets could be modified. We need your expert opinion. Please look at each option carefully. Then please indicate – separately for each option – how many percent of Qantas passengers you think would purchase carbon offsets.* This instruction, again, placed study participants into an expert role, thus avoiding socially desirable responding given that their assessments did not reflect their intentions, rather their assessment of the Australian population's intentions. The messages were rotated to ensure that each message was first and each message was last equally many times. This was done to avoid order effects manifesting in the data.

While participants were studying the messages, their eye movements were tracked using a Tobii-TX300 desktop-mounted eye tracker. Participants' fixation patterns were recorded at 300 Hz using infrared eye tracking methodology. Physiological response measures such as eye tracking procedures are prominent objective measures of visual attention (Christianson, Loftus, Hoffman, & Loftus, 1991; Krugman, Fox, & Fletcher, 1994; Rosbergen, Pieters, & Wedel, 1997; Wedel & Pieters, 2000). Eye movements consist of fixations, during which the eye remains relatively immobile, and saccades, which are rapid movements between fixation locations. Fixations reflect moments of attention to the message, whereas vision is basically suppressed during saccades (Sperling & Weichselgartner, 1995). In this study, visual attention to messages was measured using total fixation duration. Longer total fixation times are indicative of attention to the messages.

Participants' EDA was recorded using a MP150 BIOPAC system. Data were acquired using constant voltage between the two collection electrodes (0.5 V). The sampling rate of data acquisition was 2000 Hz. However, data were down-sampled offline at 10 Hz to adjust the high quality of the digitised data. Participants' activation was measured using EDA. According to Boucsein et al. (2012), EDA consists of tonic activity (slow) and phasic activity (fast). Each needs to be evaluated separately. Tonic activity reflects the basic level of conductance (skin conductance level). Phasic activity represents activation as a result of the presentation of a message (skin conductance responses). In this study, continuous decomposition analysis was used to analyse the data (Benedek & Kaernbach, 2010a, 2010b). Continuous decomposition analysis reflects the level of skin conductance in continuous measurement of tonic EDA and the level of skin conductance in continuous measurement of phasic EDA. Many skin conductance response indices are available to measure phasic activity in consumer neuroscience and psychophysiology. The commonly used quantisation technique is the sum of skin conductance responses amplitude (e.g. Groeppel-Klein, 2005). This index reflects the sum of skin conductance response amplitudes (a threshold of 0.01 μS was applied to determine the skin conductance response) within the response window. Optimally, a message aimed at increasing voluntary carbon offsetting behaviour would generate both high attention and high activation levels.

Upon completion of the eye tracking and skin conductance task, study participants answered a few more questions. Measures of their own beliefs about effectiveness and transparency of carbon offset programmes and their assessment of other Australians' beliefs towards carbon offsets were presented in the exact same way they were presented before the eye tracking and skin conductance task. However, this time they imagined the Australian population would have also seen those same messages. Asking these two groups of questions before and after the psychophysiological measures enabled testing for changes caused by exposure to messages. Finally, a few socio-demographic questions and questions about study participants' travel and booking behaviour were also gathered. At the end study participants received a $10 shopping voucher to compensate them for their time.

Although eye tracking studies are qualitative in nature, basic descriptive statistics were calculated to support the analysis and are described in the next section.

Results

Awareness and prior knowledge

Familiarity with carbon offsetting programmes among study participants was low. This provides additional empirical evidence for lack of awareness being one of the main barriers to carbon offsetting. When asked if they have ever heard of carbon offsetting, half of the study participants indicated that they had not. Those who had heard about carbon offsets admitted to only having limited knowledge about it. When asked which words come to their mind when thinking of carbon offsetting, their answers were limited to brief words (e.g. air travel, environment, interesting), supporting the notion that they had not formed clear perceptions or attitudes relating to carbon offsetting.

Attention

Two attention measures were examined across five messages: total page visit duration (the duration of respondents visiting each page containing the message and the question underneath), and total fixation duration (sum of duration of all fixations made on the message area). As recommended by the manufacturer of the eye tracking device used, a threshold of 60 milliseconds was applied to determine fixation (Tobii, 2003).

Duration of fixations depends on message features such as information type (pictorial vs. textual; Rayner, 1998) and complexity (McConkie, 1983). For the current design – given each message is different in nature – comparing total fixation duration across all messages is not optimal. Despite this limitation, all five messages were evaluated for both measures (total visit and total fixation duration) and results show no substantial difference among them. Specifically, the messages "effectiveness" and "choice" received the highest total fixation duration (on average, 31.75 and 29.55 seconds, respectively), followed by the "transparency" and "calculation" messages (24.24 and 22.56 seconds, respectively). The "Qantas" message received the lowest total fixation duration (17.05 seconds).

Looking deeper into specific elements of the messages leads to interesting insights. For this purpose, total fixation duration per surface area of each element relative to the total fixation duration of the message was evaluated. This measure was calculated separately for pictorial and text elements. The latter measure was adjusted for the number of words. Results are shown in Figure 1 for three of the messages ("effectiveness", "transparency" and "choice"). As can be seen, the elements of the messages differ substantially in the amount of attention they attract. Specifically, among the pictorial

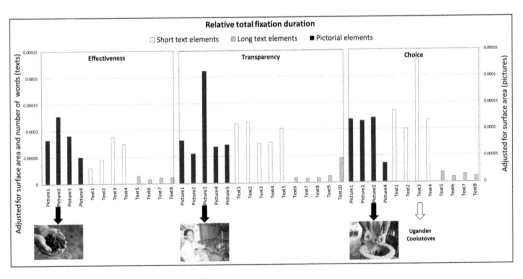

Figure 1. Attention paid to individual elements of three messages.

elements, Picture2 received the higher attention within the "effectiveness" message, Picture3 within the "transparency" message and Picture1, 2 and 3 within the "choice" message.

Results also show that some text elements (Text1 to Text4 for "effectiveness" and "choice", and Text1 to Text5 for "transparency") receive substantially higher attention than other text elements. The difference is systematic and can, at least in part, be explained by the length of the text section. Longer descriptive text elements within each message were not given as much attention as shorter ones. Those pictures which have attracted the most attention are included in Figure 1, as is the text which was viewed longest by respondents.

Activation

The sum of the amplitude peaks (Amp-Sum in units of μS) was examined to quantify phasic activity using LEDALAB V3.4.8 analysis software, which is available online (www.ledalab.de), implemented in MATLAB. Signal processing of respondents revealed two possible artefacts for two respondents due to them struggling with the mouse when first attempting to use it. The artefacts were deleted before analysis.

Figure 2(a) shows the skin conductance response amplitudes elicited by each message. Results show that the "choice", "calculation" and "effectiveness" messages elicited the highest levels of activation. The lowest level of activation results from the "transparency" message.

Attitudes

During the task, respondents assessed the percentage of passengers who, they thought, would purchase carbon offsetting by asking the question "Which percentage of Qantas passengers do you think would purchase carbon offsets if they had been presented with this information?" for each message. As can be seen in Figure 2(b), on average, the messages "effectiveness", "choice" and "transparency" were judged by study participants to have the highest impact on voluntary carbon offsetting with estimates of 58%, 56%, and 54%, respectively, of Australian purchasing offsets after seeing these messages. The "calculation" message was judged to encourage purchasing behaviour in about 47% of Australians. The "Qantas" message – mirroring the current message passengers see when they book a flight – was judged least effective with only 40% of Australians thought to respond to this message with a voluntary carbon offset purchase. Given results from prior studies indicating between 10% and 16% uptake of carbon offsetting offers on the Qantas webpage, this estimate by study participants about Australian's uptake is clearly an overestimation. This is not critical, however, because the aim of this study is not to predict uptake accurately, but to derive from the comparative assessments which of the messages holds the most promise. These comparative assessments are valid and offer two interesting insights: (1) the current Qantas message is assessed by study participants as

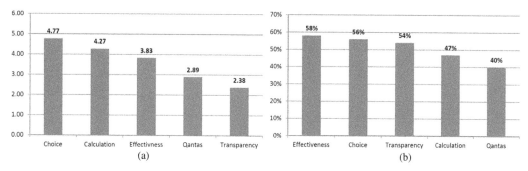

Figure 2. (a) Sum of amplitude peaks (Amp-Sum) in μs. (b) Percent of Australians purchasing carbon offsets in response to messages (as assessed by study participants).

performing worst, and (2) the "effectiveness" message which emphasises results and successes achieved as a consequence of people carbon offsetting their flights is assessed to be 45% more effective.

Three other types of attitudes were also assessed and the extent of change was evaluated by asking the same set of questions before and after showing the messages. Change of attitude toward two main barriers (effectiveness and transparency) was assessed by respondents verbally indicating how effective and transparent they think carbon offsetting programmes are ("not effective/transparent at all", "somewhat effective/transparent", and "very effective/transparent") both before and after showing the messages. Results indicate that 35% of study participants changed their attitude toward effectiveness: 15% moved from the answer option "not effective at all" to "somewhat effective" and 20% moved from "somewhat effective" to "very effective". Regarding transparency, 40% of respondents changed their attitude. Among those, four moved from "somewhat transparent" to "very transparent", one from "not transparent at all" to "very transparent" and three other from "not transparent at all" to "somewhat transparent".

Changes in stated purchase likelihood were also evaluated. Study participants verbally indicated the effect of information provided by the five messages on their likelihood to purchase carbon offsets in future. Ninety percent of study participants stated that the provided information increased their purchase likelihood.

Finally, study participants were asked to put themselves in the position of being an expert and, in this role, assess the attitudes of Australians relating to 20 statements (see Figure 3). These assessments are not a generalisation from the sample of study participants; rather they are a projective technique used to avoid social desirability bias. Study participants were presented with the same set of attitudes before and after seeing the entire suite of messages. Figure 3 shows how these assessments of attitudes changed across the full set of attitudes. Overall, all attitudes became more favourable after exposure to the messages. This means that the percentage of Australians assessed as holding negative attitudes declined and the percentage of Australians assessed as holding positive attitudes increased.

More specifically, as can be seen in Figure 3, the attitude stating "I do not understand how the price of the carbon offset is calculated" has been most affected by the messages; it improved by 40%. The attitude "It is unclear which projects are supported by the money from carbon offsets" is the second most influenced improving by 39%. In addition, people's awareness is enhanced by almost 33% as the third mostly affected attitude. The attitude most resistant to change by the

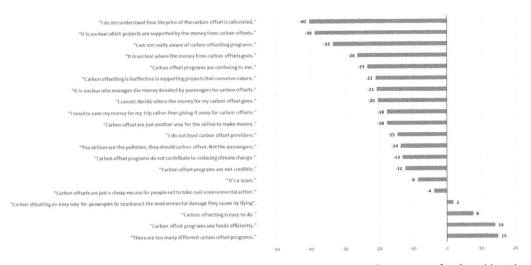

Figure 3. Study participants' estimate of Australians' attitude change after message exposure (in percentage of study participants).

messages used in this task is "Carbon offsetting programmes are an easy way to counteract the environmental damage they cause", which only improved by 2%.

The only attitude that could be seen as negative and has increased as a consequence of exposure to messages is "There are too many different carbon offsetting programmes". It is likely that this effect is a consequence of the fact that study participants were confronted with a large number of projects, given that they saw five messages. Should any of the tested messages be adopted in the online booking interface of airlines, air passengers would obviously only see one of those messages, thus reducing the cognitive load they would be facing and, as a consequence, it is expected that this particular attitude would not be as strongly affected as it was in the task.

Conclusions

Tourism-related emissions are growing due to the increase in air travel. Voluntary carbon offset schemes are becoming increasingly popular with airlines, but their adoption by consumers is low despite the potential environmental and social contribution of these schemes. Reasons for low adoption include a low awareness of carbon offsetting and confusion over offset programmes and carbon calculations and the lack of perceived effectiveness and transparency of programmes. This study tested messages aimed to sell carbon offsets for flights by using eye tracking and skin conductance methods in a laboratory environment. This approach enabled an objective assessment of participant attention and activation levels across messages. Participants were also asked to give expert advice and reflect on the attitudes of the general Australian population, using a projective technique.

The research confirmed previous findings which showed that awareness of carbon offsetting is low (Chang et al., 2010; Gössling et al., 2009). Once participants were presented with information in the lab, they believed that the general Australian population would be more likely to purchase carbon offsets. Interestingly, the current message used by Qantas received the lowest attention score, whilst the "effectiveness", "choice" and "transparency" messages attracted more attention. The messages of "effectiveness" and "choice" are also among the best achieving activation results based on the skin conductance testing.

After being exposed to the messages, participants also offered different assessments of how they thought Australians would view carbon offsets. In particular, unclear price calculation, uncertainty about the way their money would be spent on projects, unawareness, and confusing programmes showed the most improvements. However, smaller improvements were achieved concerning whether offsetting can counteract the negative impact of flying and whether offsetting is easy to do. This suggests that more communication is required to emphasise these aspects as some people can view carbon offsetting as both a cheap pardon and difficult to do (Kollmuss & Bowell, 2007). The use of positive and gain message frames recommended in social marketing (Detweiler et al., 1999; Jones et al., 2003) helps develop such communication messages, thus changing attitudes and adoption of pro-environmental behaviour.

These findings provide initial evidence that informing consumers about carbon offsetting benefits and impacts is likely to increase the adoption of offsetting. As programmes are relatively new, communications should initially focus on awareness raising, as suggested by Kim et al. (2016). Messages on airport screens in arrival and departure gates may offer an excellent opportunity, given that people are standing at the luggage carousels waiting for the luggage and thus open to entertainment, including information about carbon offsetting. Other options available to airlines are the inclusion of information in inflight magazines and into inflight entertainment which could profile specific projects successfully implemented as a consequence of air passengers' voluntary carbon offsets. Inflight announcements could also be made on the impact of specific programmes to remind travellers to offset their flights.

Findings suggest that refinement to the current messaging could increase both attention levels and emotional arousal, therefore ultimately increasing the likelihood of voluntary purchasing of carbon offsets. Specific message elements attracted more attention, which can provide insights for the design of future messages. First, short texts generated more attention compared with long texts, especially for the "transparency" and "choice" messages. This is a key insight given that air passengers typically wish to process their online booking quickly. This supports previous literature in the social marketing field highlighting the importance of short messages (Hammond et al., 2012). In the "choice" message, the text "Ugandan cook stoves" received a high level of attention along with pictures of cook stoves. The "choice" message also generated the highest activation level, pointing to programme choices related to the social benefits as a possible success strategy, an approach previously noted by Liu et al. (2015). Previous research has also suggested that promoting the additional social co-benefits of environmental offset projects in developing countries may increase adoption levels (Blash & Farsi, 2014; MacKerrom et al., 2009). Third, although shorter text did reasonably well in receiving attention for the "transparency" message, most attention was devoted to an image showing a person directly benefiting from an offset which improves their air quality and health. This again demonstrates the importance of emphasising the social benefits of offsetting, and supports social marketing studies which highlight people elements in messages (Hammond et al., 2012).

The messages tested in this study achieved substantial increases in awareness and understanding about carbon offsetting. Most importantly, however, the research shows that communication messages can change negative attitudes about carbon offsetting which are known to act as barriers to purchase decisions, such as perceived effectiveness and transparency of offset programmes. Online bookings are time-sensitive and so short text and images showing the outcomes of offsetting could encourage adoption. Our findings are of practical importance. They point to specific features about such messages that elicit stronger reactions from study participants and therefore are promising elements for use in carbon offsetting messages on actual online booking platforms. This study has also illustrated the value of using psychophysiological methods for sustainable tourism research, an area which relies heavily on measures prone to social desirability bias (Juvan & Dolnicar, 2016; Karlsson & Dolnicar, 2016).

This study has some limitations: the study sample is small and the research is not quantitative in nature. Eye tracking and skin conductance are qualitative and exploratory in nature; they offer insights. As a consequence, the messages used were not following a strict design. Rather they were quite different from each other, while each targeting a specific barrier known from prior literature and were informed by social marketing literature. The sequence of messages is also a limitation. All messages in this study were rotated in a specific sequence which may impact skin conductance results. Therefore, it would have been preferable to randomly (rather than systematically) rotate messages to make absolutely sure that sequence effects cannot manifest in the data. Another limitation is that the laboratory design and the proposed quantitative testing can only provide insight into short-term attitudinal or behaviour change. It is critical, however, to also study the long-term impacts of communications about voluntary carbon offsetting. Finally, this study assumes homogeneity of consumers, a common assumption in the field of consumer carbon offsetting research (Blasch & Farsi, 2014; Choi & Ritchie, 2014).

In future work, the most promising elements from this study will be used to develop a very small set of final messages suitable for inclusion on the webpage. These will be tested on the webpage of an airline and the number of actual offsets purchased will be used as the dependent variable to assess effectiveness of the messages. The social marketing literature outlined earlier in the paper could also be used in future research to examine message persuasiveness based on different message framing (positive vs. negative, gain vs. loss), something which was not experimentally tested in our study. Future research should also extend to acknowledge that different air passengers are likely to react positively to different kinds of messages, suggesting that a more targeted approach to communicating offsets and their outcomes may be required. For instance, some groups of consumers may lack awareness, while others may have awareness but may not have purchased offsets yet, while others may have purchased offsetting but may not continue for various reasons. The stages of change model (Prochaska & DiClemente, 1983) suggests that different interventions are required to deal with challenges people face at each stage of behaviour change. Such a model could be applied to aviation carbon offsetting behaviour and help to design appropriate communication interventions for people in each stage to move them through the stages of change. Finally, this study points to social benefits of carbon offsetting as potential key programme elements to communicate to consumers. These elements need further development and testing. Many of the carbon offset programmes have these features but they are not widely promoted. Due to concerns from some consumers over the real effects of climate change, a focus on social benefits may be wise. Such a focus may also fit in with airlines' broader corporate social responsibility activities. Based on this suggestion, further research should be undertaken to explore the influence of pro-social values and motives on carbon offsetting behaviour. This could complement the already larger number of studies that examine the influence of pro-environmental values and motives.

Acknowledgments

We wish to thank our project partners, the Carbon Market Institute and Qantas.

Disclosure statement

No potential conflict of interest was reported by the authors.

Funding

This research was supported by an Australian Research Council (ARC) [project LP150101001].

References

Andreassi, J.L. (2007). Psychophysiology: Human behavior and physiological response. Mahwah, NJ: Lawrence Erlbaum Associates.

Bagozzi, R.P. (1991). The role of psychophysiology in consumer research. In T. Robertson, & H. Kassarjian (Eds.), Handbook of consumer behavior (pp. 124–161). Englewood Cliffs, NJ: Prentice-Hall.

Benedek, M., & Kaernbach, C. (2010a). A continuous measure of phasic electrodermal activity. Journal of Neuroscience Methods, 190, 80–91.

Benedek, M., & Kaernbach, C. (2010b). Decomposition of skin conductance data by means of non-negative deconvolution. Psychophysiology, 47, 647–658.

Bureau of Infrastructure Transport and Regional Economics [BITRE] (2009). Australian transport statistics yearbook 2009. Canberra: BITRE.

Blasch, J., & Farsi, M. (2014). Context effects and heterogeneity in voluntary carob offsetting – a choice experiment in Switzerland. Journal of Environmental Economics and Policy, 3(1), 1–24.

Boucsein, W., Fowles, D.C., Grimnes, S., Ben-Shakhar, G., Roth, W.T., Dawson, M.E., & Filion, D.L. (2012). Publication recommendations for electrodermal measurements. Psychophysiology, 49, 1017–1034.

Broderick, J. (2008). Voluntary carbon offsets: A contribution to sustainable tourism? In S. Gössling, M. Hall, & D. Weaver (Eds.), *Sustainable tourism futures: Perspectives on systems, restructuring and innovations* (pp. 169–199). New York, NY: Routledge.

Brouwer, R., Brander, L., & Van Beukering, P. (2008). A convenient truth: Air travel passengers' willingness to pay to offset their CO_2 emissions. *Climatic Change, 90*(3), 299–313.

Burns, P., & Cowlishaw, C. (2014). Climate change discourses: How UK airlines communicate their case to the public. *Journal of Sustainable Tourism, 22*(5), 750–767.

Cacioppo, J.T., Tassinary, L.G., & Berntson, G. (2007). *Handbook of psychophysiology*. New York, NY: Cambridge University Press.

Chang, J.S.K., Shon, J.Z.Y., & Lin, T.D. (2010). *Airline carbon offset: Passengers' willingness to pay and reasons to buy*. Paper presented at the 12th World Conference on Transport Research (WCTR), Lisbon, Portugal.

Chen, F.Y. (2013). The intention and determining factors for airline passengers' participation in carbon offset schemes. *Journal of Air Transport Management, 29*, 17–22.

Choi, A., Ritchie, B.W., & Fielding, K. (2016). A mediation model of air travellers' voluntary climate action. *Journal of Travel Research, 55*(6), 709–723.

Choi, A.S., & Ritchie, B.W. (2014). Willingness to pay for flying carbon neutral in Australia: An exploratory study of offsetter profiles. *Journal of Sustainable Tourism, 22*(8), 1236–1256.

Christianson, S.-A., Loftus, E.F., Hoffman, H., & Loftus, G.R. (1991). Eye fixations and memory for emotional events. *Journal of Experimental Psychology: Learning, Memory, and Cognition, 17*, 693–701.

Commonwealth of Australia (2009). *National aviation policy white paper: Flight path to the future*. Canberra: Department of Infrastructure, Transport, Regional Development and Local Government.

Crowne, D.P., & Marlowe, D. (1960). A new scale of social desirability independent of psychopathology. *Journal of Consulting Psychology, 24*, 349–354.

Detweiler, J.B., Bedell, B.T., Salovey, P., Pronin, E., & Rothman, A.J. (1999). Message framing and sunscreen use: Gain-framed messages motivate beach-goers. *Health Psychology, 18*(2), 189–196.

Gillenwater, M., Broekhoff, D., Trexler, M., Hyman, J., & Fowler, R. (2007). Policing the voluntary carbon market. *Nature Reports Climate Change, 6*, 85–87.

Gössling, S., Broderick, J., Upham, P., Ceron, J.P., Dubois, G., Peeters, P., & Strasdas, W. (2007). Voluntary carbon offsetting schemes for aviation: Efficiency, credibility and sustainable tourism. *Journal of Sustainable Tourism, 15*(3), 223–248.

Gössling, S., Haglund, L., Kallgren, H., Revahl, M., & Hultman, J. (2009). Swedish air travellers and voluntary carbon offsets: Towards the co-creation of environmental value? *Current Issues in Tourism, 12*(1), 1–19.

Gössling, S., & Peeters, P. (2015). Assessing tourism's global environmental impact 1900–2050. *Journal of Sustainable Tourism, 23*(5), 639–659.

Groeppel-Klein, A. (2005). Arousal and consumer in-store behavior. *Brain Research Bulletin, 67*(5), 428–437.

Hammond, D., Reid, J.L., Driezen, P., & Boudreau, C. (2012). Pictorial health warnings on cigarette packs in the United States: An experimental evaluation of the proposed FDA warnings. *Nicotine and Tobacco Research, 15*(1), 93–102.

Haya, B. (2007). *Failed mechanism: How the CDM is subsidizing hydro developers and harming the Kyoto Protocol*. Berkeley, CA: International Rivers.

Higham, J., Reis, A., & Cohen, S. (2015). Australian climate concern and the 'attitude behaviour gap'. *Current Issues in Tourism, 19*, 1–17.

Hooper, P., Daley, B., Preston, H., & Thomas, C. (2008). *An assessment of the potential of carbon offset schemes to mitigate the climate change implications of future growth of UK aviation*. Manchester: Centre for Air Transport and the Environment, Manchester Metropolitan University.

Janiszewski, C. (1998). The influence of display characteristics on visual exploratory search behavior. *Journal of Consumer Research, 25*(3), 290–301.

Jones, L.W., Sinclair, R.C., & Courneya, K.S. (2003). The effects of source credibility and message framing on exercise intentions, behaviors, and attitudes: An integration of the elaboration likelihood model and prospect theory. *Journal of Applied Social Psychology, 33*(1), 179–196.

Just, M.A., & Carpenter, P.A. (1976). Eye fixations and cognitive processes. *Cognitive Psychology, 8*(4), 441–480.

Juvan, E., & Dolnicar, S. (2014). Can tourists easily choose a low carbon footprint vacation? *Journal of Sustainable Tourism, 22*(2), 175–194.

Juvan, E., & Dolnicar, S. (2016). Measuring environmentally sustainable tourist behaviour. *Annals of Tourism Research, 59*, 30–44.

Karlsson, L., & Dolnicar, S. (2016). Does eco certification sell tourism services? Evidence from a quasi-experimental observation study in Iceland. *Journal of Sustainable Tourism, 24*(5), 694–714.

Kim, Y., Yun, S., Lee, J., & Ko, E. (2016). How consumer knowledge shapes green consumption: An empirical study on voluntary carbon offsetting. *International Journal of Advertising, 35*(1), 23–41.

Kollmuss, A., & Bowell, B. (2007). *Voluntary offsets for air-travel carbon emissions: Evaluations and recommendations of voluntary offset companies*. Medford, MA: Tufts Climate Initiative.

Krajbich, I., Armel, C., & Rangel, A. (2010). Visual fixations and the computation and comparison of value in simple choice. *Nature Neuroscience, 13*(10), 1292–1298.

Kreuter, M.W., Bull, F.C., Clark, E.M., & Oswald, D.L. (1999). Understanding how people process health information: A comparison of tailored and nontailored weight-loss materials. *Health Psychology, 18*(5), 487–494.

Kroeber-Riel, W. (1979). Activation research: Psychobiological approaches in consumer research. *Journal of Consumer Research, 5*(4), 240–250.

Krugman, D.M., Fox, R.J., & Fletcher, J.E. (1994). Do adolescents attend to warnings in cigarette advertising? An eye-tracking approach. *Journal of Advertising Research, 34*, 39–52.

Liu, L., Chen, R., & He, F. (2015). How to promote purchase of carbon offset products: Labeling vs. calculation? *Journal of Business Research, 68*, 942–948.

Lohse, G.L. (1997). Consumer eye movement patterns on yellow page advertising. *Journal of Advertising, 26*, 61–73.

Lu, J.L., & Zhang, Y.S. (2012). Exploring airline passengers' willingness to pay for carbon offsets. *Transportation Research Part D-Transport and Environment, 17*(2), 124–128.

Macintosh, A., & Wallace, L. (2009). International aviation emissions to 2025: Can emissions be stabilised without restricting demand? *Energy Policy, 37*(1), 264–273.

MacKerron, G.J., Egerton, C., Gaskell, C., Parpia, A., & Mourato, S. (2009). Willingness to pay for carbon offset certification and co-benefits among (high-) flying young adults in the UK. *Energy Policy, 37*, 1372–1381.

Mair, J. (2011). Exploring air travellers' voluntary carbon-offsetting behaviour. *Journal of Sustainable Tourism, 19*(2), 215–230.

McConkie, G.W. (1983). Eye movements and perception during reading. In K. Rayner (Eds.), *Eye movements in reading: Perceptual and language processes* (pp. 65–95). New York, NY: Academic Press.

McKercher, B., Prideaux, B., Cheung, C., & Law, L. (2010). Achieving voluntary reductions in the carbon footprint of tourism and climate change. *Journal of Sustainable Tourism, 18*(3), 297–317.

McLennan, C.J., Becken, S., Battye, R., & So, K. (2014). Voluntary carbon offsetting: Who does it? *Tourism Management, 45*, 194–198.

Nakamura, H., & Kato, T. (2013). Japanese citizens' preferences regarding voluntary carbon offsets: An experimental social survey of Yokohama and Kitakyushu. *Environmental Science and Policy, 25*, 1–12.

Peters-Stanley, M., & Gonzalez, G. (2015). *Ahead of the curve: State of the voluntary carbon markets 2015*. Washington, DC: Forest Trends.

Pieters, R., & Warlop, L. (1999). Visual attention during brand choice: The impact of time pressure and task motivation. *International Journal of Research in Marketing, 16*(1), 1–16.

Polonsky, M.J., Grau, S.L., & Garma, R. (2010). The new greenwash? Potential marketing problems with carbon offsets. *International Journal of Business Studies, 18*(1), 49–54.

Prochaska, J.O., & DiClemente, C.C. (1983). Stages and processes of self-change of smoking: Toward an integrative model of change. *Journal of Consulting and Clinical Psychology, 51*(3), 390–395.

Qantas (2011). *Qantas data book 2011*. Sydney: Qantas.

Qantas (2015). *Fly carbon neutral - program overview*. Retrieved March 9, 2016, from http://www.qantas.com.au/travel/air lines/fly-carbon-neutral/global/en

Rayner, K. (1998). Eye movements in reading and information processing: 20 years of research. *Psychological Bulletin, 124*(3), 372–422.

Rosbergen, E., Pieters, R., & Wedel, M. (1997). Visual attention to advertising: A segment-level analysis. *Journal of Consumer Research, 24*, 305–314.

Russo, J.E., & Leclerc, F. (1994). An eye-fixation analysis of choice processes for consumer nondurables. *Journal of Consumer Research, 21*(2), 274–290.

Scott, D., Gössling, S., Hall, C.M., & Peeters, P. (2016). Can tourism be part of the decarbonized global economy? The costs and risks of alternate carbon reduction policy pathways. *Journal of Sustainable Tourism, 24*(1), 52–72.

Skumanich, S.A., & Kintsfather, D.P. (1996). Promoting the organ donor card: A causal model of persuasion effects. *Social Science & Medicine, 43*(3), 401–408.

Sperling, G., & Weichselgartner, E. (1995). Episodic theory of the dynamics of spatial attention. *Psychological Review, 102*(3), 503–532.

Stewart, D.W., & Furse, D.H. (1982). Applying psychophysiological measures to marketing and advertising research problems. *Current issues and Research in Advertising, 5*(1), 1–38.

Tobii Technology User Manual (2003). Retrieved August 4, 2016, from http://www.tobiipro.com/siteassets/tobii-pro/user-manuals/tobii-pro-tx300-eye-tracker-user-manual.pdf

Wedel, M., & Pieters, R. (2000). Eye fixations on advertisements and memory for brands: A model and findings. *Marketing Science, 19*(4), 297–312.

World Tourism Organization, United Nations Environment Programme, and World Meteorological Organization [UNWTO/UNEP/WMO] (2008). *Climate change and tourism: Responding to global challenges*. Madrid: Author.

The influence of trust perceptions on German tourists' intention to book a sustainable hotel: a new approach to analysing marketing information

Sindhuri Ponnapureddy, Julianna Priskin, Timo Ohnmacht, Friederike Vinzenz and Werner Wirth

ABSTRACT
This study examined the relationship between German tourists' trust perceptions and their intention to book a sustainable hotel, pioneering a new quantitative approach to sustainable tourism marketing. Data came from 300 respondents who participated in an online survey. Respondents were given a digital brochure to read containing information about a "fictitious" three-star beach hotel in Portugal, before completing a questionnaire that measured inter alia their intention to book this sustainable hotel. Both individual "general trust" (perception of others' trustworthiness) and "specific trust" towards the fictitious hotel in the brochure were measured. The survey also evaluated respondents' perceptions about the usefulness of the information in the brochure. Multiple regression analysis of the data indicated that general trust, trusting the hotel and perceived usefulness of the brochure were positively and significantly related to booking intentions. An interaction between general trust and perceived usefulness was also observed. This means that the higher the perception rate about the brochure's usefulness, the higher general trust was for booking intentions and vice versa. The practical implications of the results suggest that tourists could be motivated to book a hotel if its sustainability attributes and amenities were communicated in a trust inspiring way in marketing material.

Introduction

One way to achieve sustainable tourism development goals through consumer led approaches is for more consumers to book sustainable hotels. Attracting guests to sustainable hotels is challenging, despite general consumer preference shifts towards social and environmental responsibility. The proportion of consumers booking at sustainable hotels remains small (Line & Hanks, 2016). Indeed, the tourism industry has encountered numerous issues relating to consumer trust in its sustainability marketing materials. Often, sustainable hotels are recognisable by a label or certification that reflects their level of sustainable management (Peiró-Signes, Verma, Mondéjar-Jiménez, & Vargas-Vargas, 2014). Various studies suggest that certain markets defined by key socio-demographic characteristics could be considered to be more affinity with, and could be influenced by, specific sustainable hotel marketing. This leaves potential for expansion, particularly amongst non-sustainability affinity consumer markets (Company, 2014; Deloitte, 2011). Despite efforts to communicate sustainability attributes to potential guests across different markets to date, it is not clear what the marketing prerequisites are to achieve a successful booking. Yet, from an industry viewpoint this is important, particularly to determine what is useful information to potential guests that can also be trusted.

Some hotels wishing to appeal to new markets are advertised as "more sustainable" than they are in reality, which has negatively impacted on consumer's trust of the establishments' advertised services. This "greenwashing" phenomenon is rather prevalent in the tourism sector and has led to confusion, scepticism and mistrust amongst some consumers of anything that is marketed as eco, green, responsible and so on (Rahman, Park, & Chi, 2015). Not all consumer markets are predisposed to sustainable consumerism, as they have different needs and perceptions of sustainable hotel information and the trustworthiness of that information. It would seem that since mistrust is a clear barrier to booking intentions, hoteliers need to have a better understanding of how to avoid mistrust in sustainable hotel marketing. Their aim should be quite the opposite, to promote sustainably managed establishments so as to induce perceptions of useful and trustworthy information about sustainability, to enable consumers to make informed and conscious booking choices in favour of sustainably managed hotels.

Besides trusting the information consumers receive from marketing materials for sustainable hotels, they also need to perceive that information as useful, particularly if they intend to book into the establishment. Whilst sustainability and corporate social responsibility reports permit detailed accounts of a hotel's management and are considered as trustworthy in reflecting a hotel's actual management efforts, these rational communications are targeted to industry stakeholders and rarely to guests, who might otherwise have a rather poor understanding of sustainability (Miller, Rathouse, Scarles, Holmes, & Tribe, 2010; Parguel, Benoît-Moreau, & Larceneux, 2011). The achievement of higher booking rates at sustainable hotels requires consumer trust in marketing, through a format that is perceived as useful and communicates essential aspects relevant to a consumer who may not fully comprehend the complexity of sustainability. Although various sustainable tourism marketing guidelines offer concepts for hotel marketing (Villarino & Font, 2015), the perceptions of useful information that can actually lead to increased interest in booking a sustainable hotel are not clearly defined. In this context, it is challenging for sustainable hotels to market themselves appropriately, reflecting their management, when it is unclear if the information provided can be considered as useful and in what form consumers consider it as trustworthy marketing.

Besides communicating hotel services to consumers, socio-demographic variables are also relevant influences on booking intentions. The actual demand for sustainably managed tourism products is still considered a niche, restricted to less than 20% of the international travel market according to some researchers (Wehrli et al., 2014; Wehrli, Egli, Lutzenberger, Pfister, & Stettler, 2012). This pro-sustainability tourism market is commonly described as of mature age (Han, Hsu, Lee, & Sheu, 2011), with a higher than average level of both education and disposable income (López-Sánchez & Pulido-Fernández, 2016). One segmentation study based on demographics also found that mainly female, high-income individuals are willing to buy sustainable goods (Laroche, Bergeron, & Barbaro—Forleo, 2001). Other studies to date, however, failed to significantly validate the effects of social demographical variables on sustainable consumption choices (Gilg, Barr, & Ford, 2005). Clearly, the pro-sustainable tourism market is not homogenous (Hedlund, Marell, & Gärling, 2012) and to reach non-sustainability aware consumers is challenging for sustainably managed hotels. The reason for this is that such target marketing requires specific efforts to persuade consumers who may currently perceive sustainably managed hotels to be more expensive than standard alternatives, or have other barriers to booking. These consumers may also mistrust anything that is marketed as sustainable.

This paper sets out how tourist trust perceptions and their socio-demographic characteristics relate and potentially influence sustainable hotel booking intentions. The following research questions were investigated: (1) How do tourists' trust perceptions (in general and towards a sustainable hotel and its marketing brochure) influence intention to book a hotel? (2) To what extent do socio-demographic characteristics explain the intention to book a sustainable hotel? In addition, the data relating to possible interactions between trust perceptions, perceived usefulness of the information in the brochure and tourist socio-demographics with regard to booking intentions were analysed. These results provide the basis for the discussion of the practical implications of this work for sustainable hotel marketing.

Literature review

A sustainable hotel is an establishment managed with a variety of socio-economic and environmental management attributes (GSTC, 2013). Essentially, sustainable hotel management requires additional responsibility and effort to maintain high-quality guest experiences (Berezan, Millar, & Raab, 2014; ITP, 2008). Some authors also suggest that to increase bookings at sustainable hotels, additional marketing effort is required (Chhabra, 2012; Ye & Tussyadiah, 2011). These efforts are needed to enable perceptions of authenticity, to create a stronger connection to the hotel and to create trust amongst potential guests that the hotel actually performs the communicated sustainability actions (Gössling & Buckley, 2016). Trust is a concept with an established theoretical foundation that plays a key role in sustainability marketing (Belz & Peattie, 2012), where potential consumers always "use" trust to reduce their uncertainty and risk in whatever they purchase. One of the most widely cited definitions of trust is "the willingness of a party to be vulnerable to the actions of another party based on the expectation that the other will perform a particular action important to the trust irrespective of the ability to monitor or control that other" (Mayer, Davis, & Schoorman, 1995, p. 712).

Trust can be distinguished as a psychological state encompassing the intention based upon positive expectations of the intentions or behaviour of another party (e.g. to book a sustainable hotel) (Rousseau, Sitkin, Burt, & Camerer, 1998). In this study, trust is referred to as a concept that demonstrates the degree to which tourists believe a hotel's marketing and management actions, which can also be interpreted as guest belief in honesty, fairness or benevolence of the services provided. The roles, attributes and dimensions of trust have been studied extensively in many different fields although to a lesser extent in tourism. Ability, benevolence and integrity are generally considered as the most important dimensions of trust. In the context of a sustainable hotel, ability refers to the hotel's capability to fulfil its communicated promises in its marketing platforms. Benevolence is when the hotel holds consumers' interests ahead of its own self-interest and indicates sincere concern for their welfare, while integrity means the hotel acts in a consistent, reliable manner to meet its promises (Chong, Yang, & Wong, 2003; Schoorman, Mayer, & Davis, 2007).

A trustworthy relationship between a hotel and its customer has to be developed and well maintained. Therefore, trust can also be viewed as a process. Trust can be created and maintained through marketing, thereby enabling tourist's confidence with reference to a specific situation (e.g. booking a sustainable hotel). Tourists relate trust mainly to reliability, quality of the information promoted (Filieri, Alguezaui, & McLeay, 2015), even though it may not transform into bookings every time. During the process of creation, trust also acts as a point of differentiation especially when promoting a hotel to a new customer who is not familiar with its services.

When considering trust as a relevant factor for booking intentions, certain prerequisites such as being uncertain towards a particular situation are required (Doney & Cannon, 1997). In this context, when tourists are considering the process of booking a hotel, a condition exists where they are the only potential guests who need persuasion and trust towards that specific hotel. A growing body of literature dealing with online communication related to sustainable hotels has recently concentrated on examining perceptions of trust towards booking intentions (Filieri et al., 2015; Sparks & Browning, 2011; Sparks, Perkins, & Buckley, 2013). So far, the focus has been directed solely on perceptions of trust without differentiating between specific trust and general trust. Given the important role of trust in consumer behaviour, it is essential to understand the individual roles of general and specific trust.

General trust and Specific trust

General trust refers to "the general willingness to trust that others can be relied upon" Mayer et al. (1995, p. 715). It is a broad concept and acts as a basic antecedent to specific trust and refers to the extent to which a person perceives the world in general, as trustworthy (Chen & Barnes, 2007; Choi & Jin, 2015; Kantsperger & Kunz, 2010). General trust can be considered as a personality trait and an individual's propensity to trust something or someone that is independent of the situation (Kantsperger & Kunz, 2010; Rotter, 1980). For example, individuals with higher general trust believe that most people are basically trustworthy and have fair and good intentions (Mooradian, Renzl, & Matzler, 2006). Specific trust is highly influenced by the marketing activities of a company (Kenning, 2008).

Specific trust is trust towards a specific entity or situation, such as a sustainable hotel. It can be created and facilitated by appropriate marketing and promotion materials containing relevant information that helps potential consumers about a given product or service, because the presence of specific trust towards the hotel reduces the complexity of decision-making and associated perceived risk with the booking (Siegrist, Gutscher, & Earle, 2005). Both general and specific trust are interrelated and research shows that general trust influences specific trust regarding purchasing behaviours (Chughtai & Buckley, 2008; Kenning, 2008). For example, in online transactions general trust acts as an important antecedent and favours specific trust towards a particular website, because risk perceptions towards the products or services to be bought depend on individuals (Kim, Ferrin, & Rao, 2008; Siegrist et al., 2005).

The communication of rational information about product attributes is not entirely sufficient to create or facilitate trust. Therefore, other tools such as labels and certificates can help by presenting complex sets of information about a product in a short and condensed form (Sparks et al., 2013). Not surprisingly, labels often signal quality, proving their key role in creating and facilitating trust amongst some customers, which sometimes results in higher purchase intentions for certain products (Kim & Kim, 2011; Zhang, 2005). This is because certified and labelled products have been shown to have an additional differentiation point compared to standard alternatives (Peiró-Signes et al., 2014), most likely because these signal instant quality without elaborating very specific product attributes (Atkinson & Rosenthal, 2014; Dendler, 2014). To adhere to any certificate or label, product assessment by independent third party organisations are required, although this process is not explicitly documented for consumers per se. In the case of hotels, sustainability labels reflect specific responsible management policies and actions linked to the socio-economic and environmental impacts of the establishment (Grunert, Hieke, & Wills, 2014). Furthermore, few sustainable hotel labels are known to, or recognised by, consumers (James, West, Davis, & Reddick, 2010; Sandve, Marnburg, & Øgaard, 2014). Effective sustainable hotel labels are those which consumers recognise and trust, as proven by purposeful guest booking intentions.

Beside labels and certificates, the website of a hotel, its associated online-offline marketing and promotional material needs to provide additional useful and credible information to increase a likely booking intention. For example, when a hotel communicates sustainability actions as being part of its normal practice, it can facilitate positive guest perceptions towards the hotel (Font, Elgammal, & Lamond, 2016). However, sometimes the actions are not delivered transparently or in the ways suggested in promotional materials and actually overstate real hotel services thereby misleading consumers. The impact of this on consumers is disappointment, perceptions of product uncertainity and vulnerability (in a future buying context). In a sustainable consumerism context, the overstatement of claims is commonly known as "greenwashing" (Chen, 2013; Miller et al., 2010), which has been proven to reduce consumer trust and confidence (Parguel et al., 2011), increase scepticism amongst some (Albayrak, Caber, Moutinho, & Herstein, 2011) and lower specific trust towards the product or the company (Chen, 2013). Consumers in a tourism context who exhibit environmentally sustainable behaviour have been shown to be more sceptical and look for more information before trusting the environmental claims made in a company's communication (Font et al., 2016). It can take an additional effort for a marketer to convince those consumers who have lower confidence in a product.

Perceived usefulness of the information

Perceived usefulness is understood to be a source of (useful) information for the customer that is intended to increase the belief that the hotel provides what they promise and this may be a primary stage to gain trust. According to the technology accepted model, perceived usefulness is defined as "the degree to which a person believes that using a particular system would enhance his performance" (Davis, 1989). Perceived usefulness represents a significant antecedent for purchasing behaviour. Providing useful information in line with consumer needs increases familiarity with a product or a service. Additionally, it can help show understanding of consumer expectations and preferences. Offering useful information can raise trust in a product. Thus, companies can promote their attributes even to consumers who may not explicitly need or expect it. Perceived usefulness acts as a strong predictor in developing positive attitudes, which indirectly favours booking intentions (Kucukusta, Law, Besbes, & Legohérel, 2015; Morosan & Jeong, 2008). There is also positive influence between consumer trust from a particular source and perceived usefulness of the information (Lai, Huang, Lu, & Chang, 2013).

Sustainable tourists have been described to be different from the "average tourist", because they may be more prepared to participate in the sustainability actions of the hotel, such as recycling (Millar & Baloglu, 2011), and reusing towels and sheets (Reese, Loew, & Steffgen, 2014), donating funds to heritage conservation and charity funds amongst numerous other actions (Zander, Pang, Jinam, Tuen, & Garnett, 2014). The ability to trust others is highly individual and can vary significantly amongst different demographic groups. For example, trust in a specific hotel may be influenced by gender or age. Indeed, many socio-demographic factors can influence consumer booking intentions (Dolnicar, 2010) including lifestyle preferences (Berezan et al., 2014; Han et al., 2011). Various studies have shown that the German travel market has more affinity with sustainability, having an interest and willingness to book sustainable tourism products (Wehrli et al., 2012), particularly prevalent in middle-aged women, and those with above average education (Mohr & Schlich, 2016).

In this context, this research study set out to answer the following hypotheses:

H1 The higher the level of tourist trust towards the communicated sustainability attributes of a hotel, the higher the level of intention to book the hotel.

H2 The higher general trust, the higher the level of intention to book a given hotel.

H3 The higher the level of perceived usefulness of the information provided about a sustainable hotel, the higher the level of the intention to book the hotel.

H4 Tourists' socio-demographics systematically influence the booking intentions of a sustainable hotel.

It is hypothesised that the following influencing variables are predictors for the increase in booking intentions of a sustainable hotel.

H4.1 The higher the income households the greater the intention to book.

H4.2 Females have a greater intention to book than men.

H4.3 A higher education status leads to greater intention to book.

H4.4 The lower the level of age group the greater the intention to book.

Methodology

The research tested numerous influences on booking intentions with a special focus on trust. The data for this research was collected in January 2016, from an online survey administered in Germany.

The German market was chosen since Germany has a wide range of sustainably managed hotels and is considered it to be one of the most pro-sustainability tourist markets worldwide (FUR, 2014; Robecosam, 2016; Wehrli et al., 2014). Potential survey respondents were contacted by a professional polling company (Respondi AG) using an online access panel, which comprised the sample of German population in relation to age, gender, household size and income. The respondents came from a broad distribution sample in terms of gender, education levels and no mobile phones were used to complete the survey. All respondents had to be over 18 years of age and under 60. All respondents received a financial incentive for participation.

Brochure and questionnaire design

Survey participants were given the task to hypothetically plan a holiday on the Algarve Coast of Portugal. For this, they were provided with a fictitious brochure showing a three star, independent standard hotel. Portugal was chosen for the study as it is one of the preferred destinations for outbound German travellers: they are the second largest hotel users on the Algarve Coast (OECD, 2014; UNWTO, 2016). This survey used the hypothetical scenario planning method, commonly applied to predict future consumer behaviour (Karlsson & Dolnicar, 2016). This method was deemed suitable mainly because it enabled enhanced involvement of the respondents with the target behaviour of booking a specific sustainable hotel, via extensive exposure to a 16-page fictitious digital brochure, with details about standard facilities such as location, room amenities, price, quality, guest services and sustainability features covering socio-economic and environmental aspects of the advertised hotel. This method also facilitated respondents' ability to answer a detailed questionnaire about the hotel.

The digital brochure was designed by the authors using tools offered by Canva (https://www.canva.com/) and Adobe Indesign software. The brochure contained images from Portugal and text (statements) about the fictitious beach hotel named "Lumina". It was created to appear like a standard brochure that people would expect from a three-star hotel in terms of, information, layout, text style and images. The brochure's layout and features were selected from commonly available online digital brochures. To highlight the sustainability features of the hotel, a fictitious label was also developed using an open source logo design platform (https://www.hipsterlogogenerator.com/). The label's design was inspired by frequently used sustainable tourism labels currently available for industry and included a text specifically mentioning "third-party verified" (see brochures below). The label was pre-tested to verify its credible appearance and was inserted as a small logo at the bottom of every double page. In addition, a special page on which an enlarged version of the label was displayed was dedicated to explaining in detail, the hotel's sustainability management brief.

A copy of the brochure in its original German version is available at http://sushotel.github.io/lumina1/. A version translated into English is available at http://sushotel.github.io/lumina10/.

The brochure was validated by industry professionals for credibility and it was pre-tested three times prior to its final online launch. The digital brochure offered a compatible interaction between the website and tablet modus and the respondents were specifically asked not to use a phone to complete the survey. The brochure's length ensured that specific sustainability attributes could be presented in sufficient detail, using specific images. The time it took to read the brochure was also measured. This ensured that survey participants actually read the brochure before they proceeded to answer the survey questions. To avoid respondents just flicking over information, each page had one large image on the left or right side, and only one or two sentences with a heading to make it easy to comprehend and keep the participants' attention.

Once a respondent began participating in the online survey, they were given a brief introduction about the project and practical information about how to read and navigate the brochure. The first specific task the respondents were given was to read the stimuli brochure. Once this task was completed, they were redirected to the online questionnaire that included various scaled questions to assess their opinions and attitudes. The questionnaire had sections relating to trust constructs, perceived usefulness of the brochure, and booking intentions, with standard questions relating to

Table 1. Operationalisation of concepts: survey questions and measurement.

Focus	Measurement level and type
Socio-demographic variables	
Gender	Nominal (male, female)
Age	Nominal – five categories (18–24, 25–35, 36–50, 51–64, 65 and more years)
Gross annual household income	Nominal – three category (low, middle, high)
Education	Nominal – three category (primary, secondary, postsecondary)
Time spent on brochure and questionnaire	Ratio, mean = 22.31 minutes, SD = 10.85 minutes
Latent constructs	
General trust	Ratio (mean-index consisting out of five ordinal seven-point Likert scale treated as equidistant), Cronbach's alpha = 0.89, mean = 4.10, SD = 1.20
Trust (hotel)	Ratio (mean-index consisting out of six ordinal seven-point Likert scale treated as equidistant)
	Cronbach's alpha = 0.95, mean = 5.48, SD = 1.26
Perceived usefulness	Ratio (mean-index consisting out of four ordinal seven-point Likert scale treated as equidistant)
	Cronbach's alpha = 0.87, mean = 5.51, SD = 1.25
Intention to book a sustainable hotel (dependent variable)	Ratio (mean-index consisting out of five ordinal seven-point Likert scale treated as equidistant)
	Cronbach's alpha = 0.96, mean = 4.70, SD = 1.67

demographics such as gender, education, gross annual household income (Table 1). Questionnaire responses were measured on a seven-point Likert scale where 1 = strongly disagree and 7 = strongly agree. It was estimated that the questionnaire would require maximum 20 minutes to complete and the exact time spent reading the stimuli brochure was measured by the polling company. Although 310 respondents completed the questionnaire, only 300 questionnaires were retained for analysis as several respondents did not meet the questionnaire's inbuilt seriousness check.

Table 2. Measurement items, mean and standard deviation (1= strongly disagree, 7= strongly agree).

Constructs and scale items	Mean	Standard deviation
Trust (hotel)		
I suppose the promoted hotel is socially responsible	5.58	1.38
I assume that the promoted hotel is protecting the environment	5.67	1.34
I assume that the promoted hotel is following a long-term and farsighted corporate strategy	5.51	1.32
I assume that the promoted hotel generally acts in a sustainable way	5.26	1.58
In general, I trust that the hotel services are verified by an independent third-party	5.36	1.35
General trust		
Most people are basically honest	3.72	1.51
Most people are trustworthy	3.87	1.47
Most people are basically good and kind	4.13	1.44
Most people are trustful of others	3.80	1.44
Most people will respond in kind manner when they are trusted by others	4.97	1.31
Perceived usefulness		
If I were seriously looking for a hotel, I would like to use such a brochure to inform me	5.44	1.60
I would use a hotel brochure like this one, to inform me of a hotel offer	5.54	1.45
The hotel brochure contains all the important information that you can expect in a brochure like this one	5.25	1.60
Brochures like these are typical for the tourism industry	4.55	1.64
This brochure is professionally done	5.82	1.25
I think the information presented in the brochure is typical for a hotel like this one	4.98	1.51
This particular hotel brochure also contained information which is actually not typical for a standard brochure	5.11	1.55
Intention to book a sustainable hotel (dependent variable)		
I would intend to book the promoted hotel for my next vacation	4.45	1.83
I would plan to book the promoted hotel in the near future	4.73	1.75
I would be willing to book the promoted hotel for my next vacation	4.80	1.78
I can imagine to book the promoted hotel for my next stay in Portugal	5.07	1.74
I would indeed book the promoted hotel for my next vacation	4.43	1.82

The brochure served as the basis for elements of the questionnaire and four scales were created (Tables 1 and 2 in bold). These were: "1. Trust towards the hotel" (e.g. I suppose the promoted hotel is socially responsible), "2. General Trust" (e.g. Most people are basically honest), "3. Perceived Usefulness" (e.g. If I were seriously looking for a hotel, I would like to use such a brochure to inform myself) and 4. "Intention to book a sustainable hotel" (e.g. I would intend to book the promoted hotel for my next vacation). Cronbach's Alpha values of 0.70 or higher were used to estimate construct consistency and reliability. Trust towards the hotel ($\alpha = 0.95$), perceived usefulness ($\alpha = 0.87$) were self-reported items and the construct validity was refined through pre-tests. Booking intentions constructs ($\alpha = 0.96$) were measured using the elements employed by Han, Hsu, and Sheu (2010). General trust ($\alpha = 0.89$) was measured using a scale developed by (Siegrist et al., 2005; Yamagishi & Yamagishi, 1994).

Data analysis

Initial analysis of the data used descriptive statistics to show the mean, the frequencies and the standard deviation (SD) values. Then correlation analysis was applied to the data to determine how constructs related to booking intentions. Multiple regression analysis determined which patterns emerged between booking intentions (the dependent variable) and trust towards the sustainable hotel, general trust, perceived usefulness of the brochure and their demographics (the independent variables).

A multiple ordinary least square (OLS) linear regression was used using *R Studio Statistical Software* (Version 0.99.491). OLS was deemed as most appropriate as the response variable of the mean-index of booking intention was treated as a metric variable. The mean-index consisted of five ordinal seven-point Likert scales treated as equidistant, so the assumption of a metric use of the variable was acceptable. Statistical assumptions for data-set, which included homoscedasticity, normality of the error distribution and no or little multicollinearity of metric variables, were all met. The multivariate linear regression modelling was presented in two stages to test the hypothesis detailed in a previous section of this paper. An initial regression model was generated containing the variables set out in Table 1, the equation is as follows:

$$
\begin{aligned}
\text{Booking Intention} = \ & \beta_0 \\
& + \beta_1 \text{female} \\
& + \beta_2 \text{age}(25-35) + \beta_3 \text{age}(36-50) + \beta_4 \text{age}(51-64) + \beta_5 \text{age}(+65) \\
& + \beta_6 \text{primary} + \beta_7 \text{postsecondary (Education)} \\
& + \beta_8 \text{Income(high)} + \beta_9 \text{Income(low)} \\
& + \beta_{10} \text{General Trust} \\
& + \beta_{11} \text{Trust (Hotel)} \\
& + \beta_{12} \text{Perceived Usefulness} \\
& + \varepsilon.
\end{aligned}
$$

The regression formula tested the statistical relationship between the dependent variable of booking intention and several independent variables (e.g. general trust) and was modelled as a linear combination. The betas (β) in the equation are the weights (or slope) that quantified the strength and direction of influence to predict booking intentions. An optimised model was subsequently computed using the regr0 package of the *R software* for a best-fit model with interaction terms (Scheme) to identify those influencing variables that predict to a high extent the dependent variable of sustainable hotel booking intention and to test the research hypotheses. Interaction effect models were applied between general trust, trusting the hotel and perceived usefulness with regard to the brochure. Bayesian information criterion (BIC) was used as an evaluation criterion to quantitatively measure, which model maximised correspondence between the observed and predicted model. The best fit model was represented using BIC, whereby a smaller BIC indicated a better-fitting model (Raftery, 1995).

Findings

On average, the 300 survey respondents spent a total of 22.31 minutes, SD (10.85 minutes), completing the survey. The demographic profile of respondents was 54% females and 46% male: 66% of the sample was between 36 and 64 years old (Table 3). In total, 51% of the respondents were from a middle income group with gross annual household incomes between 20,000 and 55,000 Euros. Another 28% were from a low gross annual household income group and 21% were from a high gross annual household income group (Table 3). Since the regression analysis used variance data for analysis, there was no need to weight the data-set.

Descriptive statistics of the scales generally revealed positive trends (1 = totally agree and 7 = totally disagree). Respondents reported on average a high intention to book the sustainable hotel presented ($M = 4.70$, SD $= 1.67$). They also exhibited very high average trust towards the hotel ($M = 5.48$, SD $= 1.26$) even though they had somewhat lower general trust as individuals ($M = 4.10$, SD $= 1.20$). On average, respondents perceived the information presented in the brochure clearly as useful ($M = 5.51$, SD $= 1.25$). Correlation analyses indicated that general trust, trust towards the sustainable hotel and perceived usefulness of the brochure were significantly positive (Table 4). The Bravais–Pearson 0.57 correlation was significant indicating there was an association between trusting the hotel and booking intention. Since no high correlations (>0.7) resulted between the constructs, their inclusion into a multiple regression was acceptable. Moreover, the variance inflation factor (VIF) did not exceed a value of 10, which supported the decision in dealing with acceptable multicollinearity.

Table 5 summarises the initial multivariate analysis model and Table 6 illustrates the final best-fit model including interaction terms. In order to identify significant effects, t-statistics were used to test the effect of the size of an independent variable was different from zero (the closer t is to 0, the more likely that there is not a significant difference stemming from the influencing variable). Given the study's sample size, a t-value greater than 2.576 indicates a p-value of < 0.01 and 1.96 a p-value < 0.05 (e.g. if the two-tailed t-test statistics exceeds the critical value of 1.96, the null-hypothesis can be rejected at a 95% significance level).

Initial model

The variables from the initial model accounted for 45% of the variance in booking intentions where, $R^2 = 0.45, F(9, 300) = 21.13, p < .01$.

Table 3. Description of categorical variables and comparison with German census data.

Variables	Sample N	Sample %	German census %	Difference (sample- census)
Gender				
Female	162	54	49	5.0
Male	138	46.0	51	−5.0
Age (years)				
up to 24	22	7.3	9.10	−1.8
25—35	55	18.3	16.5	1.83
36–50	93	31.0	25.5	5.50
51–64	105	35.0	24.10	10.9
65 and more	23	7.67	25.0	−17.3
Education				
Primary	59	19.7	21.2	−1.5
Secondary	138	46.0	57.5	−11.5
Postsecondary	103	34.3	21.2	13.1
Annual gross household income (in 1000 €)				
Low (<20)	86	28.7	18.9	9.8
Middle (20 to 55)	153	51.0	51.5	−0.5
High (<55)	61	20.3	29.6	−9.3
Total	300			

Source: German census, see http://www.datenportal.bmbf.de

Table 4. Correlation coefficients of trust and booking intention.

Variables	M	SD	1	2	3	4	5
(1) General trust	4.10	1.2	–				
(2) Trust (hotel)	5.48	1.26	0.30**	–			
(3) Perceived usefulness	5.51	1.25	0.24**	0.61**	–		
(4) Booking intention	4.70	1.67	0.31**	0.57**	0.63**	0.11	–

$**p < 0.01$.

Table 5. Multiple regression analysis results of booking intention of a sustainable hotel (initial model).

Variables	n	F statistic	Adj. R2	β	t-Value
The model	300	21.13**	0.45		
Constant				−0.72	−1.47
Gender (female)				0.19	1.28
Age					
18–24 (Ref)				–	–
25–35				−0.60	−1.88
36–50				−0.76	−2.52*
51–64				−0.91	−2.97**
65 and more				−0.39	−1.02
Education					
Primary (Ref)				–	–
Secondary				0.18	0.89
Postsecondary				−0.01	−0.06
Income (in 1000 €)					
Low (Ref)				–	–
Middle				0.30	1.68
High				0.09	0.41
General trust				0.20	3.05**
Trust (hotel)				0.33	4.34**
Perceived usefulness				0.56	7.49**

$**p < 0.01$; $*p < 0.05$; Ref: reference category, BIC $= 1039.256$.

Trust towards the hotel also had a positive impact on hotel booking intentions ($β = 0.33$, t-value $= 4.34$, $p < .01$). The stronger the tourists' trust towards the hotel, the more likely was their booking intentions. With an increase of 1, the booking intention increased by 0.33. This proves H1 and confirms that higher trust levels about a hotel have a direct positive effect on booking intentions.

Higher general trust levels also had a positive impact and resulted in higher booking intentions ($β = 0.20$, t-value $= 3.05$, $p < .01$) which supports H2. With an increase of 1, the booking intentions increased 0.20 points.

Table 6. Multiple regression analysis results of booking intention of a sustainable hotel (final model including interaction terms).

Variables	N	F statistic	Adj. R2	β	t-Value
The model	300	32.43**	0.46		
Constant				5.31	20.09**
Age					
18–24 (Ref)				–	–
25–35				−0.49	−1.59
36–50				−0.71	−2.41*
51–64				−0.88	−2.98**
65 and more				−0.47	−1.26
General trust				0.21	2.78**
Trust (hotel)				0.44	4.69**
Perceived usefulness				0.76	7.97**
General trust * perceived usefulness			0.19	2.76**	

Note: $**p < 0.01$; $*p < 0.05$; Ref: reference category, BIC $= 1015.201$.

Perceived usefulness of the brochure (information provided) also had a high significant impact on booking intentions ($\beta = 0.56$, t-value $= 7.49$, $p < .01$). The more useful the information provided to respondents, the higher the booking intention of the sustainable hotel, which supports H3. With an increase of 1, the booking intentions increased by 0.56.

Using the same measurement level of the constructs, the effects of constructs were ranked as follows: (1) perceived usefulness, (2) trust (hotel) and (3) general trust.

The results of the initial multiple regression analysis did not confirm H4, i.e. that socio-demographics systematically influence the booking intentions to a sustainable hotel although variable "age" did influence booking intentions. Accordingly, younger respondents had higher booking intentions. For those between 36 and 50 years old (where $\beta = -0.76$, t-value $= -2.52$, $p < .05$) and those between 51 to 64 years old (where $\beta = -2.52$, t-value $= -0.91$, $p < .05$) the booking intentions were significantly lower compared to those of younger respondents aged between 18 to 24 years (Table 5).

Final model

Table 6 summarises those variables that significantly influenced the booking intentions, showing them in terms of two-fold interactions. Interpretation of the values for booking intention was based on the regression formula (Aiken, West, & Reno, 1991). Like the initial model, the variables for the final model accounted for 47% of the variance in booking intentions where, $R^2 = 0.47$, $F = 32.43$, $p < .01$. This is a better-fitting model with a BIC value of 1015.201 compared to the initial model BIC value of 1049.618. This lower BIC value indicates that the final model is better able to handle booking intention variance than the initial model. The final regression model is described by the following equation:

$$
\begin{aligned}
\text{BookingIntention} = \beta_0 \\
+ \beta_1 \, \text{age}(25-35) + \beta_2 \, \text{age}(36-50) + \beta_3 \, \text{age}(51-64) + \beta_4 \, \text{age}(+65) \\
+ \beta_5 \, \text{General Trust} \\
+ \beta_6 \, \text{Trust Hotel} \\
+ \beta_7 \, \text{Perceived Usefulness} \\
+ \beta_8 \, (\text{General Trust} * \text{Perceived Usefulness}) \\
+ \varepsilon.
\end{aligned}
$$

Variables which were not relevant to booking intentions were omitted from the final model's formula. Perceived usefulness (where $\beta = 0.76$, t-value $= 7.97$, $p < .01$), trust towards the hotel (where $\beta = 0.44$, t-value $= 4.69$, $p < .01$) and general trust (where $\beta = 0.21$, t-value $= 2.78$, $p < .01$) all acted as significant predictors of booking intentions. A significant two-way interaction of general trust by perceived usefulness was identified (where $\beta = 0.19$, t-value $= 2.76$, $p < .01$) and this interaction effect was interpreted as follows: the higher the general trust of an individual, the stronger the effect of the perceived usefulness of the brochure has on the booking intentions of that individual and vice versa: The more useful the promotional brochure information is perceived to be by an individual, the greater general trust, which in turn positively impacts the individual's intention to book a sustainable hotel.

Predicting booking intentions

A linear regression model illustrates that together the interactive effects of both perceived brochure usefulness and general trust significantly increased booking intention. Furthermore, trust towards a sustainable hotel was a significant predictor of booking intention and did not impact the other predictors. In addition, the booking intention of respondents within the 36–50 and 51–64 age groups differed from that of respondents in the 18–24 age group. Booking intention was significantly lower for the two older age groups than for the younger age group.

Figure S1 (available in the online version of this paper, under the Supplemental Data tab) shows the linear effects of the mean centred values of general trust towards booking intentions for different age groups. Perceived usefulness was held constant at the mean (= 0), facilitating the prediction of booking intention in relation to general trust, without the effect of perceived usefulness impacting the result.

Figure S2 (available in the online version of this paper, under the Supplemental Data tab) shows the effect of perceived usefulness on booking intention for different age groups. General trust was held constant at the mean (= 0), facilitating the prediction of booking intention in relation to perceived usefulness.

Figure S3 (available in the online version of this paper, under the Supplemental Data tab) shows the effect of trust (hotel) on booking intention for different age groups. Other influencing variables general trust, perceived usefulness were held constant at the mean (= 0), facilitating the prediction of trust towards the hotel.

Figure S4 (available in the online version of this paper, under the Supplemental Data tab) shows the interaction terms. This specifies focusing on general trust that depending on the value of perceived usefulness, the slope of general trust is different. For that reason, a simulation was made for fixed values of perceived usefulness (−2, 0, +2). Figure S4 (Supplemental Data) also shows the effect of general trust on booking intention for different age groups with the interaction of perceived usefulness for the values of −2, 0, +2. Hence, the effects of general trust towards booking intentions is reflected based on the respondents who perceive the information provided in the brochure as highly useful (+2), the respondents who perceive the information provided on average (0 = mean) and the respondents who perceive the brochure as not useful at all (−2). The higher the perceived usefulness of the brochure, the booking intention increases with a greater slope by higher degrees of general trust.

Figures S1–S3 (Supplemental Data) illustrate that if the interacting variables are held constant at the mean (= 0), the degree to which they influence booking intention can be ranked as follows: perceived usefulness of the information is the most influencing variable; trust in the hotel the next most influencing variable and finally general trust the least influencing variable. Figure S4 (Supplemental Data) illustrates how these main effects change due to the interaction between general trust and perceived usefulness.

Discussion and conclusions

This research contributes to the existing literature both theoretically and empirically, highlighting the relationships between trust, sustainable hotel marketing and booking intentions. It also considers social demographical variables as additional predictors of booking intentions. It provides a better understanding of the direct and interactional roles of specific trust towards a hotel, general trust and perceived usefulness of hotel brochure information on booking intentions.

General findings in the light of sustainable hotel marketing

Sustainable hotel marketing studies are generally conceptual or qualitative: only limited research has assessed the effects of trust and other scales on booking intentions empirically and in the context of a target market with an affinity towards sustainability such as Germany. The general findings of the study seem to indicate that marketers would benefit from greater investment in more effective sustainable hotel promotional material. Most of the previous studies that examined the demand side of sustainable tourism highlight that tourist markets have a limited, though increasing awareness of sustainability. They also suggest that sustainable hotel choice may be unintentional and more likely incidental, since only sustainability aware and committed consumers would deliberately book into such establishments. Given the findings about the level of booking intention in this study, it would suggest that the average mass consumers in the target market may potentially prefer a sustainable hotel. This therefore, confirms that persuasive sustainability marketing has indeed the potential to drive mass consumer markets where the younger generation are more receptive to sustainable hotels. The topic merits validation and further assessment across different travel markets.

One research question this study sought to answer was whether constructs such as tourists' general trust perceptions, specific trust towards a sustainable hotel and perceived usefulness of the information in the brochure influenced booking intentions. Previous studies on general trust, specific trust towards a hotel and perceived usefulness of marketing materials individually measured the effects on purchase intentions (Kantsperger & Kunz, 2010; Kucukusta et al., 2015). However, for this study the constructs were modelled together with respect to intentions towards booking a sustainable hotel. These factors were also found to be a reliable predictor of booking intentions and empirical analysis confirmed these constructs to be significant in understanding tourist decision-making. Previous studies did not measure the important interactional effects of the constructs on booking intentions that were done in this work.

Trust was facilitated through the use of a fictitious online hotel brochure, which clearly displayed a third party certified label, as well as details about standard hotel amenities and sustainability information relevant to the consumer. All this clearly helped integrate the determinants that show specific trust towards the hotel and the perceived usefulness of the information provided. High levels of detail about sustainability information in a specific context were found to increase trust amongst respondents (Sparks et al., 2013).

Influence of specific trust towards the hotel

The influence of specific trust in a particular state or situation on behavioural intention to execute new target behaviour has been well discussed (Pivato, Misani, & Tencati, 2008). This study supports these previous findings and contributes empirical evidence about the influence of specific trust towards a sustainable hotel on booking intentions. Sustainability information that includes all three dimensions (social, environmental and economic), as well as a label indicating sustainability certification is clearly an important element that engenders specific trust towards a sustainable hotel. As these research findings illustrate, the level of trust towards the hotel makes a difference towards booking intentions. Though all the participants got the same information, few participants trusted the information differently from the others, which clearly show that trust towards the hotel can affect the booking intention.

It would, therefore, be worthwhile for hotel marketers to ensure that they facilitate trust in their sustainable products or services and include sufficient useful information in their communication and promotional materials (Castaldo, Perrini, Misani, & Tencati, 2010). The facilitation of trust reduces the likely interpretation of information by consumers as greenwashing. Previous research also indicates that trust can be conveyed by sustainability certifications, in particular those that explicitly include messages about independent third party verification (Esparon, Gyuris, & Stoeckl, 2014; Sparks et al., 2013). Practically, specific trust towards the hotel may be partially achieved by a high degree of transparency about the sustainable management of a hotel (BSR, 2015).

Influence of general trust

This research suggests that general trust also needs to be considered as an important determinant to influence booking intentions. The findings of the study clearly show that the higher the general trust of a particular individual, the higher the booking intentions of a sustainable hotel. This means, that individuals with a higher general trust are more easily convinced to book a hotel irrespective of the specific trust towards the hotel. Additionally, when consumers have a high propensity to trust in general, it can contribute towards specific trust. A particular individual with a higher general trust responds relatively favourably to positive actions performed by an organisation, especially when the interaction between the entities is limited (Mooradian et al., 2006; Rotter, 1980). This is also important because an individual's propensity to trust can influence the consumer's product choice especially in selecting a new product or service (Siegrist et al., 2005) and this may be relevant to hotels that have only recently engaged in sustainability actions. This is highly advantageous for marketers, because focussing on specific hotel, trust-building activities would become more effective when consumers have higher levels of general trust.

Influence of perceived usefulness

The results of this research study confirm that hotel sustainability information presented in a general but detailed online brochure can be useful to persuade consumers to trust the marketing of a hotel, inducing a relatively high intention to book the hotel (Sparks & Browning, 2011). In line with commonly known marketing techniques, when consumers perceive that promotion material contains useful information about products or services, they are likely to buy them (Kucukusta et al., 2015; Morosan & Jeong, 2008). Perceived usefulness can improve the marketing effects of value-differentiated services, including sustainable hotels. The results of the study are in line with those of other research findings that suggest, in order to induce customers to book into sustainable hotels, these establishments need to provide more than just the standard marketing information (Villarino & Font, 2015). This study's findings indicate that perceived usefulness of the information in the brochure is a predictor of sustainable hotel booking intentions. Consequently, communicating sustainability in a hotel brochure may be best achieved if the sustainability text is integrated into a brochure that consumers perceive as customary or typical promotional material relevant to them. In turn, this may mean that hotel marketers should invest in attractive integrated and standard looking brochures, rather than producing special ones just focussing on the sustainable attributes. This would mean that microsites detailing the hotel's sustainability efforts are best presented in an integrated fashion along with the standard amenities and services. On a practical note, due to the increase in number of online bookings through booking.com, hotels.com, a 16-page brochure may not be regarded by tourists as a useful decision-making tool for booking decisions. The findings of the study do suggest that providing more useful and trustworthy sustainability information is important to persuade tourists to increase their booking intentions (Tables 4 and 5) but this may need to be condensed to reflect current online marketing trends (Gössling & Lane, 2015).

Interaction effects

Unlike previous studies, the current study also evaluated the significant interaction effects of perceived usefulness of the information and general trust on booking intentions. Indeed, tourists who have higher general trust as a personal trait when confronted with useful information about a sustainable hotel perceive it as valuable. The result is a higher intention to book a sustainable hotel. If the perceived usefulness is rather low, even a person with higher general trust will not have a higher booking intention. In contrast, the booking intentions will be lower with increasing trust, if the perceived usefulness is regarded as poor. The latter can be seen clearly in Figure S4 (Supplemental Data). If perceived usefulness is fixed with – 2 (after we have mean centred the range of values of the construct, indicating that people perceive the usefulness as very low), booking intention drops even with increasing trust.

Hotel marketers rarely identify travellers with high general trust regardless of marketing instruments used. However, by facilitating trust towards the hotel's actions and specifically trust towards the information and communication channels (brochures, websites and others) marketers may achieve desired booking intentions for a sustainable hotel. If these elements of specific trust towards the hotel (effectiveness knowledge) and perceived usefulness information (declarative knowledge) are aimed at consumers with a high general trust, the intention to book a sustainable hotel is highest and likewise increases the chance of a booking.

Socio-demographic factors

Research into the demand side of sustainable tourism often attempts to explain sustainable hotel booking intentions and relate these to socio-demographic profile characteristics (Han et al., 2011). Socio-demographics were considered important to trust in marketing, because one's individual knowledge and understanding tends to influence trust in sustainability products (Castaldo et al., 2010). In contrast to the literature reviewed, apart from age, the data analysis in this paper results indicate that the relationships between socio-demographic respondents' characteristics and sustainable hotel booking intentions were insignificant. Only Germans were surveyed and the data analysis shows that those respondents within the 18 to 24-year age group had a higher intention to book a sustainable hotel than those in the older age groups. A previous study undertaken in Italy had similar findings (Young, Hwang, McDonald, & Oates, 2010). The results of this study indicate that younger travellers may be more easily persuaded to book a sustainable hotel. Consequently, this younger section of the market may need to be targeted with useful, credible and trustworthy sustainability information and this merits further investigation.

Whilst this study only evaluated the German travel market's booking intentions, it is particularly important since Germany is ranked fourth for its environmental sustainability actions in tourism (Crotti & Misrahi, 2015). Various other studies also highlighted that German travellers tend to voluntarily offset flight emissions, be aware of climate change impacts and generally prefer to follow sustainability actions on vacation (Higham, Cohen, Cavaliere, Reis, & Finkler, 2016). According to the findings here, target marketing of sustainable tourism products is worthwhile, as Germans represent an important source market for many destinations worldwide.

Study limitations and future research

The principal limitations of this study were the relatively small sample size and the focus on the German travel market. Although the German travel market is appropriate when examining sustainable tourism in general, future research needs to examine other markets and identify cross cultural implications for sustainable hotel marketing. Nonetheless, the research findings provide a solid a contribution, which increases the theoretical understanding of sustainable hotel booking intentions. Additionally, the study has not measured how trust towards the hotel can be increased and what kind of information is required by different personality or consumer types to increase the perceived usefulness. Since many hotels utilise promotional flyers and brochures (both online and printed), the use of the 16-page stimuli brochure was not entirely unrealistic. Future research could test consumer booking intentions using a similar method and test trust and information usefulness in an integrated online booking platform. For example, the research could compare a conventional site such as booking.com and a pro sustainability site, such as bookdifferent.com.

Acknowledgments

This paper is the result of a cooperative research project between the Institute of Tourism at Lucerne University of Applied Sciences and the Institute of Mass Communication and Media Research at the University of Zürich. The research is partly funded by the respective institutions and by the Swiss National Science Foundation SNF (www.snf.ch).

Disclosure statement

No potential conflict of interest was reported by the authors.

Funding

The research is partly funded by the respective institutions and by the Swiss National Science Foundation SNF (www.snf.ch).

References

Aiken, L.S., West, S.G., & Reno, R.R. (1991). *Multiple regression: Testing and interpreting interactions*. Newbury Park, CA: Sage.

Albayrak, T., Caber, M., Moutinho, L., & Herstein, R. (2011). The influence of skepticism on green purchase behavior. *International Journal of Business and Social Science, 2*(13), 189–197.

Atkinson, L., & Rosenthal, S. (2014). Signaling the green sell: The influence of eco-label source, argument specificity, and product involvement on consumer trust. *Journal of Advertising, 43*(1), 33–45. doi:10.1080/00913367.2013.834803

Belz, F.-M., & Peattie, K. (2012). *Sustainability marketing – A global perspective*. Chichester: Wiley.

Berezan, O., Millar, M., & Raab, C. (2014). Sustainable hotel practices and guest satisfaction levels. *International Journal of Hospitality & Tourism Administration, 15*(1), 1–18. doi:http://dx.doi.org/10.1080/15256480.2014.872884

BSR. (2015). *Transparency, purpose, and the empowered consumer: A new paradigm for advertising*. Retrieved from http://www.bsr.org/en/our-insights/report-view/responsibility-and-transparency-in-advertising.

Castaldo, S., Perrini, F., Misani, N., & Tencati, A. (2010). The impact of corporate social responsibility associations on trust in organic products marketed by mainstream retailers: A study of Italian consumers. *Business Strategy and Environment, 19*, 512–526.

Chen, C. (2013). Greenwash and green trust: The mediation effects of green consumer confusion and green perceived risk. *Journal of Business Ethics, 114*(3), 489–500. doi:10.1007/s10551-012-1360-0

Chen, Y.H., & Barnes, S. (2007). Initial trust and online buyer behaviour. *Industrial Management & Data Systems, 107*(1–2), 21–36. doi:10.1108/02635570710719034

Chhabra, D. (2012). Proposing a sustainable tourism marketing framework for heritage tourism. *Journal of Sustainable Tourism, 17*(3), 303–320.

Choi, Y., & Jin, J. (2015). Is the web marketing mix sustainable in china? The mediation effect of dynamic trust. *Sustainability, 7*(10), 13610–13630.

Chong, B., Yang, Z., & Wong, M. (2003). Asymmetrical impact of trustworthiness attributes on trust, perceived value and purchase intention: A conceptual framework for cross-cultural study on consumer perception of online auction. *Paper presented at the Proceedings of the 5th International Conference on Electronic Commerce* (213–219). New York, NY: ACM International Conference Proceedings Series.

Chughtai, A.A., & Buckley, F. (2008). Work engagement and its relationship with state and trait trust: A conceptual analysis. *Journal of Behavioral and Applied Management, 10*(1), 47–71.

Company, T.N. (2014). *Doing well by doing good. Increasingly, consumers care about corporate social responsibility, but does concern convert to consumption?* New York: The Nielsen Company.

Crotti, R., & Misrahi, T. (2015). The travel & tourism competitiveness index 2015: T&T as a resilient contribution to national development. *The Travel & Tourism Competitiveness Report*, 13–38. Retrieved November 14, 2016, from http://reports.weforum.org/travel-and-tourism-competitiveness-report-2015/

Davis, F.D. (1989). Perceived usefulness, perceived ease of use, and user acceptance of information technology. *MIS Quarterly, 13*(3), 319–340.

Deloitte. (2011). *Hospitality 2015: Tourism, hospitality, and leisure trends*. Author. Retrieved from https://www2.deloitte.com/us/en/pages/consumer-business/articles/2015-travel-hospitality-leisure-outlook.html

Dendler, L. (2014). Sustainability meta labelling: An effective measure to facilitate more sustainable consumption and production? *Journal of Cleaner Production, 63*(0), 74–83. doi:http://dx.doi.org/10.1016/j.jclepro.2013.04.037

Dolnicar, S. (2010). Identifying tourists with smaller environmental footprints. *Journal of Sustainable Tourism, 18*(6), 717–734.

Doney, P.M., & Cannon, J.P. (1997). An examination of the nature of trust in buyer-seller relationships. *Journal of Marketing, 61*(2), 35–51. doi:10.2307/1251829

Esparon, M., Gyuris, E., & Stoeckl, N. (2014). Does eco certification deliver benefits? An empirical investigation of visitors' perceptions of the importance of eco certification's attributes and of operators' performance. *Journal of Sustainable Tourism, 22*(1), 148–169.

Filieri, R., Alguezaui, S., & McLeay, F. (2015). Why do travelers trust tripadvisor? Antecedents of trust towards consumer-generated media and its influence on recommendation adoption and word of mouth. *Tourism Management, 51*, 174–185. doi:http://dx.doi.org/10.1016/j.tourman.2015.05.007

Font, X., Elgammal, I., & Lamond, I. (2016). Greenhushing: The deliberate under communicating of sustainability practices by tourism businesses. *Journal of Sustainable Tourism, 1–17.* doi:http://dx.doi.org/10.1080/09669582.2016.1158829

FUR. (2014). *Abschlussbericht zu dem forschungsvorhaben: Nachfrage für nachhaltigen tourismus im rahmen der reiseanalyse*. Kiel: Erstellt für: Bundesministerium für Umwelt, Naturschutz, Bau und Reaktorsicherheit (BMUB). [Final research report: Sustainable tourism demand in a travel context]. Retrieved from http://www.bmub.bund.de/fileadmin/Daten_BMU/Download_PDF/Tourismus_Sport/nachhaltiger_tourismus_nachfrage_bericht_bf.pdf

Gilg, A., Barr, S., & Ford, N. (2005). Green consumption or sustainable lifestyles? Identifying the sustainable consumer. *Futures, 37*(6), 481–504. doi:http://dx.doi.org/10.1016/j.futures.2004.10.016

Gössling, S., & Buckley, R. (2016). Carbon labels in tourism: Persuasive communication? *Journal of Cleaner Production, 111, Part B,* 358–369. doi:http://dx.doi.org/10.1016/j.jclepro.2014.08.067

Gössling, S., & Lane, B. (2015). Rural tourism and the development of internet-based accommodation booking platforms: A study in the advantages, dangers and implications of innovation. *Journal of Sustainable Tourism, 23*(8–9), 1386–1403. doi:http://dx.doi.org/10.1080/09669582.2014.909448

Grunert, K.G., Hieke, S., & Wills, J. (2014). Sustainability labels on food products: Consumer motivation, understanding and use. *Food Policy, 44,* 177–189. doi:http://dx.doi.org/10.1016/j.foodpol.2013.12.001

GSTC. (2013). Global sustainable tourism criteria for hotels and tour operators. Global Sustainable Tourism Council. Retrieved October 20, 2014, from http://www.gstcouncil.org/en/gstc-criteria-hotels-tour-operators-destinations/criteria-for-hotels-tour-operators-industry.html

Han, H., Hsu, L.-T.J., Lee, J.-S., & Sheu, C. (2011). Are lodging customers ready to go green? An examination of attitudes, demographics, and eco-friendly intentions. *International Journal of Hospitality Management, 30*(2), 345–355. doi:http://dx.doi.org/10.1016/j.ijhm.2010.07.008

Han, H., Hsu, L.-T.J., & Sheu, C. (2010). Application of the theory of planned behaviour to green hotel choice: Testing the effect of environmental friendly activities. *Tourism Management, 31,* 325–334.

Hedlund, T., Marell, A., & Gärling, T. (2012). The mediating effect of value orientation on the relationship between socio-demographic factors and environmental concern in swedish tourists' vacation choices. *Journal of Ecotourism, 11*(1), 16–33.

Higham, J., Cohen, S.A., Cavaliere, C.T., Reis, A., & Finkler, W. (2016). Climate change, tourist air travel and radical emissions reduction. *Journal of Cleaner Production, 111, Part B,* 336–347. doi:http://dx.doi.org/10.1016/j.jclepro.2014.10.100

ITP. (2008). *Environmental management of hotels. The industry guide to sustainable management of hotels*. London: International Tourism Partnership.

James, J.J., West, S., Davis, S., & Reddick, L. (2010). Does sustainable certification knowledge influence tourist behaviour? *Journal of Tourism Insights, 1*(1), 1–6.

Kantsperger, R., & Kunz, W.H. (2010). Consumer trust in service companies: A multiple mediating analysis. *Managing Service Quality, 20*(1), 4–25. doi:10.1108/09604521011011603

Karlsson, L., & Dolnicar, S. (2016). Does eco certification sell tourism services? Evidence from a quasi-experimental observation study in iceland. *Journal of Sustainable Tourism, 24*(5), 694–714. doi:10.1080/09669582.2015.1088859

Kenning, P. (2008). The influence of general trust and specific trust on buying behaviour. *International Journal of Retail & Distribution Management, 36*(6), 461–476. doi:10.1108/09590550810873938

Kim, D.J., Ferrin, D.L., & Rao, H.R. (2008). A trust-based consumer decision-making model in electronic commerce: The role of trust, perceived risk, and their antecedents. *Decision Support Systems, 44*(2), 544–564. doi:http://dx.doi.org/10.1016/j.dss.2007.07.001

Kim, K., & Kim, J. (2011). Third-party privacy certification as an online advertising strategy: An investigation of the factors affecting the relationship between third-party certification and initial trust. *Journal of Interactive Marketing, 25*(3), 145–158.

Kucukusta, D., Law, R., Besbes, A., & Legohérel, P. (2015). Re-examining perceived usefulness and ease of use in online booking: The case of Hong Kong online users. *International Journal of Contemporary Hospitality Management, 27*(2), 185–198.

Lai, Y.-H., Huang, H.-C., Lu, R.-S., & Chang, C.-M. (2013). The effects of website trust, perceived ease of use, and perceived usefulness on consumers' online booking intention: Evidence from Taiwan B&B sector. *Life Science Journal, 10*(2), 1516–1523.

Laroche, M., Bergeron, J., & Barbaro—Forleo, G. (2001). Targeting consumers who are willing to pay more for environmentally friendly products. *Journal of Consumer Marketing, 18*(6), 503–520. doi:10.1108/EUM0000000006155

Line, N.D., & Hanks, L. (2016). The effects of environmental and luxury beliefs on intention to patronize green hotels: The moderating effect of destination image. *Journal of Sustainable Tourism, 24*(6), 904–925.

López-Sánchez, Y., & Pulido-Fernández, J.I. (2016). In search of the pro-sustainable tourist: A segmentation based on the tourist "sustainable intelligence". *Tourism Management Perspectives, 17,* 59–71. doi:http://dx.doi.org/10.1016/j.tmp.2015.12.003

Mayer, R.C., Davis, J.H., & Schoorman, F.D. (1995). An integrative model of organizational trust. *The Academy of Management Review, 20*(3), 709–734.

Millar, M., & Baloglu, S. (2011). Hotel guests' preferences for green guest room attributes. *Cornell University Quarterly, 53*(3), 302–311.

Miller, G., Rathouse, K., Scarles, C., Holmes, K., & Tribe, J. (2010). Public understanding of sustainable tourism. *Annals of Tourism Research, 37*(3), 627–645.

Mohr, M., & Schlich, M. (2016). Socio-demographic basic factors of German customers as predictors for sustainable consumerism regarding foodstuffs and meat products. *International Journal of Consumer Studies, 40*(2), 158–167. doi: http://dx.doi.org/10.1111/ijcs.12239

Mooradian, T., Renzl, B., & Matzler, K. (2006). Who trusts? Personality, trust and knowledge sharing. *Management Learning, 37*(4), 523–540. doi:10.1177/1350507606073424

Morosan, C., & Jeong, M. (2008). Users' perceptions of two types of hotel reservation web sites. *International Journal of Hospitality Management, 27*(2), 284–292.

OECD. (2014). *OECD tourism trends and policies 2014.* Retrieved from http://dx.doi.org/10.1787/tour-2014-33-en.

Parguel, B., Benoît-Moreau, F., & Larceneux, F. (2011). How sustainability ratings might deter 'greenwashing': A closer look at ethical corporate communication. *Journal of Business Ethics, 102*(1), 15–28.

Peiró-Signes, A., Verma, R., Mondéjar-Jiménez, J., & Vargas-Vargas, M. (2014). The impact of environmental certification on hotel guest ratings. *Cornell Hospitality Quarterly, 55*(1), 40–51.

Pivato, S., Misani, N., & Tencati, A. (2008). The impact of corporate social responsibility on consumer trust: The case of organic food. *Business Ethics, 17*(1), 3–12. doi: 10.1111/j.1467–8608.2008.00515.x

Raftery, A.E. (1995). Bayesian model selection in social research. *Sociological Methodology, 25,* 111–164.

Rahman, I., Park, J., & Chi, C.G.-Q. (2015). Consequences of "greenwashing": Consumers' reactions to hotels' green initiatives. *International Journal of Contemporary Hospitality Management, 27*(6), 1054–1081. doi:10.1108/IJCHM-04-2014-0202

Reese, G., Loew, K., & Steffgen, G. (2014). A towel less: Social norms enhance pro-environmental behavior in hotels. *The Journal of Social Psychology, 154*(2), 97–100. doi:10.1080/00224545.2013.855623

Robecosam. (2016). *Measuring country intangibles. Country sustainability rankings.* Zürich: Robecosam. Retrieved from www.robecosam.com.

Rotter, J.B. (1980). Interpersonal trust, trustworthiness, and gullibility. *AmericanPsychologist, 35*(1), 1–7. doi:10.1037/0003-066X.35.1.1

Rousseau, D.M., Sitkin, S.B., Burt, R.S., & Camerer, C. (1998). Not so different after all: A cross-discipline view of trust. *Academy of Management Review, 23*(3), 393–404.

Sandve, A., Marnburg, E., & Øgaard, T. (2014). The ethical dimension of tourism certification programs. *International Journal of Hospitality Management, 36,* 73–80. doi:http://dx.doi.org/10.1016/j.ijhm.2013.08.009

Schoorman, F.D., Mayer, R.C., & Davis, J.H. (2007). An integrative model of organizational trust: Past, present, and future. *Academy of Management Review, 32*(2), 344–354.

Siegrist, M., Gutscher, H., & Earle, T.C. (2005). Perception of risk: The influence of general trust, and general confidence. *Journal of Risk Research, 8*(2), 145–156.

Sparks, B.A., & Browning, V. (2011). The impact of online reviews on hotel booking intentions and perception of trust. *Tourism Management, 32*(6), 1310–1323. doi:http://dx.doi.org/10.1016/j.tourman.2010.12.011

Sparks, B.A., Perkins, H.E., & Buckley, R. (2013). Online travel reviews as persuasive communication: The effects of content type, source, and certification logos on consumer behavior. *Tourism Management, 39,* 1–9. doi: http://dx.doi.org/10.1016/j.tourman.2013.03.007

UNWTO. (2016). Sustainable tourism development. *Definition.* Retrieved December 16, 2016, from http://sdt.unwto.org/en/content/about-us-5

Villarino, J., & Font, X. (2015). Sustainability marketing myopia: The lack of sustainability communication persuasiveness. *Journal of Vacation Marketing, 21,* 326–335. doi:10.1177/1356766715589428

Wehrli, R., Egli, H., Lutzenberger, M., Pfister, D., & Stettler, J. (2012). Tourists' understanding of sustainable tourism: An analysis in eight countries *GSTF Journal on Business Review, 2*(2), 219–224.

Wehrli, R., Priskin, J., Demarmels, S., Schaffner, D., Schwarz, J., Truniger, F., & Stettler, J. (2014). How to communicate sustainable tourism products to customers: Results from a choice experiment. *Current Issues in Tourism*, 1–20. doi:10.1080/13683500.2014.987732

Yamagishi, T., & Yamagishi, M. (1994). Trust and commitment in the United States and Japan. *Motivation and Emotion, 18* (2), 129–166.

Ye, H., & Tussyadiah, I.P. (2011). Destination visual image and expectation of experiences. *Journal of Travel & Tourism Marketing, 28*(2), 129–144.

Young, W., Hwang, K., McDonald, S., & Oates, C.J. (2010). Sustainable consumption: Green consumer behaviour when purchasing products. *Sustainable Development, 18*(1), 20–31.

Zander, K.K., Pang, S.T., Jinam, C., Tuen, A.A., & Garnett, S.T. (2014). Wild and valuable? Tourist values for orang-utan conservation in Sarawak. *Conservation and Society, 12*(1), 27–42.

Zhang, H. (2005). Trust promoting seals in electronic markets: Impact on online shopping decisions. *Journal of Information Technology Theory and Application (JITTA), 6*(4), 5.

The role of travel agents' ethical concerns when brokering information in the marketing and sale of sustainable tourism

Alexa Mossaz and Alexandra Coghlan

ABSTRACT

Using conservation tourism as a test case, this study explores the role high-end travel agents play in selling sustainable tourism. It examines a niche marketing activity in that process. The study focuses on agents' consideration of ethics as they act as information brokers between tourists and operators. Data were collected from interviews with agents and analysed using a deductive content analysis based on six overarching concepts and theories on ethical decision-making. The findings emphasize the implicit influence within conservation tourism of tourism's ethical dimensions, whilst identifying many constraints that prevent a full consideration and/or disclosure of ethical concerns in the sales process. Most importantly, agents made assumptions using a false consensus bias about clients' preferences for service over concerns for the environment, and were not prepared to discuss the more sensitive issues surrounding conservation with their clients. A number of recommendations are proposed regarding the need to unpack conservation information, overcome the false consensus bias, and agents' reluctance to discuss ethics in the sales process. Finally, the findings have broader implications for the development of sustainable tourism, which ultimately will depend on a dialogue of ethical concerns and values within the tourism supply chain between suppliers, brokers and tourists.

Introduction

The role of the travel agent is changing; where once most tourists might access the tourism system through the intermediary of travel agents, tourism's process of disintermediation requires agents to position themselves as travel experts, or gatekeepers, with specialized knowledge (Lawton & Page, 1997; Michie & Sullivan, 1990). Agents now perform the role of information brokers, or "professional infomediaries" (Dolnicar & Laesser, 2007, p. 114) particularly where tourism supply chains involve specialized, exclusive experiences. Accordingly, travel agents can have significant power to shape the relationship between tourism products/services and the tourists themselves, preferentially selling some tours over others. Despite this, we know little about agents' role as information gatekeepers, although we do have information about travel agents in Hong Kong which demonstrates the travel trade's reluctance to grasp the concept of sustainable tourism (McKercher, Mak, & Wong, 2014). More specifically, we know little about how ethical considerations play out in the supply chains of sustainable tourism that ultimately shape the development of this sector (Chen & Peng, 2014; Lovelock, 2008; Sigala, 2013).

Discussions of ethics in tourism are not new; ethics are concerned with moral judgements, standards and rules of conduct (Holden, 2005; Jovičić & Sinosich, 2012), and usually understood as the ethical behaviour of operators or ethical choices and preferences of the tourist. Ethical concerns underpin the sector of sustainable tourism, but have not yet received detailed attention within the tourism supply chain of supply (operators), intermediaries (travel agents) and end-users (tourists). To fill this knowledge gap, this study uses conservation tourism as an example of ethically based tourism, reviews the role and performance of travel agents, and applies the literature from ethical decision-making to better understand how travel agents might act as a broker in the sale, and thus growth, of sustainable tourism sectors. This study draws on the significant body of research into organizational ethical decision-making, and examines the degree to which travel agents follow recognized patterns and processes described in ethical decision-making studies when selling conservation tourism to potential tourists. We focus on specialist, high-end travel agents who sell African conservation tourism luxury safaris within a well-established and mature tourism market in Switzerland (Dolnicar & Laesser, 2007). The power dynamic presented here is specific to high-end, niche tourism where the travel agent is a sought-after expert and the client relinquishes the decision-making process to an expert (Buckley & Mossaz, 2016).

As the first author had been a travel agent working in this area, this study adopts an emic, insider approach. This approach allowed her to access the entire population of travel agents in the French-speaking regions of Switzerland and discuss sensitive information that may not have been easily revealed to an outsider. This study therefore makes an important contribution in understanding the brokerage processes in the selling of upmarket, sustainable tourism, and is the first study in this area to focus on the process of environmental, rather than social, ethical promotion in tourism. It examines a niche activity in the marketing of sustainable tourism, but one with important potential findings for the marketing of sustainable tourism generally.

Literature review

Ethics in the tourism supply chain

Studies of ethics in the tourism realm have focused on ethical challenges at an operational level (and associated managerial decision-making), codes of ethics within the industry, the use of ethics as a marketing tool, ethics in tourism education, and finally ethical considerations about the development of tourism and its related impacts on social, cultural and natural environments (Fennell, 2006; Hultsman, 1995; Weeden, 2002; Yaman & Gurel, 2006). Conservation tourism, defined by Buckley (2010) as commercial tourism operations delivering direct conservation benefits (by comparison, eco-tourism aims to have a low impact on nature and local communities) falls into this last category, whereby tour operators design their products and services to be more conservation-oriented and underpinned by a conservation ethic (Buckley, 2010; Holden, 2009).

The specific ethical issue examined is the agents' regard and support for operators' conservation efforts as part of the selling process. The African wildlife safari and game lodge industry attracts tourists from all over the world, but particularly from wealthy developed nations, to watch iconic African wildlife in public, communal and private conservation reserves (Castley, 2010). Travel agents specialized in this subsector know that individual lodges vary in important ways; access, precise location, land tenure history, and length of habituation, and the skill and local knowledge of guides and trackers, and cooperation with neighbouring properties all influence the quality of wildlife sightings (authors withheld, in press). Views, layout, amenities, level of luxury and quality of service differ between lodges, as do their contribution to conservation and local communities. Because of this highly distributed commercial structure, the role of travel agents is critical, as both information brokers and financial intermediaries in the sales of conservation tourism. Agents have to weigh up conservation concerns against these other variables, potentially making trade-offs between environmental concerns and operators' business performance. Thus, the possible trade-off between preferentially high service quality (and potentially higher environmental footprints) or focusing on operators' conservation efforts (and potentially creating an impression of less luxury) becomes the key ethical question here: agents recognized this dichotomy as one of their primary, but by no means only, concerns.

Despite this, understanding how ethics play out in tourism has been largely neglected in the role of intermediaries within the tourism supply chain. Whilst there has been an argument that much of the tourism is undergoing a process of disintermediation, some sectors still involve intermediaries in the sale of exclusive, high-end services; African eco-safaris represent a specialized subsector where the agent's choice of operator and product can create large differences in the tourist experience and satisfaction. Agents in this sector have therefore adopted an "infomediary" role, becoming keepers of expert knowledge (Dolnicar & Laesser, 2007). In the particular case of conservation tourism, many individual agents also have their own personal views on conservation, and this may be one factor that led them to specialize in this sector. They may, therefore, book clients preferentially with operators whom they perceive as making the most significant contributions to conservation — or alternatively, they may focus on luxury, service and wildlife sightings as the core features of upmarket, African wildlife safaris.

This is an important point, as the study of ethical decision-making in tourism practitioners remains poorly understood (Yaman & Gurel, 2006) and it is not clear how the conservation activities of high-end safari within the subsector of conservation tourism are taken into consideration within the agents' sales decision-making process. Whilst models of travel agent decision-making processes do exist (e.g. Klenosky & Gitelson, 1998), these reveal relatively little about agents' values and the personal preferences of high-end agents, which are also likely to play into the agents' decision-making process when booking tours for a client (Chen & Peng, 2014). Indeed most of the "green" sales literature focuses on certification labels (and other markers) as the primary means of communication between the suppliers of green products and services and their intended market. Studies of the use of certification labels as a sales tool have shown mixed results, particularly in alternative, and sustainable tourism (e.g. Esparon, Stoeckl, Farr, & Larson, 2015). Villarino and Font (2015) describe a "sustainable marketing myopia", whereby green businesses miss opportunities to engage in persuasive communication about their green practices by focusing too much on the product rather than the client in their sales pitches. The influence of other intermediaries, such as agents, may provide an alternative means of promoting sustainable tourism.

On a practical level, specialized travel agents receive a commission on each booking and act in theory in the interest of the client, rather than the supplier (Gustafson, 2012). As specialized travel agents usually operate in low volume—high return markets, the amount of the commission does not vary greatly between operators and rarely influences travel agents' choices. This allows the agents to decide which operator to partner with to meet their own business needs, using factors other than sales commissions. With this freedom in mind, high-end travel agents' success hinges on their ability to match clients' expectations as well as shaping clients' choice with their own perception of a good product (Klenosky & Gitelson, 1998). Variables such as agent knowledge and prior experience, destination factors and trip—traveller variables, operator-supplied information and recommendations and client feedback will all be important (Hudson, Snaith, Miller, & Hudson, 2001; Michie & Sullivan, 1990).

Understanding which factors influence agents is the first step in deconstructing the importance of ethical concerns in a sales context. For instance, in a study conducted by Chen and Peng (2014), it was found that travel agents who possessed a high level of green hotel knowledge had a direct impact on the choice of green hotels by their clients. It confirmed that selling environmental friendly products required a specific body of green knowledge, which influenced sales. Addressing this knowledge gap of how the sale (and growth) of sustainable tourism is supported through the supply chain has not yet been explored through the framework of ethical decision-making (with the exception of Lovelock, 2008).

Ethical decision-making

To better understand ethical decision-making processes within the tourism chain, we borrow from the substantial body of knowledge on ethical decision-making in an organizational context (Craft,

2013). Here Rest's (1986) model is best known; he described four basic components which are (1) recognizing a moral issue, (2) making a moral judgement, (3) establishing moral intent, and (4) engaging in moral behaviour or action. Other empirical studies have highlighted the importance of dimensions such as the moral intensity of an issue (Jones, 1991), and cognitive effort, i.e. the diligent evaluation of relevant information (Street, Douglas, Geiger, & Martinko, 1997) which may influence these four basic components. Thinking styles have also been investigated as an independent variable in ethical decision-making; Groves, Vance, and Paik (2007) found that employees with a balanced thinking style, using both linear (rational, cost—benefit approach) and non-linear (emotional, gut-feeling approach) thinking, are the most likely to seek out ethically relevant information and make ethical and socially responsible decisions — a finding that is supported in tourism research by Chen and Peng (2014) and also considered in Malone, McCabe, and Smith's (2014) study of the role of emotions in choosing ethical tourism.

Sales people working within organizations have been the focus of much research within the field of ethical decision-making. This is partly because sales people are often exposed to greater ethical pressures than other employees; they work in relatively unsupervised settings, they must generate revenue for their firms, and are mostly evaluated on short-term objectives (creating high performance-related stress levels where performance criteria are met through sales volume) (Roman & Munuera, 2004). Much of the work in this area focuses on managing ethical conflicts such as fair play, honesty and full disclosure, which translate into sales activities such as selling products that meet customer needs, providing accurate information about the service or product and implementing low-pressure selling techniques (McClaren, 2000; Roman & Munuera, 2004). Studies of variables that might influence ethical decision-making behaviour of sales representatives, e.g. socio-demographic characteristics, employment variables, personal values and ethical perspectives, have, however, provided inconclusive results with limited predictive capacity. In addition, prior studies on fair play, honesty and full disclosure are a slightly different proposition to the question of how travel agents make recommendations about desirable products and services based on a broader corporate social responsibility or sustainable tourism perspective. These studies of fair play are primarily concerned with sales personnel not deliberately withholding crucial information that may affect a sales outcome (Ferrell, Johnston, & Ferrell, 2007; Roman & Ruiz, 2005).

There are some studies of sales professionals and the ethics concerned with how sellers use their own values to make recommendations, particularly where sales staff "span structural holes (missing relationships that inhibit information flow between people)" (Flynn & Wiltermuth, 2010, p. 1074). In such situations, sales agents act as brokers, occupying a position of "betweeness" centrality within the tourism value chain or stakeholder network, holding specific forms of informational advantage and power (Cheong & Miller, 2000). These studies are more akin to the types of decisions faced by agents selling high-end conservation tourism, where one of their primary considerations is to choose between discussing sensitive issues of environmental threats and impacts and selling dreams of luxury, superior service and wildlife sightings. By spanning these so-called structural holes, and deciding what aspects of the operators' business to promote, agents may unwittingly control a significant part of the discourse around ethical concerns in sustainable tourism. How an employee balances concepts of public and private moralization, including the issue of "moral muteness" and the antecedents and consequences of choices around the matching or mismatching of private and public moralization was explored by Kreps and Monin (2011).

Because of their broker role as information broker, sales agents must make intuitive assessments of the preferences of their clients, based on limited knowledge. In such cases, it is not uncommon for people to project their own preferences onto the preferences of others, sometimes through a false consensus bias (Flynn & Wiltermuth, 2010). Interestingly, Brenner and Bilgin (2011) have found that the likelihood of an option being considered in this projection process depends on its salience. Options that represent sellers' own preferences are naturally salient, as are options that are unpacked, i.e. explicitly described and explained. Taking the case of travel agents selling conservation tourism, a packed option may be "this lodge promotes conservation", whilst an unpacked option might be "this lodge employs three rangers who monitor the size, health and composition of the local lion population, and actively work on anti-poaching strategies." Unpacking an option has the effect of reducing the amount of social projection by sellers, reminding them of the less salient non-preferred option which may be overlooked if that option was to remain "packed". In other words "less preferred options are discounted more when implicitly described" (Brenner & Bilgin, 2011, p. 130). Similar strategies have also been noted by Villarino and Font (2015) to be effective in persuasive communication in marketing sustainable tourism by making "green practices" messages explicit, rather than implicit, providing more information regarding what these practices might mean for the potential tourists' experience.

In a similar vein, Wiltermuth, Bennett, and Pierce (2013) point out that the beneficiaries' ethical preferences, i.e. the ethical preferences of the tourists' buying from the agents, are also likely to affect the agents' ethical decision-making. In an empirical study of perceived ethical preferences, Wiltermuth et al. (2013) reported that individuals with a utilitarian ethical predisposition (i.e. one that considers the best moral action to maximize utility) are more likely to make their decisions based on the perceived ethical preferences of the decisions' beneficiaries. In the case of agents selling conservation tourism, agents with a utilitarian ethical predisposition are more likely to maximize the "good" sought by tourists, as opposed to formalists who will make their decisions based on the absolute right or wrong of a decision. One obvious question that arises here, is how "good" might be defined; is it the hedonistic luxury of upmarket tours, or perhaps the operators' positive outcomes for their social and natural environment or finally, is it some combination of the two? This issue also relates back to those highlighted by Kreps and Monin (2011) around moral versus pragmatic framing of business decisions and the number of reasons that an employee may privately or publically moralize an issue which may or not match their own perception of that issue.

The six theories and concepts that assist us in understanding how ethical concerns play into travel agents' sales decisions are summarized in Table 1. It must be noted here, that in a manner similar to Villarino and Font (2015, p. 4), who acknowledge that "whilst the actual inclusion of certain variables [...] is somewhat arbitrary, each of these variables has a role to play in exploring the potential

Table 1. The six ethical decision-making models and concepts explained.

Dilemma recognition, judgement, intent and action (Rest, 1986)	Individuals follow a process of recognizing that a moral dilemma exists, evaluate choices and outcomes, choose how one intends to act, and lastly act (or not) morally, the actual behaviour in the situation. If any of these steps in the process are not taken, an ethical decision will not be made.
Moral intensity and moral agents (Jones, 1991)	Moral intensity focuses on risk issues of likelihood, consequences and concentration of effect, temporal immediacy and proximity and social pressures (consensus) regarding the action. That is, moral intensity refers to how likely and severely the decision-maker perceives the effects of the decision upon him or herself. Moral agents are described by Jones as individuals who will make ethical decisions based upon a process of reasoning, through self-reflection, on the ethical dilemma.
Cognitive effort (Street et al., 1997)	This reflects the degree to which decision-makers are willing and able to expend cognitive effort in resolving ethical issues.
Thinking style (Groves et al., 2007)	Emotional responses have been found to most often trigger the recognition of an ethical dilemma. Therefore, Individuals who are receptive to non-linear thinking sources such as emotions, feelings and intuitions are more likely to recognize the moral implications of a given dilemma.
Preference projection (Brenner & Bilgin, 2011)	Decision-makers may commonly assume that others are likely to share their own preferences. Decision-makers' own preferences are more salient in their own minds and therefore likely to come to the fore when making decisions for others. Unpacking an option, making its characteristics explicit, will also enhance its salience and can help to avoid the process of preference projection.
False consensus (Wiltermuth et al., 2013)	False consensus bias represents a tendency for people to assume that others hold the same opinions as they do. This bias can be particularly strong in brokers within a social network who are assumed to possess greater insight into other's attitudes and behaviours, through their central position in that network.

message appeal", a similar approach is adopted here, focusing on themes (e.g. framing, salience, cognitive effort, the role of affect, projection bias and false consensus) that appear in various forms in the ethical organizational behaviour literature (c.f. Kreps & Monin for contemporary and highly relevant adaptations of these themes). We do acknowledge, however, that other theories and models, e.g. Srivastva's (1989) concern for personal authenticity and integrity could also have been usefully applied to the analysis. Thus our selection of theories and models, chosen for their applicability, their explanatory capacity and their operationalizabilty, represents only one of a variety of theories and models that could usefully be applied to better understand how and why sustainability is being sold (or not) to potential tourists.

Methodology

This study adopts an insider approach to interview specialized travel agents and obtain commercially confidential information on the role of conservation variables in the sale of sustainable tourism experiences. To provide illustrative examples and provide a clear focus to the interviewees, conservation aspects were centred on safari operators' efforts towards lion, leopard and cheetah conservation in southern Africa. As charismatic species, big cats are frequently used as marketing tools to increase sales, showcasing conservation activities such as lion monitoring, leopard reintroduction and cheetah rehabilitation (Okello, 2005). Furthermore, tour operators' and travel agencies' commitment to environmental sustainability is also perceived to confer a competitive advantage through value-adding (Goodwin & Francis, 2003). In the case of Switzerland for example, Wehrli, Schwarz, and Stettler (2011), found that 85% of Swiss tourists favoured sustainable tourism products, thereby adding an economic imperative to the importance of understanding ethical decision-making processes within high-end sustainable tourism products.

Reliably determining how individuals make particular decisions is a complex process as people do not always identify what factors they consider and how and why they balance and prioritize such factors, or how explicit logical and utilitarian considerations may interact with implicit emotional or affective factors (Busenitz & Barney, 1997). Moreover, individuals making decisions may not identify that their decisions incorporate ethical considerations when discussing these with a researcher in real-life contexts (Klein, 2008). The details of ethical decision-making processes may thus be hidden and subtle, even for those making the decisions.

Furthermore, most ethics research is framed using ethical dilemmas, where respondents or interviewees are offered a clear choice between two hypothetical courses of action, distinguished on the basis of some specific ethical criterion (Vitell, Singhapakdi, & Thomas, 2001). In the current case, however, there is no compulsion to make such a choice, it is up to the individual whether or not to import ethical considerations into their decisions. As such, the ethical decision-making context is closer to real life, and the researcher must make explicit an implicit process (Kwortnik, 2003). Research methods aiming to discover such details must encourage individual research subjects to reflect on decision-making processes, find the factors which they consider and reveal them to the researcher, without changing, masking or destroying the information sought (Rubins & Rubins, 1995). This is most readily achieved through mutual recognition and shared identity, e.g. using a qualitative insider approach, where the research subjects form a self-identified group to which the researcher also belongs.

This study therefore focused on a restricted and coherent group, using French-speaking Swiss agents selling upmarket African conservation tourism safaris, where the first author is herself a long-term insider member subject to the same professional pressures and standards. At the time of data collection, there were precisely 15 specialist French-speaking Swiss travel agents booking these particular operators for these particular clients (15 agents, in 10 agencies). Participants were between 30 and 60 years old, and consisted of eight females and seven males. All agents had a strong background in tourism and several years of experience in their current position. This study included all 15 of these agents, and so data were collected from a population, not a sample.

To maximize the depth of the information obtained, each respondent was interviewed three times, over an extended period. Initial conversations were open and unstructured, leading gradually to broad questions about clientele, preferred suppliers and booking procedures. Follow-up interviews were semi-structured, asking respondents to reflect on their relationships with their clients, their relationships with tour operators, their own decision-making processes, and the factors which influence those decisions. Throughout this process, the rapport established between the principal researcher (first author) and each of the research subjects through membership of the same professional group, was extended and deepened to enable trusted communication of specific information which is not typically top-of-mind. All face-to-face and electronic interviews were recorded wherever permission was granted by the interviewees, and/or notes taken either during or immediately after interviews as appropriate.

In order to ensure that the precise phraseology and tone were considered fully, the authors analysed recorded interview materials directly from the recordings as well as transcripts. The first author, a native French speaker, replayed each recording multiple times in order to extract meaning and content iteratively, and this coding was cross-checked by the second author, also a bilingual researcher A directed content analysis was undertaken to specifically test the multiple theories of ethical decision-making outlined in Table 1. Instead of identifying new themes from the data, predefined conceptual categories are used from existing theories and applied to a new concept (Humble, 2009). The key point of using a directed approach rather than the standard qualitative analytical approach is to support or deepen existing theory (Hsieh & Shannon, 2005). In this case, we compared the information obtained from the multi-step interview process, including recordings, against each of the six principal theories in turn.

The authors manually coded the transcribed interviews looking for keywords related to each of the six ethical decision-making process theories and concepts. For example, within Rest's recognition stage we searched for phrases that indicated an acknowledgement of the importance of conservation in tourism. In the judgement stage, we looked for conservation-related "should" phrases indicating support and interest. Intention was identified from statements on searching for more information, whilst action referred to specific action statements, e.g. "sending tourists" to conservation operators. Intensity and agency were coded based upon conservation importance and agents' role and responsibility statements. Cognitive effort was identified from statements of ease of finding information and priority statements, whilst thinking style focused on liking and preference statements. Preference projection was linked to statements where an agent's personal preference was attached to a decision for the client, and finally, false consensus was identified through the appearance of assumptions and a lack of discussion about the clients' views on the importance of conservation. The selected quotes are presented next, and interpreted within the context of ethical decision-making theories and concepts.

Results

The findings from the agents' interviews are presented in seven sections. First we introduce a general overview of the interviews, highlighting the authority of the agent in the decision-making process, establishing their role and responsibility in the framing (either public or private) of ethical issues. Next, we explore the interviews from the perspective of the six different theories presented in Table 1. Under each section, we present a short summary of the relevant theory or conceptual model, provide extracts of the interviews by way of illustration of these theories and models, and interpret the findings to add depth to our understanding of agents' role in ethical decision-making in tourism.

Travel agents as decision-makers

The analysis of the interviews established overall the dominant role of the agent in the decision process, evident across the 15 interviews. Agents felt empowered into authoritative figures with full ownership of the final travel decision. The agents believed that their sales message must be strong and confident, demonstrating a high level of expertise, allowing the client to surrender the responsibility of their decisions to the agent. As a result, agents appeared to impose their views for the sake of their client to reinforce their position as powerful information broker, illustrated by the quotes below:

> The clients are not asked if they have a preference for an operator, I assign my personal preferences based on what I think is best and from my own experience for the sake of my clients. I let them think that they are deciding based on my information, but in reality I own completely the decision-making process. (Agent #1)

> I can influence my client on a product that I think is a good match, but I don't let him choose. My own knowledge guides the decision-making. (Agent #6)

> The clients will listen to my recommendations. (Agent #10)

In each case, the agent is asserting his or her authority as a knowledge broker or infomediary, which in turn allows them to favour some of their own moral judgements as to the type of tour product that should be sold. These quotes reinforce the agents' role transition from booking facilitators to information specialists, where the agents retain the decision power by selling their knowledge. Interesting, this is in direct contrast to some of the findings noted by Lovelock (2008) in his study, where the client is always right and the agent is more concerned with organizational ethics that favour the proximate parties (the employer's profit and the client's right to decide) over other stakeholders.

When conservation comes into play within the sales process, it draws on ethical aspects being balanced unconsciously by the agents. To explore ethical decision-making in the context of conservation tourism, we coded the data using six different theories established in the literature as influencing the ethical decision-making process. The next step of the data analysis is to explore how conservation is perceived and integrated into the agents' decision-making process by using these different theories.

Issues of dilemma recognition, judgement, intent and action

Rest's (1986) model provides the basis of any ethical decision-making process. In this study, we applied Rest's theoretical framework to detect whether agents recognized conservation as a tourism-related dilemma, and how they integrate that recognition into their professional role.

Issues of dilemma recognition

The first step of ethical decision-making involves recognizing the existence of a dilemma or not. At the risk of over-simplifying the sales process, travel agents have two options when selling conservation tourism luxury safaris: stay focused on luxury hedonistic aspects of the product and choose to ignore conservation as it implies recognizing the existence of a moral issue, or recognize conservation as part of an ethical dilemma and act on the moral issue by favouring products that contribute to conservation. The following quotes illustrate cases where agents recognize conservation as a dilemma in their decision process, as clients may have little understanding, or appreciation, of the conservation efforts of operators.

> We contribute to conservation by sending tourists. We are very sensitive about responsible tourism and we select carefully our partners. Clients do not express a demand for a conservation-oriented product, it's quite rare, but it is our role to send them to operators who contribute to conservation. (Agent #14)

It appears, therefore, that agents are very aware of the ethical dimensions of tourism and their role in selling responsible tourism through their selection of partners and their decisions during the sales process with clients. They recognize that the latter may not hold a specific desire for sustainable tourism products that consider an ethical dimension, but the agents' own framing of these issues as an ethical one allows them to follow through with an intention to act according to an ethical framework.

> Maintaining genetic diversity is critical for lions and I think operators' involvement in these aspects is very important. [...]. But big cats are also marketing tools and probably the easiest way to get money for conservation. [...]. But I'm very keen to support lion conservation, especially in Kenya where conflicts with Maasai are a major issue.

> For me the conservation aspect is critical but the reality of conservation in Africa is so complex and harsh that it is hard to present it to clients. (Agent #11)

In the process of framing conservation tourism as an ethical one, agents are able to draw on specific issues that have moral dimensions (here, the conflict between Masaai and lion populations), as well as reflect on the pragmatics of business and tourism marketing, therefore illustrating the types of framing issues discussed by Kreps and Monin (2011) where private and public moral framing versus business framing may or may not line up. In this example above, both are clearly present, where big cat conservation is seen as an ethical issue, which can be influenced by business (tourism), when presented to clients under the guise of good marketing.

As a general pattern, agents do recognize that conservation aspects are important and that the role of the operator towards conservation efforts should not be overlooked. Conservation activities are attractive to agents and clients, in particular when charismatic high-valued species such as a lions are the target of these initiatives. Not only do they appeal to the agent as they trigger an emotional judgement, but it also represents an added-value to the product that can maximize sales when presenting a product to clients. However, the amount of information can be sometimes overwhelming to synthesize to clients, as it requires having a good understanding of the conservation background and the ability to talk about the project's aims and outcomes and provide enough details to the client to reinforce credibility and trust. As a result, conservation can be easily bypassed by the agent as the details can appear time-consuming and risky, and as these quotes illustrate, may not be requested by clients. This arguably represents a clear example of the types of issue highlighted by Kreps and Monin (2011) in their review of public versus private moralization of issues and their subsequent framing. Specifically, Kreps and Monin (2011) discuss the issue of "moral muteness" whereby powerful psychological and social pressures inhibit pubic moralization, e.g. in order to maintain harmony and/or authority.

Make a moral judgement

Agents make a moral judgement when selecting an operator influenced by its efforts for conservation. For instance, a particular conservation project promoted by an operator and which appeals to the agents can trigger the agent's moral code of ethics and influence the decision process. They will make statements of opinion as to whether conservation actions are good or not, within the context of tourism.

> I think that what some operators are doing for conservation is amazing and they lead the way forward in the industry. Some operators are beyond what is expected from them. It is important that they work on big cat conservation because I'm not sending my clients to a reserve with no cats, especially lions. But it shouldn't be just a marketing tool, I'm waiting to see tangible results from operators involvement in conservation, so far I have been a bit disappointed. (Agent #1)

This quote illustrates the basic cognitive process of the agent; when Agent #1 states that s/he would support these conservation-related actions, s/he is demonstrating a moral judgement that leans towards conservation. Not only do agents recognize the relationship between conservation and tourism as a moral issue, but in their judgement, conservation activities ought to be supported. Agents show support for conservation efforts but recognize a lack of clear information from operator; they indicate an interest in seeing results, and being able to judge the effectiveness of their partner operators to better inform their ethical sales decision-making process.

Establish moral intent

When the agent establishes moral intent, s/he recognizes the importance of conservation in the tourism product and the role of tourism operators in conservation efforts, and describes how s/he intends to act towards it.

> Local communities' involvement in conservation is the key aspect that I am looking for in an operator. While I am visiting the products on-site I would like to learn more about conservation projects and their outcomes for the communities rather than visiting all the different types of rooms in the lodge. (Agent #3)

During their familiarization trips, agents state that they are specifically seeking information that will assist them in their ethical decision-making process – the assumption underlying the quote above is that the agent will use the information about the tourism outcomes for local communities in their sales process (an intent) rather than out of simply curiosity.

> I am aware of big cat conservation issues through conflicts with local communities and habitat destruction, but I was not aware of operators' role in big cat conservation. I need more information about this, it's interesting and I would be inclined to support these actions once I know more about it. (Agent #7)

Here, intent is even more clearly indicated as the agent describes him/herself as more "inclined to support these actions", again presumably through their power as brokers in the sales of conservation tourism products to Swiss clients. In these quotes, the agents express a desire to know more about conservation aspects and less about service and room type. This is a critical turning point, as the desire to know more about conservation stems from the agent him or herself, not the client, and is guided by personal moral system linked to tourism. By establishing moral intent, the agent reinforces the importance of conservation efforts and in this particular case, prioritizes them over the service aspects of the operator.

Act on the moral concerns

The final stage of Rest's model is to undertake action based on the previous steps. In this case, agents have two options, to select or reject operators based on their conservation actions.

> No clients will be sent to an operator that is not contributing to conservation. (Agent #1)

> We do not sell a product that we do not like and that does not reflect our commitment to responsible tourism. We have a strong work ethic and care for our environment, we do not want to sell a product that does not represent our values. (Agent #13)

In both these examples, agents are indicating a definite action related to their ethical position on sustainable tourism; they will not market operators that do not reflect a commitment to responsible tourism practices. These quotes establish agents taking action in their decision process to commit to conservation efforts in tourism; they state a clear preference towards supporting those operators with a strong conservation ethic by actively sending tourists to them. This completes the ethical decision-making process according to one of the most prominent models in the field. However, other variables have been recognized to mediate the ethical decision-making process, and these are analysed next.

Concept of moral intensity and moral agents

The concept of moral intensity refers to the impact of the ethical decision on the decision-maker (Jones, 1991). A moral issue can vary depending on the degree of intensity, which directly affects the ethical intentions and behaviour by influencing one's sense of agency. This theory is applied here, in a process similar to Lovelock (2008), to understand how travel agents evaluate the moral intensity of their decision, and their sense of agency in relation to the issue. When agents based their decision upon conservation aspects by showing a willingness to contribute to conservation, they act as moral agents, identifying a certain level of moral intensity to their actions.

> I have never thought about my role in conservation but I realize that it is important to support conservation efforts for the future. I lack knowledge about conservation issues but I am willing to contribute. (Agent #10)

Many agents had not specifically considered his or her role in conservation, whilst still recognizing the issue as an important one, and one where agents have a role to play, thereby positioning themselves as moral agents capable of making a contribution in the area of responsible tourism.

> My own knowledge based on my skills and years in the industry is what I use to create a special experience for my client. What makes our agency unique is the expertise of the staff, it is our bargaining chip. I want to contribute to conservation as I guess I play a role by sending tourists to conservation tourism operators. (Agent #2)

Our role is to send our clients to operators that contribute to conservation, then it is operator's role to raise clients' conservation awareness by exposing them to conservation efforts while they are enjoying their holidays. (Agent #11)

The data presented in the previous section indicate that agents usually recognize the moral intensity of conservation in their decision process. However, it was their personal preference for an operator, rather than the moral intensity surrounding conservation, that influenced their decision process. Interviews also revealed that they whilst they often reflected on their role as moral agents, they tended to reject the responsibility of playing a role in the conservation dynamics on operators. From the perspective of agents, their professional role is limited to sending clients to operators who act responsibly, but not raising their clients' conservation awareness. Although agents can, and do, judge an operator not contributing to conservation as immoral, they might still send their clients to this operator as they balance conservation against other factors.

Cognitive effort

Cognitive efforts refer to the extent to which agents will seek information related to conservation in their decision process (Street et al., 1997). The moral cognitive development in agents' decision-making can be applied to represent the conservation aspects being balanced against more practical aspects. The following quotes illustrate the level of effort that agents are prepared to undertake to access information about conservation efforts in their decision-making process.

In sales, the conservation aspects are not the most important but indirectly are still part of the experience. (Agent #2)

This position may appear to contradict earlier statements on agents' role as moral actors. It does reflect, however, the sales nature of the agents' role. They will consider conservation aspects, but consider them as part of a suite of factors that will affect the client's experience of an operator. The next quote illustrates that that approach, in part, stems from the agents' lack of expertise to fully assess the conservation performance of operators, instead feeling more competent to comment on the service aspect of operators. Yet, this position given by Agent #10 is still a far cry from the findings of Lovelock (2008) where agents focused more on the freedom of travel for everyone and the client's right to choose, without the need to consider ethical dimensions of travel.

I lack the knowledge to evaluate the content of the information sent by operators relating to conservation so I don't go further, I keep my focus on the service and activities aspects but I realize that conservation is part of the deal too. (Agent #10)

These quotes reinforce the key concept of conservation being an important but not the sole focus of the agent, despite agents being the central interface of the conservation tourism dynamics. This theory establishes the degree to which decision-makers are willing and able to expend cognitive effort in resolving ethical issues. However, the degree to which agents are willing to expend their cognitive efforts to know more about an operator's conservation work is relatively low. As time-efficiency rules the life of travel agents, if the conservation information is not immediately available to the agents it will be bypassed. As a result, conservation is viewed as an added-value, not the core element of the sale, again suggesting the moral intensity surrounding the role of conservation in tourism is not strong.

Thinking styles

Agents' decision-making is the result of a balance between linear and non-linear thinking (Groves et al., 2007). Non-linear aspects consist of logistics, price, activities offered on-site, service and all the non-emotional factors. Linear thinking results from the agents' personal beliefs, or likability of the product, more aligned with conservation factors which require an emotional judgement from agents.

For example, big cats are charismatic species, and as a result most agents feel compelled to contribute to their conservation. This emotional factor and its role in decision-making are highlighted in the quotes provided below.

> My decision-making is largely influence by my personal feelings which is based on my experience in the field. I like what this operator is doing for conservation and I will always try to push sales with this particular operator. (Agent #6)

This agent admits to directly drawing on personal feelings as well as a "liking" for a particular operator's conservation practices to guide his/her sales decisions.

> The selling process is a trade-off between what I like, and the client's profile. Conservation has a price, and the top operators which I prefer are also the most expensive. I sell them in priority when I can because I like their work ethics but also the camps are beautiful and exclusive and they are located in areas where the wildlife is abundant. When I can send my clients to these special places I feel particularly happy! (Agent #1)

In a similar vein, this agent describes feeling happy when s/he sells a tour to an operator whose work ethics s/he likes.

> I send all my clients to AfriCat when I'm selling a trip to Namibia, because it's a great opportunity for them to see big cats from close and learn about conservation aspects. I enjoyed so much and I think they are doing a great job for conservation so my clients cannot miss it. (Agent #4)

Each of these quotes highlights the emotional component of the agents' decision-making process, or their "personal feelings"; operators that elicit positive affect around happiness and enjoyment will be sold in preference. Non-linear thinking can activate an ethical decision-making process by triggering an emotional response. However, this decision is the result of a balanced judgement, where emotional and rational factors are evaluated. Despite being attractive to the agents, the conservation product must remain "sellable". For that, it must meet certain criteria of costs, logistics and service.

Preferences projection and salience

As decision-makers have a tendency to assume that others share their preferences (Brenner & Bilgin, 2011), preferences projection and salience helps us understand and deconstruct agents' decision-making process. First, it establishes travel agents exerting a high level of power over their clients. Agents sell their knowledge by sharing their passion to their clients by sending them to places that they have personally enjoyed. This results in an unconscious projection of agents' preferences onto their client's trip. Projection is an unconscious and key strategy used by the agent facilitating the narrowing down of options, and relies on cognitive shortcuts which favour options that are most salient to them as personal preferences. In assuming the role of broker, the agent establishes basic travel parameters of the client, but then reverts back to his or her role as infomediary and decision-maker.

> I love cheetahs, they are the most beautiful species, of course I have selected special place for my clients where they can be educated about cheetah conservation, it is important for me. (Agent #8)

> I send all my clients to AfriCat when I'm selling a trip to Namibia, because it's a great opportunity for them to see big cats from close and learn about conservation aspects. I enjoyed so much and I think they are doing a great job for conservation so my clients cannot miss it. (Agent #4)

Agents tend to construct a safari that resembles what the agent themselves would personally enjoy, again representing the emotional content ("enjoyment") of the decision-making process. This is particularly true with regards to conservation aspects. Agents tend to send their clients to places where they want to support local conservation initiatives. Agents can have preferences for certain species and will then send clients to a place that they believe the clients will appreciate as much as they do. The reliance on personal preferences has implications for the salience of options (as well as the cognitive effort used to sort through options).

Unless the conservation aspects of various safari options are specifically unpacked, from a conservation point of view, by operators for agents, the latter will use their own preferences as a shortcut in the decision-making process. Unpacking, in this sense, means showcasing what lies behind "conservation tourism" tag, and making explicit the different conservation activities and outcomes of each operator. From an operator perspective, therefore, it is important to realize that conservation currently represents a packed option that needs to be unpacked to agents. Unpacking conservation could reduce the possibility of being bypassed by agents by presenting the core information instead of general information. For example, when advertising a lion monitoring project, aspects such as the threats faced by lions, the actions taken by the operator to reduce the threats, any reintroduction and anti-poaching efforts, the current number of lions being monitored and the methods employed should be provided to the agents. Moreover, this must be done in a clear and concise way that is easy to pass on to clients.

False consensus bias

The final aspect of ethical decision-making that is explored in this paper is the false consensus bias, i.e. the tendency for people to assume that others hold the same moral positions as they do (Wiltermuth & Flynn, 2013). This is particularly problematic in brokers who will often avoid moral discourse and instead discuss superficial, or socially "safe", aspects. This tendency can worsen the false consensus bias in ethical decision-making, as it may provide an illusion of consensus where, in fact, there is none.

> I care for conservation but I will not use it as a selling argument, I keep it for myself as clients want to know about service and exclusivity aspects first. (Agent #6)

Statements about what the clients want and need to know are common amongst the agents, who may choose to keep their ethical decision-making processes private, in the manner described by Kreps and Monin (2011) and focus instead on the more business-like aspects (e.g. value for money) of their decisions in their discussions with clients.

> My own desire and soft spots for some operators and places drive my decisions. (Agent #11)

The issues of good for conservation, good for the client and morally meaningful for the agent become blurred at a private level, if not at the level of discussions with the clients. Agents tend to project their own preferences for an operator on the final decision, assuming that if they like the product, their clients will like it too. This is a recurrent theme that surfaced across the majority of the interviews. Projecting one's own preferences is a false consensus bias, part of an anchoring and adjustment process to reinforce decision-making. This process confirms also the theory that decision-makers often fail to take others' perspectives, assuming that others share the same views. The general theme emerging from the data is "If I like, it my clients will like it too." Agents are powerful brokers and can influence social consensus by providing their opinion through projection.

Discussion and conclusion

The issue of sustainability in tourism, and in particular preferential adoption of forms of tourism that specifically embrace sustainability principles, has been central to tourism management since the early 1990s, most notably in the launch of the *Journal of Sustainable Tourism* (Bramwell & Lane, 1993). Whilst it is argued that progress has been made towards more sustainable practices in many areas of tourism, scholars nevertheless question why sustainability has not become more firmly embedded across the sector (e.g. Bramwell & Lane, 2013; Liu, 2003; Sharpley, 2000) and we know particularly little about how the sales decisions of intermediaries in the sustainable tourism supply chain influence the progress of sustainability-oriented practices in this sector.

Despite the process of disintermediation witnessed in mainstream tourism, the high-end, luxury safari subsector still relies heavily upon agents to act as brokers between operators and tourists (authors withheld, in press). For operators who explicitly use tourism to contribute positively towards the conservation of their natural environment, the question of how agents build these conservation outcomes into their decision-making processes when selling tours remained to be answered. Based on interviews with agents selling these types of safaris, the results suggest that the operators' conservation credentials do in fact play a role in the agents' favourable attitudes towards particular operators, which in turn influences their sales. However, the findings also indicate that the links between operators' conservation activities and travel agents' sales decisions are not straightforward and are best understood through the theories and concepts presented in organizational ethical decision-making studies.

Applying six ethical decision-making theories and models uncovered constraints to the continued development of more sustainable practices in high-end, luxury conservation tourism. Unlike Lovelock's (2008) study, our respondents reported recognizing the role tourism can play in conservation as a moral issue, judging this to be important in their sales decisions, and being willing to act upon this judgement by sending tourists to operators that actively contribute to conservation, thereby framing conservation outcomes in tourism sales as a moral issue according to Rest's model. This is a vital first step in encouraging sustainability to be considered in the tourism sales chain. However, the five additional theories used to analyse the interviews suggest a number of issues that may lead to a certain level of what Kreps and Monin (2011) refer to as moral muteness, i.e. a private moral position that does not translate to public discourse. First, agents were unsure of their role in promoting conservation through tourism – this was still seen as the operators' responsibility, indicating that moral intensity may still be relatively low (Jones, 1991). Second, cognitive effort appeared problematic – understanding conservation and transmitting the information to clients was seen as problematic (Street et al., 1997), and agents would often fall back on a "like" or "dislike" yardstick (Groves et al., 2007). Agents would then project these preferences onto their clients (Brenner & Bilgin, 2011), without necessarily unpacking conservation but rather assuming, through a false consensus bias, that clients would like what the agents like, based largely on the weighting of luxury and service versus conservation outcomes as the "good" sought by tourists in their holiday experience (Wiltermuth et al., 2013).

Based on the findings, we propose a sequential process where the framing of conservation outcomes in tourism as an ethical issue is either reinforced or weakened (Figure 1). This sequential process highlights that agents operate mostly from an emotional perspective that largely remains covert in a business context. It would appear that whilst the values and attitudes of agents are predisposed towards the selling of conservation, to avoid taking a moral stance with their clients, preferences projection and moral muteness occur (Kreps & Monin, 2011).

Therefore, conservation activities as a specific sales attribute remain problematic. Based on the patterns in our results, we propose several reasons why agents may be reluctant to explicitly and directly include conservation activities within their sales decision-making process. First, there is a question of agency and responsibility; agents did not identify a role for themselves of "pushing" conservation issues on to their clients. This is not uncommon within tourism, where other authors have identified a reluctance to "burden" the hedonistic tourism experience with issues linked to pro-environmental behaviour (Dolnicar & Grün, 2009; Wearing, Cynn, Ponting, & McDonald., 2002). Second, and linked to the first issue, conservation is heavily value laden, and the false consensus bias suggests that we are less likely to publically discuss questions of values with relative strangers – in this sense conservation joins religion, sex and politics as topics not be discussed in polite conversation.

To a large degree, this false consensus bias may be the most problematic issue facing sales in the sustainable tourism supply chain. It appears to inhibit the agents' ability to explicitly address the issue of what is "good" for the tourist; instead of questioning their clients' preference to support conservation, "good" within the context of high-end safaris is often interpreted as meaning luxury, service, and exclusivity. This reluctance to explicitly address value-laden issues (not only conservation, but

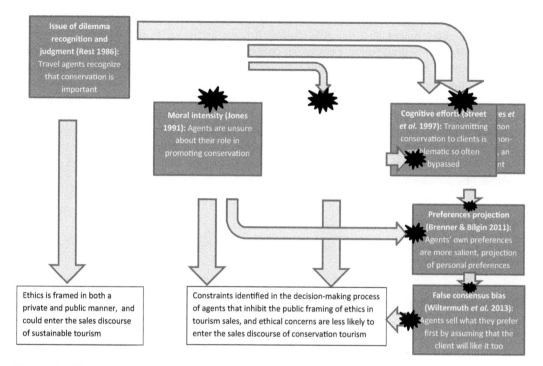

Figure 1. Possible constraints (represented by the stars), identified through the directed content analysis of interviews, where the ethical dimensions of sustainable tourism may be inhibited from entering the public (face to face) discourse of the sale of sustainable tourism.

perhaps other forms of moral dilemmas as well) may create ongoing challenges for the promotion and, more broadly, marketing of sustainable tourism. This finding lends support to Macbeth's (2005) call for a sixth tourism platform in tourism studies, an ethics platform, which will specifically interrogate the morality of tourism-related actions at all levels. Whilst we may be witnessing a broader societal shift towards sustainable tourism, on a person to person level, there may still be a reluctance to openly discuss and promote value-laden issues. This is an issue raised in other contexts, such as by Gössling, Hall, Ekstrom, Engeset, and Aall (2012) who suggest that only greater stakeholder awareness (and tourists themselves constitute a major stakeholder) will lead to systematic change in the transition towards sustainable tourism — and greater awareness will only happen through the valuing and discussion of sustainable practices within the sector.

Indeed, a study by Caruana, Glozer, Crane, and McCabe (2014) on tourists' accounts of sustainable tourism noted a clear lack of consistent discourse amongst tourists on what constitutes responsible (or ethical) tourism. Gössling and Peeters (2007) report an unwillingness to consider or discuss the moral issues of some aspects of tourism, such as the environmental impacts of flying. Thus, discourses of sustainable tourism are not currently embedded within the demand-side of tourism, despite reports of an increasing green tourism market by Bergin-Seers and Mair (2009). Furthermore, it is not clear whose responsibility it is to move to the fore this discourse of sensitive ethical issues within a hedonistic form of consumption-based leisure. Encouraging intermediaries within the tourism supply chain to include ethical concerns and moral topics may encourage the transition towards sustainable tourism. Doing this in the agents' sales decision-making may require a slow process, and will need to be facilitated by operators (e.g. by reducing cognitive effort for the agents) before it becomes fully embedded within the agents' sales rhetoric. This shift is important as "agents influence what tourists can and cannot do, where they can and cannot go, and what they select and reject" (Cheong & Miller, 2000, p. 383), thereby lending support, or impeding, the success of sustainable tourism as a sector.

In conclusion, this study has sought to contribute to the limited research on ethical concerns that underpin the development of sustainable tourism; it is the first study to specifically look at ethical decision-making in conservation tourism, and is only one of two studies to consider ethical decision-making processes of travel agents within responsible tourism (Lovelock, 2008). By adopting this framework, the study has identified some of the theoretical basis underlying the challenges facing the marketing and sale of sustainable tourism and suggests one area where we might focus our attention in order to support the ongoing development of conservation tourism. We suggest, furthermore, that the issues identified here may be similar to those faced by other forms of sustainable tourism, and recommend that a similar framework be applied to research into sustainable tourism more broadly. Extending this research into pro-poor tourism, or tourism that addresses human rights, for example, may provide fruitful avenues for future research.

Acknowledgments

The authors would like to acknowledge the support of Prof. Sparks and Prof. Buckley in their supervision of the thesis from which the data for this study are drawn.

Disclosure statement

No potential conflict of interest was reported by the authors.

References

Bergin-Seers, S., & Mair, J. (2009). Emerging green tourists in Australia: Their behaviours and attitudes. *Tourism and Hospitality Research, 9*(2), 109−119.

Bramwell, B., & Lane, B. (1993). Sustainable tourism: An evolving global approach. *Journal of Sustainable Tourism, 1*(1), 1−5.

Bramwell, B., & Lane, B. (2013). Getting from here to there: Systems change, behavioural change and sustainable tourism. *Journal of Sustainable Tourism, 21*(1), 1−4.

Brenner, L., & Bilgin, B. (2011). Preferences, projection and packing: Support theory models of judgments of others' preferences. *Organizational Behaviour and Human Decision Processes, 115*, 121−132.

Buckley, R. (2010). *Conservation tourism.* Wallingford: CABI.

Buckley, R., & Mossaz, A. (2016). Decision making by specialist luxury travel agents. *Tourism Management, 55*, 133−138.

Busenitz, L.W., & Barney, J.B. (1997). Differences between entrepreneurs and managers in large organizations: Biases and heuristics in strategic decision-making. *Journal of Business Venturing, 12*, 9−30.

Caruana, R., Glozer, S., Crane, A., & McCabe, S. (2014). Tourists' accounts of responsible tourism. *Annals of Tourism Research, 46*, 115−129.

Castley, J.G. (2010). Southern and East Africa. In R. Buckley (Ed.), *Conservation tourism* (pp. 145−175). Wallingford: CAB International.

Chen, A., & Peng, N. (2014). Recommending green hotels to travel agencies' customers. *Annals of Tourism Research, 48*, 284−289.

Cheong, S.-M., & Miller, M.L. (2000). Power and tourism: A Foucauldian observation. *Annals of Tourism Research, 27*, 371−390.

Craft, J. (2013). A review of the empirical decision-making literature: 2004-2011. *Journal of Business Ethics, 117*, 221−259.

Dolnicar, S., & Grün, B. (2009). Environmentally friendly behaviour − can heterogeneity among individuals and contexts/environments be harvested for improved sustainable management? *Environment & Behaviour, 41*(5), 693−714.

Dolnicar, S., & Laesser, C. (2007). Travel agency marketing strategy: Insights from Switzerland. *Journal of Travel Research, 46*, 133–146.

Esparon, M., Stoeckl, N., Farr, M., & Larson, S. (2015). The significance of environmental values for destination competitiveness and sustainable tourism strategy making: Insights from Australia's Great Barrier Reef World Heritage Area. *Journal of Sustainable Tourism, 23*(5), 706–725.

Fennell, D.A. (2006). *Tourism ethics*. Clevedon: Channel View.

Ferrell, O.C., Johnston, M.W., & Ferrell, L. (2007). A framework for personal selling and sales management ethical decision making. *Journal of Personal Selling & Sales Management, 27*(4), 291–299.

Flynn, F., & Wiltermuth, S. (2010). Who's with me? False consensus, brokerage, and ethical decision-making in organisations. *Academy of Management Journal, 53*(5), 1074–1089.

Goodwin, H., & Francis, J. (2003). Ethical and responsible tourism: Consumer trends in the UK. *Journal of Vacation Marketing, 9*, 271–284.

Gössling, S., Hall, C.M., Ekstrom, F., Engeset, A.B., & Aall, C. (2012). Transition management: A tool for implementing sustainable tourism scenarios? *Journal of Sustainable Tourism, 20*(6), 899–916.

Gössling, S., & Peeters, P. (2007). 'It does not harm the environment!' An analysis of industry discourses on tourism, air travel and the environment. *Journal of Sustainable Tourism, 15*(4), 402–417.

Groves, K., Vance, C., & Paik, Y. (2007). Linking linear/nonlinear thinking style balance and managerial ethical decision-making. *Journal of Business Ethics, 80*, 305–325.

Gustafson, P. (2012). Managing business travel: Developments and dilemmas in corporate travel management. *Tourism Management, 33*, 276–284.

Holden, A. (2005). Achieving a sustainable relationship between common pool resources and tourism: The role of environmental ethics. *Journal of Sustainable Tourism, 13*(4), 339–352.

Holden, A. (2009). The environment-tourism nexus: Influence of market ethics. *Annals of Tourism Research, 36*(3), 373–389.

Hsieh, H., & Shannon, S. (2005). Three approaches to qualitative content analysis. *Qualitative Health Research, 15*, 1277–1288.

Hudson, S., Snaith, T., Miller, G.A., & Hudson, P. (2001). Distribution channels in the travel agency: Using mystery shoppers to understand the influence of travel agency recommendations. *Journal of Travel Research, 40*, 148–154.

Hultsman, J. (1995). Just tourism: An ethical framework. *Annals of Tourism Research, 22*(3), 553–567.

Humble, A. (2009). Technique triangulation for validation in directed content analysis. *International Journal of Qualitative Methods, 8*(3), 34–51.

Jones, T.M. (1991). Ethical decision-making by individuals in organisations: An issues-contingent model. *Academy of Management Review, 16*(2), 366–395.

Jovičić, D., & Sinosich, R. (2012). Ethical bases of sustainable tourism. Faculty of Tourism and Hospitality Management in Opatija. In *Biennial International Congress*. Opatija: Tourism & Hospitality Industry.

Klein, G. (2008). Naturalistic decision-making. *Human Factors: The Journal of the Human Factors and Ergonomics Society, 50*, 456–460.

Klenosky, D.B., & Gitelson, R.E. (1998). Travel agents' destination recommendations. *Annals of Tourism Research, 25*, 661–674.

Kreps, T.A., & Monin, B. (2011). "Doing well by doing good"? Ambivalent moral framing in organizations. *Research in Organizational Behaviour, 31*, 99–123.

Kwortnik, R.J. (2003). Clarifying fuzzy hospitality-management problems with in-depth interviews and qualitative analysis. *Cornell Hotel and Restaurant Administration Quarterly, 44*(2), 117–129.

Lawton, G. & Page, S. (1997). Evaluating travel agent's provision of health advice to travellers. *Tourism Management, 18*, 89–104.

Liu, Z. (2003). Sustainable tourism development: A critique. *Journal of Sustainable Tourism, 11*(6), 459–475.

Lovelock, B. (2008). Ethical travel decisions travel agents and human rights. *Annals of Tourism Research, 35*, 338–358.

Macbeth, J. (2005). Towards an ethics platform for tourism. *Annals of Tourism Research, 32*(4), 962–984.

Malone, S., McCabe, S., & Smith, A.P. (2014). The role of hedonism in ethical tourism. *Annals of Tourism Research, 44*, 241–254.

McClaren, N. (2000). Ethics in personal selling and sales management: A review of the literature focusing on empirical findings and conceptual foundations. *Journal of Business Ethics, 27*, 285–303.

McKercher, B., Mak, B., & Wong, S. (2014). Does climate change matter to the travel trade? *Journal of Sustainable Tourism, 22*(5), 685–704.

Michie, D.A., & Sullivan, G.L. (1990). The role(s) of the international travel agent in the travel decision-process of client families. *Journal of Travel Research, 29*, 30–38.

Okello, M.M. (2005). A survey of tourist expectations and economic potential for a proposed wildlife sanctuary in a Maasai Group Ranch near Amboseli, Kenya. *Journal of Sustainable Tourism, 13*(6), 566–589.

Rest, J.R. (1986). *Moral development: Advances in research and theory*. New York, NY: Praeger.

Roman, S., & Munuera, J.L. (2004). Determinants and consequences of ethical behaviour: An empirical study of sales people. *European Journal of Marketing, 39*(5), 473–495.

Roman, S., & Ruiz, S. (2005). Relationship outcomes of perceived ethical sales behaviour: The customer's perspective. *Journal of Business Research, 58*(4), 439−445.

Rubins, H.J., & Rubins, I.S. (1995). *Qualitative interviewing: The art of hearing data.* London: Sage.

Sharpley, R. (2000). Tourism and sustainable development: Exploring the theoretical divide. *Journal of Sustainable Tourism, 8*(1), 1−19.

Sigala, M. (2013). Customer involvement in sustainable supply chain management a research framework and implications in tourism. *Cornell Hospitality Quarterly, 55*(1), 76−88.

Srivastva, S. (1989). *Executive integrity: The search for high human values in organizational life.* San Francisco, CA: Jossey-Bass.

Street, M., Douglas, S., Geiger, S., & Martinko, M. (1997). The impact of cognitive expenditure on the ethical decision-making process: The cognitive elaboration model. *Organizational Behaviour and Human Decision Processes, 86*(2), 256−277.

Villarino, J., & Font, X. (2015). Sustainability marketing myopia: The lack of sustainability communication persuasiveness. *Journal of Vacation Marketing, 21*(4), 326−335.

Vitell, S.J., Singhapakdi, A., & Thomas, J. (2001). Consumer ethics: An application and empirical testing of the Hunt-Vitell theory of ethics. *Journal of Consumer Marketing, 18*(2), 153−178.

Wearing, S., Cynn, S., Ponting, J., & McDonald, M. (2002). Converting environmental concern into ecotourism purchases: A qualitative evaluation of international backpackers in Australia. *Journal of Ecotourism, 1*(2−3), 133−148.

Weeden, C. (2002). Ethical tourism: An opportunity for competitive advantage? *Journal of Vacation Marketing, 8,* 141−153.

Wehrli, R., Schwarz, J., & Stettler, J. (2011). *Are tourists willing to pay more for sustainable tourism? − a choice experiment in Switzerland* (ITW Working Paper Series Tourism 003/2011). Lucerne University of Applied Sciences and Arts. Retrieved 3 February 2013 from http://www.hslu.ch/itw-working-paper-series-tourism-03-2011.pdf

Wiltermuth, S., Bennett, V., & Pierce, L (2013). Doing as they would do: How the perceived ethical preferences of third-party beneficiaries impact ethical decision-making. *Organizational Behaviour and Human Decision Processes, 122,* 280−290.

Wiltermuth, S.S., & Flynn, F.J. (2013). Power, moral clarity, and punishment in the workplace. *Academy of Management Journal, 56*(4), 1002−1023.

Yaman, H., & Gurel, E. (2006). Ethical ideologies of tourism marketers. *Annals of Tourism Research, 33,* 470−489.

Greenhushing: the deliberate under communicating of sustainability practices by tourism businesses

Xavier Font, Islam Elgammal and Ian Lamond

ABSTRACT

Greenhushing selectively communicates fewer pro-sustainability actions by businesses than are practiced; based on a perception of customers' rights to consumerism. We first studied the gap between the communication of sustainability practices in the audits and websites of 31 small rural tourism businesses in the Peak District National Park (UK). The analysis showed that businesses only communicate 30% of all the sustainability actions practiced. Their websites emphasised customer benefits, using explicit, affective, experiential and active language that legitimises the customers' hedonistic use of the landscape, while downplaying complex issues and normalising sustainability to reduce customer guilt. Just one website mentioned climate change. We found that greenhushing results from a low moral intensity, masking potentially negative consequences of perceived lower competence, whilst protecting business from more cynical consumers who may interpret their statements as hypocritical. Subsequent textual analysis and interviews were used to understand how communication constitutes these organisations. We propose that greenhushing reshapes and constitutes tourism businesses through their communications. Moreover, greenhushing is a form of public moralisation that adopts communication practices similar to greenwashing, reflecting the social norms expected from a business; however, in this case, located in a moral muteness, rather than moral hypocrisy, that businesses accept but resent.

Introduction

Most readers will be familiar with the issues surrounding "greenwashing". Fewer readers will be familiar with "greenhushing" — the converse of greenwashing – the deliberate withholding, from customers and stakeholders, of information about the sustainability practices that they employ. This paper explores why and how greenhushing is used, and its implications.

Businesses normally communicate their sustainability practices in an attempt to create a positive impression in the minds of their stakeholders. Their objective is to influence their stakeholders' behaviour towards the business and its products or services in line with their business goals, which can include increased financial gain for the business or increased societal gain from a change of behaviour (Belz & Peattie, 2012; Hall, 2014). The term *greenwashing* has been coined to identify sustainability communication without the underlying and necessary sustainability practices (Lyon & Maxwell, 2011; Peattie & Crane, 2005; Smith, 1998). Greenwashing refers to overplaying the environmental performance or benefits of their products with the objective of misleading the consumer (see Figure 1 and Delmas & Cuerel Burbano, 2011). This article contributes to the sustainability marketing literature by studying *greenhushing*, the phenomenon of under-communicating the sustainability practices in which a business engages (Martens, 2008). In this paper, we suggest that businesses use greenhushing to mitigate a potential disconnection between their perception of customer expectations and their own operational position concerning sustainability issues. This paper suggests that greenhushing is not only the result of low mastery and self-efficacy in the technical aspects of sustainability communication, but is also a conscious effort to reduce any dissonance that exists between the values of sustainability held by a business and its customers.

Most studies take an instrumental view of corporate social responsibility as a management tool to achieve business goals. This is informed by a pragmatic role of transmitting information relating to sustainability communication to achieve these goals. However, there is a deeper layer of meaning in that communication that is constitutive, as the communication itself represents sustainability problems as symbolic action (Bourdieu, 2012; Burke, 1966), i.e. as language that orients us to seeing things in a certain way. Situations are presented as meaningful by the way they bring certain elements to the fore, whilst pushing some to the back, and completely removing others. A further contribution to the literature from this article comes from understanding how organisations are shaped through their sustainability communication. The Communication Constitutes Organisations (CCO) approach redefines the sphere of study by stating that, by constituting and organising reality (Schoeneborn & Trittin, 2013), communication becomes central to the enactment of taking responsibility for being sustainable. Communication not only tells us about the values of organisations, such as what businesses think their responsibilities are and the public expectations they believe are placed on them, but more importantly, it has a role in creating such values.

Sustainability makes sense through communication because an aspect of the organisational discourse, that which constitutes it as an environmentally conscious organisation, reaches beyond the words it uses (its language) to encompass the practices in which the business is engaged and the organisational structures through which it operates. Our paper considers how the problem of sustainability is framed in communication, for it is through such discursive frames that society organises itself (see Foucault, 2002). How problems are framed establishes what counts as an acceptable solution; communication shapes the social interpretation of sustainability. To the best of our knowledge,

Figure 1. A typology of firms based on environmental performance and communication.
(Source: adapted from Delmas & Cuerel Burbano, 2011).

the perspective put forward in this paper diverges from all previous tourism and hospitality articles on sustainability communication, which have, predominantly, taken a more instrumental approach.

This study investigates the language of sustainability in public moralisation, in two contexts, communication towards sustainability experts via audited accounts compared with communication towards target customers via businesses' websites, contextualised through interviews with company owners/managers (see Kreps & Monin, 2011). Dissonant, and potentially contradictory, communicative practices tell us about the sustainability identity discourse of the businesses (Schoeneborn & Trittin, 2013). Consideration of how businesses write about sustainability can help us to understand the meaning and significance given to the term by the message producers, whilst also indicating what they expect, or consider acceptable, as a response. We will study the rhetoric of sustainability communication used by businesses to understand the discourse(s) in which the information producers are participating. This will be done through a comparison of how the businesses involved in this research have presented their sustainability communication both to their customers and within their Environmental Quality Mark (EQM) audit. The comparison will consider if they discuss environmental issues in both contexts and the language they use to do that. Such a lens allows us to study the purposeful and consequential efforts employed to influence the attitudes and behaviour of consumers through sustainability communication, as exemplified in businesses' websites, when compared to their audited sustainability reports. The focus is, therefore, on how sustainability communication both constitutes and articulates the identity of the business through the language used. The research employs interviews with the owners/managers of small rural tourism businesses.

The article is structured as follows. First, we review some practical approaches to understanding the persuasiveness of sustainability communications. Then, we reflect on the meaning behind the language used in communication as a tool to constitute organisations, which leads us to understand the organisations behind the communication. We then outline the two stage sequential mixed methods approach used in this study, comparing communication in two different contexts with different audiences: sustainability audits and the businesses' websites. The results evidence how these businesses underplay and realign their sustainability efforts to fit with what they perceive their customers' perceptions to be; we reflect on how this practice shapes the businesses' views of themselves and informs their motivations for acting sustainably as a consequence.

The practice of sustainability communication

Businesses use their websites, and other forms of communication, to persuade their target audiences to change their behaviour. The literature so far suggests that current sustainability messages have limited persuasiveness because businesses lack the technical competence to write more persuasively (Gössling & Buckley, 2016; Villarino & Font, 2015). The following paragraphs discuss four criteria of messages that have each been found to influence consumer behaviour, yet we argue there is a deeper level of analysis needed to draw conclusions on the reasons why businesses communicate in the way that they do. Our findings suggest that the willingness of an individual, or organisation, to communicate a message will reflect the communicator's interpretation of how the audience will perceive that message.

The first criterion for consideration is whether a business chooses to communicate sustainability *explicitly or implicitly*. It is the difference between a tourism business promoting local food because it reduces food miles (explicitly referring to sustainability), or because you can trust the origin of where it came from (where sustainability is implicit). Businesses will communicate explicitly either because it is believed to have a direct, and positive, bearing on the company image that they try to convey, or for the education of its customers; though the latter intention carries a high risk of appearing patronising. While earlier market research suggests there is a market for sustainable tourism products (Mintel, 2007), the communication/behaviour gap (Hall, 2014) suggests customers diffuse responsibility and select products based on selfish attributes (Hindley & Font, 2014). Tourists hold more positive, pro-environmental views of themselves than others: they adopt a mental strategy that allows them to partake in travel while diffusing responsibility and ignoring calls for behaviour change (Doran & Larsen, 2014). Because tourism is not thought of as a harmful activity by the public in general, businesses may prefer not to communicate messages that may raise negative concerns (Jones, 1991; Kong & Zhang, 2014). In addition, customers are generally cynical about sustainability messages (Brünn & Vrioni, 2001; Chan, 2013), which can dis-incentivise businesses from explicitly communicating their sustainability achievements. Therefore, businesses may choose to downplay their sustainability messages and make them implicit, while highlighting other benefits believed to be salient to the customer.

Second, where businesses choose to incorporate sustainability messages in their website content, they have a choice of using *affective or rational* language to describe their actions. Customers, particularly environmentally concerned individuals (do Paço & Reis, 2012), are more sceptical than many hotel managers think with regard to affective green hotel claims (Chan, 2013). Businesses feel confident presenting rational, factual evidence and third party endorsements (Lowry, Roberts, & Higbee, 2007) and this approach has been found in customer surveys to lead to more positive attitudes, and greater visit intention, than affective communication (Kim & Kim, 2014). This provides evidence that sustainability communication that is perceived to be objective can help address potential consumer scepticism (Alexander, 2010). Moreover, it is easier for a company to display its participation in a wider credible programme, such as a certification programme or awards, than to risk the affective impact of consumers misinterpreting a message. Yet, the results from opinion surveys are not translated into actual behaviour in quasi-experiments (Reiser & Simmons, 2005). For example, in a study of sustainability communication in holiday brochure design, all customers preferred messages with affective content, and only those customers with greater sustainability experience showed interest in rational messages (Wehrli et al., 2014). There is evidence that sustainable tourism is less virtuous and more hedonic than first anticipated, requiring businesses to emphasise the emotive aspects of experiential consumption (Malone, McCabe, & Smith, 2014).

Third, customers are more likely to respond positively to sustainability messages that refer to sustainability practices that they can *experience*. It is well known that how a message is framed impacts how customers respond to it (Tversky & Kahneman, 1981). Customers respond better to positively framed messages, where the gain for the customer is emphasised, and the benefits are made clear (Kim & Kim, 2014; Lee & Oh, 2014). Rather than giving the appearance of moralising, sustainability practices with a clearly articulated customer benefit are better framed as enhancing quality and the customer experience (Kreps & Monin, 2011; Malone et al., 2014). For example, a message that suggests customers should use the bus to enjoy better views of the landscape on their days out is positively framed, has an experiential benefit and hence is written for customers with lower environmental affect; while an alternative message that suggests customers should use the bus because otherwise their car will pollute the environment is negatively framed, does not emphasise a customer benefit and is therefore written for consumers with a high environmental affect. Customers with higher environmental affect have been shown to respond better to messages that convey an altruistic environmental benefit, although the majority of customers, with lower environmental affect, respond better when the added value is more personal (Grimmer & Woolley, 2014).

Our fourth and final criteria relates to the *active/passive* dimension of sustainability messages. Cialdini and Goldstein (2004) found that where a message producer believes a customer will gain a positive experience from participation, the message will support customer empowerment to actively choose to participate. In contrast, if it is thought that the customer will not gain a positive experience from participation, the business may communicate passively (by showing the actions taken *on behalf of* the customer). Fundamentally, as holidaymaking is not perceived as causing environmental harm (Kong & Zhang, 2014), a company is less likely to make salient aspects of sustainability that reduce customer enjoyment, or create a feeling of moral guilt, nor to exacerbate these by asking the customer to participate. For example, a restaurant may communicate the sourcing of its food as organic or local because this does not require customers to change their behaviour, but may choose not to add the carbon footprint of their different dishes because it arguably forces customers into a moral dilemma without adding to the customer experience. Prothero, McDonagh, and Dobscha (2010) argued that the public perception of tourism's neutral impact is an aspect of a dominant social paradigm that places humanity in a dominant position over nature. However, recent initiatives, they argue, are increasing awareness of the negative implications of the dominant social paradigm. With a growing population of people seeking greener tourism, there may be increased pressure to articulate the active dimension in sustainability messages. Whilst we were not able to find any research that has investigated that possible tension within small businesses, the depoliticisation of environmental responsibility, i.e. construing environmental concern as an individualised responsibility rather than a corporate or state responsibility, has been explored by Maniates (2001) and by Connolly and Prothero (2008). These studies examined green aware consumers and their relevance for understanding sustainability messages in the context of this study is unclear.

Sustainability communication constitutes the organisation

In completing this study, we could have used other criteria beyond the four dichotomies discussed above (explicit vs. implicit, affective vs. rational, high vs. low experience and active vs. passive). However, we believe these are sufficient, since our intention here is not to examine the copy writing skills of organisations, but to consider what these communication practices tell us about the values of the businesses themselves, by characterising the link between message producers and we can interpret that relationship as *structurational*; that is to say, messages are not simply the bearers of information to be communicated, they also reflect how its producer thinks the receiver will perceive them. To use Goffman's terms (1990, 2005), such reflexive behaviour frames the communication by placing certain information in the *front region*, i.e. that area where the message producer (as its *performer*) foregrounds that which they feel is most salient to the recipient. For example, message producers who believe it is a lack of sustainability awareness that limits behaviour change may simply increase the amount of information their communications contain.

As a consequence, these message producers need not necessarily communicate an attitude that is in line with their own behaviour; they are more likely to communicate messages that they believe are the ones that will present them in the best light to the recipient. With regard to messages around environmental concerns, there is extensive evidence for a gap between communicated attitude and actual behaviour (Kollmuss & Agyeman, 2002). There are, therefore, solid grounds for arguing that a study of the sustainability language would be of value. The language used by an organisation has a rhetorical impact; it frames an interpretation of how the organisation is connected to the world. The language used contributes to the construction of the reader's concept of that organisation by attributing a range of meanings to that organisation.

All business communication has a rhetorical purpose, then, it tells us something about the way a company chooses to portray itself. The language used in sustainability communication is discursively reflexive; that is, it reveals how the business construes the values of its anticipated message receiver through the way it attempts to frame that recipient's perception of the business. It is in that space, opened up by the reflexivity of the communication between the message producer and message consumer, that the question of greenwashing and greenhushing emerges. According to Alexander (2010), the main purpose of political and public environmental language is distortion, not communication, and the role of the environmentally conscious critical linguist is to understand the misrepresentation of language: most commonly understood as *greenwashing*. The converse, *greenhushing*, has not been investigated.

Alexander's arguments focus on how green consumers act in a dominant social paradigm that frames environmentally conscious consumption as the wise use of natural resources for economic growth, achieved through free markets (Kilbourne, 2004). According to Alexander (2010), the discourse of market economics is appropriating, and narrowly framing, the discourse of sustainability. Within the discourse of the free market, the rhetoric of green consumerism argues that purchasing green products can help the planet. This individuated consumer identity creates the impression that consumers are empowered to change society with their wallets (Cox, 2012; Smith, 1998). Such discourse has led scholars to develop models and theories, under an umbrella of "sustainable development", in which ecological and environmental factors are understood to be crucial to overall socio-economic progress (Haque, 2000). Sustainability discourse thus involves communication that interlinks a dominant economic framework with environmental and social issues. While an exploration of three strands of that discourse (economy, environment and society) can help to orientate tourism development towards more sustainable approaches, the dominant paradigm in the discourse of sustainable tourism development is still focused on the economic benefits over those to society and the environment, and that distortion obscures the necessity of exploring, in more depth, discourses of sustainability (Elgammal & Jones, 2007; Haque, 2000; Reed, 2013).

In keeping with Alexander's analysis, if tourism businesses are seeking to target green consumers, we would expect them to constitute themselves through a sustainability discourse. A business that felt comfortable with their sustainability practices would show little difference in the way they communicate those practices in voluntary sustainability audits and the messages they produce for their customers. If the businesses are communicating more to customers than they are delivering in practice, then it can be argued they are engaging in a practice of greenwashing. However, if it is found that they are communicating less, then it would suggest they are practicing some form of greenhushing. If businesses are engaging in more sustainability practices than they use to constitute themselves through their customer facing communication, it does raise questions concerning what other forms of discourse they are using to constitute themselves.

Methodology

We restate that the purpose of this study is to understand the relation between the sustainability practices of tourism businesses and their customer facing communication. The rationale for doing this is to better understand how the businesses constitute their identities through communication. We used a mixed methods sequential design with four interrelated stages: (1) Scope definition: refining the scope to identify suitable data from a sustainability audit that could be used in the second stage; (2) Data coding: coding and statistical analysis of text data from the audit and website to identify patterns of convergence or divergence in the discourses employed; (3) Language assessment: observation of the frequency, and common association, of words used during interviews; (4) Discourse analysis: an analysis of the interviews held with business owners/managers. The first two stages resemble previous research on greenwashing that compares facts (Bonilla, Font, & Pacheco, 2014; Clarkson, Li, Richardson, & Vasvari, 2008), while the latter two stages follow an interpretative approach common in communication (Alexander, 2010; Baxter & Babbie, 2004). This combination of methods may feel uneasy to some researchers, as only 12% (or 56) of the 468 sustainable tourism articles published in JOST over 10 years have used mixed methods and, of those, only 10 articles adopted an equivalent weighting between the quantitative and qualitative parts (Molina-Azorín & Font, 2016).

Our research took place in the Peak District, which was the first national park to be designated in England in 1951 and covers 1437 sq. kilometres. The 2014 data show the Peak District to be the third most visited national park in England, with 8.75 million visitors per year, 16% of which are overnight visitors (National Parks UK, 2015; PDNPA, 2014). There is a long tradition of tourism business networks established for the purpose of public–private partnerships in the Peak District National Park, although many businesses perceive the relation between the Park Authority and themselves as ineffective (Saxena, 2005). As part of efforts to get businesses to take more ownership for the protection of the park, in 2001, the Peak District National Park Authority established a certification programme called the EQM. This was initially subsidised by the park authority but, due to the economic recession cutting park budgets, is now operated under license by a team of qualified and experienced environmental auditors.

Our sampling frame is the 31 accommodation businesses in the Peak District National Park certified by EQM in 2014. The number of certified businesses was much greater when the National Park Authority subsidised certification and provided additional learning benefits, but, since the government budget cuts, the certification process is now paid for by the award holders, and the number of participating businesses has reduced. The businesses that are still accredited generally fall under the group that Saxena (2005) would have classified as enthusiasts or activists, where EQM membership is part of their identity or there is a loyalty to the EQM staff for the help they have provided. These businesses are all small, rural tourism businesses, often farm diversifications offering bed and breakfast or self-catering cottages and, less often, full hotel services. Examples of businesses interviewed include Wheeldon Trees Farm (nine self-catering cottages sleeping 30 people in total), Fernyford Barn (converted barn in a working farm sleeping four), Hoe Grange Holidays (four 2-bedroomed cabins specialising in wheelchair access), the fine dining country hotel Fischer's Baslow Hall and the 23 bedroom, 4 star Losehill House Hotel.

In order to analyse the discourse of actual sustainability practices undertaken, we used the EQM audit trail of these 31 businesses. To apply for EQM status, the businesses are required to complete an online form that requires them to outline their practices, in their own words, for a range of assessment criteria. Those criteria include indicators of explicit environmental practice (e.g. How do you manage your energy, water, waste and so forth?) but with a customer journey angle, enabling the businesses to consider each step with respect to their customer engagement. Examples include "In your marketing and promotional activities, how do you show potential customers and visitors what you are doing and how the Peak District is special?", "How do you show customers what you are doing to reduce your environmental impact?" and "How do you reduce the negative impact of your cleaning processes? How does the customer know?" It is important to note that in the EQM audit itself there is an emphasis on how sustainability actions are communicated to customers; this is less common in other certification programmes, and a primary reason why this research has chosen to study EQM certified businesses. The certification process is robust: qualified auditors review the application, conduct a verification visit and write a report. The application is then assessed by an independent Award Panel, who judge if the business meets the requirements of the EQM scheme. We, therefore, take the statements provided in the audits to be an accurate representation of what the 31 businesses do, to the extent that any audit can ensure this.

We tabulated 1389 statements from the 31 sustainability audits of these businesses (average 45 statements per business, ranging from 21 to 95). Those statements were then coded, using a modified coding system previously used in categorising corporate social reports (Bonilla et al., 2014; Clarkson et al., 2008), that considered (1) the relevance of the statement to the criteria; (2) whether the action taken was soft or hard (which refers to how easy it is to make a claim without much effort); (3) whether the actions taken were environmental, social and/or economic (multiple responses being allowed) and (4) whether the actions would be altruistic (benefiting the society and the environment), or would have benefits for the business, and/or the customer (again with multiple responses permitted). We chose to use dichotomous variables to simplify the analysis, except for the variable that tested how relevant the sustainability practice reported was to the audit criteria, where we felt greater level of scrutiny was needed and used a 0 to 5 scoring system. So, for example, a business providing not only extensive detail but also meaningful actions, in response to the question posed, would get a high score. One business scored 5 out of 5 in sustainability marketing by stating that (1) we have a Green Policy on our website and it mentions local food purchasing and our support of Friends of the Peak District; (2) our leaflet is printed on recycled paper and has the EQM logo on; (3) we advertise on www.responsibletravel.com and www.greentraveller.com; (4) we have a section on our website about getting to us by public transport and (5) we offer a 5% discount plus a complimentary breakfast basket to guests arriving without a car, and we offer to refund any bus travel on our local 442 bus. A different business scored 2 out of 5 for responding: (1) we have an environmental policy on the cottage website; (2) leaflets and brochures show the EQM logo and we are pleased to promote this verbally and (3) we promote leaving the vehicle and using local shops and pubs by walking from the door. We checked for cross-coder reliability by coding some entries together, then coding independently and checking cross-coder agreement; also by having regular meetings to check flagged statements.

Our analysis continued by checking whether the statements on the audit were communicated on the websites of these 31 businesses. Our analysis focused on the articulation of discourse through text. Whilst we are fully aware of the semiotic importance of visual and non-textual media, particular for website marketing, it was felt that the inclusion of too many paralinguistic features would make the analysis too large for a single journal article. However, eight separate checks were included as follows. We checked on the location of sustainability messages to see (1) whether they were on the homepage or, if not, how many clicks it took to reach them; and (2) if those messages were located on a dedicated sustainability page. We also checked for consistency between messages in the audit and website for (3) soft or hard sustainability claims (referring to how easy these are to claim without actual evidence of practising); and (4) whether their emphasis was environmental, social and/or economic emphasis. We coded web messages using four persuasiveness criteria used by Villarino and Font (2015) (as outlined earlier in the literature review) and, in doing this, we checked if the messages were (5) explicit or implicit in speaking about sustainability; (6) using affective or rational language to justify their actions; (7) outlining sustainability actions conducive to be experienced by customers or not and (8) allowing customers to actively or passively participate in these sustainability actions.

In order to triangulate any findings from the audit and web texts analysis, we conducted a series of semi-structured interviews. Out of 31 businesses, 27 businesses were contacted; 11 businesses accepted, from which we scheduled 8 interviews. Purposive sampling meant we selected businesses with different levels of thoroughness in their sustainability audits. Each interview lasted 75–90 minutes and was recorded, transcribed and analysed for evidence of articulating sustainability messages, to better assess the relationship between sustainability practices and communications (Miles & Huberman, 1994). The discourse analysis in this paper went from a general understanding of the written data to understanding the scope of the underlying motivation behind the way companies communicate sustainability (Taylor & Bogdan, 1998). We reviewed the transcripts a number of times, searching for construct ideas and patterns, then focused on bridging the transcripts with the reduced early stage of quantitative data analysis in order to come up with more robust codes. While previous literature has highlighted the use of codes and categories as a fundamental part of undertaking discourse analysis, such discussions have tended to focus on qualitative data; rather than a mix of qualitative and quantitative data. The challenge was to develop higher level codes that bridged qualitative and quantitative data; moving from a descriptive to an interpretive level of data analysis (Punch, 2013). Categories were developed that could help us make sense of the data and facilitate the analytical thinking of the researcher (Maxwell, 2012).

Finally, the language used by those businesses that participated in the interviews was compared with that used in their completion of the EQM audit. Pustejovsky, Anick, and Bergler (1993) suggest word choice (sometimes referred to as *lexical preference*) in communication plays an important role in how the communicator constructs their identity for a given audience. Bybee and Hopper (2001) and Yaeger-Dror, Granadillo, Takano, and Hall-Lew (2010) have indicated that it is important to consider how language is used because it provides an insight into the world view of the language user. Wengao (2009) and Hyland (2010) go further and argue that such lexical preferences are also indicative of the users' sense of self-identity.

Results and discussion

We find ample evidence of reflexive behaviour in the audit, website and interview data; this suggests that, when it comes to sustainability practices, the businesses are doing more than they are communicating to their customers. Adopting a CCO approach suggests that one aspect of how these businesses are constituted is through the different framing of their communications around issues of sustainability; the discourse(s) in which they are participating being indicated by what the owners/

managers of those businesses choose to put into the front region, i.e. foregrounding what they construe as most salient to the message recipient. We first analyse how these businesses communicate their sustainability practices to legitimise their clients' rights as consumers, which in turn allows us to consider how the organisations themselves are constituted through communicating their organisational identity.

These businesses legitimise that customers consume the landscape through the sustainability actions the businesses takes on their behalf, generally without being noticed by their customers. A business's environmental language aims to provide reassurance to its clients (Alexander, 2010) with the emphasis being on how the business works *in the background* to maintain the tourists' playground. In doing so, the business legitimises the tourists' use of the resource through a language of shared values, i.e. an appreciation of the value of nature. This is evidenced by (1) the fact that only 30% of sustainability practices found in the audits are communicated in the websites; (2) the different tone of communication between the audits and the websites and (3) the way these businesses explain their behaviour in the interviews, as outlined below.

The businesses select which messages to communicate according to their perception of the audience's expectations of them. We find that of the 1389 statements made by the 31 businesses in their sustainability audits (which were assessed for accuracy by auditors and therefore reliable), only 407 were communicated in their websites. The audited statements were primarily altruistic (77%), showing concern for the National Park and society at large, but also showed benefit to the business itself (68%) through eco-efficiencies and competitive advantages; the statements showed less concern for customer benefits (50%). In contrast, the messages displayed in their websites had a drop of 7% in altruism, but an increase of 4% in business benefits and, most significantly, a 15% increase in customer benefits. DePoe (1991, in Cox, 2012) suggests that there are three basic frames for green product advertising, these use nature as (1) a backdrop, i.e. promoting consumption in a natural setting; (2) a product, i.e. promoting the consumption of nature and (3) an outcome, i.e. communicating the benefits to nature as a result of the business's actions. In our inquiry, we found evidence of all three frames, although nature as an outcome was far less evident in the websites than in the audits. The fact that businesses wrote messages based on customers' expectations shows a clear understanding of how to reframe the benefits of a message and how to select messages according to their relevance, with the outcome being moral framing in the altruistic benefits and pragmatic framing in both the business and customer benefits (Kreps & Monin, 2011). We exemplify this with examples from their websites. The following is an example of a message that carries benefits for society and/or the environment (enhancing the space) and the customer (enjoying the improved space):

> By improving the exterior of our property we have helped to improve the look of the village and having started a holiday cottage business, we contribute to the local economy of Litton, as our guests spend considerable sums in the local shops and pub.

This comes across differently to the following example of a message that carries benefits for society and/or the environment (benefits the EQM members through networking and sharing knowledge) and the business (receives new ideas):

> We network with other EQM businesses at EQM events and via email to find out the best suppliers for our business.

Equally, this final example carries benefits specifically for the business:

> We ask for guests' comments and ideas on how we could improve our green credentials.

The practice of tailoring messages to perceived audience needs is evident from the analysis of the communication persuasiveness of website messages. Much of the text is explicit about sustainability practices (67%), for example, the statement "We provide you with eco washing up liquids, etc". shows the business cares about the environment because the "eco" prefix was used but the initiative does not compromise on the customer experience. There are, however, many other examples of implicit text that offer information attractive to all customers regardless of how environmentally conscious they are, for example, "Walks for all abilities are accessible directly from the front door of the cottages"; in this example, the implicit message is to reduce pollution from using transportation.

Most of the text is written in affective language (78%) such as "We would like to support visitors choosing to use public transport as much as possible", rather than rational language (22%) such as "Most of the cleaning materials are bought in bulk once every three months" and "Outside lights are fitted with infrared sensors". The emphasis on the website is on promoting the experiential benefits (86%), for example, "We use home produced and locally sourced products where possible" where arguably customers gain a personal experience of the destination visited, with fewer cases of non-experiential messages such as "…in keeping with our efforts to reduce our carbon footprint as much as possible", which the client is unlikely to experience. In general, the messages promote active engagement on the part of the clients (85%), for example, "Come and enjoy the best of British design from locally made furniture to English fine furnishings". Where framing messages with a more personal tone and emphasising customer benefit is evident, this suggests that the businesses are targeting individuals with lower environmental affect (Grimmer & Woolley, 2014) because they do not wish to be constituted as preaching to their customers (Kim & Kim, 2014; Stanford, 2014).

The composition of the sustainability messages in the audits and websites is also very different, and suggests that the businesses expect their customers to be seeking to engage with pristine nature. As part of complying with an idealised view of rurality, the businesses remove human agency from their messages, which alters the balance of their triple bottom line. The EQM audits provide the opportunity for open ended answers regarding how the business meets different generic sustainability requirements, without leading for a particular aspect of the triple bottom line. In the audits, the businesses refer to more social actions (68%) than environmental (57%), in contrast to their websites where activities with an environmental focus were communicated 17% more often, but social actions were communicated 12% less often. In addition, 55% of the actions with a benefit to the customer, reported in the audit, had an environmental focus vs. the 44% that did not have a customer benefit, and yet only 47% of actions written as benefiting customers had a social content vs. 57% that did not.

The rhetoric's constitutive role for EQM businesses shows how the environment is framed positively not negatively, i.e. not as a problem. We find the businesses distance themselves, and shelter their customers, from the negative externalities of the tourists' enjoyment. Deletion of agency, by using a generalised agent, is a well-rehearsed technique to diffuse responsibility (Alexander, 2010). Consequently, implicit messages couched sustainability practices in broader quality arguments, portraying it as an aspect of normality; this was most clearly seen in the language used in expressing active vs. passive messages. The active messages, which are more direct, compel the customer to do something (O'Keefe, 2002), and are positively framed as an immediate benefit to the destination (e.g. recycling to keep the Peak District clean). Passive messages, however, are used to communicate the less palatable sustainability requirements, i.e. those hindering the customer experience such as "environmentally friendly cleaning products are used" which the interviewees mentioned customers believe clean less thoroughly. These passive messages obfuscate responsibility by deleting the agent (Alexander, 2010) and reducing the likelihood of the customer feeling guilt (Kong & Zhang, 2014).

The purposeful positive framing of sustainability messages is best exemplified in messages pertaining to the carbon footprint of transport or the sourcing of building materials, where such factors cause a high negative impact but are necessary. During one of the interviews, a business stated that because "…our guests are paying a lot of money, we cannot restrict their stay by asking them to practice sustainability. Carbon footprint is one example of the things that we do not communicate", which shows that when sustainability is inconvenient, businesses tended to deflect attention and downplay real issues (Alexander, 2010). For example, despite most of the businesses in this study being farm diversifications, only one of them speaks of the environmental impacts of methane from cow farming (using humour and drawings in an effort to make the issue more accessible). Humour is often used to communicate sustainability messages when an organisation feels uncomfortable about how a message could be received. It is particularly meaningful that none of the businesses demonstrate on their website, or mentioned during their interviews, that they purposefully aim to attract domestic tourists in order to reduce the potential carbon footprint they cause. Conversely, some interviewees suggested that attracting international customers is a sign of pride in the quality of their business. The fact that they do not place a high value on this important factor is because of perceived causal distance, i.e. they do not feel that the impacts of transport to the destination are attributable to them (Jones, 1991; Kreps & Monin, 2011), in the same way that they consider it would be inconvenient to acknowledge certain impacts, where these might make their customers feel uncomfortable.

Our findings show that the businesses normalise sustainability practices to remove customer guilt. Normalisation enables them to construct a narrative of agency, causality and responsibility that is reassuring (Fairclough, 1992). 31% of businesses' sustainability messages are communicated within specific sustainability pages on their websites and these are more explicit, rational, non-experiential and focused on altruistic benefits than their other messages. The 69% of messages found elsewhere in their websites are more implicit, emotional, experiential and customer focused, suggesting a normalisation of green messages and integration into the broader communications that constitute the organisation (Grant, 2007; Schoeneborn & Trittin, 2013). As such, it is consistent with other forms of describing quality; we do not expect to find separate tabs for all quality marks, rather they are suggested by their integration throughout the organisation's website. By normalising, the business is allowed to use euphemisms in relation to the environment and therefore avoid having to moralise (Tenbrunsel & Messick, 2004). Businesses present an idealised view of rurality that avoids conflict for the customer (Urry, 1990); their intention is to make green look normal and showing rurality simply as an alternative to daily, urban life. This is notably different to greenwashing, which suggests that normal business practices are done specifically for sustainability reasons (Grant, 2007).

Along with the normalisation, we find that businesses increase the salience of positive actions to articulate sustainability practices. For example, "local" sourcing, which is used to refer to the sourcing of supplies, labour and other resources, appears 367 times in the audit statements, whereas the adjectives environment, social or economic, collectively, appear just 63 times. A further example is discernible in the lack of references to climate change in all three sources — the audits, the websites and the interviews. There is only one explicit entry in the audit statements "...our booking form invites guests to donate to climate change". Only one of the 31 businesses refers to climate change on their website, while others suggest car free holidays or days out without explicit reference to carbon emissions or climate change. The effort that has gone into providing car free holidays is in some cases remarkable — offering equipment for pets and babies, a food store, breakfast baskets, electric bikes, useful information on things to do from the doorstep and, of course, details on how to get to the site by public transport, all of which shows a real commitment to sustainability. Evidence from the interviews and the websites shows no mention of climate change or global warming. By framing sustainability as a normalised local practice, the business is able to frame potential areas of customer guilt as a positive message; constituting the organisation as one that offers solutions rather than raises problems. Consequently, walking and recycling appear regularly without mention of the environmental contribution these make; this is in keeping with previous evidence that customers prefer positively framed (Lee & Oh, 2014), appealing sustainability messages (Wehrli et al., 2014).

In addition, we find that businesses tend to communicate soft, palatable actions that do not challenge the presentation of an idealised rurality to customers. This is evident in the different tones used in the audit statements and the communications when describing actions. For example, we find that actions reported as soft (easy to achieve) in the EQM reports are communicated 12% more often on the website than in the reports. The hard actions reported in the EQM are data-driven facts of interest to an environmental auditor (e.g. the results of a biodiversity survey or efficiency of solar panels), whereas the soft actions are often vague statements about caring for the countryside. Only in a few cases do we see examples of soft actions in the EQM reports (such as the sourcing of food from local suppliers "whenever possible") also being marketed on the businesses' websites as hard, concrete actions, for example, dedicating space to "our local food heroes", naming suppliers and praising the quality of their produce. The examples occur when the hard evidence provides customer reassurance and, therefore, the practice communicates a positive customer experience.

Messages of holidays as escapism are reinforced on the websites and in the interviews; the emphasis is placed on customers creating social bonds to remove a sense of misplacement. As gatekeepers of the tourism experience, the businesses comply with the dominant social paradigm expectation that the countryside is a playground. We see the altruistic aspects of sustainability played down and the quality aspects highlighted. So, for example, in messages that promote walks from the accommodation's doorstep, both an altruistic (reduction in CO_2) and a consumer (convenience) benefit are emphasised, although, the EQM reports tend to focus on the former and the websites on the latter. Some of the businesses suggest that their guests are not concerned about how green their holiday is. For example, one business declares "I am happy to try new sustainability practices but not happy to publish it in my website, because not many people try to look for green holidays." Given that perspective, it is unsurprising that some organisations feel it is unnecessary to communicate sustainability practices. Other interviewees suggested that storytelling is a better fit for the ethos of their sustainability communication; it is seen as more coherent with a construal of holidays as an escape.

In summary, we find that the sustainability communication of these businesses reflects current society values (Holbrook, 1987), as they choose to not communicate many of their more onerous practices in fear that this will be met with disapproval, for holidaymakers have a sense of entitlement and lack the financial incentives to save resources (Miller, Rathouse, Scarles, Holmes, & Tribe, 2010). Instead, the businesses use choice architecture and nudging (Hall, 2014), to provide more sustainable consumption opportunities as normal (Grant, 2007) within the context of the meaning of rural holidays. Environmentally friendly practices take place in the background, which guarantees a less negative impact without having to bother the guests, while communication is reserved to "choice edited", positively perceived actions such as the selection of local suppliers to reinforce breakfast quality and the promotion of walks from the doorstep as a convenience.

We interpret these findings by suggesting that the majority of businesses interviewed are using EQM as a symbolic legitimacy boundary, a form of belonging that provides reassurance that their presence in the landscape, and local society, is justifiable. Many businesses generate narratives around their connection to the locality over specific sustainability actions and corporate responsibility initiatives. We find evidence in keeping with the corporate social disclosure literature that suggests that moral intensity and business salience increase the pressure to legitimise (Al-Tuwaijri, Christensen, & Hughes, 2004; Deegan, 2002; Jones, 1991). While we cannot discern a statistical difference between sustainability messages and the size or age of the business, the connection between communicating sustainability actions and organisational identity is clearly discernible for interviewees who are not originally from the Peak District, for whom EQM serves as a mark that they are doing their bit to look after the location. One business stated "We were living in the city before moving here. We go to courses and workshops to learn about sustainability. We are consistent in doing things according to the EQM guidelines...we do our best to help the local community." Some business owners/ managers still refer to themselves as "non-local" even when they have spent decades in the area.

Further evidence of reporting that arises from business salience comes from the connection between accommodation category and the level of sustainability communication: five star businesses communicate 40% of their actions, four star businesses 27% and three star only 12%. The gap between audited and communicated practices can act as an indicator of how the organisation constitutes its identity through communication. Higher accommodation category businesses, and those owner/managers who are incomers to the locality, seem more comfortable with articulating their identity as custodians of place, while other businesses and owner/managers seem more inclined to identify themselves as of the place, separating out their practice from what they communicate. Higher accommodation category businesses, in particular, report sustainability actions that suggest they are trying to make a difference to their local fabric. The actions communicated by higher category businesses in the interviews were often framed as making a contribution to local social well-being, not simply in environmental or economic terms. Interviewees, for example, spoke of promoting local areas and walks (Businesses 2 and 4), employing local staff (Businesses 3 and 6), sourcing milk from local suppliers (Business 2), encouraging customers to try locally produced and distributed food, value it (Business 7) and, though it may be more expensive, buy it (Business 4).

Some interviewed owners/managers, particularly those with businesses in the lower accommodation categories, suggest that they use the EQM mark purely as a signifier of their organisational identity, i.e. to reduce the dissonance between their values and the need to be commercial; in these cases, having the EQM accreditation is more for the business than for the customers. This finding is consistent with Kreps and Monin (2011) who argue that presenting sustainability actions as an essentially altruistic public good can project an image of lower organisational competence, reduce likability by sounding worthy, and increase vulnerability to seeming hypocritical. This is a point echoed by some interviewees who expressed their concerns around customers perceiving a trade-off between quality and sustainability. Reiser and Simmons (2005) also found in their research that consumers saw eco-labelling information of tourism services as irrelevant and ignored an entire section of a marketing display in a tourist office. They concluded that seeking environmentally friendly information is affective and not cognitive. In our study, while the businesses show interest in practising sustainability, there is a suggestion that some of them sense an incompatibility between identifying themselves as a quality business and as an overtly green one. An example of that perspective was expressed by the owner of Business 2, who argues that "Customers do not bother about the environment when they are in a holiday ...'5-stars' is better than 'green'; 'quality' is better than 'eco'... no one is looking at it." Business 4 supports Business 2's position by asserting "We cannot communicate much about sustainability practices because that might put guests off" and others agree that a heavy environmental message on their website would deter customers. Generally, the businesses told us they find little economic gain from communicating sustainability, which in turn means that they choose to communicate far less than they actually do. Furthermore, what they do communicate is done for their own, rather than their customers' satisfaction as they believe customers do not pay attention to it anyway.

Conclusions

The businesses under investigation not only do more than they state they are doing but they also describe what they do differently in different contexts. This finding resulted from a review of 31 sustainability certified business, using information obtained from completed EQM audits and from the websites of the businesses as source data. We find that only 30% of sustainability practices are communicated in the websites, with a greater consumer focus than in the audits but still with an altruistic and business benefit. Sustainability messages are primarily explicit, written in affective language and promote experiential benefits and active participation of the customers. The messages show an idealised view of rurality that removes human agency and diffuses responsibility, while playing down unpalatable aspects and providing reassurance to customers by emphasising the positive aspects of sustainability to support the sense of escapism from life's daily pressures. Comparing the two contexts of source data (one representing what the businesses state they do in an audit and the other being a forum through which those same businesses talk about what they do to their customers) offers us an opportunity to explore the possibility of greenhushing.

This article helps us to see how the communication of sustainability plays a part in defining organisational identity. How these businesses portray the type of product they offer explains how they represent their social identity in their websites. Following the logic of CCO, their communication also affects how these same businesses see themselves and how they influence their own perception of success and self-worth. The reasons for moral muteness have been explained for individuals in large firms as resulting from social pressures (Jones, 1991). This article suggests that the manner of communicating sustainability practices in the two contexts constitutes the organisation from the values of their owner/manager and what they perceive their customers' expectations of the organisation to be. We, therefore, find evidence that greenhushing is a combination of moral silence, by not talking about 70% of their actions, and moral muteness, defined as privately justifying acting primarily on moral grounds yet publicly taking a pragmatic approach (Kreps & Monin, 2011). Both aspects of greenhushing are influenced by the low moral intensity of tourism, i.e. that the owners/managers are less likely to moralise in relation to issues their target audience do not already see as subject to moral scrutiny (Jones, 1991).

We, therefore, argue that both greenwashing and greenhushing share the similarity of realigning business practices to our social norms. Greenhushing also contributes to the advertising industry's attempts to manipulate society's values towards consumerism through conspicuous consumption (Pollay & Gallagher, 1990), only, in this case, it is by playing down the details of what the business does to be sustainable to a level that the customer finds acceptable to enjoy their holiday. Green-washing, on the other hand, attempts to put the customer at ease by pretending that the business has taken care of potential customer concerns. Both are forms of green advertising that "as a market-ing strategy, falls within the dominant social paradigm because its primary goal is to sell more prod-ucts without regard for the limits to growth theses while shrouding itself in the cloak of social responsibility" (Kilbourne, 2004, p. 201).

The positive frame (sustainability = more enjoyment) used amongst our 31 businesses confirms Kilbourne's finding, but how these businesses communicate sustainability tells us about their values and, equally, the choices they make when communicating sustainability shape their own sense of identity and self-worth. A CCO approach helps us reframe the origin of greenhushing into one that asks how a business constitutes itself through its communications. We find that tourism businesses with sustainability values resent having to market themselves based on those values (Ateljevic & Doorne, 2000; Font, Garay, & Jones, 2014; Sampaio, Thomas, & Font, 2012). The businesses accept, but are disappointed by, the fact that they cannot communicate more of what they do and they would like their communication to show the benefits to society of their practices and not only be written for "marketing" purposes. There is a sense of wishing that customers would have a similar level of commitment to the Peak District as they themselves do and they display resentment that sus-tainability's value is reduced to having only a marketing function. They acknowledge how little they can change their customers' behaviour and how this affects their own sense of achievement in being sustainable. When these businesses choose to communicate, they prefer to state what they do, and their personal reasons for doing it, rather than engage in what they consider to be sales gimmicks. The need to market their businesses reminds them of the fact that consumers do not care about the environment as much as they do, which makes them feel uneasy about their need to make a living from clients that do not share the same values.

This article provides a first entry into a wider, more encompassing, discourse for sustainability communications, going beyond earlier technical tests on the actual persuasiveness of messages (Villarino & Font, 2015). We are aware of the fact that this study only partly explains how a business promotes its products or services, and that communication in other forms and channels should be researched. A website is only one marketing point and further communication may be available in print, on site or verbally. Further research is also needed to understand the process of, and choices behind, creating sustainability messages and both how they reflect the values of the organisation as well as how the reaction of the customers to such information shapes the values of the organisation. We are aware that the current literature suggesting that large firms practice greenwashing and small dedicated firms practice greenhushing is too crude, and a better understanding of greenhushing across cultures and organisation types is needed. Finally, it is worth studying whether or not green-hushing results from the businesses considering sustainability practices as common and therefore not worthy of communication (Lynes & Andrachuk, 2008).

In the meantime, the lessons learned through this research will inform our team's efforts to train businesses to write more sustainability messages and to make them more compelling by better understanding the links between the messages and the people behind them. The underlying approach behind most sustainability management and marketing training is a commercial business case that does not represent how all businesses choose to engage in sustainability (Font, Garay, &

Jones, 2016). Through this study, we understand that our businesses seek both reassurance that there are customers with the same values as themselves and need help in writing copy that will attract them, so that they can regain enjoyment in sharing the landscape with likeminded individuals and be the custodians of their national park.

Disclosure statement

No potential conflict of interest was reported by the authors.

References

Al-Tuwaijri, S.A., Christensen, T.E., & Hughes, K. (2004). The relations among environmental disclosure, environmental performance, and economic performance: A simultaneous equations approach. *Accounting, Organizations and Society, 29*(5–6), 447–471.

Alexander, R. (2010). *Framing discourse on the environment: A critical discourse approach.* London: Routledge.

Ateljevic, J., & Doorne, S. (2000). Staying within the fence: Lifestyle entrepreneurship in tourism. *Journal of Sustainable Tourism, 8*(5), 378–392.

Baxter, L., & Babbie, E. (2004). *The basics of communication research.* Belmont, CA: Thomson Wadsforth.

Belz, F.M., & Peattie, K. (2012). *Sustainability marketing: a global perspective* (2nd ed.). Chichester: John Wiley and Sons.

Bonilla, M.J., Font, X., & Pacheco, R. (2014). Corporate sustainability reporting index and baseline data for the cruise industry *Tourism Management, 44*, 149–160.

Bourdieu, P. (2012). *Language and symbolic power.* Cambridge: Polity.

Brùnn, P.S., & Vrioni, A.B. (2001). Corporate social responsibility and cause-related marketing: An overview. *International Journal of Advertising, 20*(2), 207–222.

Burke, K. (1966). *Language as symbolic action: Essays on life, literature, and method.* Berkeley, CA: University of California Press.

Bybee, J.L., & Hopper, P.J. (2001). Introduction to frequency and the emergence of linguistic structure. In J.L. Bybee & P.J. Hopper (Eds.), *Frequency and the emergence of linguistic structure* (pp. 1–24). Amsterdam: John Benjamins.

Chan, E. (2013). Gap analysis of green hotel marketing. *International Journal of Contemporary Hospitality Management, 25* (7), 1017–1048.

Cialdini, R.B., & Goldstein, N.J. (2004). Social influence: Compliance and conformity. *Annual Review of Psychology, 55*, 591–621.

Clarkson, P.M., Li, Y., Richardson, G.D., & Vasvari, F.P. (2008). Revisiting the relation between environmental performance and environmental disclosure: An empirical analysis. *Accounting, Organizations and Society, 33*(4–5), 303–327.

Connolly, J., & Prothero, A. (2008). Green consumption life-politics, risk and contradictions. *Journal of Consumer Culture, 8*(1), 117–145.

Cox, R. (2012). *Environmental communication and the public sphere.* Thousand Oaks, CA: Sage.

Deegan, C. (2002). Introduction: The legitimising effect of social and environmental disclosures—a theoretical foundation. *Accounting, Auditing & Accountability Journal, 15*(3), 282–311.

Delmas, M.A., & Cuerel Burbano, V. (2011). The drivers of greenwashing. *California Management Review, 54*(1), 64–87.

DePoe, S.P. (1991). *Good food from the good earth: McDonald's and the commodification of the environment.* Paper presented at the Proceedings of the Seventh SCA/AFA Conference on Argumentation, Annadale, VA.

do Paço, A.M.F., & Reis, R. (2012). Factors affecting skepticism toward green advertising. *Journal of Advertising, 41*(4), 147–155.

Doran, R., & Larsen, S. (2014). Are we all environmental tourists now? The role of biases in social comparison across and within tourists, and their implications. *Journal of Sustainable Tourism, 22*(7), 1023–1036.

Elgammal, I., & Jones, E. (2007). Using discourse analysis to explore the achievability of triple bottom line sustainability (TBLS): The case of the bluestone holiday village. In F. Jordan, L. Kilgour, & N. Morgan (Eds.), *Academic renewal: Innovation in leisure and tourism theories and methods, Volume 2 (LSA 97)* (S3−100). Eastbourne: Leisure Studies Association.

Fairclough, N. (1992). *Discourse and social change*. Cambridge: Polity Press.

Font, X., Garay, L., & Jones, S. (2014). Sustainability motivations and practices in small tourism enterprises. *Journal of Cleaner Production*, doi:10.1016/j.jclepro.2014.01.071.

Font, X., Garay, L., & Jones, S. (2016). A social cognitive theory of sustainability empathy. *Annals of Tourism Research, 58*, 65−80.

Foucault, M. (2002). *The order of things: An archaeology of the human sciences*. London: Routledge.

Goffman, E. (1990). *The presentation of self in everyday life*. London: Penguin.

Goffman, E. (2005). *Interaction ritual: Essays in face to face behavior*. Chigago, IL: AldineTransaction.

Gössling, S., & Buckley, R. (2016). Carbon labels in tourism: Persuasive communication? *Journal of Cleaner Production, 111*, 358−369.

Grant, J. (2007). *The green marketing manifesto*. Chichester: Wiley.

Grimmer, M., & Woolley, M. (2014). Green marketing messages and consumers' purchase intentions: Promoting personal versus environmental benefits. *Journal of Marketing Communications, 20*(4), 231−250.

Hall, C.M. (2014). *Tourism and social marketing*. London: Routledge.

Haque, M.S. (2000). Environmental discourse and sustainable development: Linkages and limitations. *Ethics and the Environment, 5*(1), 3−21.

Hindley, A., & Font, X. (2014). Ethics and influences in tourist perceptions of climate change. *Current Issues in Tourism*, 1−17. Retrieved from http://dx.doi.org/10.1080/13683500.2014.946477.

Holbrook, M.B. (1987). Mirror, mirror, on the wall, what's unfair in the reflections on advertising? *The Journal of Marketing, 51*(3), 95−103.

Hyland, K. (2010). Community and individuality: Performing identity in applied linguistics. *Written Communication, 27*(2), 159−188.

Jones, T.M. (1991). Ethical decision making by individuals in organizations: An issue-contingent model. *Academy of Management Review, 16*(2), 366−395.

Kilbourne, W. (2004). Sustainable communication and the dominant social paradigm: Can they be integrated? *Marketing Theory, 4*(3), 187−208.

Kim, S.-B., & Kim, D.-Y. (2014). The effects of message framing and source credibility on green messages in hotels. *Cornell Hospitality Quarterly, 55*(1), 64−75.

Kollmuss, A., & Agyeman, J. (2002). Mind the gap: Why do people act environmentally and what are the barriers to pro-environmental behavior? *Environmental Education Research, 8*(3), 239−260.

Kong, Y., & Zhang, L. (2014). When does green advertising work? The moderating role of product type. *Journal of Marketing Communications, 20*(3), 197−213.

Kreps, T.A., & Monin, B. (2011). "Doing well by doing good"? Ambivalent moral framing in organizations. *Research in Organizational Behavior, 31*, 99−123.

Lee, S.A., & Oh, H. (2014). Effective communication strategies for hotel guests' green behavior. *Cornell Hospitality Quarterly, 55*(1), 52−63.

Lowry, P.B., Roberts, T.L., & Higbee, T. (2007). First impressions with websites: The effect of the familiarity and credibility of corporate logos on perceived consumer swift trust of websites. In J. Jacko (Ed.), *Human-computer interaction* (pp. 77−85). Berlin: Springer.

Lynes, J.K., & Andrachuk, M. (2008). Motivations for corporate social and environmental responsibility: A case study of Scandinavian Airlines. *Journal of International Management, 14*(4), 377−390.

Lyon, T.P., & Maxwell, J.W. (2011). Greenwash: Corporate environmental disclosure under threat of audit. *Journal of Economics & Management Strategy, 20*(1), 3−41.

Malone, S., McCabe, S., & Smith, A.P. (2014). The role of hedonism in ethical tourism. *Annals of Tourism Research, 44*, 241−254.

Maniates, M.F. (2001). Individualization: Plant a tree, buy a bike, save the world? *Global Environmental Politics, 1*(3), 31−52.

Martens, C. (2008). Greenhushing…... Schhhhh. Retrieved from http://www.kommunikationsforum.dk/artikler/greenhushing-schhhhh

Maxwell, J.A. (2012). *Qualitative research design: An interactive approach: An interactive approach*. Thousand Oaks, CA: Sage.

Miles, M., & Huberman, A. (1994). *Qualitative data analysis: An expanded sourcebook*. Thousand Oaks, CA: SAGE.

Miller, G., Rathouse, K., Scarles, C., Holmes, K., & Tribe, J. (2010). Public understanding of sustainable tourism. *Annals of Tourism Research, 37*(3), 627−645.

Mintel. (2007). *Green and ethical consumers - UK - January 2007*. London: Mintel International Group Limited.

Molina-Azorín, J.F., & Font, X. (2016). Mixed methods in sustainable tourism research: an analysis of prevalence, designs and application in JOST (2005−2014). *Journal of Sustainable Tourism*. doi:10.1080/09669582.2015.1073739

National Parks UK. (2015). National Parks: Britain's breathing spaces. Retrieved from http://www.nationalparks.gov.uk/lear ningabout/whatisanationalpark/factsandfigures

O'Keefe, D.J. (2002). *Persuasion: Theory & research* (2 ed.). Thounsands Oaks: Sage Publications.

PDNPA. (2014). Peak district National Park visitor survey 2014 & non-visitor survey 2014. Retrieved from http://www.peak district.gov.uk/__data/assets/pdf_file/0005/538772/vistor-non-visitor-survey-2014.pdf

Peattie, K., & Crane, A. (2005). Green marketing: Legend, myth, farce or prophesy? *Qualitative Market Research: An International Journal, 8*(4), 357—370.

Pollay, R.W., & Gallagher, K. (1990). Advertising and cultural values: Reflections in the distorted mirror. *International Journal of Advertising, 9*, 361—374.

Prothero, A., McDonagh, P., & Dobscha, S. (2010). Is green the new black? Reflections on a green commodity discourse. *Journal of Macromarketing, 30*(2), 147—159.

Punch, K.F. (2013). *Introduction to social research: Quantitative and qualitative approaches*. Thousand Oaks, CA: Sage.

Pustejovsky, J., Anick, P., & Bergler, S. (1993). Lexical semantic techniques for corpus analysis. *Computational Linguistics, 19*(2), 331—358.

Reed, D. (2013). *Structural adjustment, the environment and sustainable development*. London: Routledge.

Reiser, A., & Simmons, D.G. (2005). A quasi-experimental method for testing the effectiveness of ecolabel promotion. *Journal of Sustainable Tourism, 13*(6), 590—616.

Sampaio, A., Thomas, R., & Font, X. (2012). Small business management and environmental engagement. *Journal of Sustainable Tourism, 20*(2), 179—193.

Saxena, G. (2005). Relationships, networks and the learning regions: Case evidence from the Peak District National Park. *Tourism Management, 26*(2), 277—289.

Schoeneborn, D., & Trittin, H. (2013). Transcending transmission: Towards a constitutive perspective on CSR communication. *Corporate Communications: An International Journal, 18*(2), 193—211.

Smith, T.M. (1998). *The myth of green marketing: Tending our goats at the edge of apocalypse*. Toronto: University of Toronto Press.

Stanford, D.J. (2014). Reducing visitor car use in a protected area: A market segmentation approach to achieving behaviour change. *Journal of Sustainable Tourism, 22*(4), 666—683.

Taylor, S., & Bogdan, R. (1998). *Introduction to qualitative methods: A guide and resource*. New York, NY: Wiley.

Tenbrunsel, A.E., & Messick, D.M. (2004). Ethical fading: The role of self-deception in unethical behavior. *Social Justice Research, 17*(2), 223—236.

Tversky, A., & Kahneman, D. (1981). The framing of decisions and the psychology of choice. *Science, 211*, 453—458.

Urry, J. (1990). *The tourist gaze*. London: Sage.

Villarino, J., & Font, X. (2015). Sustainability marketing myopia: The lack of persuasiveness in sustainability communication *Journal of Vacation Marketing, 21*(4), 326—335.

Wehrli, R., Priskin, J., Demarmels, S., Schaffner, D., Schwarz, J., Truniger, F., & Stettler, J. (2014). How to communicate sustainable tourism products to customers: Results from a choice experiment. *Current Issues in Tourism*, 1—20. doi:10.1080/13683500.2014.987732

Wengao, G. (2009). *Linguistic variation and identity representation in personal blogs: A corpus-linguistic approach* (PhD thesis). National University of Singapore, Singapore. Retrieved from http://scholarbank.nus.sg/handle/10635/18620.

Yaeger-Dror, M., Granadillo, T., Takano, S., & Hall-Lew, L. (2010). The sociophonetics of prosodic contours on NEG in three language communities: Teasing apart sociolinguistic and phonetic influences on speech. In D.R. Preston & N. Niedzielski (Eds.), *A reader in sociophonetics* (pp. 133—176). New York, NY: Walter de Gruyter Inc.

Tourism, information technologies and sustainability: an exploratory review

Stefan Gössling

ABSTRACT

Considerable attention has been paid in recent years to the fundamental changes in the global tourism system related to the emergence of information technologies (IT), and, specifically, the rise of social media. Opportunities to search travel-related information, to reserve and book, evaluate and judge; to receive travel advice and to communicate one's mobility patterns have all profoundly changed the practices of performing tourism, with concomitant repercussions for the management and marketing of businesses and destinations. This paper provides a discussion of the implications of these changes for the sustainability of the global tourism system. Based on an exploratory research design, key changes in the tourism system are identified and discussed with regard to their environmental, socio-cultural and psychological, as well as economic significance. The paper concludes that IT affects the tourism system in numerous and complex ways, with mixed outcomes for sustainability: while most changes would currently appear to be ambivalent — and some outright negative — there is considerable potential for IT to support more sustainable tourism. Yet, this would require considerable changes in the tourism system on global, national and individual business' levels, and require tourism academics to probe many new issues.

1. Introduction

The emergence and ubiquitous accessibility of information communication technologies (IT)[1] as well as the concomitant rise of social media represents one of the most significant changes in the global tourism system over the past decades (Buhalis & Law, 2008; Ho & Lee, 2007; Leung, Law, Van Hoof, & Buhalis, 2013; Poon, 1993; Sheldon, 1997; Werthner & Klein, 1999; Xiang & Gretzel, 2010; Zhang, Ye, Law, & Li, 2010). Tourists now use the Internet to find information about issues as diverse as weather forecasts, entrance fees or opening times (e.g. Scott & Lemieux, 2010; Xiang & Gretzel, 2010); to make reservations or to buy travel-related products and services (e.g. Buhalis & Law, 2008; Jun, Vogt, & MacKay, 2007); to evaluate and to be advised (e.g. Ayeh, 2015; Munar & Jacobsen, 2014; Sparks & Browning, 2011); and to communicate travel patterns in pursuit of social connectedness and social capital (Germann Molz, 2012; Gössling & Stavrinidi, 2015). Businesses are consequently increasingly dependent on IT to manage and market tourism, and to communicate favourable consumer opinion (Hays, Page, & Buhalis, 2013; Mauri & Minazzi, 2013).

As outlined by Buhalis and Law (2008), the use of IT in tourism has moved through different stages. Since the 2000s, IT has, with global availability and access to the Internet, become a silent but strong global transformational force in tourism, with consumer-generated content and social media having gained central importance for the economic success of destinations and businesses (e.g. O'Connor, 2008). Any tourism entity can now be judged and rated, recommended or disapproved of (Gössling, Hall, & Andersson, 2016; Law, Qi, & Buhalis, 2010), with major repercussions for consumer perceptions and choices, and the economic success of businesses (O'Connor, 2008; Öğüt & Onur Taş, 2012; Xiang & Gretzel, 2010). Online content affects customer flows and price settings, inter-business and inter-destination competition, as well as service innovation and host motivation (Gössling & Lane, 2015; Jalilvand & Samiei, 2012; Noroozi & Fotouhi, 2010; Yacouel & Fleischer, 2012; Zhang et al., 2010). Evidence is thus that IT has become perhaps the single most important new determinant in tourism's demand and supply structures, and that many of these developments have repercussions for the economic performance of local, national and global tourism systems.

As one example, Carey, Gountas, and Gilbert (1997) reported that the top 30 UK tour operators carried 17.05 million travellers in 1995, which can be compared to 850,000 bed nights reserved by individuals globally *per day* through the platform booking.com in early 2015 (Booking.com, 2015). In many tourism sub-sectors, there is evidence of the market dominance of a limited number of global platforms, some of which account for hundreds of millions of economic transactions per year (Jeacle & Carter, 2011; Jun et al., 2007). As these platforms appear to control a significant share of accommodation reservations (e.g. Booking), flight reservations (Expedia), or traveller advice and opinion (TripAdvisor), they have implications for the economic performance of businesses and destinations. This is also true for social media sites such as Facebook, which have profound implications for traveller identity formation, travel trends and mobilities (Germann-Molz, 2012; Gössling & Stavrinidi, 2015). Other platforms offer distributed, customer-to-customer (or peer-to-peer) transactions, including cheap(er) accommodation (AirBnB), accommodation exchanges (HomeExchange), "social" accommodation (Couchsurfing), or cheap(er) transportation services (Uber). These platforms have various implications from environmental and social viewpoints, as they afford and affect production and consumption patterns that are now fundamentally different from those two decades ago. In light of this, the paper seeks to provide a first, exploratory discussion of the broader implications of IT for aspects of social, environmental and economic sustainability in tourism, as seen from both supply and demand sides. As an exploratory piece, it is not seeking to provide analytical insights, rather than to stimulate debate on a broader scale about the implications of IT for sustainable tourism. It summarizes emerging questions and interrelationships, and outlines research needs.

2. IT, tourism and sustainability

Only a few authors have discussed the interrelationships of IT and sustainability. In chronological order, Liburd (2005) was one of the first to reflect on the implications of mobile tourism services for sustainable tourism with regard to aspects of equity, scale and implementation. Touray and Jung (2010), in a project on sustainable tourism development in Manchester (UK), found that tourism stakeholders considered IT as a strategic tool for sustainable tourism development, and concluded that in particular audio guides and social media networks represented useful tools to inform visitors and to encourage principles of sustainability. Scott and Frew (2013, p. 36), in presenting a survey of "eTourism experts" (*n* = 66) and their views on IT applications to support sustainable tourism, found sustainability to be a "very important factor in the design of eTourism applications", because of linkages to location-based services, destination management systems, carbon calculators, virtual reality technologies, wireless technologies, intelligent transportation systems, social media, augmented reality and recommender systems. Many of these were found to ultimately focus on consumer benefits related to discounts or other advantages, such as to visit an attraction at a time when it is less crowded. eTourism expert responses also included suggestions for future applications related to visitor management, such as control of visitor numbers, the management of tourist flows and the protection of sensitive areas. Eco-labelling was mentioned as a mechanism to aid green tourist choices. This list of potential applications to enhance destination sustainability (e.g. energy monitoring, waste management) has been expanded in Ali and Frew (2014).

Budeanu (2013) reports on a study of stakeholder dialogues in TripAdvisor, with the objective to promote sustainability in tourism. Budeanu raises various relevant issues, such as user cultures, responsible gatekeepers and rules of access. She postulates that social media can encourage demand for socially and environmentally more integrated products and services, while also exposing activities harmful for sustainability. Budeanu (2013) critically remarks that all destinations studied provide information regarding their pro-environmental initiatives in generic terms ("waste management", "renewable energy"), yet, specific information about sustainable tourism is difficult to find or entirely absent. Likewise, posts about sustainable tourism were found to be rare on TripAdvisor, even though some hotels and restaurants were labelled "sustainable". Social media, she concludes, opens up opportunities for participation in tourism decision-making and planning, allowing individuals to interact. However, this potential is far from realized, and "the interest of individuals in the sustainability of tourism provision or consumption [is] in its infancy" (Budeanu, 2013, p. 22).

The most recent and comprehensive attempt to link dimensions of sustainable tourism with IT applications has been provided by Benckendorff, Sheldon, and Fesenmaier (2014), in discussing the implications of IT for tourism resource efficiency, environmental purity and physical integrity, biological diversity, virtual substitution of travel experiences (environmental sustainability); social equity and community well-being, local control, and the cultural richness of host communities (socio-cultural sustainability); as well as economic viability and local prosperity, employment quality and capacity building (economic sustainability). In their discussion, Benckendorff et al. (2014) conclude that for tourism to become more sustainable requires constant education, monitoring and collaboration, which can be achieved on the basis of IT. They provide various examples showing how IT helps to distribute and make accessible information, to create environmental and cultural awareness, to monitor environmental resources and to reduce energy use. In this contribution, all interrelationships of tourism and IT are seen to have positive outcomes for sustainability, but these are not empirically substantiated. Notably, no critical or even negative — in sustainability terms — interrelationships were identified.

3. Method

This paper seeks to identify and discuss interlinkages between tourism, IT and sustainability. The term "sustainability" is used in this paper as a reflection on the contribution IT may make for sustainable tourism to become *more* desirable from normative societal, individual or business viewpoints in comparison to an *ex ante* situation. As there cannot be general consensus in many areas as to what would constitute a more desirable development, discussions are framed broadly, acknowledging that sustainability is an evolving, complex and adaptive concept (Hunter, 1997). Given its practice-oriented approach, definitions of sustainability as provided by UNEP and UNWTO (2005) and UNWTO (2014) "objectives for sustainable tourism development" are recognized (see, however, Aall, 2014). This is largely in line with the approach to sustainability used by Benckendorff et al. (2014), which implies a normative view of tourism as a system that aims to improve in comparison to a given situation, for instance with regard to resource efficiency and physical integrity, social equity and local prosperity. Yet, in framing this paper, somewhat broader, dimensions of sustainability also include interrelationships with consumer psychology and -cultures, and more general social change leading to altered collective and individual social identities (social sustainability); broader structural changes such as market concentration processes or competition (economic sustainability); and aspects of environmental awareness and resource use (environmental sustainability). By assuming a meta-perspective on current developments, complexities of environmental, social and economic change are examined and discussed rather than judged in order to open up a broad research agenda on tourism, IT and sustainability. This approach also seeks to avoid determinism with regard to sustainability, acknowledging that future viewpoints may be different than current ones, and that there are differences in individual perspectives on what would constitute a desirable development.

To identify linkages between tourism, IT and sustainability, the focus is on Internet-based platforms relevant for business-to-customer or traveller-to-traveller (peer-to-peer) relations, not IT per se. Platforms were identified on the basis of discussions with three colleagues at the Western Norway Research Institute, all of them specializing in Internet technologies and applications, both within and outside tourism. The choice of colleagues to derive expertise has consequently been one of convenience, representing a Eurocentric approach, and it is acknowledged that specific platforms may have been omitted, or that platforms of relevance exist in other countries. The chosen platforms' global importance was formally established by identifying user/member numbers. Even though there exist hundreds of small platforms with tourism relevance, these were thus deliberately excluded. Likewise, large platforms with indirect relevance for tourism, including, for instance, peer-to-peer transactions outside banks (Bitcoin), petitions (Avaaz), travel- or leisure-related videos (Youtube), as well as news channels and industry-focused media (Travelmole, eTurboNews), were not included. The review also excludes company websites used for business-to-customer communication, as well as technologies used to reduce specific resource use, such as measuring or metering devices/software. The overall list of platforms and sites considered is thus non-exhaustive, and the sites included serve as examples for the broader discussion of IT−tourism−sustainability interrelationships.

Table 1 shows the platforms identified, along with user/member numbers, as of March−April 2015. The list illustrates the scope, dominance and influence spheres of global platforms, which were sorted into four broad categories: (1) online reservations, (2) sharing and peer-to-peer marketplaces, (3) evaluations, opinion and advice, as well as (4) traveller identity. User/member numbers show that individual sites now reach out to a global customer base: Booking.com claims, for instance, to represent more than 600,000 accommodation businesses in 212 countries, and to process more than 850,000 room night reservations per day (Booking.com, 2015). Expedia, Lastminute and Opodo represent hundreds of airlines, and platforms such as AirBnB or CouchSurfing have tens of millions of members/users. Likewise, sites relying on consumer-generated content as well as social media sites have attracted hundreds of millions of users. As an example, TripAdvisor, one of the largest review platforms, claims to have 315 million unique monthly visitors drawing information from 200 million reviews covering 4.5 million accommodations, restaurants, attractions, resorts, destinations, beaches and islands (TripAdvisor, 2015a). Facebook as the most important social media platform with a strong (implicit) focus on travel claims to have 936 million "daily active users" (Facebook, 2015).

To evaluate potential sustainability implications of platforms, a literature review was combined with discussions involving three IT-specialized colleagues at the Western Norway Research Institute, as well as with six colleagues working at various institutions in western countries on topics related to IT, and IT and sustainable tourism. Again, this may have resulted in a Eurocentric perspective. The topics identified were summarized and structured in a preliminary keyword list. Each of these keywords (e.g. "car sharing") was subsequently researched in specific searches for related scientific papers, using the EBSCO database, as well as Google Scholar. Where relevant papers were identified, this often spawned new searches for articles highlighted in these papers.

The process resulted in a large amount of material, which was structured in three categories, i.e. depending on the papers' primary focus on social, environmental or economic sustainability. Within each of these categories, preliminary lists of "aspects of sustainability" were developed, based on the manual interpretation of paper content within a thematic analysis approach (Guest, Namey, & Mitchell, 2015). This yielded a total of 12 categories in which IT can be seen as relevant for broader aspects of sustainability, with 4 of these categories subsumed under each of the three dimensions of sustainability (social, economic and environmental sustainability; see Sections 4.1−4.3). This

Table 1. Platforms and user numbers.

Platform type (source)	User number (March/April 2015)
Online reservations	
Booking (2015)	>647,000 accommodations in 212 countries; 850,000 bed nights booked per day
Agoda (2015)	625,000 hotels
HRS (2015)	250,000 hotels
	80 million users
Hotels (2015)	240,000 hotels
Venere (2015)	200,000 hotels and accommodation establishments
Expedia (2015)	400 airlines, 435,000 hotels
Orbitz (2015)	8 million visitors per month
Lastminute (2015)	300 airlines, 120,000 hotels
Opodo (2015)	>500 airlines, 150,000 hotels, 20,000 cruises, 7000 car rental locations
Trivago (2015)	Compares 721,714 hotels on 262 sites
Sharing and peer-to-peer marketplaces	
AirBnB (2015a)	More than 1 million offers in 190 countries
	More than 25 million guests
CouchSurfing (2015)	10 million members
HomeExchange (2015)	More than 65,000 homes
Uber, Lyft, CarMa	Not disclosed by websites
Online travel agents	
Expedia (2015)	400 airlines, 435,000 hotels
Orbitz (2015)	8 million visitors per month
Lastminute (2015)	300 airlines, 120,000 hotels
Opodo (2015)	>500 airlines, 150,000 hotels, 20,000 cruises, 7000 car rental locations
Trivago (2015)	Compares 721,714 hotels on 262 sites
Evaluation, opinion and advice	
TripAdvisor (2015a)	315 million unique monthly visitors; 200 million reviews covering 4.5 million accommodations, restaurants and attractions
HolidayCheck (2015)	25 million visits per month, 11 million reviews
Zoover (2015)	185 million visitors per year, contains 2.6 million reviews covering 356,000 accommodations in 45,0000 destinations
Fodor's Travel (2015)	20 million page views in a single month
Wayn (2015)	23 million members
Traveller identity	
Facebook (2015)	936 million daily active users; 1.44 billion monthly active users
Instagram (2015)	300 million members
FlyerTalk (2015)	593,250 members

Source: Own review.

categorization is not necessarily straightforward, because IT often initiates changes with implications for various dimensions of sustainability, sometimes promoting one, while diminishing another. The categorization thus follows a subjective principle of "best fit", and interrelationships are discussed to emphasize linkages.

It should also be noted that the list of sustainability aspects identified is not necessarily complete, and does omit several of the topics identified in the literature (e.g. Benckendorff et al., 2014; Budeanu, 2013), partially because these refer to business-to-business interactions, which are not considered in this paper, or because the categories identified are too broad or vague ("local prosperity"), demanding refinement to allow for a more analytical discussion. The following sections discuss each of the 12 sustainability categories, drawing on insights from different disciplines, such as sociology, transport studies, psychology and management/economics. Given that this approach is inherently subjective and non-exhaustive, the following discussion needs to be seen as an exploratory examination of the subject.

4. Interrelationships of tourism, IT and sustainability

4.1. Social sustainability

Social sustainability is usually defined as comprising various dimensions of social and cultural change, as exemplified by UNEP and UNWTO's (2005, p. 11) "Respect the socio-cultural authenticity of host communities, conserve their built and living cultural heritage and traditional values, and contribute to inter-cultural understanding and tolerance" (for a similar definition see Beckendorff et al., 2014). The following section is framed more broadly and introduces "psychological" sustainability, as an aspect of social sustainability. Psychological sustainability relates to mental well-being, an issue that has received growing recognition in recent years (e.g. Cacioppo & Patrick, 2008), also in the context of the use of IT and in particular social media platforms (e.g. Turkle, 2011). There are also links between tourism, the use of IT and personal/collective identities, the quality of relationships, social and network capital, and opportunities for sociality (e.g. Germann Molz, 2012; Hibbert, Dickinson, Gössling, & Curtin, 2013). Furthermore, social sustainability includes perspectives of hosts and changing consumer cultures. The review of the material subsumed under social sustainability consequently generated four major themes: "glamorization of travel and tourism"; "traveller identity"; "social status and competitive travel"; and "social connectedness" (Table 2).

4.1.1. Glamorization of travel and tourism

Mobility is an increasingly important signifier of social status and a generator of network capital (Urry, 2007, 2011). In contemporary society, social status is expressed through a wide range of mechanisms, including ideas and objects of admiration (Cohen & Gössling, 2015). Admiration of tourism and travel-related consumption has, until the rise of social media, primarily been linked to objects, such as powerful cars, yachts, private aircraft, or the semiotics of status-coloured frequent flyer cards (Thurlow & Jaworski, 2006). These representations of admiration still exist, but they are increasingly expressed to wider audiences through social media such as Facebook and other platforms visualizing mobility patterns on the basis of maps depicting frequency and geographical distribution of movement, as well as iconic places visited, or places lived (Cohen & Gössling, 2015; Gössling & Stavrinidi, 2015). These mechanisms of travel glorification are also employed by corporate users of Facebook, as exemplified by Expedia's "travel profiles" assigning "travel points", and assessing the global share of countries visited (Expedia 2015a). Other examples include FlyerTalk, a platform devoted to a community of frequent flyers, as well as FlightMemory, a platform allowing people to register flights and to compare one's travelness to fellow members in form of various measures such as number of flights made, distances covered, or "[Lifetime] flight time: 1496 hours or 62.3 Days, or 8.9 Weeks, or 2.08 Months, or 0.171 Years". Social media have thus fundamentally changed perceptions of distance and mobility as a socially desirable activity, with concomitant repercussions for transport volume growth and greenhouse gas emissions, i.e. environmental dimensions of sustainability.

4.1.2. Traveller identity

Desforges (2000) shows that self-identity is closely connected to mobility, and that travel is shaping perceptions of self through comparison (Urry, 2000; see also Noy, 2004). Traveller identity is thus related to society's views on mobile lifestyles, as well as the views of peers in physical and virtual

Table 2. Categories of social sustainability.

Sustainability aspect	Relevant platforms (examples)
Glamorization of travel and tourism	Instagram, FlyerTalk, FlightMemory
Traveller identity	Facebook, Instagram, Wayn
Social status and competitive travel	Facebook, FlightMemory, FlyerTalk
Social connectedness	Facebook, Instagram

networks (Zhao, Grasmuck, & Martin, 2008). Hibbert et al. (2013) discuss how travel choices and the general desire to travel are driven by perceptions of self. Social media such as Facebook foster these processes by providing markers, which can be related to identity, agency, sociality and spatiality (Gössling & Stavrinidi, 2015), and profile owners in social media have been found to present themselves within the limitations and guiding themes implied by the system (e.g. Facebook's "Where are you now?"), and against the social desirability of specific activities within their respective networks. Ultimately, this can result in the assumption of liquid identity, i.e. identities modelled on movement (Gössling & Stavrinidi, 2015). As outlined by Hibbert et al. (2013), where identities are at stake, there is very limited scope for environmental concern, and travellers with mobile identities are unlikely to change behaviour out of environmental concern. Social media are thus powerful agents fostering mobile identities, and the desire to move physically, leading to growth in transport volumes.

4.1.3. Social status and competitive travel

In social media platforms, users compete for attention over posted content (Garcia, Tor, & Schiff, 2013). Facebook, as the largest such platform, has more than 900 million daily active users, who simultaneously witness, testify and judge (Germann Molz, 2006; Gössling & Stavrinidi, 2015). As social status is to a considerable extent derived out of movement (Larsen & Guiver, 2013; Pappas, 2014) and in the case of Facebook, as well as other social media platforms, seen in comparison to the mobility of other network members (Cohen & Gössling, 2015), these foster social processes that encourage, but also force network members to embrace mobility in competitive ways (Gössling & Stavrinidi, 2015). Mechanisms of competitive mobility have also been identified in the context of frequent flyer programmes, which reward mobile lifestyles with more mobility (Gössling & Nilsson, 2010), and which are made comparable through platforms including FlightMemory or FlyerTalk. Social mechanisms of competitive travel, aided by IT, consequently result in transport volume growth. Other changes of immediate importance for destinations include the possibility of a decline in average length of stay, as the exploration of destinations loses importance in comparison to the number of sites visited. These developments may thus have various economic and environmental implications. Socially and psychologically, the quest for social capital is not necessarily problematic, but, as a competitive process, it can trigger negative emotions and affect psychological well-being (e.g. Fox & Moreland, 2015).

4.1.4. Social connectedness

A key element of travel is social connectedness, i.e. the opportunity to share time with family, friends and relations (Pearce, 2005). Social connectedness has been identified as one of the most fundamental aspects of human life, essential for the sense that one's life has meaning (Williams, 2001). Social media are means to connect over distance, as they allow for co-presence, i.e. to be physically in one location and virtually in another (Germann Molz, 2012). However, the consequences of sharing attention and receiving attention at a distance are complex. For travellers, they provide virtual mooring (Germann Molz & Paris, 2015), thus making travel psychologically more bearable, for instance because travellers may overcome feelings of loneliness (Ryan & Xenos, 2011). Yet, as outlined by Turkle (2011), social media also affect sociality and the way we interact, relate and love. Smartphones as tools of multitasking, and in particular the use of social media, have been found to divide attention, to the degree where people are no longer mentally present. Excessive smartphone use has been described as an addiction linked to narcissism and neuroticism (Pearson & Hussain, 2015). This has implications for close relationships, which require a sense of security of the other's responsiveness (Reis, Clark, & Holmes, 2004), i.e. frequent and strong responses to the other person's thoughts, feelings and behaviour (Berscheid, Snyder, & Omoto, 1989). As considerable amounts of time may now be spent communicating with those not physically present (Turkle, 2011), opportunities for building strong relationships are reduced, and holidays as an opportunity to focus on family and friends may have lost part of their function as a space in time to reflect and interact. To be constantly online also diminishes opportunities to overcome work-related stress. As Turkle (2011, pp. 288–289) emphasizes: "To experience solitude you must be able to summon yourself by yourself; otherwise, you will only know how to be lonely. [...] many find that, trained by the Net, they cannot find solitude even at a lake or beach or on a hike." Findings such as these have implications for sociality, as well as its flipside, loneliness, as a growing social phenomenon (Cacioppo & Patrick, 2008). The inability to mentally embrace free time has also been linked to reduced creativity, as there is evidence that boredom and daydreaming foster creativity (Mann & Cadman, 2014). IT, and specifically social media, have, therefore, complex interrelationships with individual and collective psychologies, which are largely unexplored in the context of tourism.

4.2. Environmental sustainability

UNEP and UNWTO (2005, p. 11) define environmental sustainability as to "Make optimal use of environmental resources that constitute a key element in tourism development, maintaining essential ecological processes and helping to conserve natural heritage and biodiversity." This definition again resonates with Benckendorff et al.'s (2014) environmental sustainability categories, including efficient use of resources, preservation of environmental purity and physical integrity, and biodiversity conservation. Benckendorff et al. also highlight the importance of environmental education. Sustainability categories, as included in the following discussion, consequently include "environmental learning" and the importance of "deep experiences" as elements of environmental awareness; "traveller consumer cultures"; opportunities to make "sustainable choices"; and "sharing". Ultimately, the latter aspects refer to the influence of IT to directly or indirectly enhance or reduce resource use (water, energy, food), emissions of greenhouse gases (e.g. CO_2), solid waste and sewage (Table 3).

4.2.1. Environmental and cultural learning and deep experiences

Learning is a central element of tourism (Falk, Ballantyne, Packer, & Benckendorff, 2012). An important distinction is, however, that people learn both *formally and consciously*, i.e. with a specific purpose, as well as *obliviously* through comparison of values, norms and customs, the experience of new environments, cultures, or the consumption of (new) tourism-related products and services. It has been shown that travel contributes to practical skills, knowledge and practical wisdom, with implications for intellectual and personal growth, intercultural awareness, foreign language learning and professional development (Falk et al., 2012). From a sustainability viewpoint, learning processes can thus have positive outcomes for conservation (Ballantyne, Packer, Hughes, & Dierking, 2007), intercultural understanding and respect (e.g. Dolby, 2004), knowledge of environmental processes (e.g. Ballantyne, Packer, & Falk, 2011), ecosystem change (e.g. Lemelin, Dawson, & Stewart, 2013), or individual species' biology (e.g. Tisdell & Wilson, 2001). Ballantyne and Packer (2011) argue that the tourism industry has a responsibility to engage visitors in transformative learning experiences to foster and support processes of sustainability, and, importantly, that the impact of a tourism experience can be enhanced through social networking. While this view opens up a positive potential of tourism to promote sustainability, it may also be argued that the outcome of travel experiences is often more complex. As an example, a wildlife safari may generate insights about wildlife ecology, and potentially increase awareness of global ecological crisis, but travellers may also learn — obliviously — that

Table 3. Categories of environmental sustainability.

Sustainability aspect	Relevant platforms (examples)
Environmental and cultural learning & deep experiences	Facebook
Traveller consumer culture	Facebook, Wayn
Sustainable choices	TripAdvisor
Sharing	HomeExchange, AirBnB, Couchsurfing

travel is psychologically rewarding, specifically when experiences can be turned into social capital through social media, leading to a growing interest in continuous experience consumption and high-carbon lifestyles based on aeromobility (Cohen & Gössling, 2015). As noted by Hall (2013), the global rise in research on sustainability does not appear to have led to any progress on sustainability issues, and there is little evidence that greater environmental knowledge would actually translate into more environmentally friendly behaviour (Juvan & Dolnicar, 2014a, 2014b). As the quest for social capital is competitive, experiences may also be consumed at increasingly faster rates, and with little interest in their deeper meaning. This would contradict the notion of "deep" experiences with the potential to change travellers (Ballantyne & Packer, 2011), and rather indicate a prevalence of, and interest in, "showcase" experiences that can be turned into social capital. A considerable share of learning effects may thus not be related to sustainability, but to rewards for personal psychologies. It is notable that debates on environmentally friendly consumption, but also forms of social control of peers, in the sense that travellers are "told off" (Randles, 2009) for participating in environmentally harmful behaviour appear to be suspiciously absent from social media communications (Gössling & Stavrinidi, 2015).

4.2.2. Traveller consumer culture

Tourism can be seen as a powerful mechanism fostering specific forms of consumption, as virtually all "desirable" consumption in travel media is luxurious, high-carbon consumption. This is also true for airports as arenas of materialism, characterized by the ubiquitous presence of luxury brands and conspicuous forms of consumption. Airports also interlink aeromobile and automotive consumption through the exhibition of powerful cars, and they create notions of superiority of frequent flyer classes (Adey, Budd, & Hubbard, 2007). Similar things may be said about various forms of accommodation, and in particular upscale accommodation, where buffets are presented as limitless forms of consumption, characterized by high-protein food compositions, indulgence and wastage. Tourism is deeply entangled with oblivious learning processes about desirable forms of consumption, though that entanglement is not unique to tourism. These processes are fostered and facilitated by IT, with QR codes allowing fast-recording of desirable objects and practices, also presented in digital form in traveller reviews, recorded in photographs and posted on social media sites. Often, this will include forms of indulgence in the consumption of upscale brands or unsustainable products and services – including, for instance, forms of auto and aeromobility, which may also contribute to notions of consumer entitlement. While evidence would suggest that such patters of consumer behaviour change mostly embrace luxurious brands and forms of resource-intense consumption, platforms such as Facebook also allow liking sustainable tourism choices, indicating that different consumer culture pathways may be aided by IT.

4.2.3. Sustainable choices

Given the importance of platforms for destination-, accommodation- and transport choice, there is, in theory, a huge potential for these platforms to also guide consumer decisions towards more sustainable choices, as proposed by Ali and Frew (2014) and Benckendorff et al. (2014). To date, only few such attempts are visible, however (Budeanu, 2013), and it is difficult to identify any that do work unambiguously to the advantage of sustainability. This is illustrated by a discussion of three platforms, TripAdvisor and its GreenLeader programme; Directflights, a global distribution platform providing travellers with a "smart score"; and Bookdifferent, a recently founded reservation platform that assigns CO_2 emission values to hotel nights. Essentially, all three platforms provide additional information on environmental sustainability, hence empowering travellers to make more sustainable choices, a key sustainability demand identified by Miller, Rathouse, Scarles, Holmes, and Tribe (2010).

TripAdvisor assigns bronze, silver, gold or platinum status to hotels participating in its GreenLeader programme, indicating various degrees of environmental commitment. The programme was developed in cooperation with the United Nations Environment Programme, UK Green Building Council, International Tourism Partnership and Carbon Trust. However, TripAdvisor does not allow businesses to be ranked by environmental achievement, which would increase their visibility, nor does TripAdvisor provide an overview of environmentally friendly accommodation, which prohibits strategic pro-environmental choices by travellers. In the current version (April 2015), travellers have to look out for the GreenLeaders symbol, a green leaf, and it is not evident what the difference between the four levels of certification is. The impact of the label is thus limited. Directflights identifies flight options between any two destinations, accompanied by a "smart score". The smart score considers price and schedule, comfort and amenities, as well as environmental impact. A higher score would represent low price, good comfort and low fuel use. Paradoxically, however, more seating space would increase the smart score, even though negative in environmental terms, as lower seat density increases per passenger fuel use and greenhouse gas emissions. This raises the question whether different, potentially contradictory choices can be integrated into one indicator. Finally, Bookdifferent provides information about all listed hotels' carbon footprints, expressed in kg CO_2, as well as a coloured "footprint" symbol that can be either red, orange, yellow or green, with green representing a more sustainable choice. The platform also forwards 25% of the commission it receives to one of 100 charities. The site thus increases both "carbon capability" (Whitmarsh, Seyfang, & O'Neill, 2011) and the interest in making donations, an important positioning in times where levels of empathy in society may be declining (Konrath, O'Brien, & Hsing, 2011). However, as with TripAdvisor's GreenLeaders programme, no information is provided on how environmental performance — in this case carbon emissions — is measured and calculated, or how the platform's economic distribution system works: Bookdifferent uses Booking's database, and has to pay 50% of the overall commission to Booking. It may thus be argued that this opens up another (green) market for Booking, which may previously have been retained by smaller platforms such as Sleepgreenhotels. Ultimately, this may further increase Booking's global market share (see also section on economic sustainability).

Sustainable choices can also be fostered through rankings. One such example is the Atmosfair Airline Index (Atmosfair, 2014). The index ranks airlines on the basis of their environmental performance, measured as emissions of CO_2 per net load km, allowing a comparison of airlines on the basis of their actual performance. Results exposed various airlines previously considered environmentally friendly (Mayer, Ryley, & Gillingwater, 2012) as particularly emission intense, and results were communicated widely on the Internet, also by those airlines leading the rankings, as a means of advertisement, sales and public relations (Hvass & Munar, 2012). Rankings would consequently be important because they can create competitive patterns for greater sustainability, and benefit transparency because of third-party assessments and growing public awareness. In conclusion, platforms have various options to highlight more sustainable choices: whether access to such information will significantly influence behavioural choices is a complex question, however (Juvan & Dolnicar, 2014a, 2014b).

4.2.4. Sharing and peer-to-peer marketplaces

The sharing economy has received considerable attention in recent years (e.g. Belk, 2014). An increasing number of people seem to be willing to share, rather than own, goods and products, for reasons of convenience and financial savings. Many goods owned by people are also underutilized, a prominent example being car seats being driven around empty. A growing number of websites now facilitate sharing, and many are relevant for tourism, including home sharing (e.g. HomeExchange), and shared-use mobility. The latter includes multiple transport use (e.g. Moovel), car sharing (e.g. Stadtmobil.de); public bicycle sharing (Bayareabikeshare); ride-sharing (e.g. Lyft, Carma); parking space sharing (e.g. Justpark); as well as combinations of ride-sharing, rental and taxi-services (Uber). For all sharing approaches, IT has an important role in matching supply and demand, i.e. by providing information on availability periods and locations, departure times and connections.

Shared-use platforms have grown rapidly in recent years, with for instance bike sharing platforms including at least 165 cities, and more than 237,000 rental bikes (Shaheen & Guzman, 2011). Environmental implications of bike rental platforms are clearly positive, as various studies show that their existence leads to a decline in sales and use of motorized vehicles (Fishman, Washington, & Haworth, 2014; Martin, Shaheen, & Lidicker, 2010). Other platforms, such as Uber, allow requesting and offering rides, thus reducing costs and environmental impacts, as travellers split fares while underutilized transport capacity declines. The platform, which is rapidly globalizing, also simplifies transport sharing through standardization, as its app works in an increasing number of countries. Yet, the platform also fosters unsustainable travel patterns by encouraging luxurious car choices (Uber, 2015), and has invited debates regarding safety and monopolization.

Sharing patterns can also be found in accommodation, and may have two potentially contrary outcomes. First, sharing leads to travel cost reduction, which is an important, though insufficiently researched aspect of environmental sustainability. Sites such as Couchsurfing or HomeExchange offer accommodation that is often cheaper (or even free of charge) than accommodation booked through reservation sites. This is obvious in the case of home exchanges, as users only pay a fee to use a matching site's services. Couchsurfing is another way of reducing the price for accommodation, and works on the basis of mutual visits, i.e. also involving a social encounter, which may be seen as a positive outcome from a social sustainability viewpoint. The effects of AirBnB are more difficult to assess. The platform provides both cheap accommodation (unused, private housing), as well as commercial exchanges (often apartments or flats). The latter may include privately owned flats marketed through AirBnB to achieve a higher rate of return, but with the potential downside of reducing local people's access to housing, and potentially unregistered properties avoiding tax payments.

All platforms have in common that low-cost or free accommodation may cause travellers to spend a greater share of their holiday budgets on transport, to visit more destinations, or to engage in additional travel/trips. Contrasting this view, it is also possible that travellers decide to stay longer or spend more money in the destination, with a positive effect for local economies. As with many other examples, these relationships and their sustainability outcomes are as yet insufficiently understood.

4.3. Economic sustainability

Economic sustainability challenges were defined by UNEP and UNWTO (2005, p. 11) as to "ensure viable, long-term economic operations, providing socio-economic benefits to all stakeholders that are fairly distributed, including stable employment and income-earning opportunities and social services to host communities, and contributing to poverty alleviation." Again, this definition is mirrored in Benckendorff et al. (2014), who include economic viability and local prosperity, employment quality and capacity building in their list of economic sustainability challenges. The following sections refer to changes that have implications for sustainability goals with regard to "market concentration and dominance"; "online reputation and business ethics"; "competitive structures and notions of scarcity"; and "guest expectations and consumer judgement cultures" (Table 4).

4.3.1. Market concentration and domination

The rapid growth of IT use in tourism has led to concentration processes. For instance, in accommodation, market leader Booking (2015) reports having contracts with more than 600,000 hotels. The scale of such market concentration is unprecedented in tourism history, and has various implications. First, an increasing share of commissions previously paid to a greater number of intermediaries is concentrated in the hands of a few global players. Destinations with their own platforms, as well as hotel chains with their own distribution channels face a concomitant decline in turnover, notably in a

Table 4. Categories of economic sustainability.

Sustainability aspect	Relevant platforms (examples)
Market concentration and domination	Booking, Expedia, Uber
Online reputation and business ethics	TripAdvisor, HolidayCheck
Competitive structures and notions of scarcity	Trivago, Opodo, Booking
Guest expectations and judgement cultures	Booking, Agoda

situation where new processes of competition may cause a downward adjustment of prices and a decline in overall revenue (Gössling & Lane, 2015). Destinations consequently face leakage of financial resources due to the involvement of global platforms, i.e. resources that may previously have secured more diversified employment and a higher regional multiplier. In line with these developments, individual businesses are increasingly dependent on specific platforms, with hotels reporting to sell up to 80% of their room capacity through Booking (Gössling & Lane, 2015). This implies various vulnerabilities, as businesses become enmeshed in new dependency structures, while losing control over content and online reputation (see below). However, observational evidence also suggests that small businesses appear to be the winners by using global platforms, reaching out to global customer bases at low cost, while often being rated highest by customers. Overall, processes of market concentration and globalization made possible by IT are visible throughout tourism, and their implications for the economic sustainability of tourism are potentially huge. These interrelationships have, however, as yet been insufficiently understood.

4.3.2. Online reputation and business ethics

Ratings and business success are closely related and increasingly becoming inseparable (Öğüt & Onur Taş, 2012). As businesses are dependent on online evaluations, they become more service-oriented (Lacey, 2012; Melián-González, Bulchand-Gidumal, & López-Valcárcel, 2013), but also more vulnerable, particularly where businesses have as yet received few online reviews, or where they are competing on a best-in-class basis. In such a situation, even a single negative review can potentially affect business position, and have significant detrimental consequences for consumer demand and turnover. A response to dealing with consumer opinion is to engage in measures to control online content (Phillips, Zigan, Santos Silva, & Schegg, 2015; Zhang & Vásquez, 2014), and for many managers, online reputation management is now a business priority (Gössling et al., 2016). As Buhalis (1998, p. 409) correctly predicted, "Only creative and innovative suppliers will be able to survive the competition in the new millennium." However, where pressure increases, businesses are more likely to engage in ethically questionable activities to improve online reputation (Gössling et al., 2016). With growing dependencies on single platforms and increasing pressure on managers to perform, such strategies are likely to become more prevalent, introducing an element of dishonesty in global tourism. Reviews and ratings have also been revealed as a source of frustration and suspicion among business managers, owners and staff (Gössling & Lane, 2015; Gössling et al., 2016). These developments would clash with economic and social sustainability goals.

4.3.3. Competitive structures and notions of scarcity

Platforms foster competition in tourism between different types of businesses, and on both supply and demand sides. For instance, AirBnB (2015b), which entered the market in 2008, claims 60 million customers and more than 2 million listings in November 2015, i.e. more than twice the number of accommodation opportunities listed only half a year earlier (AirBnB, 2015a). TripAdvisor (2015b), on its Paris site, offers reviews of 1794 hotels and 5797 vacation rentals (November 2015), indicating the growth and relevance of new forms of accommodation. Platforms and meta-search sites make visible differences in accommodation, prices and guest evaluations, introducing a competitive element that is global and ubiquitous. As an example, Booking informs new partners: "Your content score is x%. Your competitors have an average content score of y%." From the outset, it is made clear that the common denominator of the platform is competition and that it is important to perform better than others in order to be successful. Such competitive structures may also result in declining average prices charged per room night (a potential benefit for customers). Competitive mechanisms are also employed to create notions of scarcity, for instance by showing the share of booked capacity in a destination, both to distribute demand in time and to force consumers into rapid reservation decisions. To achieve the latter, Booking also reports on the number of rooms left, and the time it may take until no further rooms will be available: "It is likely that this businesses will be sold out within the next x hours." While in one sense a consumer service, this is also a mechanism of creating competition between consumers, and one that can be used to "artificially" create notions of scarcity by withholding capacity ("only 2 rooms left"). Competition is however, most evident in ratings, which theoretically range between 5.0 and 10.0, and which can be directly compared. Other platforms may use different, but related mechanisms, such as guest recommendation ratings ("x% of customers recommend this business"). Overall, reservation platforms have thus established competition on price and business reputation as expressed in guest ratings as the new basis for global business, while simultaneously communicating scarcity to guests. However, how these mechanisms work, and the implications they have for consumers and businesses as well as, ultimately, economic sustainability, remain insufficiently investigated.

4.3.4. Guest expectations and judgement cultures

Reservation platforms are efficient and easy to use for consumers, and they contribute to price comparison benefits. However, platforms have also changed guest expectations, with potentially highly relevant consequences for businesses and destinations. First, due to more competitive structures, guest expectations have been raised, and there may be changes with regard to price perceptions, the timing of bookings and cancellation policies. Competition also introduces changes in consumer cultures, as review opportunities encourage "cultures of critique" (Gössling et al., 2016), both empowering customers but also supporting criticism: platforms *demand* judgment. To assess is no longer a choice rather it is an obligation, with evidence that consumers increasingly understand their power over reputation (McQuilken & Robertson, 2011). The relevance of the phenomenon is such that TripAdvisor rhetorically asks: "As a business representative, how can I report that a guest threatened me with a bad review?" (TripAdvisor, 2014), an indication that guests may use and abuse their power over business reputation. Management concerns include in particular loud, demanding guests; reviews perceived as unjustified or badmouthing; as well as the impossibility to post replies, and thus being exposed to opinion (Gössling & Lane, 2015; Gössling et al., 2016).

5. Discussion and conclusions

This paper has sought to discuss interrelationships between tourism, IT and social, economic and environmental dimensions of sustainability. Several key findings have emerged from this exploratory review: First, only limited research has addressed the implications of IT for tourism sustainability, and with the exception of Touray and Jung (2010), Scott and Frew (2013) and Budeanu (2013), no empirical studies appear to exist. Yet, there is consensus that IT has far-reaching consequences for the ways in which tourism is supplied and consumed, paired with optimism that IT does already make considerable contributions to tourism sustainability, and that there are opportunities to further develop positive outcomes (Ali & Frew, 2014; Benckendorff et al., 2014).

In contrast to these findings and the expectation that implications of IT for tourism sustainability could be identified, evidence suggests that the outcome of global IT adoption and its mainstreaming in tourism is difficult to discuss in deterministic terms: IT—sustainability interrelationships are always complex, and cannot be easily judged from the normative viewpoint of socially or individually more "desirable" developments. There are various reasons for this. First, changes initiated by IT are complex and potentially antipodal, as implications for social, environmental and economic sustainability may contradict each other. As an example, sharing sites, such as Couchsurfing, may promote social sustainability, as the site facilitates meaningful connections between visitors and local hosts; yet, it may also diminish social sustainability when free accommodation and sociality are provided in non-reciprocal relationships. Sharing sites may promote economic sustainability by distributing hospitality profits more widely throughout the local community, but may also reduce economic sustainability by taking customers away from established businesses or working around tax codes. Environmentally, sharing sites may promote efficient use rather than wasting resources, but they may also foster more energy-intense spending on transport, or free financial resources to fund more frequent trips.

To disentangle these and other contradictions requires considerable additional (empirical) research efforts.

The discussion in this paper also calls for analysis at greater analytical depth, and on an interdisciplinary basis: Benckendorff et al. (2014), for example, postulate that IT's potential to contribute to education and environmental learning is considerable. However, there is growing evidence that environmental knowledge and awareness does not automatically translate into behavioural change (e.g. Juvan & Dolnicar, 2014a, 2014b). How should such developments be valued from societal viewpoints, as there is also evidence of problematic learning outcomes, such as the framing of resource-intense luxurious consumption as desirable, or the glamorization of travel and tourism through social media, resulting in lifestyles modelled on movement, and the emergence of competitive mobilities? As growing travel volumes are one of the main challenges with regard to climate change, and closely related to problems such as global food production and species loss, these issues have great relevance. In contrast, whether it is likely that travel will be replaced by virtual reality, perhaps under resource use constraints (Benckendorff et al., 2014), remains questionable: it is also imaginable that such restrictions, even though for the best of the environment, will be opposed by travellers and industry.

Yet, it is clear that IT could have a far more important role in the development of sustainable tourism. There are numerous examples of platforms highlighting more sustainable choices, and there are a growing number of platforms specifically devoted to forms of sharing. These have a potential to contribute to greater environmental sustainability, because they can influence knowledge and awareness, and, more importantly, create "green trends" by highlighting "greener" services as higher quality choices. None of the larger platforms identified in this paper is currently unambiguously supporting such processes, however, and many smaller platforms lack transparency in terms of assessment criteria or methodologies used. Likewise, the visibility of environmental performance parameters is as yet limited on many platforms, even though positive examples have been identified.

Finally, economic sustainability challenges were found to be equally complex. Just a few years ago, Buhalis and Law (2008, p. 611) suggested that the Internet would challenge the role of intermediaries, as an increasing number of people would make reservations directly through hotel websites. This prediction has not come true, as a rapidly growing number of accommodation establishments now rely on a limited number of online global intermediaries. Even where peer-to-peer transactions are facilitated by platforms, these are likely to charge membership fees or commissions. Paradoxically, however, global platforms can empower small businesses, providing global visibility, while simultaneously fundamentally disrupting local business structures because of global market integration. Ratings and rankings are an important feature of platforms, influencing customer flows, and ultimately determining business success. Yet, there is evidence that ratings and rankings have also led to growing awareness of online reputation and changing guest expectations, with potentially controversial outcomes, as exemplified by "cultures of critique" and the empowerment of particularly demanding guests, a development not anticipated by Miller et al. (2010).

Overall, the paper has shown that IT, and specifically social media, have a wide range of implications for sustainability that are insufficiently understood, calling for a new research agenda on the interrelationships of tourism, IT and sustainability. This research agenda may specifically focus on economic value chains and the flow of financial resources; the consequences of IT for the rise of new mobility cultures and travel identity, and the consumption of distance for reasons related to sociality and social capital; as well as the opportunities of IT to guide consumer choices, including sustainability information and the marketing of more sustainable forms of tourism. Given the importance of these issues for the development of more sustainable tourism, as well as the global relevance of the phenomena outlined, this research agenda should receive immediate attention. A notable new opportunity, which this paper cannot explore here, is that research into tourism sustainability interrelationships has been given a series of new research opportunities stemming from IT-based methods: Germann Molz's (in press) paper on family voluntourism is a recent example.

Note

1. The terms "information communication technology" (ICT) and "information technology" (IT) are used interchangeably in this paper, subsuming social media.

Acknowledgments

The author is grateful to his colleagues at the Western Norway Research Institute, who are always willing to share their knowledge on the latest developments in social media, platforms, apps and IT more generally. Thomas Vith helped to collect data on platform user numbers. A special thanks goes to Bernard Lane, for his always careful editing.

Disclosure statement

No potential conflict of interest was reported by the author.

References

Aall, C. (2014). Sustainable tourism in practice: Promoting or perverting the quest for a sustainable development? *Sustainability, 6*(5), 2562−2583.

Adey, P., Budd, L., & Hubbard, P. (2007). Flying lessons: Exploring the social and cultural geographies of global air travel. *Progress in Human Geography, 31*(6), 773−791.

Agoda. (2015). Info (Facebook page). Retrieved 13 May 2015 from https://www.facebook.com/agoda/info?tab=page_info

AirBnB. (2015a). About us. Retrieved 13 May 2015 from https://www.airbnb.com/about/about-us

AirBnB. (2015b). About us. Retrieved 7 November 2015 from https://www.airbnb.com/about/about-us

Ali, A., & Frew, A.J. (2014). ICT and sustainable tourism development: An innovative perspective. *Journal of Hospitality and Tourism Technology, 5*(1), 2−16.

Atmosfair. (2014). Atmosfair Airline Index 2014. Retrieved 14 May 2015 from https://www.atmosfair.de/documents/10184/882239/AAI2014_DE/4e22246c-1b1c-4aca-9e8d-7ae89b6a818c

Ayeh, J.K. (2015). Travellers' acceptance of consumer-generated media: An integrated model of technology acceptance and source credibility theories. *Computers in Human Behavior, 48*, 173−180.

Ballantyne, R., & Packer, J. (2011). Using tourism free−choice learning experiences to promote environmentally sustainable behaviour: The role of post−visit 'action resources'. *Environmental Education Research, 17*(2), 201−215.

Ballantyne, R., Packer, J., & Falk, J. (2011). Visitors' learning for environmental sustainability: Testing short-and long-term impacts of wildlife tourism experiences using structural equation modelling. *Tourism Management, 32*(6), 1243−1252.

Ballantyne, R., Packer, J., Hughes, K., & Dierking, L. (2007). Conservation learning in wildlife tourism settings: Lessons from research in zoos and aquariums. *Environmental Education Research, 13*(3), 367−383.

Belk, R. (2014). You are what you can access: Sharing and collaborative consumption online. *Journal of Business Research, 67*(8), 1595−1600.

Benckendorff, P.J., Sheldon, P.J., & Fesenmaier, D.R. (2014). *Tourism information technology*. Wallingford: CABI.

Berscheid, E., Snyder, M., & Omoto, A.M. (1989). The relationship closeness inventory: Assessing the closeness of interpersonal relationships. *Journal of Personality and Social Psychology, 57*, 792−807.

Booking.com. (2015). Overview. Retrieved 14 May 2015 from http://www.booking.com/content/about.en-gb.html?dcid=4&lang=en-gb&sid=71f964d406607e8d0ee2a836ccf86bc3

Budeanu, A. (2013). Sustainability and tourism social media. In A.M. Munar, S. Gyimóthy, & C. Liping (Eds.), *Tourism social media: Transformations in identity, community and culture* (pp. 87−103). Bingley: Emerald.

Buhalis, D. (1998). Strategic use of information technologies in the tourism industry. *Tourism Management, 19*(5), 409−421.

Buhalis, D., & Law, R. (2008). Progress in information technology and tourism management: 20 years on and 10 years after the Internet − the state of eTourism research. *Tourism Management, 29*(4), 609−623.

Cacioppo, J.T., & Patrick, W. (2008). *Loneliness: Human nature and the need for social connection*. New York, NY: W.W. Norton.

Carey, S., Gountas, Y., & Gilbert, D. (1997). Tour operators and destination sustainability. *Tourism Management, 18*(7), 425–431.

Cohen, S., & Gössling, S. (2015). A darker side of hypermobility. *Environment and Planning A*, DOI: 10.1177/0308518×15597124

Couchsurfing. (2015). About us. Retrieved 13 May 2015 from http://about.couchsurfing.com/about/

Desforges, L. (2000). Travelling the world: Identity and travel biography. *Annals of Tourism Research, 27*(4), 926–945.

Dolby, N. (2004). Encountering an American self: Study abroad and national identity. *Comparative Education Review, 48*(2), 150–173.

Expedia. (2015a). Front page. Retrieved 13 May 2015 from http://www.expedia.com/?v=b

Facebook. (2015). Investor relations: Facebook reports first quarter 2015 results. Retrieved 13 May 2015 from http://investor.fb.com/releasedetail.cfm?ReleaseID=908022

Falk, J.H., Ballantyne, R., Packer, J., & Benckendorff, P. (2012). Travel and learning: A neglected tourism research area. *Annals of Tourism Research, 39*(2), 908–927.

Fishman, E., Washington, S., & Haworth, N. (2014). Bike share's impact on car use: Evidence from the United States, Great Britain, and Australia. *Transportation Research Part D: Transport and Environment, 31*, 13–20.

FlyerTalk. (2015). Front page. Retrieved 13 May 2015 from http://www.flyertalk.com/

Fodor's. (2015). Where do travelers want to go in 2015? Fodor's reveals popular destinations and emerging hotspots. Retrieved 13 May 2015 from http://www.fodors.com/press-room/press-releases/where-do-travelers-want-to-go-in-2015-fodors-reveals-popular-destinations-a

Fox, J., & Moreland, J.J. (2015). The dark side of social networking sites: An exploration of the relational and psychological stressors associated with Facebook use and affordances. *Computers in Human Behavior, 45*, 168–176.

Garcia, S.M., Tor, A., & Schiff, T.M. (2013). The psychology of competition: A social comparison perspective. *Perspectives on Psychological Science, 8*(6), 634–650.

Germann Molz, J. (2006). 'Watch us wander': Mobile surveillance and the surveillance of mobility. *Environment and Planning A, 38*(2), 377–393.

Germann Molz, J. (2012). *Travel connections: Tourism, technology and togetherness in a mobile world*. London: Routledge.

Germann Molz, J. (in press). Making a difference together: Discourses of transformation in family voluntourism. *Journal of Sustainable Tourism*, DOI: 10.1080/09669582.2015.1088862

Germann Molz, J., & Paris, C.M. (2015). The social affordances of flashpacking: Exploring the mobility nexus of travel and communication. *Mobilities, 10*(2), 173–192.

Gössling, S., Hall, C.M., & Andersson, A.C. (2016). A conceptualization of online review manipulation strategies by accommodation managers. *Current Issues in Tourism*. Submitted. Retrieved from http://dx.doi.org/10.1080/13683500.2015.1127337

Gössling, S., & Lane, B. (2015). Rural tourism and the development of Internet-based accommodation booking platforms: A study in the advantages, dangers and implications of innovation. *Journal of Sustainable Tourism, 23*(8&9), 1386–1403.

Gössling, S., & Nilsson, J.H. (2010). Frequent flyer programmes and the reproduction of mobility. *Environment and Planning A, 42*, 241–252.

Gössling, S., & Stavrinidi, I. (2015). Social networking, mobilities, and the rise of liquid identities. *Mobilities*, DOI: 10.1080/17450101.2015.1034453

Guest, G., Namey, E.E., & Mitchell, M.L. (2015). *Collecting qualitative data*. Thousand Oaks, CA: Sage.

Hall, C.M. (2013). Framing behavioural approaches to understanding and governing sustainable tourism consumption: Beyond neoliberalism, "nudging" and "green growth"? *Journal of Sustainable Tourism, 21*(7), 1091–1109.

Hays, S., Page, S.J., & Buhalis, D. (2013). Social media as a destination marketing tool: Its use by national tourism organisations. *Current Issues in Tourism, 16*(3), 211–239.

Hibbert, J.F., Dickinson, J.E., Gössling, S., & Curtin, S. (2013). Identity and tourism mobility: An exploration of the attitude-behaviour gap. *Journal of Sustainable Tourism, 21*(7), 999–1016.

Ho, C.-I., & Lee, Y.-L. (2007). The development of an e-travel service quality scale. *Tourism Management, 28*(6), 1434–1449.

HolidayCheck. (2015). About HolidayCheck. Retrieved 13 May 2015 from http://www.holidaycheck.com/aboutus.php

HomeExchange. (2015). About HomeExchange. Retrieved 13 May 2015 from https://www.homeexchange.com/en/about/

Hotels. (2015). About us. Retrieved 13 May 2015 from http://de.hotels.com/customer_care/about_us.html

HRS. (2015). HRS at a glance. Retrieved 13 May 2015 from http://www.hrs.de/web3/showCmsPage.do?clientId=ZW5fX05FWFQ-&cid=52-2&pageId=standard-01841

Hunter, C. (1997). Sustainable tourism as an adaptive paradigm. *Annals of Tourism Research, 24*(4), 850–867.

Hvass, K.A., & Munar, A.M. (2012). The takeoff of social media in tourism. *Journal of Vacation Marketing, 18*(2), 93–103.

Instagram. (2015). About us. Retrieved 13 May 2015 from https://instagram.com/about/us/

Jalilvand, M.R., & Samiei, N. (2012). The impact of electronic word of mouth on a tourism destination choice: Testing the theory of planned behavior (TPB). *Internet Research, 22*(5), 591−612.

Jeacle, I., & Carter, C. (2011). In TripAdvisor we trust: Rankings, calculative regimes and abstract systems. *Accounting, Organizations and Society, 36*(4), 293−309.

Jun, S.H., Vogt, C.A., & MacKay, K.J. (2007). Relationships between travel information search and travel product purchase in pretrip contexts. *Journal of Travel Research, 45*(3), 266−274.

Juvan, E., & Dolnicar, S. (2014a). Can tourists easily choose a low carbon footprint vacation? *Journal of Sustainable Tourism, 22*(2), 175−194.

Juvan, E., & Dolnicar, S. (2014b). The attitude−behaviour gap in sustainable tourism. *Annals of Tourism Research, 48*, 76−95.

Konrath, S.H., O'Brien, E.H., & Hsing, C. (2011). Changes in dispositional empathy in American college students over time: A meta-analysis. *Personality and Social Psychology Review, 15*(2), 180−198.

Lacey, R. (2012). How customer voice contributes to stronger service provider relationships. *Journal of Services Marketing, 26*(2), 137−144.

Larsen, G.R., & Guiver, J.W. (2013). Understanding tourists' perceptions of distance: A key to reducing the environmental impacts of tourism mobility. *Journal of Sustainable Tourism, 21*(7), 968−981.

Lastminute. (2015). Über lastminute.de. Retrieved 13 May 2015 from http://www.lastminute.de/company/ueber-last minute-de.html

Law, R., Qi, S., & Buhalis, D. (2010). Progress in tourism management: A review of website evaluation in tourism research. *Tourism Management, 31*(3), 297−313.

Lemelin, H., Dawson, J., & Stewart, E.J. (Eds.). (2013). *Last chance tourism: Adapting tourism opportunities in a changing world*. Abingdon: Routledge.

Leung, D., Law, R., Van Hoof, H., & Buhalis, D. (2013). Social media in tourism and hospitality: A literature review. *Journal of Travel & Tourism Marketing, 30*(1−2), 3−22.

Liburd, J.J. (2005). Sustainable tourism and innovation in mobile tourism services. *Tourism Review International, 9*(1), 107−118.

Mann, S., & Cadman, R. (2014). Does being bored make us more creative? *Creativity Research Journal, 26*(2), 165−173.

Martin, E., Shaheen, S.A., & Lidicker, J. (2010). Impact of carsharing on household vehicle holdings. *Transportation Research Record: Journal of the Transportation Research Board, 2143*(1), 150−158.

Mauri, A.G., & Minazzi, R., 2013. Web reviews influence on expectations and purchasing intentions of hotel potential customers. *International Journal of Hospitality Management, 34*, 99−107.

Mayer, R., Ryley, T., & Gillingwater, D. (2012). Passenger perceptions of the green image associated with airlines. *Journal of Transport Geography, 22*, 179−186.

McQuilken, L., & Robertson, N. (2011). The influence of guarantees, active requests to voice and failure severity on customer complaint behavior. *International Journal of Hospitality Management, 30*(4), 953−962.

Melián-González, S., Bulchand-Gidumal, J., & López-Valcárcel, B.G. (2013). Online customer reviews of hotels as participation increases, better evaluation is obtained. *Cornell Hospitality Quarterly, 54*(3), 274−283.

Miller, G., Rathouse, K., Scarles, C., Holmes, K., & Tribe, J. (2010). Public understanding of sustainable tourism. *Annals of Tourism Research, 37*(3), 627−645.

Munar, A.M., & Jacobsen, J.K.S. (2014). Motivations for sharing tourism experiences through social media. *Tourism Management, 43*, 46−54.

Noroozi, A., & Fotouhi, Z. (2010). The influence of semantic web on decision making of customers in tourism industry. *International Journal of Information Science and Management*, Special Issue 1, 77−98.

Noy, C. (2004). This trip really changed me: Backpackers' narratives of self-change. *Annals of Tourism Research, 31*(1), 78−102.

O'Connor, P. (2008). User-generated content and travel: A case study on Tripadvisor.com. In P. O'Connor, W. Höpken, & U. Gretzel (Eds.), *Information and communication technologies in tourism* 2008 (pp. 47−58). Vienna: Springer.

Öğüt, H., & Onur Taş, B.K. (2012). The influence of internet customer reviews on the online sales and prices in hotel industry. *The Service Industries Journal, 32*(2), 197−214.

Opodo. (2015). About us. Retrieved 13 May 2015 from http://www.opodo.com/about_us/

Orbitz. (2015). Orbitz. Retrieved 13 May 2015 from http://careers.orbitz.com/orbitz.html

Pappas, N. (2014). The effect of distance, expenditure and culture on the expression of social status through tourism. *Tourism Planning and Development, 11*(4), 387−404.

Pearce, P.L., & Lee, U.-I. (2005). Developing the travel career approach to tourist motivation. *Journal of Travel Research, 43* (3), 226−237.

Pearson, C., & Hussain, Z. (2015). Smartphone use, addiction, narcissism, and personality: A mixed methods investigation. *International Journal of Cyber Behavior, Psychology and Learning, 5*(1), 17−32.

Phillips, P., Zigan, K., Santos Silva, M.M., & Schegg, R. (2015). The interactive effects of online reviews on the determinants of Swiss hotel performance: A neural network analysis. *Tourism Management, 50*, 130−141.

Poon, A. (1993). *Tourism, technology and competitive strategies*. Wallingford: CABI.

Randles, S., & Mander, S. (2009). Aviation consumption and the climate change debate: 'Are you going to tell me off for flying?' *Technology Analysis & Strategic Management, 21*(1), 93–113.

Reis, H.T., Clark, M.S., & Holmes, J.G. (2004). Perceived partner responsiveness as an organizing construct in the study of intimacy and closeness. In D.J. Mashek & A.P. Aron (Eds.), *Handbook of closeness and intimacy* (pp. 201–225). Mahwah, NJ: Lawrence Erlbaum Associates.

Ryan, T., & Xenos, S. (2011). Who uses Facebook? An investigation into the relationship between the Big Five, shyness, narcissism, loneliness, and Facebook usage. *Computers in Human Behavior, 27*(5), 1658–1664.

Scott, D., & Lemieux, C. (2010). Weather and climate information for tourism. *Procedia Environmental Sciences, 1*, 146–183.

Scott, M.M., & Frew, A.J. (2013). Exploring the role of in-trip applications for sustainable tourism: Expert perspectives. In Gretzel, U., Law, R. & Fuchs, M. (Eds), *Information and Communication Technologies in Tourism 2010* (pp. 36–46). Berlin: Springer.

Shaheen, S., & Guzman, S. 2011. Worldwide bikesharing. Retrieved 13 May 2015 from http://tsrc.berkeley.edu/worldwide%20bikesharing

Sheldon, P.J. (1997). *Tourism information technology*. Wallingford: CABI.

Sparks, B.A., & Browning, V. (2011). The impact of online reviews on hotel booking intentions and perception of trust. *Tourism Management, 32*(6), 1310–1323.

Thurlow, C., & Jaworski, A. (2006). The alchemy of the upwardly mobile: Symbolic capital and the stylization of elites in frequent-flyer programmes. *Discourse & Society, 17*(1), 99–135.

Tisdell, C., & Wilson, C. (2001). Wildlife-based tourism and increased support for nature conservation financially and otherwise: Evidence from sea turtle ecotourism at Mon Repos. *Tourism Economics, 7*(3), 233–249.

Touray, K., & Jung, T. (2010). Exploratory study on contributions of ICTs to sustainable tourism development in Manchester. In Gretzel, U., Law, R. & Fuchs, M. (Eds), *Information and Communication Technologies in Tourism 2010* (pp. 493–505). Berlin: Springer.

TripAdvisor. (2014). As a business representative, how can I report that a guest threatened me with a bad review? Retrieved 2 February 2014 from: https://www.tripadvisorsupport.com/hc/en-us/articles/200614417-As-a-business-representative-how-can-I-report-that-a-guest-threatened-me-with-a-bad-review-

TripAdvisor. (2015a). About TripAdvisor. Retrieved 13 May 2015 from http://www.tripadvisor.com/PressCenter-c6-About_Us.html

TripAdvisor. (2015b). About TripAdvisor. Retrieved 7 November 2015 from http://www.tripadvisor.com/PressCenter-c6-About_Us.html

Trivago. (2015). Who we are. Retrieved 13 May 2015 from http://www.trivago.com/static/company/company

Turkle, S. (2011). *Alone together: Why we expect more from technology and less from each other*. New York, NY: Basic Books.

Uber. (2015). Uber. Retrieved 14 May 2015 from www.uber.com

UNEP & UNWTO. (2005). *Making tourism more sustainable – a guide for policy makers*. Paris: Author.

UNWTO. (2014). Concept note – towards the development of the 10YFP sustainable tourism programme. Retrieved 28 April 2015 from http://dtxtq4w60xqpw.cloudfront.net/sites/all/files/docpdf/10yfpstpconceptnotedec2014.pdf

Urry, J. (2000). *Sociology beyond societies: Mobilities for the twenty-first century*. London: Routledge.

Urry, J. (2007). *Mobilities*. Cambridge: Polity Press.

Urry, J. (2011). Social networks, mobile lives and social inequalities. *Journal of Transport Geography, 21*, 24–30.

Venere. (2015). Our services. Retrieved 13 May 2015 from http://www.venere.com/aboutus/page_template.html?ab_3_en

Wayn. (2015). About us. Retrieved 13 May 2015 from http://www.wayn.com/aboutus

Werthner, H., & Klein, S. (1999). *Information technology and tourism: A challenging relationship*. Vienna: Springer.

Whitmarsh, L., Seyfang, G., & O'Neill, S. (2011). Public engagement with carbon and climate change: To what extent is the public 'carbon capable'? *Global Environmental Change, 21*(1), 56–65.

Williams, K.D. (2001). *Ostracism: The power of silence*. New York, NY: Guildford.

Xiang, Z., & Gretzel, U. (2010). Role of social media in online travel information search. *Tourism Management, 31*(2), 179–188.

Yacouel, N., & Fleischer, A. (2012). The role of cybermediaries in reputation building and price premiums in the online hotel market. *Journal of Travel Research, 51*(2), 219–226.

Zhang, Y., & Vásquez, C. (2014). Hotels' responses to online reviews: Managing consumer dissatisfaction. *Discourse, Context & Media, 6*, 54–64.

Zhang, Z., Ye, Q., Law, R., & Li, Y. (2010). The impact of e-word-of-mouth on the online popularity of restaurants: A comparison of consumer reviews and editor reviews. *International Journal of Hospitality Management, 29*(4), 694–700.

Zhao, S., Grasmuck, S., & Martin, J. (2008). Identity construction on Facebook: Digital empowerment in anchored relationships. *Computers in Human Behaviour, 24*, 1816–1836.

Zoover. (2015). Jobs. Retrieved 13 May 2015 from http://www.zoover.de/jobs

An environmental social marketing intervention in cultural heritage tourism: a realist evaluation

Diana Gregory-Smith ⓘ, Victoria K. Wells, Danae Manika and David J. McElroy

ABSTRACT

Following Pawson and Tilley's principles of realist evaluation and the *context–mechanism–outcome* (CMO) framework, this paper conducts a process evaluation of an environmental social marketing intervention in a heritage tourism organisation. Social marketing and employee environmental interventions have received relatively scant attention in tourism. Additionally, prior literature mostly focused on the evaluation of intervention outcomes (i.e. how far the intervention produces precise targeted outcomes) and ignores the importance of process evaluation (i.e. identifying what works, for whom, under which circumstances and how, plus issues of intervention maintenance). This paper fills this literature gap using realist evaluation theory and academic perspectives, as well as via the reflections of practitioners involved in intervention design and delivery. Findings suggest that a good understanding of the tourism and organisational *context* (regarding the dimensions of structure, culture, agency and relations) and the use of tailored, action-focused *mechanisms* (for each context dimension) are critical to achieving transformational *outcomes* in environmental interventions in cultural heritage organisations. Based on these findings, it is concluded that the CMO is a useful framework for assessing environmental social marketing interventions in tourism (both for heritage and other tourism organisations). Implications for tourism practice and further research directions are also discussed.

Introduction

Sustainable and responsible tourism has broadly embraced marketing (Caruana, Glozer, Crane, & McCabe, 2014; Chhabra, 2009) but one area of marketing that has received relatively scant attention is social marketing, which uses marketing techniques and strategies to encourage behaviour change and to benefit society (Lee & Kotler, 2015). Where social marketing has been used in tourism, the focus has been on demarketing tourism and tourists' sustainable behaviour (Hall, 2014, 2016). Sustainable and responsible tourism have also focused on corporate social responsibility (CSR) (Nicolau, 2008), particularly environmental issues (Font, Walmsley, Cogotti, McCombes, & Häusler, 2012). However, CSR research in this area has generally focused on the environmental behaviour of tourists (Cheng & Wu, 2015; Miller, Merrilees, & Coghlan, 2015) and marketing managers (El Dief & Font, 2010). This reflects the focus in mainstream CSR, which generally overlooks the micro-level of environmental behaviour within organisations, i.e. the employees. It is at this micro-level that social marketing and CSR join forces, in the understanding of and in conducting interventions[1] to encourage employees' pro-environmental behaviour (PEB). Some work has begun to look at this area (Chou, 2014; Wells, Manika, Gregory-Smith, Taheri, & McCowlen, 2015) but much is still to be understood. Important progress has been made in the hospitality sector: Zientara and Zamojska (in press) present a useful summary.

Understanding employee behaviour towards the environment helps the process of marketing pro-environmental thinking to them as on-site agents. It can also help employees to market sustainability messages to their visitors, a process discussed in Warren, Becken, and Coghlan (in press).

In the field of social marketing interventions, a clear distinction must be made between process evaluation and outcome evaluation (Linnell, 2014). Existing frameworks such as Lee and Kotler's (2015) Social Marketing Planning Process and McKenzie-Mohr's (2011) Community-Based Social Marketing Planning Process include stages dedicated primarily to outcome evaluation. However, practitioners and researchers alike are starting to propose a new view on what needs to be evaluated to allow a deeper and more broadly useful assessment of interventions. This paper, therefore, focuses on this process evaluation, which prioritises the process rather than the outcome(s) and highlights "the types and quantities of services delivered, the beneficiaries of those services, the resources used to deliver the services, the practical problems encountered, and the ways such problems were resolved" and it is particularly "useful for understanding how program impact and outcome were achieved and for programme replication" (Linnell, 2014). Therefore, through the focus on process evaluation, this paper fills a gap in both social marketing and tourism literatures in the context of employee pro-environmental interventions and behaviour.

First, this paper contributes to prior literature by conducting a detailed process evaluation of a social marketing sustainability intervention within heritage tourism. This process evaluation builds on a prior outcome evaluation, the details of which can be found in Wells et al. (2015), and is conducted from two perspectives – academic (i.e. via realist evaluation theory) and practitioner (i.e. reflections of practitioners involved in the intervention design/delivery). The process evaluation takes an interdisciplinary perspective consistent with the view that "research on sustainable tourism within society is increasingly likely to examine it through the use of 'critical' assessments that draw on general social science approaches, theories, and concepts" (Bramwell & Lane, 2014, p. 1). Specifically, the process evaluation of the social marketing intervention within heritage tourism was undertaken by employing Pawson and Tilley's (1997) realist evaluation theory and applying their "trio of explanatory components" (p. 77) also known as the context—mechanism–outcome (CMO) framework.[2] This builds on the proposed case for critical realism, which has been made in the context of tourism research by Platenkamp and Botterill (2013). It will be the first of its kind.

The present process evaluation utilises a case-study approach of an environmental intervention within a cultural heritage tourism organisation, which was designed and delivered by social marketing practitioners from Global Action Plan (GAP – a leading UK environmental behaviour change charity, which designs and leads environmental behaviour changes interventions in workplaces, communities and schools [http://www.globalactionplan.org.uk/]. None of the authors of this paper are GAP practitioners involved in the design or the delivery of the intervention). The intervention took a downstream social marketing approach, focused on influencing individual employee behaviours within the heritage organisation such as changing energy use (i.e. lighting and heating) and recycling (i.e. waste reduction) behaviours. This was delivered via a "Sustainability Toolkit" (containing information from line managers, stickers, posters, newsletters) and which could be tailored according to the needs and infrastructure of the locations where the intervention (four sites and the head office of the heritage organisation). Based on a field experiment methodology (Bamberg, 2002) undertaken by GAP practitioners, the intervention was a success and saved 1888.42 kWh at site level over a period of one year (equating to a £255.31 saving) as well as resulting in attitudinal and behavioural outcomes (for full details, see Wells et al., 2015). However, the focus of the current paper is the realist evaluation of the process and, therefore, data from a range of sources are used: (1) qualitative data collected prior the intervention (this secondary data were collected by GAP practitioners as part of their design, delivery and outcome evaluation); (2) documentary evidence (i.e. GAP's practitioner report to the client heritage organisation); and (3) qualitative interviews conducted by the authors of this paper with the GAP practitioners who developed and delivered the intervention. This was used to provide a practitioner reflection on the process of designing and delivering the intervention.

Second, the paper contributes to prior literature, with a discussion of the implications of using CMO in the tourism context (both heritage and broader tourism) for evaluating similar interventions and with recommendations for future research. Next, the paper will review the relevant literature, followed by the methodology, analysis and results.

Literature review

Social marketing, pro-environmental behaviour and CSR in tourism

Social marketing is defined as "the systematic application of marketing alongside other concepts and techniques to achieve specific behavioural goals, for a social good" (French & Blair-Stevens, 2007, p. 32) and as "an approach used to develop activities aimed at changing or maintaining people's behaviour for the benefits of individuals and society as a whole" (Hopwood & Merritt, 2011, p. 4). Social marketing has been used to tackle a wide range of social issues including general PEB (McKenzie-Mohr, 2000), specific behaviours such as waste reduction and recycling (Mee, Clewes, Phillips, & Read, 2004), water conservation (Dolnicar & Hurlimann, 2010) and energy saving behaviours (Steg, 2008). Within the workplace, social marketing has been used to target and understand employee's PEBs (Gregory-Smith, Wells, Manika, & Graham, 2015; Smith & O'Sullivan, 2012) due to close relationships between employees and consumers (Coles, Fenclova, & Dinan, 2013) and their responsibility for implementation of CSR strategy (Costa & Menichini, 2013).

However, the role social marketing plays in tourism is under-researched, especially related to employee's PEBs. For example, Chou's (2014) study of employee environmental behaviour in tourism examined individual (environmental beliefs, personal environmental norms, self-reported environmental behaviour) and organisational variables (green organisational climate), as well as demographics to explain employee behaviour but did not examine the impact of an intervention/campaign. Only one paper has examined a social marketing campaign in tourism (Wells et al., 2015) and found that though it is a beneficial approach to influencing heritage organisation employees' PEBs, knowledge and awareness of environmental solutions are often lacking. Beyond these studies, little is known about the potential success factors for social marketing interventions within tourism; hence further evaluation and understanding are required.

Evaluation: outcomes versus process

Social marketing has developed as a field over the last 40 years, but it is generally agreed that there is room for improvement in its practice and one of the most significant areas for development is evaluation (Biroscak et al., 2014). Increasingly, social marketers are focusing on evaluation (Polit, 2012), which is clearly an essential element, largely because of increasingly stretched resources and the need to demonstrate best value for money (Lister & Merritt, 2013). However, research into evaluation within social marketing is in its infancy and to date has largely focused on specific outcomes (e.g. reductions in water/electricity used, increases in amounts of paper recycled, etc.) rather than taking a deeper and broader approach to evaluation.

One area of intervention evaluation research, which has developed more significantly, is that of public health interventions (Linnan & Steckler, 2002). Social marketing could learn much from the strategic and planned approaches, tools and methodologies available in this area. Process evaluation is such an approach and it is particularly suitable for social marketing, as it has been demonstrated to be of value in intervention evaluations as wide ranging as drug/substance use/abuse (Harachi, Abbot, Catalano, Haggerty, & Fleming, 1999) and workplace stress (Biron & Karanika-Murray, 2014).

Process evaluation is not concerned with whether a programme works or does not, but why and under what circumstances (Harachi et al., 1999; Saunders, Martin, & Joshi, 2005) it might work. It has been described as examining the "black-box" of an intervention (Saunders et al., 2005) and focuses on implementation elements (which may explain variability in results), contextual elements and questions elements such as intervention practitioners' self-efficacy, enthusiasm, preparedness and confidence, and any bottlenecks or problems encountered (Harachi et al., 1999; Hulscher, Laurant, & Grol, 2003). It is the chance to "disentangle the factors that ensure successful outcomes, characterise the failure to achieve success, or attempt to document the steps involved in achieving successful implementation of an intervention" (Linnan & Steckler, 2002, p. 1). Process evaluation can be used both formatively and summatively and provides input for future planning of interventions, or the application of an intervention in a different setting (Saunders et al., 2005).

Earlier process evaluation approaches were relatively basic and there is not a specified process evaluation framework that has gained attention in social marketing. Hence, this paper uses a more sophisticated approach, using realist evaluation theory, for a deep understanding of all evaluation elements (Moore et al., 2014) and to assess the success of an environmental social marketing intervention. The realist evaluation focuses on the evaluation of the process, within which outcomes are only one element, and therefore is a superior method of evaluating interventions.

Realist evaluation and the CMO framework

Realist evaluation focuses on "what works for whom in what circumstances and in what respects, and how?" (Pawson & Tilley, 2004, p. 5). While a case for critical realism has been made in the context of tourism research (Platenkamp & Botterill, 2013), the principles of realist evaluation have been only recently and scarcely applied to tourism-related areas such as heritage crime prevention (Grove & Pease, 2014), analysis of travel blogs (Banyai & Havitz, 2013) and community-based programmes (Nilsson, Baxter, Butler, & McAlpine, 2016).

In this paper, the realist evaluation of an environmental social marketing intervention will be carried out using the CMO framework, with a specific focus on the *context* and *mechanism* dimensions (detailed below). As noted earlier, this evaluation will be the first of its kind. A brief analysis of the *outcome* dimension will be included to reflect a general assessment. (Description of specific planned outcomes, e.g. cost savings, energy savings, change in attitude and behaviour-related variables, etc. can be found in Wells et al. (2015) as noted in the introduction). Subsequently, reflections on the lessons learnt and recommendations for tourism organisations are discussed.

In realist evaluation, *context* is described as the conditions under which the programme is introduced, works or has worked (Pawson & Tilley, 2004). These conditions are relevant to the choice and use of subsequent *mechanism(s)* as per CMO. The *context* includes elements such as interpersonal/ social relationships, technology, economic conditions, location, demographics material resources, rules and systems (Pawson & Tilley, 2004). Context is an important aspect in heritage, tourism and sustainability/conservation research (e.g. Chabra, 2009; Wickham & Lehman, 2015) and Adger et al. (2003) has highlighted the need for context-specific solutions in sustainability and decision-making research, while Nilsson et al. (2016) reflected on the numerous aspects of context (e.g. culture, logistics, knowledge/cognitions, time) that influence the outcomes of community-based conservation programmes, e.g. natural parks, ecotourism, wildlife protection. Hence, a detailed assessment of the *context* is critical to the implementation, success and durability of an intervention in the tourism arena.

Mechanism(s) are those resources that enable/disable the programme subjects to make the programme work (Pawson & Tilley, 2004) and can be divided into structural, cultural, agential and relational mechanisms each of which will produce various outcomes (de Souza, 2013). *Outcomes* follow *mechanisms* in the CMO framework. The consideration of relevant mechanisms is also critical because programmes have to be designed in a way that will "activate the underlying causal mechanisms situated within pre-existing social structures to generate change or a different potential existing within the action context" (de Souza, 2013, p. 146).

Outcome(s) include intended and unintended consequences of the intervention, as a result of activating different mechanisms. Therefore, the outcomes of an intervention can show mixed patterns of behaviour. In a realist evaluation, unlike traditional evaluations, the aim is not to test hypotheses such as "does intervention x on subject y produce outcome z?" (Pullin & Stewart, 2006), but rather the focus will be showing which aspects of the programme are key for maintaining the programme and which ones were (not) useful or successful (Pawson & Tilley, 2004). The size of specific outcomes (e.g. financial savings, return on investment, number of energy bulbs replaced, etc.) is less important than the lessons learnt (Tilley, 2000).

Methodology

This paper takes a case-study approach to complete a realist evaluation of an environmental social marketing intervention with a focus on process evaluation in heritage tourism. In doing so, this evaluation also takes two perspectives: (1) academic (via realist evaluation theory) and (2) practitioner (via reflections of being on the front line of intervention design/delivery).

Case studies provide an up-close and in-depth understanding of a case set within a real-world context (Yin, 2009), and are useful when asking descriptive (what is happening?) and explanatory questions (how and why did something happen?). This is aligned with the realist evaluation approach (Pawson & Tilley, 2004) and hence suitable for the present study (Yin, 2011). Case studies draw on multiple sources of evidence (Yin, 2011) as do process evaluations (Linnan & Steckler, 2002; Moore et al., 2014) and this study draws on hybrid data, using triangulated qualitative data (Edmondson & McManus, 2007). In this paper, both data triangulation and method triangulation are used (primary qualitative data from interviews with GAP practitioners who designed and delivered the intervention and the employees of the heritage organisation who received the intervention; focus groups with employees of the heritage organisation and secondary data drawn from the official report). Through triangulation, the limitations and biases of using one particular methodology or just one stakeholder's opinion are overcome (Decrop, 1999).

As a contribution, this paper focuses on the novel insights provided by the data gathered from interviews with the GAP practitioners who designed and delivered the intervention in the heritage organisation. These interviews sought to understand GAP practitioners' involvement with, and contribution to, the intervention, if and how they carried out the evaluation of the intervention, and their reflections on the process and decisions. This data is key to a realist evaluation of the intervention and to provide reflections on the lessons to be learnt and implications for tourism and social marketing. Individual semi-structured interviews that lasted 40–60 minutes were conducted with three practitioners. The GAP practitioners were the managing partner (who liaised with the senior management of the heritage organisation and oversaw the strategic dimension of the project); the project manager (who developed the intervention, organised site visits, developed materials and delivered most on-site visits and training); and the project assistant/ambassador (who carried out on-site interviews and focus groups with the heritage organisation's employees). In the analysis below, the quotes from the GAP practitioners will be listed as P1 – managing partner; P2 – project manager; P3 – project assistant. Additionally, data from 57 separate heritage organisation employees (i.e. from 42 short individual interviews and 6 focus groups prior to the intervention) are used this paper. This included a range of full-time heritage organisation employees (e.g. site managers, shop assistants, office employees), seasonal staff and volunteers. The availability and the setting in which they were conducting their daily activities dictated the choice between the two methods. In this paper, the qualitative data from the heritage organisation's employees will be used to delineate the realist evaluation of the intervention in terms of its *context* and the enabling or disabling *mechanisms* (rather than their attitudinal and behavioural outcomes which are reported in a different analysis in Wells et al., 2015). Below, quotations from the heritage organisation employees will be referred to as E1, E2, etc. Finally, the official report to the heritage organisation management from the GAP practitioners (a secondary data source) was also analysed, and extracts from it will be signposted in the analysis below using the abbreviation OR.

A copy of the general protocol used in the interviews and focus groups with the employees can be found in Supplemental Material Table S1, available in the online version of this paper.

All the interviews and focus groups (from heritage organisation employees and GAP practitioners) were audio-recorded and transcribed verbatim. All the data were analysed using thematic analysis (Braun & Clarke, 2006). More specifically, using Strauss and Corbin's (1990) guidelines, three sequential coding procedures were used: open coding, axial coding and selective coding. Following the emergence of new categories and themes, the data were continuously re-evaluated and re-organised by two coders, who used Pawson and Tilley's theoretical framework and definitions to resolve any differences. All the data analyses were aligned to the CMO framework and followed de Souza's (2013, p. 149) elaboration approach. This approach focuses on analysing the context in terms of structure (with mechanisms including roles/positions, practices, resources and processes), culture (with mechanisms connected to ideas/propositional formulations about structure, culture, agency and relations), agency (with mechanisms related to beliefs and reasons for action or non-action) and relations (with mechanisms including mechanisms connected to duties/ responsibilities, rights and power).

Data analysis and discussion

Aligned with realist evaluation principles, the analysis below focuses on the process evaluation using the CMO framework, with particular attention given to the *context* and *mechanism* dimensions and a brief overview of process outcomes. This analysis follows de Souza's (2013) elaboration. Figure 1

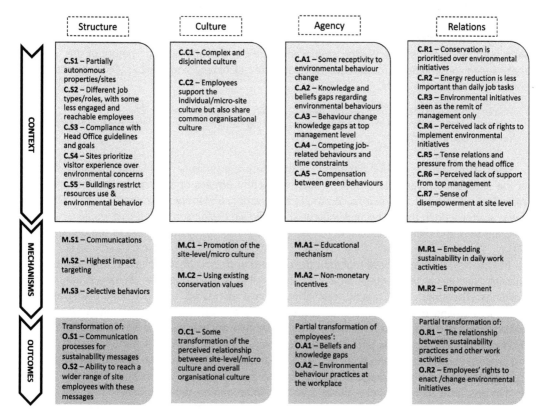

Figure 1. Summary of CMO-based evaluation.

provides a summary of the analysis and findings, which match the CMO elements breakdown and four dimensions for each of these (i.e. structure, culture, agency and relations). The detailed analysis below as well as the summary present in Figure 1 is based on the qualitative data multiple sources (GAP practitioners, heritage organisation employees and official report).

Context

Regarding context, the data revealed several particularities of the structure of the heritage organisation. The practitioners described the organisation as having "…properties [which] are all largely autonomous and operate individually" (P1) but which also need to comply with head office sustainability-related guidelines/goals: "they've set themselves a lot of targets, they got EMS [environmental management system] they are developing and embedding within all of the sites" (P2). However, at the site level, the priority was the visitor experience, not sustainability:

> On a cold day if obviously it's quite difficult for a visitor attraction, so during open hours to the public there will be doors open throughout the building. (E7)

The complexity of this structure and the different priorities was subsequently acknowledged by GAP practitioners, but there is little evidence that it was considered at the earlier stage of identifying mechanisms and designing the intervention; therefore, this may have affected intervention outcomes. Thus, the official report only acknowledges the challenge needed "to balance the demands of energy saving and visitor experience" in certain busy areas of the heritage organisation's sites (OR, p. 6). Additionally, in terms of job types, the organisational structure included a range employees such as full time, part time, casual workers, volunteers, the latter proving to be less engaged and likely to be reached as they "are not paid [and] have erratic work hours" (P1). This probably affected the implementation of the intervention.

Other context-related issues noticed by GAP practitioners from their own assessment and discussions with the heritage organisation employees were the age and heritage nature of the buildings that needed conservation considerations (P1); and the lack of recycling facilities (OR), which restricted some sustainable behaviours:

> We can't have gas in here because we are a sixteenth century building so it's electric. (E4)
> …because of the castle's historic nature we can't do anything about the windows… [and] because of access we can't have doors closed. (E5)

When assessing the cultural dimension of the context, a similarly complex and disjointed culture of the organisation was noted, with "… lots of different entities of an organisation that have own individual cultures but also share a common [organisational] identity and culture…" (P1). Therefore, it was acknowledged that "[The challenge was]…could we design something that would work across different sites and different areas and rely on them sharing the overall culture of the organisation?" (P1).

The aspects discussed above highlight the complex and somewhat conflicting organisational and cultural structures of the heritage organisation, as well as issues around the physical structure of the buildings. Therefore, GAP practitioners should have pondered and activated/deactivated the enabling/disabling mechanisms related to positions, practices, resources and culture. A thorough consideration of the potential and, more importantly, relevant mechanisms would have led to a better design of the intervention and ultimately to even a more successful intervention. Issues concerning organisational, cultural and building-related characteristics appear to be of particular importance to large and/or complex heritage tourism organisations, with multiple sites and distinctive features, as they are more likely to involve bureaucratic organisational systems with shared as well as divergent priorities, local practices and culture (Ashworth, 2000). Therefore, future environmental interventions in large heritage organisations should consider carefully these issues and ensure that a systematic assessment of the mechanisms is carried out in order to implement a suitable and bespoke environmental intervention.

Part of context, the agency dimension (i.e. relating to beliefs and reasons for action/lack of action) must also be evaluated pre-intervention. The project assistant who carried out the initial interviews with the heritage organisation employees commended some employees' receptivity to environmental behaviour change (P3) but:

> Staff in the properties themselves had belief gaps. I am not sure people felt they could do very much. There was not too much awareness of how they as an individual impact on the energy use of the property. (P1)

which meant they were less likely to be motivated to behave sustainably and probably less responsive to an intervention due to knowledge and beliefs gaps (P1, P3).

Similarly, there were issues regarding agency not only with employees working on sites but also at higher levels: "The knowledge gaps at the management levels were more about how to we help people to change these behaviours, what steps do we take, what interventions do we need…" (P1). Other reasons for lack of action were job-related competing behaviours and priorities, as well as time constraints:

> I do a reasonable amount but I try to keep it to the essential or where I really need to, partly because if I do too much I don't have time to get on with the actual work….time and convenience is a big element. (E10)

Finally, as observed by GAP practitioners, some employees tended to compensate between behaviours as "people felt they were doing something and therefore they tackled the environment or environmental issues…'Well, I'm recycling already what else do I need to do?' (P3).

Based on the analysis of the agency dimension, the practitioners should have considered more carefully the mechanisms favouring employees' reasons for actions and counteracting the reasons for non-action.

Finally, the relations dimension was also a most complex dimension of context. As per the pre-intervention interview with heritage organisation employees, there was an issue related to their perceptions of duties and responsibilities, and the fact that employees did not see value in environmental initiatives. These were described as a "move away from the conservation side of things and started to become more business-orientated, less respect for the property and the history of the architecture" (E3). Some employees did not prioritise environmental behaviour due to other job tasks: "I've got far more things to worry about [than energy use] … [it's]clients … because we have [events] functions [so] very very busy night working" (E9). Other employees noted environmental initiatives are the remit of site management and displayed a lack initiative or interest: "I don't actually get involved in anything like that, it goes to…the general manager" (E2). Additionally, employees mentioned the lack of perceived ownership and ability or the rights to change:

> We discussed before about the gardens department here making use of food waste for composting….I don't understand all of the information about it myself, but I know that's why we didn't particularly go down that route…. (E6)

The employee pre-intervention interviews also revealed some issues around power relations and alluded to tense relations with, and pressure from, the Head Office. Despite suggested support for the implementation of the environmental intervention from the Board of Directors, Head of CSR and the Head of Communications (according to P1), the project assistant also noted this tension and:

> there were significant differences between different sites, between site managers…some under a great deal of pressure … and who saw perhaps the interview as a bit of an inconvenience or they were quite defensive in some respect. It was almost like they were being audited…perhaps they didn't really understand the focus of the interview. (P3)
> There was not too much awareness of how they as an individual impact on the energy use of the property; there was a sense of disempowerment. (P1)

Therefore, the intervention should have considered enabling/disabling mechanisms connected to several aspects of the agency dimension (i.e. duties, rights and power) at intervention design stage.

Mechanisms

Several mechanisms related to the structure used by GAP practitioners during the intervention were identified following data analysis; only some mechanisms seemed well connected to the context analysis or applied fully.

Regarding role/positions and processes, a particular focus was given to mechanisms regarding communication. They were used by GAP practitioners to reach heritage organisation employees with different roles/positions and communicate to employees at site level about environmental actions and behaviours. These communication mechanisms were designed to be multi-channel, personalised and to engage various types of employees, which was aligned with the context analysis that revealed a dual central and site-level culture and structure of the heritage organisation:

> We had workshops at each of the different sites, we had remote support through calling and emails. A lot of the materials were delivered digitally and either printed locally or adapted locally. (P1)

The data triangulation indicated the communication mechanism was the most developed intervention mechanism and that attention was paid to a wide range of aspects (i.e. messages, messengers, creative strategies and communication channels). This is aligned with recent research on the communication of sustainability practices that have a positive effect on employees' organisational commitment and a negative effect on turnover intentions (Kim, Song, & Lee, 2016). Heritage literature had mainly focused on general external communication strategies with visitors (e.g. Chhabra, 2009). Only recently, research into the role of communications for CSR purposes has started to emerge. Recent models of communication of sustainability practices propose communicating with a range of internal and external stakeholders, including employees (see Wickham and Lehman' s (2015) museums study). More generically, in the casino industry, Kim et al. (2016) found aspects of CSR (i.e. economic, legal, ethical and philanthropic responsibility) and aspects of internal marketing (i.e. welfare system, training, compensation, communication and management support) have a positive effect on employees' organisational commitment and a negative effect on turnover intentions (see also Zientara & Zamojska, in press). This evidence concurs with the suitability of choosing a communications mechanism for the environmental intervention. However, overall, there is limited research on the role of the internal sustainability communications for heritage employees, with the present paper making some initial contributions. Moreover, internal marketing communications using new media (e.g. email, intranet, internet), some of which are used in this intervention, have been highlighted as an effective tool for employee motivation and as a two-way communication that can enhance trust in the organisation and enable change of organisational practices (De Bussy, Ewing, & Pitt, 2003). Nevertheless, this has not been examined in a heritage tourism context before the present study. Therefore, communication via new media tools could be beneficial to the employee interventions (Sanchez, 1999).

For ensuring better reach and success, GAP practitioners used the highest impact targeting and selective behaviours mechanisms according to where more resources were used for heating, lighting and appliances, waste and catering (OR, p. 12). As mentioned by the project manager (i.e. GAP practitioner):

> we were trying to reach a little bit of everybody but there were key areas of the sites where we wanted to have a bigger impact – 1) the shops because that's where a lot of waste was being generated, both material/paper waste and food waste; 2) the key facilities managers were the people we wanted to engage with; 3) and any of the house-based staff so people who were actually based within the buildings themselves where there were issues like lighting and heating. (P2)

These mechanisms appeared relevant to heritage organisation employees who performed certain behaviours as

> ...departments were very interested...because they had budgets that they had to keep to so if they could reduce their impact or reduce their costs in terms of utilities then they might have more to spend on their other activities. (P3)

However, no specific mechanisms were used to overcome some of issues revealed in the *context* analysis regarding perceptions of practices (i.e. complete site compliance with head office guidelines and goals; and site-level employees prioritising visitor experience over energy saving).

As per the *context* analysis, the organisation had a complex culture as both site-level culture and the broader (i.e. off-site level) organisational culture co-existed and conflicted sometimes. This means GAP practitioners should have considered activating/deactivating relevant mechanisms regarding ideas or formulations about culture. In response to this, two culture-related mechanisms have been employed. First, a mechanism promoting the site-level/micro-culture was used through the intervention toolkit, which was designed to allow a certain degree of personalisation to reflect stories, news and actions taking place at site level. However, this toolkit could have been initially designed to reflect better the individual site-level cultures rather than delegating each site to adapt general guidelines. While it can be assumed that a coherent and unique overall organisational culture is required for an enduring and successful organisational identity and image (Jo Hatch & Schultz, 1997), recent research on the wine industry (Zamparini & Lurati, in press) shows that it can be beneficial for strategic and competitive purposes for organisations to claim legitimate distinctive identities. This offers some support for the mechanism used in this intervention and its partial success. Nonetheless, more research is required in this area. The management and human relations literatures have previously examined the theme of micro-culture or subculture by looking into the reflection of subcultural differences in employees' perceptions of cultural practices (Liu, 2003). However, this area remained unexplored in the field of cultural heritage. Even within broader tourism research, the focus seems to be largely on the generic organisational culture, mostly within the hospitality industry.

The second culture-related mechanism that was used in the intervention to motivate sustainable behaviour amongst heritage organisation employees was the mechanism appealing to conservation values, rather than mechanisms appealing to financial savings or incentives. The former were clearly shared by employees:

> Yeah I think it would be money we're saving in the long term but I would like to think it would be for conservation and environmental issues rather than money. (E8)

While the motivation of the heritage organisation might have encompassed both (i.e. conservation as well as the environment needs money, so employees need to be informed about that, as the main reasons for the intervention and targeted behaviours).

In the heritage tourism literature, the employees' conservation motivations are scarcely researched compared to those of tourists. However, a research stream on volunteers in heritage organisations confirms employees such as volunteers can be highly motivated by conservation concerns (i.e. the so-called "conservers" – Stebbins & Graham, 2004, p. 27). Nonetheless, a barrier to enabling this values-related mechanism was the fact that "there seem to be disparate views and ideas about sustainability" (P3). This is somewhat aligned with research from the wider tourism literature indicating that the PEB of some managers is only partially explained by organisational environmental values, while their personal environmental values do not influence at all their PEB (Dief & Font, 2010).

Moreover, while GAP practitioners recognise that "the [heritage organisation] has a responsibility towards the environment, and they were clear on the link between sustainability and the [heritage organisation's] core values" (OR, p. 9) this was not always recognised at the site/employee level, due to existing practices and prioritises (the discussion in relation to context). As noted by both GAP practitioners and heritage organisation employees (P2; E1), employees' longevity and commitment to the organisation could benefit the intervention. However, these ideas and views about the relations dimension were not further explored; neither mechanisms connected to these characteristics of culture have been used. Therefore, more attention should have been dedicated to identifying and using appropriate culture-related mechanisms by GAP practitioners.

Regarding agency, several mechanisms were used to tackle the reasons for lack of action and to boost employees' existing reasons for action. First, an educational mechanism was used to tackle the belief and knowledge gaps identified at the context analysis stage. Belief gaps such as "we can't change the lighting because it's a listed building" were tackled by using "examples from other properties in the organisation that had done those actions" (P2) and knowledge gaps with actions such as:

> we did some focus groups…on lighting, with specifically different bulb types…LED, energy efficient lighting… heritage-designed LED lighting [and a person came to demonstrate]…getting them to think that 'not all of your sites are heritage', you do have modern parts where you do have more freedom so do things…often shops or visitors entrance spaces, ticket halls. (P2)

The use of this educational mechanisms is aligned with past research that considers knowledge building is important in sustainable tourism (Cole, 2006), thought its results can be mixed and highly dependent on contextual factors (Nilsson et al., 2016). Nieves and Haller (2014) highlighted the role of employee's knowledge in achieving dynamic capabilities in the hotel industry and, specifically, the importance of procedural organisational knowledge "which is linked to more routine processes [to] act as a reference to provide foundations for building learning processes to facilitate the introduction of changes" (Nieves & Haller, 2014, p. 227), such as this current paper's environmental social marketing intervention. As part of implementing this educational mechanism, "a toolkit was designed to provide user-friendly information to staff and volunteers using the key communication routes: face-to-face team meetings [staff huddles] and the property newsletters" (OR, p. 2).

Additionally, a mechanism highlighting relevant non-monetary benefits to employees was used to encourage people to take action. This was done by converting the financial savings into visitor membership money equivalents:

> rather than talking about energy saving as being £60 a year, which doesn't sound like very much, we'd be expressing that as "one membership" and suddenly it is more tangible to people…or "just as signing up one person a day" and suddenly they'd go "oooh!!" and they can see the value in that cause they know how difficult it is to get those memberships but they cannot quantify money in the same way because they are not the ones paying the energy bills for that site. (P1)

This mechanism was built on employees' desire to prioritise visitor experience and conservation over financial savings, and it increased employees' receptivity to the intervention and their desire to behave more environmentally friendly. This choice is aligned with previous research findings (Lee, De Young, & Marans, 1995; Marans & Lee, 1993) that found financial incentives do not motivate employees' sustainable behaviour. In the context of heritage tourism, research about the most suitable types of employee incentives for PEB at the workplace is lacking. However, some studies in the field of nature conservation highlighted the use of tools as total economic value (TEV) to assess the importance of biodiversity and ecosystem services to individuals/local communities. TEV incorporates a measure of "non-use values such as which include altruistic values (the satisfaction of knowing that other people have access to nature's benefits), bequest values (the satisfaction of knowing that future generations will have access) and existence values (satisfaction of knowing that a species or ecosystem exists)" (Christie, Fazey, Cooper, Hyde, & Kenter, 2012, p. 68). This agrees with the present research findings on the non-monetary/conservation-related benefits valued by the heritage employees.

Nonetheless, as per the previous context dimensions analysis, other agency mechanisms should have been considered/used, i.e. mechanisms related to tackling competing job tasks and behaviours; mechanisms counteracting employees' rationalisation techniques (Chatzidakis, Smith, & Hibbert, 2006); and their green compensatory behaviours and beliefs (Gregory-Smith, Smith, & Winklhofer, 2013).

The first relations-related mechanism used in the intervention was that of embedding sustainability into employees' daily activities or particular events, so that eventually sustainability can become embedded in their job. This helped tackle the barriers related to competing workplace duties/responsibilities and issues around time pressure:

> ...we sent them all Christmas quiz questions that they could feed into activities that they were doing that were sustainability themed to nudge them and ask them to continue to take part in the programme. (P2)

This approach matches findings from hospitality that recognise the involvement of hotel management/staff and a change in routines as success/failure factors in the adoption of environmental tools for sustainable tourism (Ayuso, 2006). Therefore, the present findings contribute to the scarce literature in this area and show how attempts to merge environmental practices with daily duties can pay off.

The second relations-related mechanism was the empowerment mechanism that aimed to deal with some of the relations-related issues, uncovered before the intervention and discussed previously. This mechanism was employed to overcome heritage organisation employees' and site managers' perceived lack of ownership, rights and ability to change things without the Head Office approval, as well as to overcome the perceived lack of support from top-level management regarding site-level environmental goals or initiatives. This was largely achieved by allowing employees and site-level managers to participate in the local delivery of the intervention along with GAP practitioners and to tailor their internal marketing communications (i.e. to tailor the toolkit, emails, newsletters and other employee engagement methods). This supports the some theoretical assumptions made about the role of communications in the tourism and heritage context (see De Bussy et al., 2003), particularly related to new media communication technologies that "empower employees and contribute to the democratization of the workplace" (De Bussy et al., 2003, p. 157). These findings also corroborate with some evidence that empowerment has found to be an effective tool for behaviour change in natural heritage locations, i.e. programmes connected to ecotourism (Scheyvens, 1999) and conservation (Nilsson et al., 2016). Overall, in the case of the present case study, the use of the empowerment mechanism was concordant with the micro-culture of each site and has heightened the sense of autonomy in the decision-making process.

Despite the use of this mechanism, the context analysis revealed that one unresolved problem was the conflict between the duties/responsibilities and the prioritised benefits, as seen by the employees and top-level management in the heritage organisation (i.e. responsibility to the visitors' experience and building conservation principles versus responsibility to cut costs and adopting a business model of running the sites and overall organisation). It should be also noted that given the interrelations between the context dimensions identified, the mechanisms identified and employed in the intervention at times tackle issues across context dimensions (e.g. the communications mechanism).

Outcomes

As mentioned before, the analysis of specific outcomes (e.g. cost, energy savings, change in attitude and behaviour-related variables) is not the focus of this paper (see details in Wells et al., 2015), but rather the evaluation of process (i.e. intervention design and delivery). The focus here is on learnt lessons regarding what works, for whom, under which circumstances and how (Pawson & Tilley, 2004, p. 5). While organisations and policy-makers search for definite, "clear-cut" and "one-fits-all" answers/ solutions, most realist evaluations of interventions offer partial answers and context-tailored advice (Pawson & Tilley, 2004, p. 21); which is beneficial for the present research within the heritage tourism context. Pawson and Tilley's (2004) guidelines on outcomes evaluation are used by answering the following questions to address this research gap.

What worked? Overall, the academic assessment carried out in this paper showed that GAP practitioners carried out a good evaluation of the four dimensions of context, according to de Souza's

(2013) classification (even though not due to their knowledge of the framework but rather based on their experience). Based on the qualitative data, several adequate mechanisms were identified and used in the intervention in response to the context analysis, with particular good use of the educational mechanism that tackled most of the employees' knowledge and beliefs gaps. The intervention involved heritage employees via hands-on activities (e.g. team huddles and the toolkit), while other elements (e.g. intranet and emails communications) required less participation and suited employees working in a non-office environment or volunteers. There was also a good selection of benefits that motivated heritage organisation employees' environmental behaviour.

What didn't work and which aspects were not successful? Some mechanisms were overlooked; therefore, some of context-related issues were not tackled properly (see Mechanisms section). For example, the issues around the complex and disjointed organisational culture and the existence of a micro-culture at site level were only partially explored/dealt with. While not per se the focus of the environmental intervention, the issues related to culture were found to act as barriers. Additionally, a better assessment of the roles/job types, their requirements and how they might support or hinder the intervention should have been carried out and reflected in the intervention design. Compared to the employee level, little was done to tackle the knowledge gaps at top management level, except by providing some post-intervention information in the official report. The issue of compensation for green behaviours at work (e.g. recycling compensates for disregard of energy use) has also not been tackled through adequate mechanisms during the intervention.

For whom it worked, in what circumstances and in what respects? The intervention had both effective and less effective elements, leading to mixed outcomes. However, this does not minimise its benefits, which is consistent with Pawson and Tilley's (2004) view that intervention outcomes can show mixed patterns of behaviour despite overall intervention success. The intervention worked better for the employees who: focused on the non-financial benefits of their environmental behaviour; were more receptive to behaviour change; did compensate between workplace green behaviours; were less time-constrained/pressured in their daily job; could be reached via multiple channels; and who were more likely to take environmental initiatives. However, the intervention targeted too many types of behaviours and employees, and could not reach or highly engage all employees, e.g. volunteers.

Will it have a long lasting effect and what aspects can enhance the long-term effects of the intervention? The intervention relevance and durability have been enhanced by GAP practitioners who included the empowerment mechanisms and who allowed employees/sites to partially personalise the intervention. Nonetheless, social marketing intervention effects are known to minimise as time passes (Lee & Kotler, 2015), which was also noted by GAP practitioners who lacked monitoring on some sites, leading to lower levels of involvement. Thus, monitoring could potentially extend long-lasting effects, besides employee support, empowerment and regular feedback on their environmental behaviour. These could also enhance visitor experience.

Should the intervention be deployed on a larger scale? Overall, the intervention was successful and, thus, could be implemented across all the organisation's sites. However, the previously highlighted areas of improvements and outstanding issues should be addressed beforehand; only simple replication might lead to similar or less substantial results.

Recommendations for tourism practice and future research

In the case of the environmental social marketing intervention discussed in this paper, the GAP practitioners largely focused on outcome evaluation rather than process evaluation; and they did not use any particular framework in the evaluation. Therefore, GAP's own evaluation did not identify all relevant mechanisms that would have further enhanced the success of the intervention. Nonetheless, through the academic assessment carried out in this paper, important lessons can be learnt and several recommendations can be made for tourism practice and future research.

Some mechanisms related to organisational structure were overlooked by GAP practitioners (i.e. negative attitude of each site towards complying with head office guidelines and goals; and employees' predisposition towards the prioritisation of visitors' experience over environmental concerns). Open acknowledgement by heritage managers (at site, regional and national levels) of these attitudinal predispositions as enabling/disabling mechanisms should be considered in collaboration with practitioners and addressed in the development of environmental interventions. This is consistent with broader tourism and hospitality industry views (Kusluvan, Kusluvan, Ilhan, & Buyruk, 2010, p. 193) about the importance of internal consistency and complementarity to minimise internal conflicts, aside from being in line with the organisation's strategy, characteristics and competitive position.

Similarly, a better understanding of issues around organisational culture should be carefully assessed and considered. This is because the co-existence of a general organisational cultural and micro-/site-level cultures could be detrimental to organisation's identity, image (Jo Hatch & Schultz, 1997) and its environmental initiatives, if perceived by employees to be in conflict with their priorities and environmental values.

A detailed consideration of context-related aspects (e.g. structure, employee relations and job requirements) is critical to heritage/tourism organisations, since these are likely to vary across organisations by sector, size, types of ownership and service/product offering. Dewhurst and Thomas (2003) found motivations for environmental practices vary across types of small tourism organisations, and Garay and Font (2012) found these practices vary even within the same industry (i.e. accommodation enterprises). Therefore, it is vital for successful environmental interventions that heritage tourism managers should be receptive to and promote context analysis within their organisation and at each site.

Non-monetary benefits were selected as the mechanism for motivating employees' PEB. These should be, however, implemented continuously by heritage managers for long-lasting effects. Additionally, drawing from lessons learnt in prior community nature-based conservation programmes, the most effective incentive type may vary by types of employees, stakeholders, organisations and countries, according to their level of development and cultural values (see Waylen, Fischer, McGowan, Thirgood, & Milner-Gulland, 2010). Thus a thorough context analysis and, potentially, pretesting of alternative incentives are needed.

Before conducting similar interventions within heritage tourism organisations, the type of compensation behaviour of green beliefs (as seen in the consumer behaviour/psychology literatures) and neutralisation techniques used by employees should be considered and used pre-intervention for employee segmentation within the organisation (see Gregory-Smith et al., 2015). Following this, it could be concluded that specific mechanisms (e.g. psychological and communication mechanisms to counteract different types of neutralisation techniques) should be used for each of the employee segments identified. Additionally, the intervention empowered the organisation's employees and managers at site level to personalise and run tailored communications, indicating that future interventions should employ a co-creation approach to developing a sustainable cultural heritage product offerings (e.g. Gössling, Haglund, Kallgren, Revahl, and Hultman (2009) study on environmental values co-creation in the airline travelling context) and a participatory approach for successful behaviour change interventions (see Matthies & Krömker, 2000).

While a series of lessons have been learnt from this case-study intervention, following Pawson and Tilley's (2004, p. 5) realist evaluation perspective, interventions should be regarded as open systems, influenced by externalities such as "unanticipated events, personnel moves, physical and technological shifts … practitioner learning, … organisational imperatives, performance management innovations". Therefore, this will influence the ability of replicating similar interventions across similar organisations within the heritage or wider tourism industry. Consequently, the design and implementation of environmental interventions within the tourism must be accommodating, flexible and follow a bespoke approach rather than "one-fits-all" approach (Manika, Wells, Gregory-Smith, & Gentry, 2015). This tailored intervention approach should be built on a detailed assessment of the context, with perspectives drawn from all types of employees, managers and stakeholders such as visitors and local communities.

Regarding the limitations of this paper, more mechanisms and contexts are likely to exist and require further elaboration and action than the ones emerging from the data used here. Additionally, interviewer and single-case study biases should be addressed in future research. Finally, despite the usefulness of de Souza's (2013) outline of how to elaborate and apply the CMO framework, it was found that its application to the present heritage organisation and intervention was not always straightforward. This is due to the overlap between context dimensions and types of mechanisms. Moreover, the classification of mechanisms portrayed in this framework may not be always relevant across interventions and case studies, within the tourism context.

In conclusion, this paper offers the first ever process evaluation of an environmental social marketing intervention in cultural heritage tourism (i.e. identifying key aspects to intervention maintenance and which ones are useful/inappropriate, successful/unsuccessful). This is achieved via a case-study methodology, using realist evaluation and the CMO framework, and via the reflections of practitioners who delivered the intervention. Overall, CMO is a useful framework for evaluating environmental interventions in tourism, which can lead to the development of clear recommendations for practice.

Notes

1. In this paper, the terms intervention and programme will be used interchangeably.
2. In some research papers and studies (e.g. de Souza, 2013), this is referred to as the "context–mechanism–outcome configuration (CMOc)".

Disclosure statement

No potential conflict of interest was reported by the authors.

ORCID

Diana Gregory-Smith (iD) http://orcid.org/0000-0001-9828-0933

References

Adger, W.N., Brown, K., Fairbrass, J., Jordan, A., Paavola, J., Rosendo, S., & Seyfang, G. (2003). Governance for sustainability: Towards a "thick" analysis of environmental decision making. *Environment and planning A, 35*(6), 1095–1110.

Ashworth, G.J. (2000). Heritage, tourism and places: A review. *Tourism Recreation Research, 25*(1), 19–29.

Ayuso, S. (2006). Adoption of voluntary environmental tools for sustainable tourism: Analysing the experience of Spanish hotels. *Corporate Social Responsibility and Environmental Management, 13*(4), 207–220.

Bamberg, S. (2002). Effects of implementation intentions on the actual performance of new environmentally friendly behaviours – results of two field experiments. *Journal of Environmental Psychology, 22*(4), 399–411.

Banyai, M., & Havitz, M.E. (2013). Analyzing travel blogs using a realist evaluation approach. *Journal of Hospitality Marketing & Management, 22*(2), 229–241.

Biron, C., & Karanika-Murray, M. (2014). Process evaluation for organizational stress and well-being interventions: Implications for theory, method, and practice. *International Journal of Stress Management, 21*(1), 85–111.

Biroscak, B.J., Schneider, T., Panzera, A.D., Bryant, C.A., McDermott, R.J., Mayer, A.B., ... Hovmand, P.S. (2014). Applying systems science to evaluate a community-based social marketing innovation: A case study. *Social Marketing Quarterly, 20*(4), 247–267.

Bramwell, B., & Lane, B. (2014). The "critical turn" and its implications for sustainable tourism research. *Journal of Sustainable Tourism, 22*(1), 1–8.

Braun, V., & Clarke, V. (2006). Using thematic analysis in psychology. *Qualitative Research in Psychology, 3*(2), 77–101.

Caruana, R., Glozer, S., Crane, A., & McCabe, S. (2014). Tourists' accounts of responsible tourism. *Annals of Tourism Research, 46*, 115–129.

Chatzidakis, A., Smith, A., & Hibbert, S. (2006). "Ethically concerned, yet unethically behaved": Towards an updated understanding of consumer's (un) ethical decision making. In C. Pechmann & L. Price (Eds.), *NA – Advances in Consumer Research* (Vol. 33, pp. 693–698). Duluth, MN: Association for Consumer Research.

Cheng, T.-M., & Wu, H.C. (2015). How do environmental knowledge, environmental sensitivity, and place attachment affect environmentally responsible behavior? An integrated approach for sustainable island tourism. *Journal of Sustainable Tourism, 23*(4), 557–576.

Chhabra, D. (2009). Proposing a sustainable marketing framework for heritage tourism. *Journal of Sustainable Tourism, 17*(3), 303–320.

Cole, S. (2006). Information and empowerment: The keys to achieving sustainable tourism. *Journal of Sustainable Tourism, 14*(6), 629–644.

Christie, M., Fazey, I., Cooper, R., Hyde, T., & Kenter, J.O. (2012). An evaluation of monetary and non-monetary techniques for assessing the importance of biodiversity and ecosystem services to people in countries with developing economies. *Ecological Economics, 83*, 67–78.

Chou, C-J. (2014). Hotels' environmental policies and employee personal environmental beliefs: Interactions and outcomes. *Tourism Management, 40*, 436–446.

Coles, T., Fenclova, E., & Dinan, C. (2013). Tourism and corporate social responsibility: A critical review and research agenda. *Tourism Management Perspectives, 6*, 122–141.

Costa, R., & Menichini, T. (2013). A multidimensional approach for CSR assessment: The importance of the stakeholder perception. *Expert Systems with Applications, 40*, 150–161.

Decrop, A. (1999). Triangulation in qualitative tourism research. *Tourism Management, 20*(1), 157–161.

De Bussy, N.M., Ewing, M.T., & Pitt, L.F. (2003). Stakeholder theory and internal marketing communications: A framework for analysing the influence of new media. *Journal of Marketing Communications, 9*(3), 147–161.

Dolnicar, S., & Hurlinmann, A. (2010). Australians' water conservation behaviours and attitudes. *Australian Journal of Water Resources, 14*(1), 43–53.

de Souza, D.E. (2013). Elaborating the context-mechanism-outcome configuration (CMOc) in realist evaluation: A critical realist perspective. *Evaluation, 19*(2), 141–154.

Dewhurst, H., & Thomas, R. (2003). Encouraging sustainable business practices in a non-regulatory environment: A case study of small tourism firms in a UK national park. *Journal of Sustainable Tourism, 11*(5), 383–403.

Dief, M.E., & Font, X. (2010). The determinants of hotels' marketing managers' green marketing behaviour. *Journal of Sustainable Tourism, 18*(2), 157–174.

Edmondson, A.C., & McManus, S.E. (2007). Methodological fit in management field research. *Academy of Management Review, 32*(4), 1246–1264.

El Dief, M., & Font, X. (2010). The determinants of hotels' marketing managers' green marketing behaviour. *Journal of Sustainable Tourism, 18*(2), 157–174.

French, J., & Blair-Stevens, C. (2007). *Big pocket guide: Social marketing*. London: National Social Marketing Centre.

Font, X., Walmsley, A., Cogotti, S., McCombes, L., & Häusler, N. (2012). Corporate social responsibility: The disclosure–performance gap. *Tourism Management, 33*(6), 1544–1553.

Garay, L., & Font, X. (2012). Doing good to do well? Corporate social responsibility reasons, practices and impacts in small and medium accommodation enterprises. *International Journal of Hospitality Management, 31*(2), 329–337.

Gössling, S., Haglund, L., Kallgren, H., Revahl, M., & Hultman, J. (2009). Swedish air travellers and voluntary carbon offsets: Towards the co-creation of environmental value? *Current Issues in Tourism, 12*(1), 1–19.

Gregory-Smith, D., Smith, A., & Winklhofer, H. (2013). Emotions and dissonance in 'ethical' consumption choices. *Journal of Marketing Management, 29*(11–12), 1201–1223.

Gregory-Smith, D., Wells, V.K., Manika, D., & Graham, S. (2015). An environmental social marketing intervention among employees: Assessing attitude and behaviour change. *Journal of Marketing Management, 31*(3–4), 336–377.

Grove, L., & Pease, K. (2014). A situational approach to heritage crime prevention. In L. Grove & S. Thomas (Eds.), *Heritage crime: Progress, prospects and prevention* (pp. 107–127). Basingstoke: Palgrave Macmillan.

Hall, C.M. (2014). *Tourism and social marketing*. Abingdon: Routledge.

Hall, C.M. (2016). Intervening in academic interventions: framing social marketing's potential for successful sustainable tourism behavioural change. *Journal of Sustainable Tourism, 24*(3) 350–375.

Hopwood, T., & Merritt, R. (2011). *Big pocket guide to using social marketing for behaviour change*. London: National Social Marketing Centre.

Harachi, T.W., Abbot, R.D., Catalano, R.F., Haggerty, K.P., & Fleming, C.B. (1999). Opening the black box: Using process evaluation measures to assess implementation and theory building. *American Journal of Community Psychology, 27*(5), 711–731.

Hulscher, M.E.J.L., Laurant, M.G.H., & Grol, R.P.T.M. (2003). Process evaluation on quality improvement interventions. *Quality and Safety in Health Care, 12*(1), 40–46.

Jo Hatch, M., & Schultz, M. (1997). Relations between organizational culture, identity and image. *European Journal of Marketing, 31*(5/6), 356–365.

Kim, J.S., Song, H.J., & Lee, C.K. (2016). Effects of corporate social responsibility and internal marketing on organizational commitment and turnover intentions. *International Journal of Hospitality Management, 55*, 25–32.

Kusluvan, S., Kusluvan, Z., Ilhan, I., & Buyruk, L. (2010). The human dimension a review of human resources management issues in the tourism and hospitality industry. *Cornell Hospitality Quarterly, 51*(2), 171–214.

Lee, N.R., & Kotler, P. (2015). *Social marketing: Influencing behaviors for good* (5th ed.). Thousand Oaks, CA: Sage Publications.

Lee, Y.-J., De Young, R., & Marans, R.W. (1995). Factors influencing individual recycling behavior in office settings: A study of office workers in Taiwan. *Environment and Behavior, 27*(3), 380–403.

Linnan, L., & Steckler, A. (2002). Process evaluation for public health interventions and research. In L. Linnan & A. Steckler (Eds.), *Process evaluation for public health interventions and research* (pp. 1–30). San Francisco, CA: Jossey-Bass, a Wiley Imprint.

Linnell, D. (2014). Process Evaluation vs. *Outcome Evaluation*. Retrieved 15 August 2016 from http://tsne.org/blog/process-evaluation-vs-outcome-evaluation

Lister, G., & Merritt, R. (2013). Evaluating the value for money of interventions to support behavior change for better health (behavior change evaluation tools). *Social Marketing Quarterly, 19*(2), 76–83.

Liu, S. (2003). Cultures within culture: Unity and diversity of two generations of employees in state-owned enterprises. *Human Relations, 56*(4), 387–417.

Manika, D., Wells, V.K., Gregory-Smith, D., & Gentry, M. (2015). The impact of individual attitudinal and organisational variables on workplace environmentally friendly behaviours. *Journal of Business Ethics, 126*(4), 663–684.

Marans, R.W., & Lee, Y.-J. (1993). Linking recycling behavior to waste management planning: A case study of office workers in Taiwan. *Landscape and Urban Planning, 26*(1–4), 203–214.

Matthies, E., & Krömker, D. (2000). Participatory planning – a heuristic for adjusting interventions to the context. *Journal of Environmental Psychology, 20*(1), 65–74.

McKenzie-Mohr, D. (2000). Promoting sustainable behavior: An introduction to community-based social marketing. *Journal of Social Issues, 56*(3), 543–554.

McKenzie-Mohr, D. (2011). *Fostering sustainable behavior: An introduction to community-based social marketing* (3rd ed.). Gabriola Island: New Society Publishers.

Mee, N., Clewes, D., Phillips, P.S., & Read, A.D. (2004). Effective implementation of a marketing communications strategy for kerbside recycling: A case study from Rushcliffe, UK. *Resources, Conservation and Recycling, 42*(1), 1–26.

Miller, D., Merrilees, B., & Coghlan, A. (2015). Sustainable urban tourism: Understanding and developing visitor pro-environmental behaviours. *Journal of Sustainable Tourism, 23*(1), 26–46.

Moore, G., Audrey, S., Barker, M., Bond, L., Bonell, C., Cooper, C.,... Baird, J. (2014). Process evaluation in complex public health intervention studies: The need for guidance. *Journal of Epidemiology & Community Health, 68*, 1–2.

Nicolau, J.L. (2008). Corporate social responsibility: Worth-creating activities. *Annals of Tourism Research, 35*(4), 990–1006.

Nieves, J., & Haller, S. (2014). Building dynamic capabilities through knowledge resources. *Tourism Management, 40*, 224–232.

Nilsson, D., Baxter, G., Butler, J.R., & McAlpine, C.A. (2016). How do community-based conservation programs in developing countries change human behaviour? A realist synthesis. *Biological Conservation, 200*, 93–103.

Pawson, R., & Tilley, N. (1997). *Realistic evaluation*. London: Sage.

Pawson, R., & Tilley, N. (2004). Realist evaluation. Retrieved 1 August 2016 from http://dmeforpeace.org/sites/default/files/RE_chapter.pdf

Platenkamp, V., & Botterill, D. (2013). Critical realism, rationality and tourism knowledge. *Annals of Tourism Research, 41*, 110–129.

Polit, S. (2012). The organizational impacts of managing social marketing interventions. *Social Marketing Quarterly, 18*(2), 124–134.

Pullin, A.S., & Stewart, G.B. (2006). Guidelines for systematic review in conservation and environmental management. *Conservation Biology, 20*, 1647–1656.

Sanchez, P. (1999). How to craft successful employee communication in the information age. *Communication World, 16*(7), 9–15.

Saunders, R.P., Martin, E., & Joshi, P. (2005). Developing a process-evaluation plan for assessing health promotion program implementation: A how-to guide, *Health Promotion Practice, 6*(2), 134–147.

Scheyvens, R. (1999). Ecotourism and empowerment of local communities. *Tourism Management, 20*, 245–249.

Smith, A.M., & O-Sullivan, T. (2012). Environmentally responsible behaviour in the workplace: An internal social marketing approach. *Journal of Marketing Management, 28*(3–4), 469–493.

Stebbins, R.A., & Graham, M. (Eds.). (2004). *Volunteering as leisure/leisure as volunteering: An international assessment.* Wallingford: CABI.

Steg, L. (2008). Promoting household energy conservation. *Energy Policy, 3*(12), 4449–4453.

Strauss, A., & Corbin, J. (1990). *Basics of qualitative research* (Vol. *15*). Newbury Park, CA: Sage.

Tilley, N. (2000, September). Realistic evaluation: An overview. Founding Conference of the Danish Evaluation Society, Copenhagen. Retrieved 1 August 2016 from http://healthimpactassessment.pbworks.com/f/Realistic+evaluation+an+overview+-+UoNT+England+-+2000.pdf

Warren, C., Becken, S., & Coghlan, A. (in press). Using persuasive communication to co-create behavioural change – engaging with guests to save resources at tourist accommodation facilities, *Journal of Sustainable Tourism*, DOI: 10.1080/09669582.2016.1247849

Waylen, K.A., Fischer, A., McGowan, P.J.K., Thirgood, S.J., & Milner-Gulland, E.J. (2010). Effect of local cultural context on the success of community-based conservation interventions. *Conservation Biology, 24*, 1119–1129.

Wells, V.K., Manika, D., Gregory-Smith, D., Taheri, B., & McCowlen, C. (2015). Examining the role of employee environmental behaviour in cultural heritage tourism environmental CSR. *Tourism Management, 48*, 399–413.

Wickham, M., & Lehman, K. (2015). Communicating sustainability priorities in the museum sector. *Journal of Sustainable Tourism, 23*(7), 1011–1028.

Yin, R.K. (2009). *Case study research: Design and methods* (4th ed.). Thousand Oaks, CA: Sage Publications.

Yin, R.K. (2011). *Applications of case study research (applied social research methods).* Thousand Oaks, CA, Sage Publications.

Zamparini, A., & Lurati, F. (in press). Being different and being the same: Multimodal image projection strategies for a legitimate distinctive identity. *Strategic Organization*, DOI: 10.1177/1476127016638811

Zientara, P., & Zamojska, A. (in press). Green organizational climates and employee pro-environmental behaviour in the hotel industry, *Journal of Sustainable Tourism*, DOI: 10.1080/09669582.2016.1206554

Index

For Product Safety Concerns and Information please contact our EU
representative GPSR@taylorandfrancis.com
Taylor & Francis Verlag GmbH, Kaufingerstraße 24, 80331 München, Germany

www.ingramcontent.com/pod-product-compliance
Ingram Content Group UK Ltd.
Pitfield, Milton Keynes, MK11 3LW, UK
UKHW051831180425
457613UK00022B/1209